In *Challenging codes*, leading social theorist Alberto

ONE WEEK LOAN

Challenging codes

Cambridge Cultural Social Studies

General editors: JEFFREY C. ALEXANDER, *Department of Sociology, University of California, Los Angeles, and* STEVEN SEIDMAN, *Department of Sociology, University at Albany, State University of New York.*

Editorial Board
JEAN COMAROFF, *Department of Anthropology, University of Chicago*
DONNA HARAWAY, *Department of the History of Consciousness, University of California, Santa Cruz*
MICHELE LAMONT, *Department of Sociology, Princeton University*
THOMAS LAQUEUR, *Department of History, University of California, Berkeley*

Cambridge Cultural Social Studies is a forum for the most original and thoughtful work in cultural social studies. This includes theoretical works focusing on conceptual strategies, empirical studies covering specific topics such as gender, sexuality, politics, economics, social movements, and crime, and studies that address broad themes such as the culture of modernity. While the perspectives of the individual studies will vary, they will all share the same innovative reach and scholarly quality.

Titles in the series
ILANA FRIEDRICH SILBER, *Virtuosity, charisma, and social order*
LINDA NICHOLSON AND STEVEN SEIDMAN (eds.), *Social postmodernism*
WILLIAM BOGARD, *The simulation of surveillance*
SUZANNE R. KIRSCHNER, *The religious and Romantic origins of psychoanalysis*
PAUL LICHTERMAN, *The search for political community*
KENNETH H. TUCKER, *French revolutionary syndicalism and the public sphere*
ERIK RINGMAR, *Identity interest and action*
ALBERTO MELUCCI, *The playing self*

Challenging codes

Collective action in the information age

Alberto Melucci
University of Milan

CAMBRIDGE
UNIVERSITY PRESS

PUBLISHED BY THE PRESS SYNDICATE OF THE UNIVERSITY OF CAMBRIDGE
The Pitt Building, Trumpington Street, Cambridge, United Kingdom

CAMBRIDGE UNIVERSITY PRESS
The Edinburgh Building, Cambridge CB2 2RU, UK
40 West 20th Street, New York, NY 10011–4211, USA
477 Williamstown Road, Port Melbourne, VIC 3207, Australia
Ruiz de Alarcón 13, 28014 Madrid, Spain
Dock House, The Waterfront, Cape Town 8001, South Africa

http://www.cambridge.org

First published 1996
Reprinted 1999, 2001

Printed in the United Kingdom at the University Press, Cambridge

A catalogue record for this book is available from the British Library

Library of Congress Cataloguing in Publication Data
Melucci, Alberto, 1943–
    Challenging codes: collective action in the information age /
Alberto Melucci.
      p.   cm. – (Cambridge cultural social studies)
      ISBN 0 521 57051 4. – ISBN 0 521 57843 4 (pbk.)
      1. Collective behaviour.   2. Social action.   3. Social movements.
    4. Group identity.   I. Title   II. Series.
    HM281.M42   1996
303.48′4–dc20   96-3883   CIP

ISBN 0 521 57051 4 hardback
ISBN 0 521 57843 4 paperback

On ne connait que les choses qu'on aprivoise
(We only know things that we have been able to
domesticate)

Antoine de Saint-Exupery, *Le Petit Prince*

Contents

Preface and acknowledgements

The ideas and findings presented in this book were assembled over the last twenty years from a great deal of field research and an ever growing body of literature, and through an ongoing discussion with many students and colleagues in various parts of the world. My former students and associates of Lams (Laboratory of Research on Social Change) at the University of Milano contributed directly to some of the ideas on contemporary movements presented here. Together with its companion *The Playing Self*, the first version of this book was written with the linguistic assistance of Adrian Belton and at its intermediate stage it was improved substantially by the careful and supportive editing work of Timo Lyyra, to whom I am deeply endebted. I am grateful to Jeffrey Alexander and Steven Seidman, who wanted the two books to be part of the series on Cultural Social Studies. I wish also to thank Catherine Max, social sciences editor at Cambridge University Press for her support in the editorial and production process.

I would like to dedicate this book to my family, my roots in the everyday; and to my readers in different regions and cultures of our incoming planetary society: together we share the responsibility of this little portion of knowledge represented by the present book.

Introduction

Prophet: the one who speaks before

Movements in complex societies are disenchanted prophets. The charmed universe of the *heroes* has definitively dissolved under the impact of an era taking cognizance of itself as a planetary system riven by molecular change, as a system which constantly generates tensions and then in turn adapts to them by striving to control them. Movements are a sign; they are not merely an outcome of the crisis, the last throes of a passing society. They signal a deep transformation in the logic and the processes that guide complex societies.

Like the prophets, the movements 'speak before': they announce what is taking shape even before its direction and content has become clear. The inertia of the old categories may prevent us from hearing the message and from deciding, consciously and responsibly, what action to take in light of it. Without the capacity of listening to these voices, new forms of power may thus coalesce, though multiple and diffuse and no longer reducible to any linear and easily recognizable geometry.

Contemporary movements are prophets of the present. What they possess is not the force of the apparatus but the power of the word. They announce the commencement of change; not, however, a change in the distant future but one that is already a presence. They force the power out into the open and give it a shape and a face. They speak a language that seems to be entirely their own, but they say something that transcends their particularity and speaks to us all.

This book was born over the last twenty years as an attempt to listen to the voices and read the signs of precisely that which collective action is proclaiming. But the mind that sets about to regard the societal actors today must in a similar manner proceed within a disenchanted framework. The intellectuals who claim to represent the good conscience or the true ideology of a movement have always participated in preparing the way for the advent of the Prince, only to end up as either his victims or his courtiers. The contemporary transformations of social actors parallelling the shift in the focus of conflicts and the changes in the forms of power have rendered the situation even more problematic. Both passionate and critical, involved and detached, the analysis of collective action is confronted with new challenges it itself must recognize, lest 'those who speak before' should go unheeded and the walls of stone or of silence muffle their message.

When looking at contemporary movements, we can assume one of two different attitudes – that of 'resolving' or that of 'listening.' Modern technology with its practice of intervention, wherein success is measured in terms of the efficacy of the given technique, claims victory for the 'resolutionary' approach and renders listening impossible. Under the influence of the general predisposition to immediate remedial action, social movements are taken into consideration solely on account of their capacity (or lack thereof) to modernize institutions or to produce political reform. But this is to forget, or to ignore, that the reduction of contemporary social movements to their political dimensions alone is tantamount to solving the 'symptom', to suppressing the message contained in their specifically communicative character ('symptom' literally means 'to fall together') and simply moving about the problem in the background.

Reflection on the analysis of social movements, however, is not warranted for the sake of scholarship only. At the same time, it may become a topical antidote in society: the work of analysis can contribute to the culture of the movements themselves, enhancing their resistance to the illusion that the word they bear is sacred and undermining the urge to totality that will swiftly turn them into churches or new powers that be. Heightened awareness of the possibilities and constraints of action can transform the word of the movements into language, culture, and social relationships, and may out of collective processes build a practice of freedom.

The continuum which ranges from protest and rebellion by a social group to the formation of a mass movement and a large-scale collective mobilization comprises a huge variety of intermediate forms of action, and any attempt to classify them seems at first sight all too formidable an undertaking. Indeed, one doubts whether such an operation might even reward the effort, since it remains questionable whether any continuity or homogeneity among the phenomena considered can actually be found. Here, more than in any other field of sociology, misunderstandings reign supreme. Terms such as 'collective violence', 'collective behaviour', 'protest', 'social movements', or 'revolution' often denote diverse phenomena and generate ambiguities, if not outright contradictions. It is not by chance that this confusion rotates around phenomena which closely involve the fundamental processes whereby a society maintains and changes its structure. Whether wittingly or not, the debate on the significance of collective action always embraces the issue of power relationships, and on closer examination derives its energy from defending or contesting a specific position or form of dominance. But the increasing prominence of the problem does not first and foremost stem from an ideological confrontation. It is social reality itself which presents us with a variety of collective phenomena, of conflictual actions, of episodes of social revolt which evade interpretation guided by traditional political categories, thus calling for new tools of analysis. Behind random protest or manifestations of cultural revolt in our complex planetary society – which by now also includes the developing societies of the 'South' – there of course always lie diverse problems and social structures. In this situation, the increasing diffusion of these phenomena and their diversification is, paradoxically, matched by the inadequacy of the analytical tools available to us.

In a certain sense, then, this book constitutes a venture into the uncertain terrain of a theory still to be constructed. In this search – which at the present stage can only proceed by trial and error – the capacity of a theory to rely exclusively on its own analytical foundations is necessarily limited. From this fact derives the importance of the growing body of research into cases of social movements and episodes of collective action, which in recent years has enriched theoretical analysis with a large quantity of empirical material relating to actual behaviour in society. From this point of view, the nonlinear progress of any analysis that attempts to come to grips with the theme of social movements and collective action is also understandable, obliged as it is to rely upon overspecific observations to fill gaps in the theory, just as it is, by the same token, forced to run the risk of general hypotheses where empirical material is scarce or nonexistent on the other hand.

In the last thirty years, analysis of social movements and collective action has developed into an autonomous sector of theory formation and research within the social sciences, and the amount and quality of the work in the area has grown and improved. Not incidentally, the autonomy of the conceptual field relating to the analysis of social movements has developed parallel to the increasing autonomy of noninstitutional forms of collective action in complex systems. The social space of movements has become a distinct area of the system and no longer coincides either with the traditional forms of organization of solidarity or with the conventional channels of political representation. The area of movements is now a 'sector' or a 'subsystem' of the social.

Recognizing this autonomy forces us to revise dichotomies like 'state' and 'civil society', 'public' and 'private', 'instrumental' and 'expressive'. The crisis of such polar distinctions signals a change in our conceptual universe. The notion of 'movement' itself, which originally stood for an entity acting against the political and governmental system, has now been rendered inadequate as a description of the reality of reticular and diffuse forms of collective action.

Contemporary 'movements' assume the form of solidarity networks entrusted with potent cultural meanings, and it is precisely these meanings that distinguish them so sharply from political actors and formal organizations next to them. We have passed beyond the global and metaphysical conception of collective actors. Movements are not entities that move with the unity of goals attributed to them by ideologues. Movements are systems of action, complex networks among the different levels and meanings of social action. Collective identity allowing them to become actors is not a datum or an essence; it is the outcome of exchanges, negotiations, decisions, and conflicts among actors. Processes of mobilization, organizational forms, models of leadership, ideologies, and forms of communication – these are all meaningful levels of analysis for the reconstruction from the within of the action system that constitutes the collective actor. But, in addition, relationships with the outside – with competitors, allies, and adversaries – and especially the response of the political system and the apparatuses of social control define a field of opportunities and constraints within which the collective action takes shape, perpetuates itself, or changes.

Contemporary forms of collective action are multiple and variable. They are located at several different levels of the social system simultaneously. We must therefore begin by distinguishing between the field of conflict on the one hand and the actors that bring such conflict to the fore on the other. In the past, studying conflicts implied analysing the social condition of a group and submitting what was known of that condition to deductive reasoning in order to wrest the causes of the collective action from it. Today, we must proceed by first singling out the field of conflict, and then explain how certain social groups take action within it.

Since no actor is inherently conflictual, the nature of action assumes a necessarily temporary character, and it may involve different actors and shift its locus among the various areas of the system. This multiplicity and variability of actors makes the plurality of the analytical meanings contained within the same physical phenomenon even more apparent. The totality of a given empirical collective action is usually attributed a quasi-substantial unity, when it is instead the contingent outcome of the interaction of a multiple field of forces and analytically distinct processes.

The inner differentiation of action is reinforced by the fact that in a planetary system social reality becomes synchronic: in the contemporaneity created by the media system, all the 'geological strata' of human history are simultaneously present. In the unity of the present, movements thus contain in one problems and conflicts that have different historical roots. Adding to this, movements attract the forms of discontent and marginalization that the social system generates, while the forming elites exploit conflict to seek opportunity to affirm themselves or to consolidate their positions.

An analytical perspective that draws on these insights helps us clarify one of the issues recurrently debated over the last decades. It concerns the 'newness' of contemporary conflicts: What is 'new' in the 'new social movements' is still an open question. Bearing the responsibility of the one who introduced the term 'new social movements' into sociological literature, I have watched with dismay as the category has been progressively reified. 'Newness', by definition, is a relative concept, which at the time of its formulation in the context of the movements research had the temporary function of indicating a number of comparative differences between the historical forms of class conflict and today's emergent forms of collective action. But if analysis and research fail to specify the distinctive features of the 'new movements', we are trapped in an arid debate between the supporters and critics of 'newness'.

On the one hand, there are those who claim that many aspects of the contemporary forms of action can be detected also in previous phenomena in history, and that the discovery of their purported newness is in the first place attributable to the bias shown by numerous sociologists blinded by emotional involvement with their subject matter. On the other hand, the defenders of the novel character of contemporary movements endeavour to show that these similarities are only formal, or apparent, and that the meaning of the phenomena is changed when they are set in different systemic contexts.

However, both the critics of the 'newness' of the 'new movements' and the proponents of the 'newness paradigm' commit the same epistemological mistake: they consider contemporary collective phenomena to constitute unitary empirical objects, seeking then on this basis to define the substance of their newness or to deny or dispute it. When addressing empirical 'movements', one side in the debate sets out to mark out differences with respect to the historical predecessors, the other stresses continuity and comparability.

The controversy strikes one as futile. In their empirical unity, contemporary phenomena are made up of a variety of components, and if these elements are not analytically separated, comparison between forms of action that belong to mutually distinct historical periods becomes an idle activity. It will be extremely difficult to decide, for instance, the extent of the 'new' in the modern 'women's movement', as a global empirical phenomenon, compared with the first feminist movements of the nineteenth century. Paradoxically, the result of the debate on 'new movements' has been the accelerating decline of the image of movements-as-entities. Through comparative work on different historical periods and different societies, we know now that contemporary movements, like all collective phenomena, bring together forms of action which involve various levels of the social structure. These encompass different points of view and belong to different historical periods. We must, therefore, seek to understand this multiplicity of synchronic and diachronic elements and explain how they are combined in the concrete unity of a collective actor.

Having clarified this epistemological premise, we may however still ask ourselves whether a new paradigm of collective action is not at the moment taking shape: not in the empirical sense – that is, in terms of the observed phenomenon as a whole – but analytically, in terms of certain levels or elements of action. It is thus necessary to inquire as to whether there are dimensions to the 'new' forms of action which we should attribute to a systemic context different from that of industrial capitalism.

This question is dismissed by critics of 'new movements', who trace such phenomena on an exclusively political level. The resulting reductionism dispenses with the question of the emergence of a new paradigm of collective action without, however, having first provided any answers as to its pertinence. Moreover, it ignores those specifically social and cultural dimensions of action that feature so significantly in the 'new movements'. This gives rise to a different bias, to the exclusive concentration on the visible and measurable features of collective action – such as their relationship with political systems and their effects on policies – at the expense of the production of cultural codes; but it is the latter which is the principal activity of the hidden networks of contemporary movements and the basis for their visible action.

Do contemporary collective phenomena comprise antagonist conflicts that are systemic in nature, or do they rather belong to the phenomena of social emargination, of aggregate behaviour, of adjustment by the political market? So general a question can only be answered by first exploring alternative explanations of collective action, formulated for example in terms of dysfunctions or crises, or with reference to political exchange. Many of the contemporary conflicts can be explained through recourse to the workings of the political market, commonly as the expression of excluded social groups or categories pressing for representation. Here, however, there is no antagonistic dimension to the conflict; there is only the pressure to join a system of benefits and rules from which one has been excluded. When the confines of the political system are rigid, such a conflict may even turn violent. However, this needs not necessarily entail antagonism towards the logic of the system; it may, instead, express a simple demand for a different distribution of resources or for new rules. Similarly, a poorly functioning organization may be subject even to an intense conflict, the aim of which, however, is not to dismantle that organization but rather to restore it to its normal state.

After exhausting the explanatory capacity of these dimensions, it, still remains to be asked – and this is important – whether there is anything left to account for. And here we must preserve a sufficient theoretical space in which to formulate the question of systemic conflicts; otherwise the issue will be glossed over without answers being provided or the questions themselves having been shown to be pointless. Today, we refer to the changes under way in contemporary systems using allusive terms (complex, post-industrial, postmodern, late capitalist society), the implicit assumption being that they follow a logic significantly different from that of industrial capitalism. But to do so is to neglect or to suppress the theoretical problems this very assumption raises.

The question of the existence of antagonistic conflicts of systemic scope, however, keeps open a number of issues with which theoretical analysis must now come to grip: for example, whether one can conceive of a dominant logic that disperses itself over a variety of areas of the system, producing thereby a great diversity of conflictual sites and actors.

'If God gave me the choice of the whole planet or my little farm, I should certainly take my farm', wrote Ralph Waldo Emerson. Today we can no longer take the farm, since we have already been obliged to take the whole planet by virtue of the fact that the planet has become a whole. The Gulf War of 1991 has been the most recent and shocking demonstration of the global interdependence of our destiny as human beings on this planet and of the crucial role of information in shaping our reality. While we might not yet be fully aware of the reality of this fundamental change, contemporary social movements act as signals to remind us that both the external planet, the Earth as our homeland, and the internal planet, our 'nature' as human beings, are undergoing radical transformations. The reality in which we live has in its entirety become a cultural construct, and our representations of it serve as filters for our relationship with the world. For the first time in the history of the human species, this assertion is also true in a literal sense. In fact, the world of which we speak today is a global world of planetary scale, and this is made possible only by information, or the cultural processes with which we represent our world to ourselves. The consequences of this change are enormous. But the emergence of the transnational dimension to issues and social actors, more than a political question, is in the first place a sign of the fact that human action by now is capable of culturally creating its own space. The planet no longer designates just a physical location; it is also a unified social space which is culturally and symbolically perceived.

Interest in cultural analysis has grown in the last two decades alongside the extraordinary cultural transformation of planetary society. We are witnessing, with mixed feelings of amazement and fear, the impressive development of communication technologies, the creation of a global media system, the disappearance of historical political cleavages, the collision of cultural differences within national societies and at the world scale. Never before have human cultures been exposed to such a massive reciprocal confrontation, and never has the cultural dimension of human action been as directly addressed as the core resource for production and consumption. It therefore comes as no surprise that social sciences are rediscovering culture, that a new reading of the tradition is taking place through the lens of this key concept, and that a wave of interest in cultural analysis is bringing a new vitality to theoretical debates in sociology.

Social movements too seem to shift their focus from class, race, and other more traditional political issues towards the cultural ground. In the last thirty years emerging social conflicts in complex societies have not expressed themselves through political action, but rather have raised cultural challenges to the dominant language, to the codes that organize information and shape social practices. The crucial dimensions of daily life have been involved in these conflicts, and new actors have laid claim to their autonomy in making sense of their lives. Contemporary society with its tightly woven networks of high-density information requires for its proper functioning the development of a distinct degree of autonomy of its component parts. It must presuppose and depend on individuals, groups and subsystems, which act as self-regulating units capable of sending, receiving, and processing information. To this end, development of formal skills of action, decision-making, and continuous learning is encouraged. However, increasing systemic differentiation simultaneously threatens social life with fragmentation, lack of communication, atomized individualism, and calls for deeper integration of individual and collective practices. The key focus of control shifts from the manifest forms of behaviour to motives and the meaning of action, to those hidden codes that make individuals and groups predictable and dependable social actors.

Social conflicts tend to emerge in those fields of social life which are directly exposed to the most powerful and intense flow of information, and where at the same time individuals and groups are subject to the greatest pressure to incorporate in their everyday behaviour the requirements and the rules of systemic normality. The actors involved in these conflicts are transient, and their action serves to reveal to and caution the society of the crucial problems it faces, to announce the critical divisions that have opened up within it. Conflicts do not express themselves through action taken in accordance with the purposive norms of efficacy. The challenge is made manifest in the upsetting of cultural codes, being therefore predominantly formal in character.

In contemporary systems, signs become interchangeable and power operates through the languages and codes which organize the flow of information. Collective action, by the sheer fact of its existence, represents in its very form and models of organization a message broadcast to the rest of society. Instrumental objectives are still pursued, but they become more precise and particular in their scope and replaceable. Action does still have effects on institutions, by modernizing their culture and organization, and by selecting new elites for them. At the same time, however, it raises issues that are not addressed by the framework of instrumental rationality. This kind of rationality is devoted to the effective implementation of whatever has been decided by anonymous and impersonal powers operating through the apparent neutrality of technical expertise.

Actors in conflicts recast the question of societal ends: they address the differences between the sexes, the ages, cultures; they probe into the nature and the limits of human intervention; they concern themselves with health and illness, birth and death. The action of movements deliberately differentiates itself from the model of political organization and assumes increasing autonomy from political systems; it becomes intimately interweaved with everyday life and individual experience.

Increasing control is applied to people's routine existence by the apparatuses of regulation which exact identification and consensus. Conflicts involve the definition of the self in its biological, affective, and symbolic dimensions, in its relations with time, space, and 'the other'. It is the individual and collective reappropriation of the meaning of action that is at stake in the forms of collective involvement which make the experience of change in the present a condition for creating a different future. Movements thus exist also in silence, and their presence is fundamental for the vitality of information societies. The challenge embodied in the movements' action keeps raising questions about meaning, beyond the technical neutrality of procedures which tends to install itself in institutions and governs their role in the society.

This dimension, however, does not exhaust the significance of collective action. Contemporary collective action weaves together its different roots in multiple meanings, legacies from the past, the effects of modernization, resistances to change. The complexity, the irreducibility, the intricate semantics of the meaning of social action is perhaps the most fundamental theme of this book. Only a society that is able to accommodate the thrust of the movements by providing an unconstrained arena for the fundamental issues raised by collective action, as well as democratic channels of representation and decision-making, can ensure that complexity is not ironed out, that differences are not violated. Keeping open the space for difference is a condition for inventing the present – for allowing society to openly address its fundamental dilemmas and for installing in its present constitution a manageable coexistence of its own tensions.

PART I

Theory of collective action

1

The construction of collective action

Traditions

When talking of social movements and collective action, one is usually referring to empirical phenomena with a certain degree of external unity. Movements are often described in terms similar to those used in addressing personalities or personages in tragic theatre, characters with a distinct and coherent role. Yet what in fact is in question are heterogeneous and fragmented phenomena, which internally contain a multitude of differentiated meanings, forms of action, and modes of organization, and which often consume a large part of their energies in the effort to bind such differences together. Movements, characteristically, must devote a considerable share of their resources to the task of managing the complexity and differentiation that constitutes them.

It is, furthermore, customary to refer to movements as the effects of a particular historical situation, or as an outcome of a particular conjuncture (such as an economic crisis or contradictions within the system). In doing so, however, one ignores the motives for, and the meaning and components of, collective action, by assuming that the ways in which such action comes into being and persists over time are irrelevant when compared to the interplay of 'structural' variables. These manners of considering social movements as either historical characters or results of structural determinants are not just commonplace notions of everyday discourse; they also stamp many of the current analyses of contemporary collective action.

They indeed demonstrate how wide the gap still is that separates the established linguistic convention, or the political interest that issues in the talk of 'social movements', from the possibility of giving an adequate theoretical basis to the analysis of collective action. Too often, a movement is still portrayed as the incarnation of an essence or the secondary effect of the 'tendential laws' of a structure. The *collective action* of a movement is thus always related to something other than itself; properly speaking, it does not even exist.

It is important to react against such theoretical liquidation of an object so salient in daily discourse and theoretical debate, and with so crucial a role in contemporary social processes. Beyond linguistic convention, only a theory of *collective action* can provide a meaningful basis for analysis of social movements. A discipline that sets out to study social movements can accomplish its task meaningfully only if it starts out from a theory that can account for the specificity and autonomy of social *action*, and can give a foundation to its *collective* character as something different from the sum total of aggregate individual behaviours.

Up until the 1960s, those interested in these issues in the sociological field drew, directly or indirectly, either on Marxist theory or on the sociology of collective behaviour. One has not much to say about the former, for I believe that, strictly speaking, there exists no specifically Marxist branch of analysis of social movements today in the proper sense of the term, only studies (sometimes very accurate) of the crisis of the capitalist mode of production and of its transformations. Marxism has provided a theoretical framework for the historical analysis of class action, but its explicit contribution to the theory of social movements has been poor, indirect, or frankly derivative (see Calhoun 1982; Pakulski 1995). On the other side, one finds the scholars who in the 1960s ventured to examine collective behaviour within the functionalist and interactionist traditions, the most influential among them being Smelser and Turner (Smelser 1962, 1968; Turner 1969; see also Turner and Killian 1987). Even though many differences divide and sometimes oppose to each other the functionalist and the interactionist perspectives, they both rely on a theory of shared beliefs, applied to various kinds of collective behaviour ranging from panic to revolution. The great spectrum of behavioural phenomena drawn to these analyses likewise dissolves the object 'social movements'; it now becomes a particular case of generalized belief, a specific way of restructuring the field of collective normative patterns. When norms or shared values are threatened by some form of imbalance or crisis, the response through which an attempt is made to reestablish social order is centred around a common belief which, while often fictitious, mobilizes collective energies.

In the legacy of these intellectual traditions, two ingenuous epistemological assumptions still persist that have left their mark on the study of collective phenomena. The first one is the supposition that *factual unity* of the phenomenon, as perceived or believed to be there by the observer, actually exists. The proximity in space and time of concomitant forms of individual and group behaviour is elevated from the phenomenological to the conceptual level and thus granted ontological weight and qualitative homogeneity; collective reality, as it were, exists as a unified thing. A second assumption now enters into the process of reification: the *collective dimension* of social behaviour is taken as a given, as a datum obvious enough to require no further analysis. How people actually manage acting together and becoming a 'we' evades the problematic as it is taken for granted.

However, in contemporary societies affected by accelerated change and permanently on the brink of a catastrophe, it has in the meantime become evident that social processes are products of actions, choices, and decisions. Collective action is not the result of natural forces or of the iron laws of history; but no more is it the product of the beliefs and representations held by the actors. On the one hand, research traditions have located the roots of all conflicts in the social fabric (in the economic structure in particular) and explained them in terms of an historical necessity of some sort. The most significant example of this tendency is given to us in the dilemma that, at least since the Second International, has divided Marxist scholarship: is class action born out of voluntarist orientation, emerging spontaneously from the condition of the proletariat, or is it a necessary effect of the contradictions of a capitalist production system marked by fate for a collapse? This question has remained unresolved in the Marxist traditions, and the fact bespeaks all the difficulties that arise when collective action is taken to be a phenomenon without its own autonomy from 'structural determinants'. Various attempts have been made to bridge this gulf between the contradictions of the capitalist system and class action, sometimes by emphasizing the determinism of structural laws, at others by stressing the voluntarism of mobilization. This dualistic legacy is still alive in current debates on the relationship between structure and agency (Sewell 1992; Berejikian 1992).

On the other hand stand those who seek to explain collective behaviour in terms of the beliefs held by actors, such as are manifest, for example, in common objectives or shared values. Actors, it is claimed, respond to certain dysfunctions of the social system by creating a collective set of representations which fuel action. In this case, too, the problem of how the collective subject of action comes about and persists in time is left unresolved. The actors' own beliefs will not provide a sufficient ground for an account of their actions, for such beliefs always depend on the broader relations in which the actors are involved. Analysis cannot simply identify action with that which the actors report about themselves, without taking into account the system of relationships in which goals, values, frames, and discourses are produced.

Thus, explanations based on the common structural condition of actors take for granted the actors' ability to perceive, evaluate, and decide what they have in common. That is, such explanations ignore the processes which enable actors to define a 'situation' as a field of shared action. On the other hand, actors' motives, beliefs, discourses and individual differences again are never enough to provide an explanation of how certain individuals or groups recognize each other and become part of a 'we'.

Between these two poles of the dualism bequeathed to us by research tradition there stretches an open, still unexplored theoretical space: it concerns the ways in which actors *construct* their action. During the last twenty-five years, to be sure, some progress has been made towards resolving the evident impasse created by the dualistic tradition. European authors on one hand have contributed to a better understanding of the process through which collective action is formed in highly differentiated – or postindustrial – systems (Touraine 1977, 1981, 1985; Habermas 1984, 1987, 1990; Giddens 1984, 1987, 1990). American proponents of the Resource Mobilization Theory, on the other, have provided a framework for the analysis of the actual mobilization process ((available resources, entrepreneurs, opportunity structures) (McCarthy and Zald 1973, 1977; Zald and McCarthy 1979, 1987; for a review, Jenkins 1983). Other authors have extended in original ways this paradigm (Oberschall 1973; Gamson 1990; Gamson, Fireman and Rytina 1982; Tilly 1978; McAdam 1982; Klandermans 1984; Tarrow 1989a). In my previous work I have tried to bridge these approaches by stressing the constructive dimension of collective action (Melucci 1980, 1984, 1988, 1989) and other authors have increasingly supported the necessity of reducing the gap between European and American tradition (Cohen 1985; Tarrow 1988b; Klandermans, Kriesi and Tarrow 1988; Klandermans and Tarrow 1988; McAdam, McCarthy and Zald 1988; Gamson 1992a). More recent contributions are building on these advances and are explicitly addressing the processes through which actors give meaning to their action (Klandermans 1989a, 1992; Tarrow 1992, 1994; Morris and Mueller 1992; Mueller 1992, Larana, Johnston and Gusfield 1994, Johnston and Klandermans 1995). Today we are in a better position to build a new framework for the analysis of collective action by both acknowledging the legacy of the past and overcoming its deficiencies.

Collective action as a construct

Should we want to draw up a balance sheet summing up the contribution of classical and recent sociology to the study of social movements and collective action, one can point out a number of fundamental insights which constitute indispensable points of reference for the ongoing debate on, and theoretical analysis of, collective action.

The tradition of Marxism has taught us that collective action cannot be analysed without addressing its relationship to a 'structural' (or, better, 'structured') field of relationships which provides resources and constraints for the action itself. Moreover, it has persuasively demonstrated the importance of social conflicts and the fact that some of them are of an antagonist nature. It is within this legacy that recent European contributions (Touraine 1988a, 1994a; Habermas 1989, 1990; Giddens 1990, 1991) have tried to understand the changes that modern, postindustrial systems are undergoing today.

Within the classic functionalist approach, Merton's well-known distinction between deviance and nonconformism goes beyond the limited and sometimes ideological perspective from which Parsons examines social conflicts. This distinction – with whose terminology one may or may not agree – raises a crucial problem for analysis of social movements. It rejects any reduction of collective action to the status of a mere symptom of the degradation of the social system (not by coincidence, identification of every form of collective action with deviance is a feature typical of the ideology of the dominant groups). It also permits a further distinction to be drawn between collective processes that stem from disaggregation of the system and those which rather seek to rebuild that system on a different basis.

The analyses by the Chicago School and the contribution of the sociology of collective behaviour (particularly such authors as Smelser and Turner) have taught us that it is not possible to distinguish, to use the common label in the dominant discourse, 'normal' social behaviour from a 'pathological' social behaviour, of which the forms of collective action would be an index. Analysis of collective action must be conducted using the same categories that are applied to other components of the social system: the tools employed in analysis of collective phenomena must be framed by some general hypotheses on the social system.

Symbolic interactionism building on the work of Blumer, on the other hand, has taught us that collective action is not the expression of irrationality or of psychological suggestion that the crowd psychology of the nineteenth century assumed (LeBon 1960; Tarde 1969); it is, instead, *meaningful* behaviour (see Turner 1983): there is a logic of collective action which entails certain relational structures, the presence of decision-making mechanisms, the setting of goals, the circulation of information, the calculation of outcomes, the accumulation of experience, and learning from the past.

Finally, resource mobilization theory in all its variants has demonstrated to us that collective action does not result from the aggregation of atomized individuals. Rather, it must be seen as the outome of complex processes of interaction mediated by certain networks of belonging. Collective action, therefore, is not unstructured behaviour in the sense that it would not obey any logic of rationality. It involves an articulated structure of relations, circuits of interaction and influence, choices among alternative forms of behaviour. It only appears unstructured when set against the dominant norms of the social order, and against the interests which that order wishes to maintain (as in the discourse that labels collective action as marginal, deviant, rootless, irrational).

But beyond the specific contribution of the sociology of social movements, an understanding of contemporary collective action could hardly take place without referring to the implications of cultural changes for a theory of social action. The central role of culture in shaping social action has been one fundamental reminder of the recent developments in sociological theory by authors different in many respects as Alexander (Alexander 1988a, 1988b, 1989) and Bourdieu (1977, 1984, 1990a, 1990b). Within a paradigm that stresses the capacity of human action to construct meaning and making sense of reality, my particular understanding of the cultural dimension of collective action builds on the work of Norbert Elias (1991, 1994), Mary Douglas (1970, 1986, 1992) and Clifford Geertz (1973, 1983).

If one discards the simplistic image of collective action as the upshot of irrational and perhaps suggestive processes, along with the naive assumption that collective phenomena are simply empirical aggregations of people acting together, it becomes of critical importance to develop a theoretical model to account for the nature and the emergence of this type of action through the identification of the general and specific factors of its formation. We can now identify at least five distinct problems upon which to concentrate our inquiry. A first level of analysis concerns the definition of *collective action* and involves both the devising of analytical criteria and the empirical delimitation of the field. Another issue is establishing the processes that give rise to collective action, its *formation* in the social structure. At this level, it will be important to distinguish between structural conditions and conjunctural factors. Thirdly, analysis is called for of the *components* that structure collective action, that is, of the system of relations which which give it continuity, adaptability, and effectiveness. Closely connected with this level of analysis is the problem of the *forms* assumed by collective action (and particularly by contemporary social movements). Finally, the *field* of collective action must be examined, as the set of social relationships providing resources for and constraints to the action. In this chapter I will address the first of these analytical problems, while the remaining chapters of part I (the theory of collective action) will be devoted to a closer examination of the questions involved in the second and third issues. The third issue will also be extensively addressed in part IV (internal dimensions of collective action). Part II (actors) of this book will discuss in detail contemporary social movements, while Part IV touches upon the forms of collective action in general. Part III (the systemic field) addresses the environmental conditions for collective action and in particular lays out the political system and the state as that particular field against which all collective action must measure itself in a concrete society and through which other systems of opportunities and constraints become evident.

The first question to be addressed is whether, and to what extent, it is possible at all to identify the analytical criteria which enable us to make more specific distinctions within the general category of collective action. Is it possible to establish a homogeneity of pattern between a panic and a revolt? Or, conversely, what is it that authorizes us to talk of social movements as sociologically specific phenomena? The sociology of collective behaviour, for instance, moves within the perspective of the former problematic. It defines collective behaviour as a general analytical level of social action which enables panic, fashion, crazes, and revolutions to be explained altogether using the same criteria. All that differs from one phenomenon to the other is the degree of generality in the components of action affected and restructured by collective behaviour. Smelser's theory, for example, is the first explicit attempt to develop an analytical framework which encompasses all the different forms of 'collective behaviour'. What in 'crowd psychology' was confused and implicit becomes, for Smelser, methodological requirement in the construction of theory. For early researchers, the irrationality of deep urges was the implicit analytical level at which to situate crowd behaviour. According to Smelser, however, it is generalized belief which is the feature common to all collective forms of behaviour, enabling us to decipher their analytical significance.

But is the category of generalized belief analytically precise enough to allow distinctions to be drawn among the various empirical forms of collective action? For this purpose, 'collective behaviour' is too general a container, bringing together under its categorial unity a great multitude of different empirical phenomena ranging from 'spontaneous' panic to planned revolutions. The only common feature shared by this heterogeneity is ultimately the 'collective' character of each phenomenon in concern, which simply describes an empirical contiguity but remains unsatisfactory for us set about to analytically differentiate among these phenomena.

My perspective builds on a strictly phenomenological point of departure: collective phenomena are those sets of social events that comprise a number of individuals or groups exhibiting, at the same time and in the same place, behaviours with relatively similar morphological characteristics. These phenomena are variously defined in sociological literature as collective behaviour, social movements, protest events, crowd behaviour, and the like, but the assumption that all these social practices share some common features stops short at the mere recognition of their common 'collective' character (for an example, see Hardin 1982). Beyond this phenomenological trait it is difficult to assume some kind of qualitative unity or homogeneity without making a conceptual assumption about the *analytical* nature of the phenomena. Even the choice between collective 'behaviour' or collective 'action' implies a different theoretical frame which needs to be explicitly addressed. Consequently, as a starting point, I will define collective action as a set of social practices (i) involving simultaneously a number of individuals or groups, (ii) exhibiting similar morphological characteristics in contiguity of time and space, (iii) implying a social field of relationships and (iv) the capacity of the people involved of making sense of what they are doing. This definition already contains some of the theoretical assumptions which will be discussed in the following pages, but it is also the minimal and the most general starting point for a different approach to the empirical phenomena that are usually referred to when speaking of collective action, social movements, and other similar commonsense notions.

First of all, escaping the dualistic inheritance of the sociological tradition in the study of collective phenomena will only be possible if we reverse the naive assumption regarding collective action as a unitary empirical datum. Instead of taking it as a starting point, we should examine that very datum in order to discover how it is produced, and disassemble its unity so as to reveal the plurality of attitudes, meanings, and relations that come together in the same whole of the phenomenon. Addressing the problem of how a collective actor takes shape requires recognition of the fact that, for instance, what is empirically called 'a movement' and which, for the sake of observational and linguistic convenience, has been attributed an essential unity, is in fact a product of multiple and heterogeneous social processes. We must therefore seek to understand how this unity is built and what different outcomes are generated by the interaction of its various components.

This approach signifies a real change of perspective. Historical studies and the sociology of work, for example, have shown the multiplicity of levels present in what, almost by linguistic convention, is called 'the workers' movement' and which, despite its analytical heterogeneity, stemmed from a common, underlying social condition (Calhoun 1982; Fantasia 1988; Hirsch 1990a). Strikes have never been homogeneous phenomena, for, internally, they have brought together a host of mutually conflicting demands, including those aimed at the organizational system of the firm, those addressed to the political system, and elements of class struggle against the capitalist mode of production as such (Badie 1976). This differentiation of objectives and interests is even more evident in contemporary collective phenomena, which moreover are not rooted in a shared social condition.

I propose to differentiate the general category of collective action and to shift from an empirical to an *analytical* point of view. Within this broader framework, as we will see in section 3.4 of this chapter, I specifically propose to use the notion of 'social movement' not as an empirical categorization of certain types of behaviour but as an *analytical concept*: understood this way, it addresses a *particular level* of collective action that should be distinguished from other levels present in the empirical collective phenomena. No phenomenon of collective action can be taken as a global whole since the language it speaks is not univocal. An analytical approach to those phenomena currently called 'movements' must be firmly placed within a theory of collective action, and it must break down its subject according to *orientations of action* on the one hand and the *system of social relationships affected by the action* on the other. For example, campaigning for functional changes in an organization is not the same thing as challenging its power structure; fighting for increased participation in decision-making is different from rejecting the rules of the political game. Only by distinguishing among the different analytical meanings and relational fields of the collective action under consideration can we begin to understand the contents of a concrete 'movement' as the vehicle for multiple and often contradictory demands.

Thus conceived, the *concept* of social movement, along with all the other concepts to be presented for analytical purposes in the following section, are always *objects of knowledge constructed by the analyst*; they do not coincide with the empirical complexity of the action. The study of collective action is still prisoner of an 'objectivist' assumption about his categories and it seems rarely aware of the epistemological turn introduced by hermeneutics (Ricoeur 1974, 1976, 1981, 1984; Gadamer 1976) and the cognitive revolution (Bruner 1986, 1990). An awareness of the constructive operation of our conceptual tools is today an epistemological requirement if we are to abandon for good the naive assumption that social phenomena are 'out there' existing in full independence from our point of view, and if we wish to be able to assume responsibility for the role that knowledge plays, and can play, in contemporary social life.

Principles for analysis of collective action

Analysis must distinguish between a reaction to a crisis and the expression of a conflict.

As stated, the appearance of collective action has often been linked to a *crisis* in one sector of the system or the another, the crisis denoting breakdown of the functional and integrative mechanisms of a given set of social relations. Collective action has thus been often viewed as a pathology of the social system. A *conflict*, on the other hand, is defined by a struggle between two actors seeking to appropriate resources regarded by each as valuable. The actors in a conflict join battle in a shared field for control of same resources. For an event to constitute a conflict, the actors must be definable in terms of a common reference system, and there must be something at stake to which they both, implicitly or explicitly, refer. Without a distinction between conflict and crisis it would be impossible to make sense of many historical and recent forms of collective action. Had working-class struggle, in the history of capitalism, been nothing more than a reaction to economic exploitation and cyclic crises, it would have been over as soon as the workers won better pay and improved working conditions. But the conflictual character of the workers' movement derived rather from the fact that it was a struggle against the very logic of industrial production under capitalist conditions (Katznelson and Zolberg 1986).

Conflicts, therefore, are not only conceptually distinct from crises, but among them are included those in which the adversaries enter the strife on account of the antagonistic definitions of the objectives, relations, and means of social production they assert and defend. A conflict of this kind within a social system may be brought to the surface by particular situations of crisis internal to the system itself. But when a collective actor by its action makes visible a conflict which is antagonistic in nature, this should not be confused with a simple reaction referring back to the crisis that, at this particular juncture, has provoked or accelerated that action.

A crisis always arises from the processes of disaggregation of a system, having to do with dysfunctions in the mechanisms of adaptation, imbalances among parts or subsystems, paralyses or blockages in some of these, difficulties of integration. The scope and the intensity of a crisis naturally depend on the particular levels of the system affected. A crisis provokes disintegration and the subsequent reaction of those who seek to redress the balance, whereas an antagonistic conflict makes manifest a clash over the control and allocation of crucial resources (Collins 1975). In the history of any particular society, these two dimensions are often meshed together, rendering the analysis of the processes of collective mobilization even more difficult.

The difference between a crisis and an antagonistic conflict, then, emerges as a distinction of great consequentiality. In practical reality, it is played out in the fact that the dominant groups always tend to define movements as simple reactions to crises, that is, to a dysfunctional mechanism of the system. Admitting that they are something else would entail recognition of collective demands that challenge the legitimacy of power and the current deployment of social resources.

> *Analysis should distinguish among different orientations of collective action.*

We can discriminate between sets of basic orientations of collective action that are helpful in establishing *analytical* distinctions among various kinds of behaviour. They are as follows:

1 Some collective phenomena involve *solidarity*; that is, the ability of actors to recognize others, and to be recognized, as belonging to the same social unit. In other cases, collective action arises as an aggregation of atomized behaviours (Alberoni 1984). This latter orientation I will designate as *aggregation*: (a) Aggregative orientations do not involve solidarity and they only express spatio-temporal contiguity; (b) they can be broken down to the level of the individual without the loss of their morphological features; and (c) they are wholly oriented towards the outside rather than towards the group.

Collective orientations of this kind usually form in response to a crisis in the social system or to accelerated change, and they result from the aggregation of atomized individuals through a generalized belief, in the sense given to the term by Smelser. The operation of such a belief – which is not a system of solidarity but an object of affective identification by individuals – joins together actions which in themselves are separate. An aggregate results from the temporal and spatial proximity of the repetitive multiplication of individual behaviours.

The phenomena which can be most readily assigned to this category are those that the sociology of collective behaviour has studied closely (crowd behaviour, panic, booms, crazes, fashion) (Smelser 1963; Turner and Killian 1987; Weller and Quarantelli 1974; Marx and Wood 1975; Aguirre *et al.* 1988). One should not forget, however, that these empirical phenomena likewise have different analytical meanings: a fashion, for example, is never an aggregate phenomenon pure and simple, since it is also the result of changes in production modes, of the workings of the market, and of the emergence of new needs. On the other hand, even the most highly structured social movements contain aggregate elements which manifest themselves, for example, in rituals, in the broadcasting of symbols, in mass events, and so on. Thus the empirical object should always be broken down analytically to reveal the multiple meanings it contains within itself.

2 Some collective phenomena involve *conflict*, that is, the opposition of two (or more) actors who seek control of social resources valuable to each of the protagonists. Others, again, come into being through *consensus* over the rules and procedures governing the control of valued resources.

3 Lastly, some collective orientations involve a *breach of the limits of compatibility* of the system of social relationships within which the action takes place. I define 'the limits of compatibility' as the range of variability in systemic states that enables a system to maintain its structure (or the set of elements and relations that identify the system as such). Orientations of collective action break the limits of compatibility when they are propelled beyond what is covered by the range of such variations that the system can tolerate without altering its structure. Other kinds of collective action have *order-maintaining* orientations, in that their effects remain within the limits of structural variability of the given system of social relations.

A simple breach of the compatibility limits of the reference system is not enough for an action to signify social conflict: it merely signals the disruptive character of the action. A breach of the rules or the rejection of the shared norms do not necessarily imply a struggle between two actors over something at stake, but is instead symptomatic of deviant behaviour: here the actor is defined by marginality with respect to a system of norms, reacting to the control that such norms exercise without nevertheless challenging their legitimacy – without, that is, identifying a social adversary and a set of contested resources or values. Deviance, as the product of breakdown in the order or as the inadequate assimilation of norms by individuals, resolves itself into the search for particularist rewards outside accepted norms and behaviour. In this case, too, I treat *deviance* as an analytical category endowed with autonomous weight. The empirical analysis of those forms of behaviour that are commonly classified as deviant is, then, a different matter altogether. The criticism of the functionalist framework longtime employed by sociological analysis of deviance has allowed numerous misunderstandings. It has been rightly pointed out that deviant behaviour cannot be reduced to social pathology, and that such behaviour is often implicitly critical of the dominant normative system. But preoccupation with specifying labelling processes and the processes of social production of deviance (Spector and Kitsuse 1973; Kitsuse 1975) has often obscured the best achievements of the functionalist paradigm: its focus on phenomena engendered by dysfunctions in the integrative mechanisms of a social system. Only by preserving the analytical distinction between simple disruptive behaviour and conflictual processes can we avoid both the reductionism that treats all forms of dissent as social pathology (as in the classical version of functionalism) and the attribution of an innovative or even revolutionary potential to every act that breaks the order (as in some radical extension of labelling theory).

On the other hand, if a conflict is not pushed beyond the limits of the reference system, what is in question is an opposition of interests within a certain normative framework. In such a case, action seeks to improve the relative position of the actor, to overcome functional obstacles, to change authority relationships. Conflict observes the limits set by the partners' joint preoccupation with ensuring the compatibility of the system as defined above and respecting the rules of the exchange. This kind of behaviour – common in large organizations, systems of industrial relations, and in the political systems of complex societies – can be defined as *competition*: its analytical content concerns the presence of contending interests and acceptance of set 'rules of the game'.

These basic orientations can be plotted as axes along which the various forms of collective action can be arranged and identified (figure 1).

The analytical field of collective action depends on the system of relationships within which such action takes place and towards which it is directed.

The reference systems of collective action should not be confused with the concrete sites of social praxis in which action effectively takes place (institutions, associations, organizations, and the like). The physical workings of a certain social arrangement always combine a number of different processes: the school, the factory, the city are all the result of the interaction of productive structures, of systems of stratification, of decision-making processes, of symbolic systems, of forms of power, and so on.

The reference systems of collective action should therefore be understood as analytical structures, as specific forms of social relationships which can be differentiated in terms of the nature of the social link binding individuals or groups together. Any analysis that, implicitly or explicitly, introduces the notion of the 'breaking of limits' must define a reference system. Sociologists, however, have often failed to recognize the full importance of this imperative – for example, when they have looked at 'protest' and usually

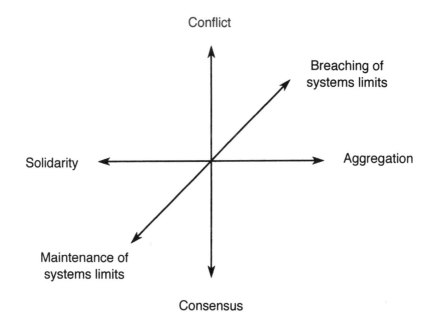

Conflict

Breaching of
systems limits

Solidarity

Aggregation

Maintenance of
systems limits

Consensus

Figure 1

defined it as a form of *disruptive* action (Lipsky 1968; Eisinger 1973; Di Nardo 1985; Lofland 1985; Epstein 1990a). But what are the confines that the protest breaks or transcends ('disrupts')? Without a definition of the reference system, the notion of protest is, analytically speaking, meaningless.

The first question is: What is meant by a 'system'? An approach to the social reality in terms of systems refuses to characterize this reality as any kind of essence or a metaphysical entity, and instead considers it to be a coincidence of interdependent relationships. A system is simply the complex of the relationships among its elements. A system does not possess a privileged nucleus that would contain the meaning of the whole. Each element stands for itself in relation to the others, and each variation in these relations affects the whole. To analyse society as a complex of social relations is tantamount to declining the invitation both to reduce the social to the natural and to turn it into an expression of essence (of man, of Spirit, of morality). Social action is not the effect of mechanical laws or natural determinism, but nor is it the incarnation of the spirit or a progeny of values; it is the result of relationships which tie together a plurality of social actors producing meaning for what they do (Alexander 1988a; Collins 1981, 1988, 1989; Schelling 1978).

Different systems which may be defined according to the specific types of relations that characterize them. Minimally, we must thus distinguish between (1) the system that *ensures the production* of a society's resources; (2) the system that *makes decisions* about the distribution of these resources; (3) the system of roles which *governs the exchange* and deployment of the latter; and (4) the lifeworld or the system of *reproduction* in everyday life:

1 The first of these systems consists of antagonistic relationships that comprise the production, appropriation, and allocation of a society's basic resources. This level of relations defines the modes by which society produces and appropriates its basic resources, incorporating imbalances of power and manifesting a basic conflict over the means and orientation of social production. As regards production, we should remember that the historical experience of the era of industrial capitalism has supported the ascendance of the reductivist identification of the mode of production with economic activity. The social relations of capitalist production, which in industrial society were culturally defined in material terms, have been overgeneralized to stand for production as such, obscuring thereby the understanding of the cognitive, symbolic, and relational components that have always given the social activity of producing its very character.

2 The political system (see chapter twelve) constitutes the level of a society at which, within a framework of shared rules and through processes of representation, normative decisions are made between competing interests. This analytical level not only coincides with political systems in the strict sense but can today be identified in all complex organizations, decentralized administrative systems, and the like as well.

3 The third system, the organizational system, comprises the relationships whose purpose it is to ensure the society's internal equilibrium as well as its adaptation to the environment through processes of integration and exchange among different parts of the system (in particular through exchange among roles, or systems of normatively regulated, reciprocal expectations of behaviour). This analytical level applies equally to a global society and to an individual organization or institution.

4 The lifeworld, or the reproductive system, is that level of social relations within which the basic requirements of social life are maintained and reproduced through interaction and communication. In everyday life intimate interpersonal relations allow individuals to make sense of their world. Physical reproduction and affective primary bonds rely on face to face relationships governed by the fundamental dynamics of identification and differentiation.

From this multiplicity of the systems making up the social structure, it is clear that each one of such systems is 'incomplete' in itself, and that each of them reaches out to other systems, to relations and meanings, to goals and interests beyond their individual confines. There is a hierarchy whereby one system imposes on others a greater burden of limitations than what the others may accomplish with respect to it; this, however, is not a mechanical, predetermined relationship, but one of autonomy and dependence. Dependence is manifest in the fact that the possibilities and the limits in the functioning of one system are determined by another. Autonomy arises where each system has developed processes and rules of its own, and each has the capacity to create constraints on the system upon which it depends. Thus social production sets specific limits on the functioning of the political system; and the political system, in turn, establishes the rules for social organizations and everyday life. Each of these systems, however, is also governed by its own internal logic and constituted by specific relations (opposition between different societal ends, the play of pressure and influence in decision-making, exchange and interaction between roles, interpersonal and affective communication in lifeworlds). Moreover, each system can affect the others, among them even those with respect to which the system's balance sheet of mutual constraint remains negative: for example, the meaningfulness or the emptiness of primary relations, and the equilibrium, or lack thereof, of the role system can affect the political system and the mode of production, just as openness or rigidity in political decision-making mechanisms can retroact on the relations of production and on the appropriation of social resources.

This set of analytical distinctions enables us to differentiate among the multiple fields of collective action that combine in various ways with the orientations listed above in the concrete phenomena that are currently called by the observers, or call themselves, 'social movements'. Through this set of analytical categories, competition regulated by interests that operate within the confines of the existing social order can be distinguished from forms of solidarist action which force the conflict to the point of breaking through the system's compatibility limits; the atomized sum of individual behaviours present in certain aggregate phenomena can be differentiated from deviant behaviour which pushes beyond shared rules but does not reach conflictual dimensions, and so forth.

> *The notion of a social movement is an analytical category. It*
> *designates that form of collective action which (i) invokes solidarity,*
> *(ii) makes manifest a conflict, and (iii) entails a breach of the limits*
> *of compatibility of the system within which the action takes place.*

Within the framework of the principles just laid out, I propose to transform the notion of social movement from an empirical generalization into an analytical concept. As an empirical generalization the notion of social movement is currently applied to various empirical phenomena of collective action ranging from political protest to different kinds of 'disruptive' behaviour. The empirical features selected by the observer normally lead to differing definitions of what a social movement is, with a low and erratic degree of comparability among the various definitions (for recent examples with different theoretical backgrounds, see Boggs 1986; Diani 1992; Epstein 1990b; Tarrow 1994). I propose, instead, to define the concept of 'social movement' through certain analytical dimensions which indicate specific qualities within the broader field of collective action. One can speak of a 'social movement' only when these analytical conditions required by the definition are met. Or, better yet, one can employ the concept as an analytical tool to detect in the variety of empirical behaviours the presence of those analytical dimensions that identify a specific type of collective action.

The epistemological shift I thus propose implies an equivalent shift in the attitude of the observer-analyst: that from simply mirroring empirical reality under the assumption of its 'objective' existence, towards a more explicit and conscious acknowledgment of the active role of our analytical tools in selecting among the mass of empirical 'data' and in constructing our 'objects' of knowledge.

In this specific case, such a shift nevertheless involves a linguistic problem. In our ordinary language, we still hold on to the notion of social movement to indicate various empirical collective actors (as when we speak of 'youth movement', 'women's movement', 'peace movement', and the like). Confusingly, thus, the same term is used to designate at once an analytical concept and a variety of empirical phenomena. The persistence of this linguistic ambiguity, however, depends on the life expectancy of the notion of a social movement itself. Its crisis is related to, and settled together with, the crisis of the general paradigm to which it belongs and which gave birth to it: that of the industrial capitalism. We cannot rid ourselves of old languages as long as we remain imbedded in the old paradigm of which they are an organic part; and at the establishment of a new paradigm the old problem ceases to exist altogether as it comes to be defined in a different way, generating thereby entirely new concepts. At the present, I see no alternative but provisionally to accept the uncomfortable linguistic ambiguity while at the same time intensifying the efforts to push the notion of social movement towards a creative self-destruction.

Under this conscious theoretical discomfort, I wish to define a social movement as a concept that comprises three analytical dimensions. A movement is the mobilization of a collective actor (i) defined by specific solidarity, (ii) engaged in a conflict with an adversary for the appropriation and control of resources valued by both of them, (iii) and whose action entails a breach of the limits of compatibility of the system within which the action itself takes place. A movement, therefore, does not just restrict itself to expressing a conflict; it pushes the conflict beyond the limits of the system of social relationships within which the action is located. In other words, it breaks the rules of the game, it sets its own non-negotiable objectives, it challenges the legitimacy of power, and so forth.

In order to identify a movement – as a category of analysis rather than as an empirical phenomenon – we therefore have to verify three conditions, each one of which must be met before we can speak of a 'social movement' in any analytical sense. These dimensions also allow a clear distinction from other kinds of collective action theoretically bordering on social movements.

> *A 'social movement' refers to just one specific form of collective action among many others that combine orientations and fields of different kinds.*

My purpose here is to suggest elements of a method rather than engage in a typological exercise. We must at all times keep in mind the limits of any typology: they depend on the dimensions of action that are originally selected by the observer. A refinement or improvement in the analytical procedures along the lines I have proposed would produce different typologies. For that reason, my remarks are intended to address questions of method instead of aiming to contribute to production of a comprehensive summary of the various forms of collective action.

From this starting point, we may proceed to next examine more closely some of the possible observable combinations of the categories presented above that refer to actual forms of collective action bordering on social movements.

(i)   *Social movements* were already defined as those forms of action analytically implying conflict, solidarity and a breaching of the system limits.

(ii)   In general terms, one may talk of *competition* when conflict and solidarity are confined within the boundaries of the given system.

(iii)   At the opposite pole, forms of behaviour which breach these compatibility limits without, however, implying solidarity and constituting a conflict can be identified as *deviance*.

(iv)   *Cooperation* designates the area of collective action that is based on solidarity but not oriented towards a conflict, and which is entirely located within the limits of compatibility of the system.

(v)   Up to this point, social movements literature, my own work included, has been mainly devoted to oppositional movements, revealing an explicit bias of the majority of the students of collective phenomena. With some important exceptions, much less attention has been paid to what we can call *reaction*, that area of collective action where solidarity is employed to defend social order even by breaching the system limits. The literature on right-wing movements and counter-movements (see Mosse 1975; Billig 1978; Lo 1982; Zald and McCarthy 1987; Blee 1991) provides good examples of such an orientation. These forms of action turn increasingly towards an explicit fascist character as they move from the organizational level to the mode of production.

Other areas of collective action are less prone to a categorization that would inevitably imply a detailed typology. My methodological purpose is fulfilled here by the simple warning that what we empirically call 'social movements' are in fact composite phenomena of collective action comprising a multiplicity of analytical dimensions. The specific level of collective action that I have analytically called 'social movement' is empirically surrounded by and intertwined with many other forms of action implying differing orientations and affecting different fields. However, one should never forget that collective action takes place not only where it manifests itself in visible mobilizations against public authorities. Collective action is also present in forms of behaviour that apparently never reach any comparable prominence:

(vi)   *Individual resistance*, like the slowdown of work rhythms or sabotage in capitalist factories (Dubois 1976), is not just an individual behaviour. As shown by many studies, such seemingly atomized behavior is a primitive form of conflictual resistance to capitalist power in the workplace, an embryo of class consciousness without which the more visible forms of collective action could not be explained. It is an action which expresses a conflict and breaks the system limits, but which takes the form of an aggregate behaviour. Other forms of elementary resistance which precede more organized forms of behaviour have been analysed in rural societies (see Hobsbawm 1959; Scott 1986; Colburn 1989; Abu-Lughod 1990).

(vii)   On the other hand, *individual mobility* is sometimes an alternative to collective competition, when the channels for the improvement of individual conditions are open and the costs for mobilization are high (see the classic exit-voice model by Hirschman 1975). Individuals express a conflictual orientation within the limits of the system in an aggregate form that does not reach the level of solidaristic action and looks for atomized individual advantages.

(viii) At the opposite pole, collective *rituals* that publicly celebrate and reinforce social order may sometimes be carriers of social movements, their womb or their mentors (Turner 1969, 1982; Ozouf 1988; Mosse 1975). They are aggregate phenomena that imply consensus and take place within the limits of a given system.

All these levels of collective action should be of main interest for the students of social movements because some of them are always associated with the big processes of collective mobilizations and can provide useful hints for the understanding of the multiple meaning of collective action (figure 2 provides a summary of the present discussion in a graphic form).

A further step in the differentiation of analytical levels of action consists in articulating them with the different systemic fields. This exercise could end up in a rigid typology, which as already stated is not my purpose. I will therefore just give some examples to show the possible applications of the criteria adopted here, knowing that none of these forms of behaviour is by definition 'pure'.

1 Where forms of competition are concerned, *claimant action* and *political competition* can be used to address those conflicts that lie, respectively, within the confines of an organizational and a political system. *Cultural innovation* is a form of action which is in conflict with the bases of the mode of production, but which, at least for a while, keeps within the system's compatibility limits.

2 In the case of deviance, behaviours can be examined, first of all, at the lifeworld and the organizational level. This is the case with most of the behavioural forms that the classical literature on deviance identifies as the product of dysfunctions in integrative mechanisms, in processes of socialization, and in the agencies of social control. At the political level, we may refer to forms of political violence which break the rules of a political game without any reference to institutional change or to the modification of power relationships. Many forms of expressive violence and terrorist action (which often come to coincide) assume this feature. Certain forms of extreme alienation seek to jolt the fundamental logic of the mode of production by totally, and typically through violent means, rejecting it. However, such action does not develop into conflict, lacking as it does the identification of the stakes and/or of the social adversary. Here the presence of an unborn conflict is detected by its absence, by its negative imprint,

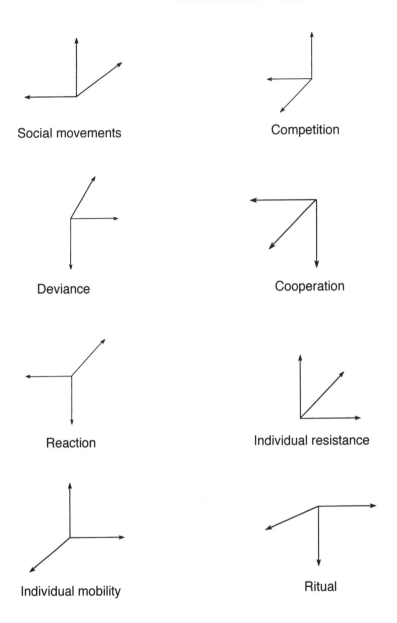

Social movements

Competition

Deviance

Cooperation

Reaction

Individual resistance

Individual mobility

Ritual

Figure 2

as it were; precisely for this reason such a form of behaviour constitutes a signal that should be read all the more carefully (for a significant example in the case of youth, see Dubet 1987).

As for cooperation, a distinction among the levels of action is easily exposed to the risk of confusing analytical categories with natural phenomena. Many forms of altruism and community action correspond to these analytical orientations at the everyday life and organizational level respectively. Voluntary action can manifest this orientation in the political system, particularly in campaigning, fund-raising, and lobbying activities. Press and intellectual campaigns are approximate examples of activities carrying this orientation and affecting the mode of production.

Distinguishing among the various levels of aggregate behaviour, here too, is made more difficult by their nebulous and scattered nature, and by the increased risk of confusing analytical categories with natural phenomena. None the less, drawing on the existing literature on collective behaviour, at the lifeworld or organizational level we can identify those kinds of behaviour which link up most closely with a crisis or a change in either the functional processes or the instrumental apparatuses of a system (panics, booms). As regards the political system, one may speak of crazes and riots as phenomena that indicate aggregate response to a crisis or a change in the decision-making apparatus. Finally, bearing in mind the conceptual difficulty inherent in referring aggregate behaviour back to a mode of production, fashions are probably forms of behaviour which, at the aggregate level, are one reaction to a crisis or transformation in the production and appropriation of social resources.

Social movements can be distinguished according to the field of their action.

We can now apply the same general criteria to the specific category of social movements. They too can be classified into four analytically different types of behaviour according to the system invested by collective action.

(a) If the conflict and the breaking of the rules take place at the lifeworld level, we can talk of a *conflictual networking*. Molecular action is taken against the rules governing social reproduction in everyday life through the creation of networks of conflictual social relations. Forms of popular resistance are always present in society, creating a free space that precede visible action (Evans and Boyte 1986; Fantasia 1988; Colburn 1989; Scott 1986, 1990b).

(b) Within an organizational system characterized by roles and functions, action may be appropriately called a *claimant movement*. The collective actor presses for a different distribution of resources within an organization and strives for a more efficient functioning of the apparatus. Such action, however, clashes with the power that imposes the rules and decides on the division of labour. The action taken may be in defence of the advantages enjoyed by a distinct category, it may mobilize a group of underprivileged workers, or it may seek to bring about a different distribution of roles and rewards. In doing so, however, it tends to exceed the established limits of the organization and its normative framework. The conflict moves beyond the operative level to affect the production of norms.

(c) A *political movement* expresses conflict by breaking the confines of the political system. It campaigns to extend the criteria for participation in decision-making and fights against the bias in the political game that always privileges some interests above others. It seeks to improve the actor's influence over the decision-making processes, or to ensure its access to them, and endeavours to open up new channels for the expression of previously excluded demands, by pushing in any case participation beyond the limits set by the existing political system.

(d) An *antagonist movement* consists of collective conflictual action aimed at the production of a society's resources. It not only contends the specific way in which resources are produced, but equally challenges the goals of social production and the direction of development as such.

Antagonist movements are by definition the most abstract of the categories proposed so far, since no collective actor can ever be wholly 'antagonistic'. Set within a concrete society, what is currently called a 'movement' operates through everyday networks, organizational systems and the mechanisms for political representation and decision-making. What, then, is the meaning of making this distinction?

There are two points. Firstly, the dominant groups in a society tend to deny the existence of conflicts which involve the production and appropriation of social resources. At the very most, they acknowledge the existence of grievances or political claims, seeking however then to reduce all conflictual phenomena to these only. Secondly, we must acknowledge that not all forms of collective action are antagonistic in their nature and that the functional or political problems of a society have their own autonomous existence.

Moreover, the degree of autonomy or specificity of political systems and organizational mechanisms *vis-à-vis* the constraints of social production is a key factor in assessing the impact of antagonistic demands within such systems. There are no antagonist movements in undiluted form, unmediated by the political system or the social organization. A 'pure' antagonist movement, unprepared to equip itself with an instrumental base and without any relationship with the mechanisms of representation and decision-making, tends to break up and disintegrate along the two dimensions that define its action. Conflict and the breach of the compatibility limits are divorced, and the conflict loses its social rootedness and its antagonistic connotations, terminating in a mere symbolic search for alternative – a search easily assuming the features of an escapist and marginal counter-culture unable to exert any influence on the crucial mechanisms of the society. Or, on the other hand, limit-breaking action becomes deprived of any conflictual referent (adversary and stake) and turns into that obsessive rejection which, as an end in itself, finds its only form of expression in violent alienation.

In the more undifferentiated societies of the past where the functions of unification and centralization were performed by the state, social movements were unable to express themselves without the mediation of collective action tied to the social organization or the political system. As a result of the increasing differentiation of societies and the greater autonomy of the various systems that constitute them, it is now easier to pursue antagonist action without the mediation of organizations or institutions. Thus we can today witness the appearance of forms of antagonist action which state the issue of control over key collective resources in directly cultural terms. Complete lack of any kind of mediation, however, renders these forms of action extremely fragile. In any case, they probably anticipate, in an embryonic form, the advent of antagonist action that is less constrained by organizational and political mediation, and hence more likely to 'explode' in the two directions I described above.

The movements of the late 1970s and the 1980s were the first signs of the transition from movements as organizational or political actors to movements as *media*. The movements of the nineteenth century were at the same time social actors – class actors – *and* political actors, acting for the inclusion of the working class within the bourgeois political system and the bourgeois state (Tilly 1975, 1990; Katznelson and Zolberg 1986). In complex systems these two aspects are breaking apart, creating different and separate processes. On one hand, there are political actors, engaged in action for reform, inclusion, new rights, the opening of the boundaries of the political systems, redefinition of the political rules, and so on. And on the other hand, there are actors addressing the issues in a pure cultural form, or in pure cultural terms – bringing the issue to the fore, to the public. When the issue is *named*, it can at once be processed through political means, but if it is not named, and until it is not named, it is simply acted through structures, powers, imbalances, domination, and so forth. A movement as a pure medium is a form of action that simply brings to the light the fact that there is a societal dilemma and a conflict concerning some basic orientations of society. Of course, the observable empirical forms of action never reach such 'purity', but we can still expect these two trends to remain increasingly separate.

This transition will not be linear, since political actors will still be needed as we continue living in historical societies with political systems, within borders of states, and so on. Without political action, change cannot be institutionalized in complex societies, but movements increasingly act as new media by their very existence. When they escape the risk of pure symbolic counterculture (see, for example, Marx and Holzner 1975) or marginal violence, they fulfil their role and transform themselves into new institutions, providing a new language, new organizational patterns and new personnel. This outcome, however, depends on what it is possible to *process* politically and on the degree of openness and flexibility of the given political systems.

Every concrete form of collective action has a plurality of analytical meanings.

The aim of our discussion so far has been to suggest elements of a method for the analysis of 'social movements' more than to provide an exhaustive empirical account of them (which at this point could only be descriptive and classificatory). The distinctions I have drawn are analytical. That is to say, they are conceptual instruments to be used in analysing empirical phenomena. A concrete collective actor is always a complex and heterogeneous process which unfolds in reality and which contains meanings of action that are addressed by the various analytical categories I have set forth in what goes before. A collective actor operates within various organizational systems at once; it lies within one or more political systems; it acts within a society comprising various coexisting modes of production. Its action therefore involves a whole range of problems, actors, and objectives.

One dimension may outweigh the others and thus give a particular character to a movement. Alternatively, the dimensions may combine in different ways. An empirical 'movement' within an historical society is often the confluence of the marginal and deviant groups present in a system, and aggregate behaviours form and coagulate within it. On its borders, action dissolves into mere negotiatory behaviour or violent rupture according to whether it becomes wholly integrated within sphere of the rules and limits of the system or loses its capacity to locate an adversary and a common field for conflict. For the meaning and direction of a collective actor to be understood, this magma of empirical components must first be deconstructed by analysis and then reconstructed into a system of meaningful relations.

This operation, however, does not proceed in a straightforward fashion. In particular, it is not easy to identify the elements that allow one to speak of an antagonistic orientation of collective action:

(i) The *way in which a system affected by collective action responds* to the conflictual impulse is a first indicator of the meaning of that action. The adversary – controlling more resources and having thus more to lose – will not permit itself a broad margin of error. The interests under attack react in those areas where they are perceived to be threatened the most, and when a movement is antagonistic this response usually occurs at a systemic level higher than the one that is directly affected by the movement's action. Protest arising within an organizational system and directly challenging the setup of power provokes intervention by the political system and the repressive apparatus of the state. A political movement which pushes beyond the allowed limits of participation arouses a reaction which involves the mode of production (for example, economic crisis, a halt in innovation, the rise of new elites).

(ii) Secondly, an antagonist movement, using the language of its own cultural system, tends to describe the situation as *a struggle between those who produce crucial social resources and those who appropriate them.* Whether directly or indirectly, what is at stake in this struggle is always the control over these resources – that is, the society's mode of production.

(iii) Finally, in moving from everyday networking to a claimant movement, to a political movement, and then to an antagonistic one, action passes along a spectrum consisting of the following dimensions:

> *Increasing symbolic content.* An antagonist movement campaigns for objectives that always concern the fundamental identity of the actors. This is no longer an issue of control over immediate resources or of acquisition of material advantages, but of the fundamental nature of social production itself; what is at stake is the possibility of giving a different form to, and profoundly reorganizing, the structure and goals of the appropriation of social resources. In this sense, antagonistic conflict strikes at the heart of the cultural foundations of a society.

Decreasing divisibility (or negotiability) of goals. When conflicts are internal to an organization or a political system it is easier to adopt partial strategies and to negotiate about intermediate goals. Antagonist movements embody goals and forms of action that are not negotiable with the existing arrangement of social power and with the forms of political hegemony exercised by dominant interests.

Decreasing reversibility of conflicts. Conflict resolution becomes progressively more difficult as action completes the passage from the claimant movement type to an antagonist movement, and the stakes become increasingly more important for the group concerned.

Decreasing calculability. The ratio between the costs and benefits of the action is clearer, and calculation of the effects of various courses of action is easier, when that which is at stake is more readily quantifiable and when it is possible to identify various alternative solutions. When the stakes concern general cultural orientations of society not everything can be calculated and the affective and emotional dimension (which is not irrational!) becomes ever important.

Solution tending towards zero sum. The further one moves along the spectrum towards antagonist movements, the closer the conflict approximates a zero sum solution. In struggles for the control of social production the stakes are indivisible, whereas in an organization or a political system all parties to the conflict may hope to gain a partial advantage, and victory for one of them induces only a relative imbalance of gains and losses.

Every form of collective action is a system of action.

The collective action of an empirical 'movement' is the outcome of purposes, resources, and limits. Put differently, it is a purposive orientation built on social relations within a field of opportunities and constraints. It therefore cannot be considered as either the simple effect of structural preconditions or the expression of values and beliefs. Individuals and groups acting collectively construct their action by means of organized investments: in other words, they define in cognitive and affective terms the field of possibilities and limits which they perceive, and they simultaneously activate their relationships to create meaning out of their joint behaviour, so as to give sense to their 'being together' and to the goals they pursue.

The empirical unity of a social movement should be considered as a result rather than a starting point, a fact to be explained rather than something already evident. Collective action is a multipolar system of action which combines different orientations, involves multiple actors, and encompasses a system of opportunities and constraints which shapes the actors' relationships. Actors produce collective action because they are able to define themselves and their relationship with the environment (other actors, available resources, present opportunities and obstacles). The process of creating such definitions is, however, not linear: the events in which a number of individuals act collectively are the product of the interaction, negotiation, and opposition between different action orientations. The actors construct a 'we' (more or less stable and integrated according to the type of action) by rendering common, combining and then painstakingly adjusting three different kinds of orientations: those relating to the *ends* of the action (to the meanings that the action has for the actor), to the *means* (that is, to the possibilities and limits of action), and finally to relationships with the *environment* (to the field in which the action takes place).

The multipolar system of action of a collective actor thus organizes itself along a number of polarities: the three axes (ends, means, environment) constitute a set of interdependent vectors in reciprocal tension. In fact, collective action has to be able to handle within its own field mutually conflicting needs, it has to meet multiple and contrasting requirements in terms of ends, means, and environment. It is never the simple expression of one goal-directed impulse; it builds itself out of the resources available to the actors and located within the field of possibilities and limits of a particular environment. Collective mobilizations can occur and even continue because the actor has succeeded in realizing, and in the course of the action continues to realize, a certain integration between those contrasting requirements. Constant tensions arise among ends, means, and environment: Goals no longer match means or vice versa; the environment is either poor or rich in the requisite resources; the means are more or less congruent with the field of action. Even within each one of these three axes, tensions are continually generated: over the definition of ends, between short- and long-term ends, over the choice of means, over the choice between allocating resources for the pursuit of efficiency and for building solidarity, over relationships with the environment, between internal equilibrium and exchange with the outside.

Collective actors constantly negotiate and renegotiate these aspects of their action. This 'social construction' of the 'collective' through repeated negotiation is continually at work when a form of collective action occurs. A failure or a break in this constructive process makes the action impossible. Leadership and organizational forms represent attempts to give a more stable and predictable structure to to this multipolar system, which is permanently subject to stress (see chapters 16 and 17). Usually, when one considers collective phenomena, attention is focused on the most visible aspects of the action (events, mobilizations); but these presuppose the generally ignored analytical level to which I have already drawn attention (see chapter 4 for further development). Visible action is born and persists over time because the actor manages to achieve a certain degree of integration among the various orientations just described. Undoubtedly, the emergence of concrete actions is aided by conjunctural factors (such as the structure of political opportunities, the existence of entrepreneurs, the extent of equilibrium or crisis in the environment). But it would be impossible for these factors to exert any influence were the actor not able to perceive them and to integrate them into the system of orientations which frames the action.

2

Conflict and change

The emergence of collective action

The most simple explanation of the origin of social movements is the one
provided by the ruling groups in the society. The ideology of the constituted
order defines collective action as irrational and always regards it as ultimately stemming from a conspiracy or a contagion (Moscovici 1981;
Graumann and Moscovici 1987; McPhail 1991). Such a theory of bad faith
customarily interprets collective action as comprising a 'decent' majority
which, however unwittingly, becomes guided by deception or by suggestion
– and in actuality against its own true interests – by a minority of agitators.
Another standard feature of this account is the persecutorial representation of the subject as a threatening, unitary, and organized adversary.

This ideology, which in a subtle manner permeates a great many analyses of episodes of collective action, not only asserts an arbitrary and unsci-
entific anthropology of the deficiencies of human nature, but also bluntly
rejects all empirical evidence. In fact, no phenomenon is of greater importance for the analysts of social movements than the complexity of the relations and divisions internal to the collective actor, and the difficulties
involved in building unitary action.

If we leave aside these presociological attempts at explanation and
instead inspect the contributions made by the sociological tradition, we
find a variety of proposals wide enough to resist every attempt at typological classification. Eckstein (1965), in a classic essay seeking to establish an
'etiology of internal wars', has assigned the various theories of collective
action into five categories: (a) theories which stress 'intellectual' factors,
according to which revolts, social movements, and revolutions stem from a
breakdown in socialization, a conflict of values and ideologies, and/or a
betrayal of the system by the intellectuals; (b) theories which give emphasis to economic factors (increasing impoverishment or rapid economic

growth, disequilibria between production and the distribution of resources, or a combination of these); (c) theories which focus on aspects of the social structure such as a breakdown in cohesion, excessive or scant mobility, anomie, or the ascent of new classes; (d) theories which concentrate on political factors (the government's failure to satisfy political demands, closure of channels of participation, too rapid an expansion of these channels); (e) theories which give priority to the general characteristics of change, such as too drastic a pace of the changes, their random and erratic or asymmetric nature. This typology already covers a wide range of theoretical approaches. If, however, we proceed nowhere beyond the activity of the mere enumeration of causal factors, it becomes difficult to orient oneself among the various explanatory frameworks offered, as all of these models have some basis in empirical evidence.

A more reliable approach would instead be to first fix certain criteria for a sociological explanation and then use such criteria to frame a discussion of the various theories. The first general condition for a sociological approach to the problem is that the explanation be couched in terms of *social relationships*. This, of course, might appear an obvious agreement; yet it remains a fact that many of the discourses on collective action still very frequently take a covert recourse to a concept of human nature. They do so espousing either the negative and pessimistic version of it, propounded by the dominant discourse equating collective action with irrationality, or in the form of blind acceptance of the humanistic triumphalism of certain images purveyed by social movements of themselves. The main difficulty, however, lies not in avoiding such ideological pitfalls but in succeeding to analyse collective action as a set of relationships. The fact that what is conventionally considered to be the specific and separate object of analysis is either rebellious action or the response to it by the dominant system easily leads to the risk of reifying social actors by separating them from their social relationships. It is necessary, instead, to base analysis on the field relationship, even when one's consideration is centred on only one of the parties involved. A concept which implies this relational perspective is, for example, that of the *potential* of collective action, which, adopting a suggestion by Eckstein (1965; see also Klandermans 1984; Klandermans and Oegema 1987), I define as the relationship between the forces which work for collective action and the forces which work against it. Thus, from this point of view collective action should always be seen as a *resultant* in a field.

The second condition for a properly sociological analysis is this: sociological explanation must identify the point at which the analysis of 'structures' and 'systems' and the analysis of forms of behaviour meet. 'Action' is, conceptually, this meeting point. The *raison d'être* of sociology lies, I believe, precisely in the possibility of this encounter, and the theme of collective action forms a critical staging area along the way. Refusing to identify itself with actors, with their own representations, with their motivations, sociological explanation must account for behaviour on the basis of a field of social relationships. At the same time, however, it must not relegate such behaviour to the merely epiphenomenal, into the results of mechanical determination by the system. Actors themselves, with their different orientations, constitute the various systems of social relations which form the 'structure'.

Lastly, sociological explanation must encompass meaningful criteria which enable distinctions to be drawn among different forms of behaviour. The confusion noted above in the definitions of collective action should also be avoided in the analysis of its emergence. It is not enough to indicate the factors responsible for a collective phenomenon *en large* (a 'riot', a 'movement', or a 'revolution'); one must also identify those differential factors which give rise to one kind of action rather than another.

How an antagonistic conflict is born

The theorists of pluralism and the sociology of conflict were right on target when they showed the inadequacy of the Marxist class paradigm set against the multiplicity of the groups and interests that interweave in complex societies. But in doing so, they deliberately ignored, for a priori ideological reasons, the existence of general conflicts of antagonistic scope. The most significant examples of such neoliberalist positions that have deeply influenced scholarship are those provided in the 1960s by Dahrendorf (1972) and in the 1970s by Crozier (Crozier and Friedberg 1978). Similar assumptions are also implicit in neoutilitarian theories of the political market (e.g. Lindblom, 1977), in the liberal critique of the welfare state (e.g. Dahrendorf, 1988), and in theories of rational choice (see Coleman 1982, 1990; for a critique of the rational choice model, see Heath 1976).

Utilitarianism, whether in its optimistic or pessimistic versions, explains conflict in terms of the acquisitive nature of *homo oeconomicus*. It relies on an elementary anthropology, on a philosophy of human nature in its positive form of acquisitive needs or in its negative form of *homo homini lupus*, for explanation of the clash of interests.

Marxism, on the other hand, maintains that conflict derives from the necessary contradictions of the class systems. However, on the sociological level, the reliance on necessary contradictions sets off an endless chain of determinisms which reduces social relations to natural relationships and deprives them of their specificity. The question arises, where do these contradictions derive from (for example, those between production relations and productive forces, in standard Marxist language) if not from certain social relationships?

Conflict is thus portrayed as either generated by the inevitable growth of productive forces beyond the limits allowed by production relationships, being thus the necessary effect of capitalist crises, or it is considered an expression of human essence, of the nature of the elite or of the masses. Determinism and voluntarism are the negation of sociology – that is, of the explanation of social action on the basis of social relationships.

Even a writer of the stature of Touraine (1977, 1988), who has pushed criticism of social philosophies to its furthest and sought to lay a basis for a theory of action, still preserves a sort of metaphysics of conflict as an original dimension of society. The problem, however, is how to explain conflict in terms of social relations without turning it into a primal dimension. This is to say that what needs to be done is to construct an analytical space within which to frame antagonistic social relationships.

I shall call this space a theory of production or of the relation to objects. Industrial capitalism has accustomed us to associating 'class relationships' with the metabolism of material production, with the work that transforms nature and produces goods. Instead, we need a theory of production which severs the equivalence relation inserted between production and economic relationships: these two are but one specific form of a social relationship and as such inseparable from other kinds of relation. It was only under the conditions of capitalist production during a distinct phase of the development of Western industrial societies that this temporary coincidence between economic 'form' and social relationships of production came into existence.

A sociological theory of social production as a relationship with objects is therefore required; and every effort should be made to divest it of its historical ties with capitalist industrialization so as to prepare for an adequate account of the production conditions in highly complex societies.

I therefore define social production as the shaping or reshaping of objects through application of certain means of production to a raw material within specific social relationships. The analytical components of social production are thus: (i) a form of action; (ii) raw material; (iii) the means of production; (iv) a social relationship. The shaping or reshaping of objects, or the action that modifies the human environment, takes place within a social relationship and also within the framework of a dual 'non-social' constraint. Human action is purposive behaviour capable of reflexivity – capable, that is, of producing its own orientation and also of recognizing it. It is at the same time social behaviour, behaviour defined by the interdependence and the symbolic exchanges that tie people together. The dual 'non-social' constraint signals the anti-idealist character of the definition of production. There exist conditions which represent the system of constraints governing the shaping and reshaping of objects. The natural environment of the action (raw material) and its instrumental base (means of production) indicate that human behaviour which transforms the environment is never the pure expression of an essence, of an intention, of a will.

Social production is therefore part of Nature, since it is from Nature that social production extracts those crucial (biological, energy, instrumental) resources that make it possible, and it is from Nature that its constraints simultaneously derive. But a specific feature of this natural process – in other respects similar to the behaviour of other living systems – is that the shaping of the environment takes place coupled to the production of meaning and symbolically mediated relations.

Social production always transforms Nature into Culture and the paradox of this junction lies at the core of human action. Production therefore entails recognition of the product as the result of the producer's action. But the attribution of belonging, in a situation of relational interdependence, presupposes certain reciprocity of recognition. Under these conditions, appropriation of the product is possible, giving rise to a certain orientation or destination of the produced goods. Production as a symbolically mediated social act is therefore the point at which human action and other living systems both meet and separate (Morin 1980, 1986). Production is a social relationship which involves reciprocal recognition of the identity of the producers and which, because of the fact, makes exchange possible. Exchange, and even more so the gift in which the values exchanged are no longer comparable, presupposes the producer's ability to recognize and to appropriate. Exchange and gift are possible because each party is able to recognize its own products and because, at the same time, there is a certain reciprocity of recognition between the two. A theory of social production therefore implicates a theory of identity.

Constructing an analytical space of this kind – which precedes the identification of antagonistic social relationships – enables us to reflect on the process by which groups in conflict are formed and on the various features they assume. The formation of antagonistic groups (which in the history of capitalist industrialization take the name of 'classes') should always be analytically related to a breakdown in the reciprocity of recognition among the actors participating in the production of basic social resources. The division between production and recognition on the one hand, and appropriation and orientation on the other, take the form of opposition among antagonistic social groups striving for control of the same resources.

The present book is not the place to analyse how such a breakdown comes about; the answer must come from historical studies or from the comparative anthropology of human societies. In the case of each mode of production, this breakdown develops along a particular trajectory and assumes a specific form, which should be analysed within its own social context. Its salient features, however, are the privileged control by certain groups over social forms of accumulation and investment, and the role of other groups in producing the resources which 'make' society and reshape it.

A still unresolved and crucial question concerns the manner in which the split between the dominants and the dominated first opened up in the passage from a society of reproduction and integral exchange to one of accumulation and investment.

Some hints of the possible directions for an answer come from powerless societies like those analysed by Clastres in his studies on one of the last isolated indigenous groups of Amazonia (Clastres 1977). These are societies with no or little accumulation, and in which total reciprocity governs the social relationships (with the sole exception of the fundamental, almost presocial, division between men and women). Only language breaks the circle of transparency and equality in this situation of integral interdependence among the members of the group. A taboo prohibits the hunter from eating the meat he has himself provided, so that everyone depends on everyone else for survival. The chief is expected to ritually remind the group of the beliefs, principles, and rules governing social life, but when he speaks nobody pays attention to his words. The hunters have but their nocturnal songs in the circle around the fire to affirm their individual differences; the chief can only rely on words to assert his command.

Clastres' analysis of this culture, so remote from contemporary society, demonstrates that the roots of conflict nevertheless lie at the very heart of social action: in the unresolved tension between recognition and reciprocity, in the impossibility of enclosing associative human behaviour within the transparent circularity of exchange.

Even in societies with practically no accumulation – those without an unequal distribution of power based on the privileged control of specific accumulated resources by one particular group – social relationships create the potential for breakdown in reciprocity. If the societies of the nomadic hunters of the Amazonian forests are to survive in a harsh environment where resources are scarce, they must ensure that it is the integrative impulse of the group that prevails. Power and conflict find expression in the symbolic medium of language alone; they are never exercised as such. The chief speaks to the group in the purely ritual capacity of communicating what is already known, with no one expected to listen: power is asserted and simultaneously denied its capacity of dividing the group and sundering apart the reciprocity of social bonds. The lonely song of the hunters at night, as they sing together, each celebrating his personal feats and superiority over the others, expresses and channels individual differences but simultaneously keeps the potential conflict and its disruptive energy within the ritual circle of the group. Again, social bond is challenged and reinforced at once. In these rituals, through language, we can find the seeds of the possible division, and also the instruments for the neutralization of the potential for breakdown.

Even here, all the integral reciprocity notwithstanding, the multiple does not then reduce to one, equal and different do not stand together unencumbered by tension. Even where the social bond is inescapable and rendered near-transparent by an egalitarian interdependence, where the necessity of survival neutralizes power and contains conflict within a ritual narrative – there too the seeds of division and inequality are present.

Recognition and reciprocity may fracture, but the social form of such division is not a metaphysical necessity: conflict always depends on the way the society is structured and on its relationships with the environment. It must, therefore, be explained socially.

Addressing the social dimension of change

Theories and definitions of change ordinarily start from the naive assumption of change depicting it as an existing reality, as the flow in which social life is embedded: *Panta rei*, as Heraclitus put it – everything flows and nothing is stable and fixed for ever. From this undeniable empirical observation is derived the postulation that social life is undergoing permanent change, and what one has to explain is therefore how change affects this or that aspect of social reality (Sztompka 1994). This almost naturalistic conception of change belongs not only to our common sense as its unreflected part, but it has left its mark as well in sociological analyses and theories, particularly in those dealing with collective action, either explained in terms of breakdown of the existing structure or connected to the appearance of new solidarities (Useem 1980). The naive social evolutionism still lying at the basis of many approaches is the last legacy of the philosophies of the nineteenth century. In any closer scrutiny, however, it becomes obvious that this assumption provides a very weak underpinning for sociological inquiry, and not only for reasons internal to the history of ideas burdening it but specifically because it denies the very *social* dimension of change.

First of all, one should be aware of the fact that the idea of *social* change is a very modern representation of social life. Societies of the past have not thought of themselves in terms of change, and even less of change as a linear progress in time. Change as a social and cultural product is an idea which belongs to societies which have acquired a high power of intervening in their environment and in themselves. Societies of the past have referred change to *metasocial* forces (gods, myths of foundation) and represented it as the eternal and cyclical renewal of the primary events constitutive of the group's identity. Change was perceived as a cyclical return of the same, repeating and reiterating a primordial, atemporal event and governed by sacred powers. The Judeo-Christian tradition preserved the cyclical image of time but also introduced the notion of a linear progression, of a path of salvation whose final meaning was redeemed by its fulfilment at the end of human history. In every case, change is referred to forces and powers which operate *beyond* the reach of social life and social relationships.

The modern ideas of progress and revolution are but desacralized versions of the Christian legacy, and they continue to rely on a nonsocial notion of change. Change is divested of its religious references and brought down to its natural dimensions. Now the forces which govern it are *infrasocial,* they lay *below* the visible dimension of social relationships as the expression of Nature or of History, understood as the visible unfolding of natural laws. The great social thinkers of the nineteenth century pushed the modern conception of change to its extreme consequences and started revealing the social nature of social relationships; yet they still shared the positivist idea of the basically presocial determinism on which social phenomena depend (the invisible hand of Adam Smith and the *homo oeconomicus* of classical political economists, the evolutionist faith of Spencer and Comte, the necessary development of productive forces in Marx's terms, the constraining nature of social solidarity in the language of Durkheim).

To think of change in *social* terms is then a relatively recent idea which belongs to societies that through their action on themselves make the social nature of social relationships visible and undeniable. It is only when the survival of the human species and its environment entirely come to depend on human choices that the social nature of change can be addressed as such.

Being aware of our socially located point of view on *social change,* we can now turn from a naive idea of change as a natural flow manifest in all things to a definition of change as an *analytical concept.* In this perspective, the paradigm shift introduced in contemporary science by the systems theoretical approach has allowed a conceptualization of the social dimension of change and has provided us with a language to circumscribe it (for an overview, see Morin 1980, 1986; Maturana and Varela 1980).

If we refer to a social system as a set of elements (individuals or groups) connected by interdependent relationships (implying, that is to say, that any variation in one element has effects on all the others), we can at any given moment identify a recognizable pattern describing the character and quantity of elements and relationships; we may refer to this pattern as the structure of a system. A system is defined by its internal boundaries (maintenance of its structure) and by the fact that it is delimited in relation to its environment. The existence of a system moreover implies that the whole of its elements and their mutual relationships is qualitatively different than the simple sum total of these same elements.

Two consequences can be derived from this perspective. First, definition of social change is not possible without the preceding definition of a system and its boundaries. Second, this conceptual operation is always relative to the position of an observer (which means that at any given moment we can always establish a new point of view, a metasystem including the previous 'system' *and* the observer).

We can now address social change in analytical terms and draw from the foregoing the following methodological consequences:

(i)   Social change cannot be addressed as a homogeneous social phenomenon, but only as a process which should be differentiated according to the systemic point of reference (elements or levels of a system involved);

(ii) Social change should be referred to an observer's point of view, which delimits the boundaries of the system under consideration;

(iii) The point of view of an observer does not entail coincidence with the subjective perception of social actors for two reasons: (a) there is a crystallization and solidification of social structures which stabilizes social relationships and transforms them to a variable degree into 'objective' constraints; (b) systemic relationships are not immediately accessible to social actors and they imply a measure of opacity or non-transparency; the relational point of view needs as its supplement an access to a metalevel which is different from the ordinary position of actor (social actors can of course have such an access, but only insofar as it is made possible by an at least temporarily distantiation from their position as actors and the adoption of the observer's position).

Under these conditions we can define social change as *any variation in a social system perceived by an observer* and we can make the following distinctions:

(i)   It is necessary to distinguish the synchronic point of view (definition of the system and its structure) from the diachronic point of view (analysis of the processes though which a system changes); in this becomes clear the distinction between *structural* and *conjunctural* factors triggering social change that is derived from the analytical difference between these two perspectives;

(ii) Furthermore, it is necessary to distinguish *adaptive changes* from *changes of structure*: the former refer to variations which take place within the limits of compatibility of a system (as the range of variations which does not affect the structure, see chapter 1); the latter refer to variations that entail a redefinition of the character and quantity of elements and their relationships;

(iii) It is necessary to accept that, ignoring for the moment catastrophic events, it is unlikely that a social system can be affected by change in all its elements and relationships *simultaneously*: structural changes are affected as the work of combined processes taking place at different levels and different times.

(iv) Finally, it is necessary to distinguish between *endogenous* and *exogenous* factors affecting social change, according to the boundaries established for a given system.

Integration and change

We are thus brought on to examine the relationship between collective action and change. In the many theories of movements, change has always been taken to be the given datum of which movements are a product, generating in turn further changes. Whether one talks of growing expectations, of economic development, of differentiation, or of the contradiction between productive forces and production relations, change is either related to external causes or taken to be the result of immanent historical necessity.

My intention instead is to explain change in terms of the same conceptual system that I have used to define collective action, and without resorting to a *deus ex machina* external to the system under consideration. This is not to deny the importance of external factors in inducing change in a system; but the operation of external factors becomes meaningful only if it can be shown that they affect the inner workings of a system and modify it. Otherwise the recourse to external factors will amount to nothing but one way of papering over the cracks in the theory.

In accordance with the foregoing, the first step in this task is to draw the distinction between the synchronic and the diachronic dimensions, between the structural workings of a system and the changes occurring in it over time. Logically speaking, synchronic analysis must necessarily precede diachronic analysis if we are not to attribute change to the inevitable progress of history. Only through a structural analysis of the components of a system and their relations can we show how, why, and to what extent changes take place.

The conflict that sets groups producing the crucial resources of a society against those that exercise the ultimate control over them, should be viewed as a synchronic dimension of the system, since, as I have maintained above, it is rooted in the very structure of social production (which assumes different historical connotations in different kinds of society). This structural antagonism within a system generates extremely high costs, distributed among the various groups, and creates disintegrative pressures which add to the centrifugal forces provoked by complexity and differentiation in the first place. Potential conflict must therefore be brought under control, a task allocated to the functions performed by the integrative mechanisms of the system. Such mechanisms, however, are not solely the expression of dominant interests; they operate in accordance with purely systemic imperatives, responding to the systems requirement of subduing any threat to structural integrity. In other words, we may claim that there are no integrative functions (and power is an integrative force par excellence) within a system that do not enjoy a certain amount of public consensus regarding the role they perform for the maintenance of the system as a whole.

None the less, integration also serves to safeguard the structure of the dominant interests and the particular social relationships that characterize them. This means that integrative functions are overburdened by the need to maintain under control the structural tension that defines production relationships. Change internal to a system should therefore not be seen only as the process of adaptation required to cope with the 'natural' variability of elements and their relations, and with changes in the environment. It also results from the exigencies of maintaining the system within the compatibility limits of its dominant social relationships. The action of external factors obviously increases the threat of imbalance and intensifies the need for regulation.

It is here that the notion of contradiction – stripped of its deterministic overtones – enters consideration. I define contradiction as the incompatibility among the elements or parts of a system. Incompatibility can in turn be defined as an anomaly which prevents a system (or a part of it) from maintaining its structure. Incompatibility among systems (subsystems or elements) arises when one system is unable to preserve its own structure because of variations in another (subsystem or element). In diachronic terms, any remedial action taken to keep a system within its compatibility limits tends to produce contradictions. These contradictions, furthermore, generate a form of collective action which, depending on the area one is referring to, will fall under one of the various categories analysed above. Incompatibilities among the inner elements of a specific system (for example, within a political system or an organization) and incompatibilities between different systems are the factors which activate social movements and other forms of collective action.

The appearance of forms of collective action and, in particular, social movements gives rise to still further contradictions. The system reacts to such new situations by instituting supplementary internal modifications (functional modernization, political reform, cultural and technical innovation), provided it is able to absorb the conflictual pressures; otherwise it is forced to alter its elements and their relations en bloc, thus yielding to the push for a change in structure. A change of this kind may affect a society in its entirety, or parts of it, or its subsets (for example, a change of regime is a change in the structure of a political system). In complex societies, however, change in their various parts or subsystems nonetheless takes places in piecemeal fashion and to imagine a structural change that simultaneously involves all the levels of the actual society is to entirely misconstrue the workings of such societies.

Social movements, and above all antagonist movements, thus tie contradiction and conflict together; for they are situated at the intersection of structure and change. Social movements are in fact rooted in the structural, synchronic operation of a system, but are activated by contradictions that emerge and manifest themselves in its evolution and historical conjuncture. The theoretical problem is first to distinguish between these two levels and then to define their mutual relations. Empirically, one must first define a movement in terms of its reference system and then single out the conjunctural factors that have contributed to its appearance. The concrete features of a movement will depend on the relative weight of each of the two levels of analysis and on their various combinations.

3

Action and meaning

Action made invisible

Without a reference to the systems of action that explain the complexity of the actor and the actor's relations with the whole of the social field, analysis of collective action will not be able to achieve a clear grasp of its subject matter. Below, I shall discuss a number of different interpretative models contained in the literature that make an attempt at precisely this direction, and then take them as examples in trying to show the dependency of movements research on certain implicit assumptions upon which the relative validity of these models rests. As I want to claim, behind their manifest argument they all *presuppose a theory of action and identity* of the kind I have outlined in the previous chapters and I will complete in chapter 4. An explication of such a covert theory, against which only the explanatory power of these models can be examined, is in order if we are to provide a proper foundation for their claims and redeem the (potentially) enduring value contained in them.

The first such model, which I will call the expectation–reward model, encompasses a broad field of applications (Geschwender 1968; Davies 1969; Gurr 1970; Oberschall 1973; Klandermans 1984, 1989a). It sets to explain collective action in terms of a gap between the expectations and the rewards attached to the outcome of the action and, ultimately, between frustration and aggression. The model states that the discrepancy between the expectations developed regarding the results from action (anticipated gratification) and its actual results engenders processes leading to collective mobilization, which then may or may not take a violent turn but will nevertheless fall outside the institutionalized forms of behaviour. This is also the underlying thesis of, for example, most of the theories that analyse collective action in terms of the economic cycle and which, in particular, link the wave of mobilizations or violent action to abrupt interruptions in the growth trend of prosperity ('rise and drop'), or to a flattening of the rewards curve after a long upswing ('rising expectations'). The same framework is used by the model of 'relative deprivation', which suggests that action is triggered when people compare their own situation to that of a reference group relative to which they develop expectations, which then are disappointed. Similarly, it is incorporated in the model of 'downwards mobility', which constitutes a special case of relative deprivation, as well as in the explanations built around the model of 'status inconsistency', according to which mobilization takes place because critical dimensions of status – prestige and income, for example – fail to coincide.

Behind all these theories lies the built-in assumption that takes for granted that the gap between expectations and rewards induces frustration, which in turn arouses a collective response in the form of aggression. The actor is presumed to have been deprived of the expected gratification (and, moreover, to be conscious of the fact), with the resulting frustration generating an aggressive mobilization through which is sought the restoration of the balance between expectations and achievements. At the level of collective action, such propositions, for that matter, can be seen as an extension of the experimentally-based model developed by psychologists at Yale University in the 1930s. While this is not the place for a detailed analysis of the heuristic merits of the frustration–aggression model (for a discussion of the work of Dollard and his associates, see Berkowitz 1969, 1972), or of the legitimacy of its application outside the experimental setting in which it was formulated, we can point out that the model has been criticized for overgeneralizing the two terms of reference it employs, and for unjustifiably seeking to extend the results of laboratory experiments conducted under very specific conditions to encompass social behaviour in general. This, however, is not the real issue: one can certainly translate the logical structure of the model into sociological terms and apply it to collective action. By so doing – albeit none of the various theories described has ever made the attempt – we could formalize the assumptions of the model as follows: (a) There is a necessary link which ties the perceived discrepancy between expectations and rewards (frustration, or denial of expected gratification) to a collective response of a conflictual type (aggression); (b) this entails the notion of critical threshold, or a level of tolerance beyond which conflict is triggered.

Let us now consider briefly these assumptions, which consequentially enough have never been made explicit in the many theories based on the expectation–reward model or, as it stands, on 'naive' extensions of the frustration–aggression paradigm.

Both assumptions relate to the premises of an underlying theory of action and identity of the kind I am sketching out in the part I of this book; and, as said, it is only through the clarification of this hidden framework that we can assess precisely the validity of these assumptions. In what follows, I want to ignore the terms 'frustration' and 'aggression' in order to create distance to their too marked psychological bent, and will, instead, refer to the perceived gap or shortfall between expectations and rewards (or denial of an expected gratification) and to the collective conflictual response.

The first assumption to warrant examination concerns the necessary link between the two key terms of the model. The relation it posits presupposes a theory of distributive justice to the extent that collective subjects expect rewards at least commensurate to their investments. In fact, for a perception of the gap (what is termed 'frustration') to be possible, we must presume that the rewards expected by the actor are at least proportional to the investments, and that mobilization occurs when the received rewards remain below what was expected. Secondly, the model suggests a linear cause-and-effect relation between the two terms, without specifying any intermediate term. Thus presented, however, both of these assumptions remain open to considerable qualifications.

The assumption that actors have expectations of rewards at least proportional to their investments in fact implies a theory of social action that is based on the central notion of identity. Expectations of rewards commensurate with investments presuppose a situation of relative reciprocity of exchange – that is, a situation where the actors mutually recognize each other's control over the effects of their respective actions and the right to attribute such effects to themselves. Each actor recognizes the products of that actor's action as belonging to her/himself through the intimate connection to them established in the performed action, and anticipates from others in turn a recognition to that same effect. Expectations of proportionate rewards are in fact based on the possibility of having one's investments recognized. The actor expects certain rewards because s/he recognizes, and attributes value to, her/his own investments (the effects of the action) and looks to others for them to lend that same recognition.

There is, therefore, a second problem involved in assessing the ratio between investments and rewards. How can one estimate whether the rewards actually are more or less commensurate with the resources invested in the action? Here, too, measuring requires a standard to which to refer, a yardstick in the actor's field of identity which makes possible a comparison between investments and rewards; without it the whole undertaking would no doubt be inconceivable.

In conclusion, the assumption of distributive justice, which implies that a subject has expectations proportional to her/his investments, then relies on an implicit theory of identity; in itself, it generates a chain of other assumptions (people can compare investments and rewards; they have a standard reference) which also need an accompanying theory of action and identity to sustain their validity. How can people compare their investments with the results of their action; how is a yardstick established? These questions can be answered only by referring to a theory that explains how people define themselves, recognize the outcomes of their action, and secure recognition from others.

The same is true for the allegedly linear link between the two terms of the relation ('frustration/aggression'). In actual situations, there is a broad range of alternative responses to the registered discrepancy between expectations and rewards. Far from being the only possible reaction, violent/conflictual action is in fact rarely resorted to, and even when it is this only takes place under specific conditions. For a collective actor, there is a number of other courses of action available from which to choose in accordance with the dictates of the situation, or towards which to deflect under the present circumstances.

There is, first of all, the option of restructuring the means and/or the ends of the action itself. Once aware of the inadequacy of the rewards as compared with the investments, the actor restructures the field of the action by redefining its goals, or the instruments used to achieve them, or both. This is the most common response in relatively institutionalized situations where negotiative or contractual relationships obtain; adaptation, negotiations, and the devising of strategies are ways of restructuring the field and adjusting the means and the ends in accordance with accumulated experience.

Another possible response is what we might call the 'depressive option'. Having experienced a gap between expectations and rewards, the actor draws back into her/himself and breaks off relations with social partners. This kind of response may take two principal forms: either a complete withdrawal, as the actor severs relations with the outside and renounces all courses of action, or a designation by the group of an internal scapegoat, who is charged with the responsibility for the privation suffered. In its two versions, the depressive response rules out any conflictual action, and turns its aggressive energies onto the group itself, paralyzing its capacity for action or, worse still, activating destructive processes.

Further, there is the 'exit-voice' alternative (Hirschman 1975, 1982). The inadequacy of results compared with investments discourages conflictual collective action on a motivational level and opens the way for individualistic mobilization. Individual actors search for particularistic rewards, for example through individual upward mobility; alternatively, a contest may begin for specific advantages for individuals or subgroups. The cyclical waves of commitment and withdraw bare witness to this possibility (Hirschman 1982).

Another common reaction is what we can call 'sublimation'. Perception of the shortfall between investment and rewards induces the actor to mobilize its symbolic resources, to construct an ideal self-image, to take refuge in myth. The group rapidly transforms itself into a commune, a sect or a church, creates or appropriates its sacred texts, develops rituals and priestly functions, and so forth (Kanter 1972, 1973; Abrams and McCulloch 1976; Wilson 1990a; Robbins 1988). Rewards found to be unattainable in real life are sought in sacral self-celebration or through obliteration of the self in an abstract and all-embracing symbolic universe, with all the anachronistic implications of displaced religious metaphysics. In this case, even if the practical effects were the consolidation of the group solidarity and the avoidance of disaggregation, the possibilities for a conflictual mobilization remain very remote.

Finally, there is the kind of response which is 'aggressive', but symbolically projected outside the actor's social reference system. The action is not directed against the social adversary present in the reference system, but against a symbolic adversary which has no concrete relationship with the actor's experience. Hence, this option does not involve any redefinition of the field of action; nor does it produce any effects in that field. Conjuring up a distant, unreachable enemy does not provoke conflictual collective action, but instead engenders ideology, myth, and rites. As in the previous case, this may easily give way to an emergence of sects; but here a beleaguered mentality prevails and the liturgy becomes more dramatic in tone. Thus, it is not possible to point out a necessary relationship between denial of an expected gratification and conflictual collective behaviour. Are there nevertheless conditions under which this connection holds? Again, for an answer we must draw on the theory of action and identity. In order for the conflictual response to an expectations-rewards shortfall to be chosen from among the many alternative lines of action, at least three conditions must obtain.

Firstly, there must be a temporal continuity of the actor, which allows the comparison between the two different conditions involved using the same yardstick. That is, the actor must perceive her/his own consistency and continuity between time T and time T_1 in order to be able to decide that an expectation arising at T has been disappointed at T_1. One of the dimensions of the actor's identity is constituted by precisely this continuity.

Secondly, if the action is not to be directed towards a mythical adversary, against a fantastic enemy, the cause of the deprivation or shortfall must be socially defined in terms included in the actor's frame of reference. For the reaction not to be restricted to ritual invective or anathema, as in a sect, but, instead, to have the possibility of developing into collective action and struggle, a tangible antagonist whose action affects the actor's reference field must be identified.

Finally, in order for the denial of an expected object to possess the power to mobilize conflictual energies, the actor must feel a sense of ownership over the object. It must be possible for the actor to consider the object around which the strife is centred as something that belongs to her/himself as a justly held right or as a deep-rooted possession (Moore 1978; Gamson, Fireman and Rytina 1982). Otherwise the very notion of 'frustration' loses its meaning.

These three conditions are all grounded in a theory of action and identity. Without an actor able to define its own identity, without a relation of opposition in which the actor is located as one of the poles, and without a field from which is derived the meaning of what the actor fights for or feels it has been deprived of – without an adequate account of these, establishing a link between expectations and rewards and, especially, explaining why collective actors mobilize themselves will be possible only by bypassing the whole understanding we now have of the capacity of actors to act meaningfully and by reducing 'aggression' to a mechanistic behavioural reaction.

We may now turn to the second general assumption of the model under scrutiny: the assumption of a critical threshold. While the necessary nexus of frustration–aggression is presupposed by the model in its static form, its dynamic presupposition is the critical threshold. In fact, for the situation of deprivation to become explosive there must be a breaking point (whether qualitative or quantitative, is left undefined) which is gradually approximated. It becomes immediately obvious that it is well-nigh impossible to establish a priori, and without it being wholly arbitrary, the point at which the gap between expectations and rewards becomes intolerable and at which the conflictual reaction is triggered. Such an explanation is necessarily *post factum* and restricts itself to recording the occurrence of the 'aggressive' response. Why does this gap between expectations and rewards set in motion the actor's conflictual response; why is this not triggered below the threshold; and why, all other conditions remaining unchanged, different actors do not react in the same way – these are all questions which a theory modelled on the frustration–aggression thesis cannot answer.

In fact, the whole notion of a threshold remains meaningless insofar as it is not related to the compatibility limits of the system in which the action takes place, that is, to the limits beyond which the customary means for achieving goals and obtaining rewards no longer produce the desired result. One must therefore examine not the generic and abstract discrepancy between expectations and rewards, but the actor's field of action with its specific compatibility limits; the conflictual response takes place whenever the breach of these confines occurs.

If, for example, the actor's self-definition relies on the terms of a system of roles, the scope of the action will be determined by the set of normative and functional requirements and by the type of power that govern those roles. In the case of a political actor, the rules of the decision-making game mark out the area of the decidable, thereby establishing accepted procedures. A situation or an event is liable to produce 'aggressive' effects only when the degree of the perceived shortfall between the actor's expectations and rewards is greater than what is allowed by the system's room for adaptation – that is, when they exceed the system's actual or potential capacity to modify its operations to fill that gap without radical restructuration.

In other words, only if the system is unable to bridge the recognized gap by using its habitual mechanisms for controlling and regulating tensions will 'aggression' come about. And this is the case when the expected rewards are in any case incompatible with the practical possibilities permitted by the limits of the reference system.

At this point we can draw a distinction between a quantitative notion of accumulating tension and the eminently qualitative notion of the critical threshold. Perception of a gap between expectations and rewards may give rise to redistributive demands that do not necessarily assume an aggressive character. For an 'aggressive' noninstitutionalized mobilization to be possible, an extension of the scope or a quantitative accumulation of deprivation will not suffice; the demands must relate to objectives that reach beyond the system's actual compatibility limits and be qualitatively incompatible with it.

Lastly, the notion of the threshold requires one further specification. Here I shall use a diachronic conception – which should not be confused with synchronic, structural analysis – of how a conflict is born and takes shape. The precise nature of the shortfall perceived by the actor – how remediable or not it might seem – necessarily depends on the system's compatibility limits. There are demands or expectations that are structurally incompatible with a given reference system. But a perception of such incompatibility, the crossing over the critical threshold that triggers conflict, occurs in a diachronic process, and is helped or hindered by specific conjunctural factors. Identification of these factors requires careful historical analysis. Theories based on the frustration–aggression model never concern themselves with an analytical distinction between the synchronic and the diachronic, and they fail to spell out the notion of the critical threshold implicit in them. As a result, they tend to confuse the qualitative nature of the discrepancy produced by incompatible expectations with the conjunctural factors which bring the discrepancy to the surface and activate noninstitutionalized conflict.

Interests and action

Another model contained in the literature, one which has been considerably developed in the work of Charles Tilly (starting from Tilly 1970; Tilly *et al.* 1975), hinges upon the notion of 'collective interest'. This model has the twin merit of providing an extremely broad quantitative and qualitative basis for research into collective violence on the one hand, and focusing attention on the relationship between collective action and the political system on the other. In Tilly's terms, collective violence occurs whenever an actor finds itself entering a political system or exiting from it. Those already located within a political system define its rules of membership, administering thereby the power at their disposal to block the entrance to it by those outside of its parameters; or, at the very least, they will not miss an opportunity to impose selective restrictions on the criteria for access to the system where it is possible. As a response, such an exclusionary action provokes processes of mobilization and even violence on the part of those seeking to penetrate the system. Likewise, groups in decline within a certain political system and in the process of being forced out of it, naturally resist the intended outcome, mobilizing themselves for collective action and at times resorting to violence in order to delay and obstruct the process. Tilly's model, which states the classical Marxist thesis in more precise and sophisticated form, takes collective interests to be a determinant factor of action. Those who try to enter a political system share the interest of broadening the gates governing access to it, and those already part of the system have a common interest in keeping those gates closed as far as possible, or in reacting to protect their established position within that system whenever it becomes threatened by newcomers. In assigning a role to shared interests, however, the model makes two assumptions.

First, it implies the situation of 'frustration' that is the gap between the expectations and the outcome of action. We are led back to our previous discussion. Upwardly mobile social groups develop expectations regarding entrance into the system which, however, become frustrated; or, alternatively, expectations may exist of a permanent stay within the system on the part of the groups with long-fought positions conquered in it, when, in fact, they are facing a decline and are currently in the process of being forced out of it. Moreover, groups which have acquired resources on other markets expect to have them recognized by the political system: an improvement in their economic position, for example, or an increase in their numerical or organizational strength, induces expectations of access to representation by these groups. By contrast, those groups whose resources, for a longer or shorter period of time, have been recognized by the political system expect such recognition to go undisturbed. In both cases, the expectations are disappointed: in the former case, by the closure of the system; in the latter, by the loss of position. The violent collective reaction falls therefore wholly within the framework of the analytical model analysed above: it is the response to the gap between expectations and rewards.

But there is another, more significant assumption at work here: namely, that there actually exists a shared, collective interest in gaining access to the system (or in obstructing that access), or in terminally remaining inside it. In dealing with this assumption, Olson's (Olson 1965) by now classic argument still appears as forceful as ever. The fact that there exists an interest in obtaining a collective good does not sufficiently explain collective mobilization designed to acquire it. In fact, individuals belonging to a large collectivity may very well enjoy the benefits accruing from the collective good without participating in the costs necessary to obtain it. The existence of interests is equated with the capacity of the group to take action in order to defend or promote them. But in social structures which can be analytically described in terms of a market structure (such as the political system), the common interest of the members of the group in achieving a certain goal does not necessarily imply that each one of them has an equal desire to assume the responsibility for the costs involved. Selective incentives are called for even in large interest-based organizations so as to induce the participation of its individual members, since this would not be stimulated by the mere sharing in the pursuit of collective goals alone.

Olson's argument has been received with a great deal of criticism, especially as regards its reductive premise that collective action is a sum total of instances of individual behaviour and the result of atomized cost-benefit calculation. It has been pointed out that direct participation in order to obtain certain highly symbolic or ethical goods does not require selective incentives, and that solidarity plays an important role in the calculation of the costs and benefits of action (Tilloch and Morrison 1979; Fireman and Gamson 1979; Oliver 1984; Oberschall 1993; Oliver and Marwell 1993).

Yet, despite all qualifications by such criticism, Olson's thesis has helped to clear the ground for advances in the theory of collective action by undermining the naive assumption that the existence of a collective interest constitutes a sufficient motive for action, thus opening up a very fertile avenue for research. Collective interests can no longer be taken as given; the question of how they are formed and maintained has instead been submitted for demonstration.

Pizzorno (1978, 1986, 1993a), while building on the critical foundations of Olson's argument, has reversed its logic to show that collective identity is the condition for cost-benefit calculation of action. Every social action aims at benefits which are proportional to the costs of obtaining them. For the rewards gained from social exchange to be expendable, he maintains, there must be a socially specific market which recognizes them. And it is collective identity that specifically guarantees this market and allows investments in mobilization to be calculated. Within the market provided by a collective identity, an individual can calculate the costs and benefits of action and count on a certain predictability of conduct. When processes of transformation erode the basis for the rational calculation of social relations, these relations become less predictable, the rules of exchange are altered, resources are no longer recognized and can no longer be disposed of at will. It is at this point that mobilization in the defence of the affiliation system or in search for new markets or new collective identities takes place. In both cases the idea is to preserve (or to construct) an area of recognition which permits individuals to calculate the effects of their actions.

Thus, on the one hand, the simple premise of common interest is not enough to explain mobilization without the introduction of a structure of incentives and individual advantages – in other words, the possibility for a rational estimate of the costs and benefits of action – in the picture. On the other hand, Olson's premise, which views collective decisions as the sum total of individual choices in a market of micro-exchanges, forgets that it is precisely the individual's affiliation with a network of associative or community relations which is the necessary condition for the calculation of the effects of action to be possible. Pizzorno's argument contributes both to a critique of the naive assumption of collective action based on shared interests, and to the possibility of overcoming the Olsonian individualism. Here, too, we must retrieve the underlying theory of action and identity to lend a foundation to the model of shared interests. Deducting nothing from the critical force of Olson's argument (common interest in itself is not a sufficient motive for collective action), it will still be possible to bypass the apparent dead end of the logic of the 'free rider' with the postulates of such theory in mind. Interests and mobilization can be coupled only if one refers to the concept of collective identity – that is, if theory provides an understanding of the 'we' through which people recognize themselves, confer meaning and give continuity to their action, and thus enable the calculation of costs and benefits.

Moreover, Tilly himself, in later developments of his theory, seems to have shifted towards a more complex definition of collective action (e.g. Tilly 1978, 1986, 1993). Although interests retain their connotation of objective givenness (they are, in fact, gains and losses resulting from the interaction of one group with others), the passage from interests to action is now articulated through an analysis of the role of the organization, of mobilization processes, and of the opportunity structure of the system in which the action takes place (the nature of the adversaries, available resources, and so forth).

Recognizing what is common

All the models discussed above presuppose a broader theory of action, however hidden its presence in their explanatory models. What is needed is the analysis of an intermediate level that is comprised of the processes by which individuals recognize and assess what they have in common when they decide to act together. It is on this intermediate level, therefore, that work seeking to render the European and American approaches compatible has concentrated in the 1980s. One proposal, which can usefully serve to map out this analytical level, is to distinguish between mobilization potential, recruitment networks, and motivation to participate (Klandermans 1984; 1988, Klandermans and Oegema 1987; McAdam 1988; Friedman and McAdam 1992). The concept of mobilization potential usually refers to that proportion of the population which, on account of its position in society, is favorable towards a movement or a certain issue. It cannot, however, be understood as a subjective attitude based on objective preconditions; this would raise again the insoluble problem of the relationship between social condition and group consciousness that I have already discussed. If one begins with a dualistic assumption, then a *deus ex machina* (the intellectuals, the party, the organization) is required which connects objective preconditions and subjective attitudes together, and translates the latter into action. If unity cannot be conceptualized right from the beginning, it will never be forthcoming at the end, either. Mobilization potential should be conceived in itself as a set of social relations, as an interactive and negotiated perception of the opportunities and constraints of action shared by a certain number of people.

Recruitment networks likewise perform an important role in the process of becoming involved in collective action. No mobilization is born in a vacuum, and contrary to the tenets of the theory of mass society

(Kornhauser, 1959; see also Hoffer 1951; for a discussion Halebsky 1976; Gusfield 1995), isolated and rootless individuals never mobilize. The relational networks that ramify through the social fabric facilitate involvement processes and make it less costly for individuals to invest in collective action (Granovetter 1973; Oberschall 1973; Wilson and Orum 1976 Snow *et al.* 1980; McAdam 1982, 1986). Networks constitute an intermediate level which is crucial for understanding mobilization processes. Within these networks, individuals interact, influence one another, and engage in negotiations as they produce the cognitive and motivational schemata necessary for action.

Finally, motivation to participate should not be mistaken for a variable that relates exclusively to an individual. To be sure, it is rooted in individual psychological differences and in personality traits; but it is through interaction that it is built and strengthened. A decisive influence on motivation is exercised by the structure of incentives, which is variably attributed value precisely through the relational networks that tie the individuals together.

The authors working within the resource mobilization theory (RMT) have shown that the amount of discontent always present in a system is not enough to account for mobilization processes. They stress the importance of the 'discretionary resources' and the 'opportunities structure' that makes the action possible. The critique advanced by writers associated with RMT has brought up the fact that expectations are constructed through assessment of the chances and limits present in the environment. This has highlighted the importance of an intermediate level which has been completely ignored by the models that assume a direct link between discontent and mobilization. However, RMT, too, remains a prisoner of the very same limitation that constrains the theories it criticizes, as far as the same implicit assumption of an action and identity theory is concerned: as a matter of fact, concepts like 'discretionary resources' or 'opportunity structure' do not relate to 'objective' entities, but, rather, imply the ability of actors to perceive, evaluate, and decide on the possibilities and limits offered by the environment. They are premised on a theory of identity, which, although never explicit, provides the sole foundation of the heuristic capacity of such concepts.

RMT thus does postulate some kind of a process by which the actor constructs an identity, though without paying any particular attention to the relevant level of analysis. However, precisely such neglected aspects have been recently explored by a number of analyses close to RMT which stress the active role of the actors in constructing their cognitive frames and relations (Snow *et al.* 1986; Snow and Benford 1988; Gamson and Modigliani

1989; Gamson 1995). Whatever the merits of such advances, it nevertheless remains imperative to move decisively beyond the restricted framework of RMT and its postulate of actor behaviour exclusively based on calculation.

In its theory of collective action, RMT basically provides a rational choice model (Kerbo 1982; Kitschelt 1991; Zald 1991, 1992; Ferree 1992; see also Rule 1989) to explain how people get together or act together under certain conditions, and how they make use of available resources, recognize them, and organize them for the purposes of achieving mobilization. One can agree with many of the assumptions of RMT, while it is nevertheless necessary to recognize the need to criticize its presentation regarding the foundation of the model of calculation at the core of its theory of action. Here I will draw on Pizzorno's argument against the 'free rider' model. The gist of his argument has persuasively demonstrated the impossibility of any such calculation without a system of reference which in itself is not subject to calculation. To put it simply, a yardstick to measure the investments and rewards is necessary for the estimation of relative yield from the various possible courses of action, and such a standard is formed previous to the performance of calculation itself, emerging in closer investigation as that which I call identity. Identity is what people choose to be, the incalculable: they choose to define themselves in a certain way not only as a result of rational calculation, but primarily under affective bonds and based on the intuitive capacity of mutual recognition. Such a remarkable affective dimension is fundamentally 'nonrational' in character without yet being irrational. It is *meaningful* and provides the actors with the capacity of making sense of their being together. Within the premises of a rational choice framework, this constitutive dimension is simply excluded from the account altogether or, alternatively, relegated to its blank margins as an irrational, that is, analytically irrelevant part of the analysis. Yet it is not the question of either/or that decides the rationality of the affective dimension; what sets it outside the considerations of rational choice is simply the fact that it is never submitted to the logic of purposive calculation. The affective elements themselves play a significant part in a meaningful creation of connections and bonds both with the others and also within our selves, which in turn provides the basis for identity construction. Even on the level of our personal choices, we bring into being a certain combination of the different needs, wants, desires that constitute our selves, and the choice that the self so constructed makes is not made by inference from all the different calculations completed in preparation for it, but to a significant extent with reference to a definition of a self, which, both intuitive and affective, is charged with emotion and meaning and directs the orientation of action. The calculation of the chances and feasibility of action that provides the centre of the hypotheses of RMT is thus performed with reference to precisely such an inner definition which precedes all subsequent comparison of advantages and losses that may affect the onset and direction of action.

Both the models based on expectations and RMT inadvertently presuppose a theory of identity which alone can buttress their theses. Expectations are constructed and measured against reality (against rewards, for example, but also against the opportunities structure) only based on a negotiated definition of the internal constitution of the actor, and of that actor's field of operation. The formation of expectations and the assessment of the possibilities and limits of action presuppose that the actor is able to define itself and its environment. I define this process of building an action system as *collective identity* – a concept that has entred sociological debate through the work of writers such as Touraine and Pizzorno (see Cohen 1985 for a discussion). Despite their innovative categorial achievements, however, to this day these authors have failed to clarify the processes by which the collective actor is constructed through interactions and negotiations and in a relationship with the environment. In the case of Touraine, identity is simply taken as a given, as a sort of an essence of the movement, whereas Pizzorno apparently still adheres to the Marxist tradition by anchoring that concept in objective interests.

I shall instead treat collective identity as an interactive process through which several individuals or groups define the meaning of their action and the field of opportunities and constraints for such an action. This common definition must be conceived as a process, for it is constructed and negotiated through the ongoing relationships linking individuals or groups. The process by which a collective identity is constructed, maintained, and adapted always has two sides to it: on the one hand, the inner complexity of an actor, its plurality of orientations; on the other, the actor's relationship with the environment (other actors, opportunities/constraints). This process provides the basis for the building of expectations and for the calculation of the costs and benefits of action. Constructing a collective identity entails continuous investment and unfolds as a process: identity crystallizes into forms of organization, systems of rules, and leadership relationships the closer the action draws towards the more institutionalized forms of social behaviour. In collective action, the construction of identity assumes the character of a process that must be constantly activated if action is to be possible. In the following chapter we shall move on to analyse precisely this process.

4

The process of collective identity

Defining collective identity

The concept of collective identity was introduced in my previous contributions to the analysis of contemporary social movements (Melucci 1988, 1989, 1994), and has already stimulated a promising discussion (Bartholomew and Mayer 1992; Gamson 1992a; Mueller 1994; Proietto 1995). In recent sociological debates we are witnessing a renewed interest in cultural analysis which corresponds to a shift towards new questions about how people make sense of their world, how they relate to texts, practices, and artifacts rendering these cultural products meaningful to them (see Swidler 1986, 1995; Wuthnow *et al.* 1984; Wuthnow 1987; Wuthnow and Witten 1988; Clifford 1988; Alexander 1990; Alexander and Seidman 1990). The contributions of social psychology in terms of scripts (Schank and Abelson 1977; Abelson 1981), social representations (Farr and Moscovici 1984; Moscovici 1988), the rhetorical construction of arguments and thoughts (Billig 1991, 1992, 1995), as well as the reflections on the discursive construction of identity (Gergen 1982, 1985, 1989, 1991; Shotter and Gergen 1989; Shotter 1993b; Harré and Gillett 1994) are also part of this shift towards a better understanding of the human capacity to construct meaning and to make sense of action.

The present interest in culture and meaning is paralleled by a growing discussion on the topic of identity, both at the individual and collective level, which crosses different disciplinary fields in social sciences (for an introduction see Hirsch 1982; Weigert *et al.* 1986 Berkowitz 1988; Abrams and Hogg 1990; Burkitt 1991; Breakwell 1992; Barglow 1994). The interest is focused on critical issues such as the continuity-discontinuity of identification processes and the multiplication of the facets of identity in contemporary society (Berger *et al.* 1973; Parfit 1984; Elster 1985; Taylor 1989; Gergen 1991; Strathern 1991; White 1992; Burke 1992; Melucci 1996).

These new questions raised by the recent reflection on culture, identity and meaning are paralleled by the increasing evidence of the weaknesses of traditional sociological theories when confronted with contemporary social movements. So far, the study of social movements has been divided among those who continue to work under the premises of the dualistic legacy discussed in chapter 1. As a result, we are still struggling to bridge the gap between behaviour and meaning, between 'objective' conditions and 'subjective' motives and orientations, between 'structure' and 'agency'. Explanations based on 'structural determinants' on the one hand and 'values and beliefs' on the other can never answer the questions of how social actors come to form a collectivity and recognize themselves as being part of it; how they maintain themselves over time; how acting together makes sense for the participants in a social movement; or how the meaning of collective action derives from structural preconditions or from the sum of the individual motives.

The development of a new interest in culture, and the related attention to hermeneutics, linguistics (Barthes 1970, 1975), and to the many methodological warnings issuing from ethnomethodology and cognitive sociology (Garfinkel 1967; Cicourel 1974, 1982) have also made more evident the low level of epistemological awareness and self-reflexivity typifying traditional research on collective phenomena (see also chapter 20). With few exceptions (such as Eyerman and Jamison 1991; Diani and Eyerman 1992; Johnston 1995), research on social movements has up to the present been informed by a widespread 'realistic' attitude toward the object, as if collective actors existed in themselves as unified ontological essences, readily offered for the comprehension of the researcher through reference to some underlying structural condition or upon sorting the motives behind the various behaviours. The position of the observer is of course that of an external eye, as objective as possible, and very little attention is paid to questions such as how the relationship of the researcher to her/his field contributes to its construction, even if we can see signs of a turning point on these matters and of an increasing epistemological awareness (on social movements, see Johnston and Klandermans 1995; Darnowsky, Epstein and Flacks 1995).

A thorough rethinking of the concept of collective identity is necessary to productively confront the dualism between structure and meaning. The concept, as we will see, cannot be separated from the production of meaning in collective action and from some methodological consequences in considering empirical forms of collective action (see chapter 20). This strategic role of the concept in dealing with the questions that are arriving to the forefront of contemporary sociological debates probably explains the parallel interest in both cultural analysis and collective identity. By asking the question of how individuals and groups make sense of their action and how we may understand this process, we are obliged to shift from a monolithic and metaphysical idea of collective actors towards the processes through which a collective becomes a collective. A processual approach to collective identity helps to affect such a theoretical and methodological shift. But the concept risks being incorporated in recent social movements studies (see Taylor and Whittier 1992; Friedman and McAdam 1992; Hunt *et al.* 1994) in a reified fashion, as a new *passepartout* that simply substitutes the old search for a core 'essence' of a movement: without, that is, taking into account its theoretical and methodological implications. In the present chapter, I want to outline a processual approach to collective identity, relying on the constructivist view of collective action developed in this book. Such an approach, moreover, carries important epistemological consequences for the way the observer/observed relation is construed in social research, and it affects the research practices themselves, as we shall see in chapter 20.

The question of how a collective actor is formed at this point assumes a decisive theoretical importance: what was formerly considered a datum (the existence of the movement) is precisely that which needs to be explained. Analysis must address itself to the plurality of aspects present in the collective action and explain how they are combined and sustained through time. It must tell us, therefore, what type of 'construct' we are faced with in the observed action and how the actor himself is 'constructed.'

Action and field: a definition

I call *collective identity* the process of 'constructing' an action system (see chapter 1). Collective identity is an interactive and shared definition produced by a number of individuals (or groups at a more complex level) concerning the *orientations* of their action and the *field* of opportunities and constraints in which such action is to take place. By 'interactive and shared' I mean that these elements are constructed and negotiated through a recurrent process of activation of the relations that bind actors together.

(i) Collective identity as a process involves *cognitive definitions* concerning the ends, means, and the field of action. These different elements, or axes, of collective action are defined within a language that is shared by a portion or the whole of society, or within one that is specific to a group; they are incorporated in a given set of rituals, practices, cultural artifacts; they are framed in different ways but they always allow some kind of calculation between means and ends, investments and rewards.

This cognitive level does not necessarily imply unified and coherent frameworks (unlike cognitivists tend to think: see Neisser 1976; Abelson 1981; Eiser 1980); rather, it is constructed through interaction and comprises different and sometimes contradictory definitions (see Billig *et al.* 1988; Billig 1995).

(ii) Collective identity as a process refers thus to a network of *active relationships* between actors who interact, communicate, influence each other, negotiate, and make decisions. Forms of organization and models of leadership, communicative channels and technologies of communication are constitutive parts of this network of relationship.

(iii) Finally, a certain degree of *emotional investment* is required in the definition of a collective identity, which enables individuals to feel themselves part of a common unity. Collective identity is never entirely negotiable because participation in collective action is endowed with meaning which cannot be reduced to cost-benefit calculation and always mobilizes emotions as well (Kemper 1978, 1981, 1990; Hochschild 1979, 1983; Scheff 1990). Passions and feelings, love and hate, faith and fear are all part of a body acting collectively, particularly in those areas of social life that are less institutionalized, such as the social movements. To understand this part of collective action as 'irrational', as opposed to the parts that are 'rational' (a euphemism for 'good'), is simply nonsensical. There is no cognition without feeling and no meaning without emotion.

Let us try now to understand more closely this interactive and communicative construction, which is both cognitively and emotionally framed through active relationships.

Process and form

The term 'identity' is most commonly used to refer to the permanence over time of a subject of action unaffected by environmental changes falling below a certain threshold; it implies the notion of unity, which establishes the limits of a subject and distinguishes it from all others, and a relation between two actors which allows their (mutual) recognition. The notion of identity always refers to these three features: namely, the continuity of a subject over and beyond variations in time and its adaptations to the environment; the delimitation of this subject with respect to others; the ability to recognize and to be recognized.

The notion of a certain stability and permanence over time seems to contrast with the dynamic idea of a process. At any given moment social actors no doubt try to delimit and stabilize a definition of themselves; so do the observers. But the concept of collective identity as defined above can precisely help to understand that what appears as a given reality, something more or less permanent, is always the result, at least to a certain extent, of an active process which is not immediately visible.

Such a process involves continual investments and as it approaches the more institutionalized levels of social action it may increasingly crystallize into organizational forms, systems of rules, and leadership relationships. The tendency and need to stabilize one's identity and to give it a permanent form create a tension between the results of the process, which are crystallized in more or less permanent structures, in more or less stable definitions of identity, and the process itself which is concealed behind those forms.

The concept of collective identity can be of help addressing the interactive and sometimes contradictory processes lying behind what appears as a stable and coherent definition of a given collective actor. We should, however, take notice of the fact that the term 'identity' remains semantically inseparable from the idea of permanence and may, perhaps for this very reason, be ill suited for the processual analysis for which I am arguing. Nevertheless, I have retained 'identity' as a constitutive part of the concept of 'collective identity' for the simple reason that for the present, no better linguistic solution seems available. Because, as I will argue, such collective identity is as much an analytical tool as an object to be studied, it represents by definition a temporary solution to a conceptual problem, and should be replaced if and when other concepts prove themselves more adequate. In the meantime, my work continues situated within the limits of the available language, confident that the inevitable shift towards new concepts will not amount to a mere matter of different terminology but to an overall emergence of a new paradigm. The way out of the legacy of modernity will be a difficult process, and our time will notice its completion only at the end, when, as in any major scientific shift, we find ourselves already in a new conceptual universe. Meanwhile, for the sake of communication, we cannot but continue using old words to address new problems.

One way to overcome the apparent contradiction between the static and the dynamic dimensions implied by collective identity is to think of it in terms of action. Collective identity enables social actors to act as unified and delimited subjects and to retain control over their own action; conversely, however, they can act as collective bodies because they have completed, to some extent, the constructive process of collective identity. In terms of the observed action, one may thus speak of collective identity as the ability of a collective actor to recognize the effects of its actions and to attribute these effects to itself. Thus defined, collective identity presupposes, first, a self-reflective ability of social actors. Collective action is not simply a reaction to social and environmental constraints; it produces symbolic orientations and meanings which actors are able to recognize. Secondly, it entails that they have a notion of causality and belonging; they are, that is, able to attribute the effects of their actions to themselves. This recognition underpins their ability to appropriate the outcomes of their actions, to exchange them with others, and to decide how they should be allocated. Thirdly, identity entails an ability to perceive duration, an ability which enables actors to establish a relationship between past and future and to tie action to its effects.

The relational dimension of collective identity

Collective identity thus defines the capacity for autonomous action, a differentiation of the actor from others within the continuity of that identity. However, autoidentification must also gain social recognition if it is to provide the basis for identity. The ability of a collective actor to distinguish itself from others must be recognized by these 'others'. It would be impossible to speak of collective identity without referring to its relational dimension.

Social movements develop collective identity in a circular relationship with a system of opportunities/constraints. Collective actors are able to identify themselves when they have learned to distinguish between themselves and the environment. Actor and system reciprocally constitute themselves, and a movement only becomes self-aware through a relation with its external environment, which offers to social action a field of opportunities and constraints, that in turn are recognized and defined as such by the actor.

In this way, the unity of collective action, which is produced and maintained by autoidentification, rests on the ability of a collective actor to locate itself within a system of relations. A collective actor cannot construct its identity independently of its recognition (which can also mean denial or opposition) by other social and political actors. In order to act, any collective actor makes the basic assumption that its distinction from other actors is constantly acknowledged by them, if only in the extreme form of denial. There must be at least a minimal degree of reciprocity in social recognition between the actors (movement, authorities, other movements, third parties) even if it takes the form of a denial, a challenge, or an opposition (Gamson, Fireman and Rytina 1982). When this minimal basis for recognition is lacking there can only be pure repression, an emptiness of meaning nullifying the social field in which collective identity can be produced.

The autonomous ability to produce and to recognize the collective reality as a 'we' is then a paradoxical situation: in affirming its difference from the rest of the society, a movement also states its belonging to the shared culture of a society and its need to be recognized as a social actor. The paradox of identity always consists of the fact that difference, in order to be affirmed and lived as such, presupposes a certain equality and a degree of reciprocity.

Identity and conflict

Collective identity as a process can be analytically divided and seen from the internal and external point of view. This separation of two sides is obviously a way of describing what should be seen as a basically unified process. Collective identity contains an unresolved and unresolvable tension between the definition a movement gives of itself and the recognition granted to it by the rest of the society.

Conflict is the extreme example of this discrepancy and of the tension it provokes. In social conflicts reciprocity becomes impossible and the struggle for scarce resources begins. Both subjects involved deny each other their respective identities, refusing to grant their adversary that which they demand for themselves. The conflict severs the reciprocity of the interaction; the adversaries clash over something which is common to both of them but which each refuses to confer to the other. Beyond the concrete or symbolic objects at stake in a conflict, what people fight for is always the possibility to recognize themselves and be recognized as subjects of their action. Every conflict which transgresses a system of shared rules, whether it concerns material or symbolic resources, is a conflict of identity. Social actors enter a conflict to affirm the identity that their opponent has denied them, to reappropriate something which belongs to them because they are able to recognize it as their own.

During a conflict the internal solidarity of the group reinforces identity and guarantees it. People feel a bond with others not because they share the same interests, but because they need that bond in order to make sense of what they are doing. The solidarity that ties individuals to each other enables them to affirm themselves as subjects of their action and to withstand the breakdown of social relations induced by conflict. Moreover, they learn how to gather and focus their resources in order to reappropriate that which they recognize as theirs. Participation in forms of collective mobilization or in social movements, involvement in forms of cultural innovation, voluntary action inspired by altruism – all these are grounded in the need for identity and help to satisfy it.

Collective identity over time

Collective identity is a learning process which leads to the formation and maintenance of a unified empirical actor that we can call a 'social movement'. As that process passes through various stages, the collective actor develops a capability to resolve problems posed by the environment and becomes increasingly independent and autonomous in its capacity for action within the network of relationships in which it is situated. The process of collective identity is thus also the ability to produce new definitions by integrating the past and the emerging elements of the present into the unity and continuity of a collective actor.

It is above all in situations of crisis or intense conflict that the identity of a collective actor is put to challenge, when it is subjected to contradictory pressures which set a severe test for the ability of the collective actor to define its unity. It can respond by restructuring its action according to new orientations, or it can compartmentalize its spheres of action, so as to be still able to preserve a certain amount of coherence – at least internally to each of these spheres. The most serious cases provoke a breakdown or fragmentation of the collective actor or a breach of its external confines. This can lead to the incapacity to produce and maintain a definition of the 'movement' that could exhibit a certain stability or, vice versa, to the compulsive assumption of a rigid identity from which it is impossible to escape, as in sects or terrorist groups.

Collective identity ensures the continuity and permanence of the movement over time, it establishes the limits of the actor with respect to its social environment. It regulates the membership of individuals, it defines the requisites for joining the 'movement', and the criteria by which its members recognize themselves and are recognized. The content of this identity and its temporal duration vary according to the type of group concerned.

When we consider organizational structures, leadership patterns, membership requisites, we deal with levels of collective action which presuppose the notion of collective identity: they incorporate and enact the ways a collective actor defines ends, means and field of his action. One should consider those levels as empirical indicators of a possible collective identity and, conversely, should use this concept as an analytical tool to dismantle the 'reified' appearance of those empirical dimensions of a social movement and to attain the constructive process behind them.

De-reification of collective identity

One cannot treat collective identity as a 'thing', as the monolithic unity of the subject; it must, instead, be conceived as a system of relations and representations. Collective identity takes the form of a field containing a system of vectors in tension. These vectors constantly seek to establish an equilibrium between the various axes of collective action, and between identification declared by the actor and the identification given by the rest of the society (adversaries, allies, third parties).

Collective identity in its concrete form depends on how this set of relations is held together: this system is never a definite datum; it is instead a laborious process where unity and equilibrium are reestablished over and over again in reaction to shifts and changes in the elements internal and external to the field. Collective identity therefore patterns itself according to the presence and relative intensity of its dimensions. Some vectors may be weaker or stronger than others, and some may be entirely absent. One may imagine it as a field which expands and contracts and whose borders alter with the varying intensity and direction of the various forces that constitute it.

At any given moment both actors and observers can give an account of this field through a unified, delimited, and static definition of the 'we'. This tendency for 'reification' is always part of a collective actor's need for continuity and permanence. But today this unavoidable necessity has to confront important changes in the ways identification takes place.

Identification processes have been gradually transferred from the outside of society to its interior. From entities that are transcendent and metaphysical, from metasocial foundations such as myths, gods, ancestors, but also from the more recent avatars of God such as History or the Invisible Hand of the market, identification processes shift to associative human action, to culture, communication, and social relations. As identity is progressively recognized as socially produced, it becomes obvious that notions like coherence, limit maintenance, and recognition only describe it in static terms; in its dynamic connotation, however, collective identity increasingly becomes a process of construction and autonomization.

For recent social movements, particularly those centred around cultural issues, collective identity is then becoming ever more conspicuously the product of conscious action and the outcome of self-reflection, and, correspondingly, loses its status based on a set of given or 'structural' characteristics. The collective actor tends to construct its coherence and recognize itself within the limits set by the environment and social relations. Collective identity tends to coincide with conscious processes of 'organization' and it is experienced not so much as a situation as it is an action.

To express this increasingly self-reflexive and constructed manner in which contemporary collective actors tend to define themselves, I suggest using the term *identization*. Within the boundaries of our language, it is a rough and provocative acknowledgement of a qualitative leap in the present forms of collective action, and also a call for an equivalent leap in our cognitive tools.

The lens of collective identity: what one can see through it

Collective identity is a concept, an analytical tool and not a datum or an essence, a 'thing' with a 'real' existence. As far as concerns concepts, one should never forget that we are addressing not 'reality', but rather instruments or lenses through which we read reality. The concept of collective identity can function as a tool only if it helps to analyse phenomena, or dimensions of them, that cannot be explained through other concepts or models and if it contributes to the formation of new knowledge and to the understanding of these same phenomena.

As was stated in the opening section, the concept of collective identity was devised to overcome the shortcomings of the dualistic legacy still present in the study of collective action, and the difficulties of the current approaches in explaining some dimensions of contemporary social movements, particularly the central role of culture and symbolic production in these recent forms of action. It also addresses the naive epistemological assumptions, often only implicitly present in the many approaches to the study of social movements. It is then a concept that is intended to introduce changes in our conceptualization of social movements and for this very reason should contribute to a different understanding of the changing significance of social movements in contemporary society.

These two levels, changes in conceptualization and changes in our understanding of the practical-political significance of collective phenomena, are connected by a circular relation. The circle is not a vicious one if concepts help us to see more of the phenomena to which they apply, to see them differently. Reversely, if these empirical phenomena are filtered and interpreted through the conceptual lenses, they may help us to refine and improve the quality of the lenses themselves.

1 The notion of collective identity is relevant to sociological literature because it brings along with it a field perspective on collective action and a dynamic view of its definition. It implies the inclusion of the social field as part of the movement construction and it means that beyond the formal definitions (public speeches, documents, opinions of participants) there is always an active negotiation, an interactive work among individuals,

groups or parts of the movement. This again shifts the attention from the top to the bottom of collective action and does not consider only the most visible forms of action or the leaders' discourse. It looks to the more invisible or hidden forms and tries to listen to the more silent voices.

Processes of mobilization, organizational forms, models of leadership, ideologies and forms of communication – these are all meaningful levels of analysis for the reconstruction from within of the system of action that constitutes a collective actor. The whole of part IV will be devoted to a consideration of these aspects. But also relationships with the outside, with competitors, allies, adversaries, and especially the reaction of the political system and the apparatus of social control, must be taken into account to understand how the collective actor takes shape, perpetuates itself or changes. The importance of this dimension has been stressed for example by authors like Gamson (Gamson, Fireman and Rytina 1982), Tarrow (1989, 1994) McCarthy (Mc Carthy *et al.* 1991; McCarthy 1994) and will be developed in particular in part III.

2 The concept of collective identity can also contribute to a better understanding of the nature and meaning of the emerging forms of collective action in highly differentiated systems. As the quantity and quality of work in the area has increased and improved our understanding of recent phenomena (Rucht 1988, 1990, 1991; Scherer-Warren and Krischke 1987; Dalton and Kuechler 1990; Pakulski 1991; Koopmans *et al.* 1992; Kriesi 1993; Kriesi *et al.* 1995; Giugni 1995; Ahlemeyer 1995; Proietto 1995), we know that contemporary 'movements' increasingly address cultural issues and tend to differentiate themselves from the model of political action. The concept of collective identity aids in the making of distinctions that mark off this cultural level from all others, and particularly from dimensions that are political in the proper sense. Such dimensions do not disappear from the scene, but come to play different roles that can be captured only if one relies on conceptual tools that allow the recognition of the complexity of present collective actors, tools that do not take for granted 'social movement' as a unified and homogeneous reality.

3 Collective actors are neither historical heroes nor villains. By identifying specific levels that enter the construction of collective identity, movements can be seen as action systems. They are not 'subjects' that act with the unity of purposes that leaders, ideologues, or opponents attribute to them. They are always plural, ambivalent, often contradictory.

4 The concept of collective identity has important consequences in clearing up the misunderstanding on the so-called new social movements. The notion of 'newness' that I introduced as a temporary and relative qualification of emergent collective action (Melucci 1980) has been criticized by

comparing different historical cases (see as examples of critics of the 'newness' Kivisto 1986; D'Anieri *et al.* 1990; Scott 1990a; Calhoun 1993), or it has been attributed to recent movements as a whole as their intrinsic quality (Offe 1985a; Dalton and Kuechler 1990). Contemporary movements are not 'new' or 'old' in themselves, but rather comprise different orientations with their components belonging to different historical layers of a given society. The notion of collective identity can help to describe and explain this connection between the apparent unity, which is always our empirical starting point, and the underlying multiplicity, which can be detected only by an appropriate analytical tool.

5 Another important consequence of the concept of collective identity has to do with the theory of domination and conflict. The notion of collective identity can prevent sociological analysis from ridding itself too quickly of the theoretical question of whether there are dimensions of contemporary collective action which express new systemic conflicts and challenge new forms of social domination in complex societies. To dismiss this question by reducing recent movements only to their political dimension is to hide or deny the new location of power.

I have suggested that collective action of many recent social movements constitutes a communicative act which is performed through the form of action itself, making visible new powers and the possibilities of challenging them. Action still pursues political goals or instrumental advantages, but within a limited scope and with a degree of interchangeability. But in so doing it also throws light on hidden issues that are not accounted for by the rationality of dominant apparatuses.

6 However, this antagonist dimension cannot explain everything, and the concept of collective identity is a permanent warning about the necessity of recognizing a plurality of levels in collective action. This is perhaps the most important contribution that the concept of collective identity can bring to the field of social movements studies.

7 Finally, collective identity has some radical methodological implications. Sociological analysis is not free from the risk of reducing collective action to just one of its levels – which in fact is often the 'official' definition of a movement – and of considering it as a unified empirical object. When sociology still rests on an essentialist idea of social movements as characters acting on the stage of history, it may contribute, even unwillingly, to the practical denial of difference, to a factual and political ignorance of that complex articulation of meanings that contemporary movements carry in themselves. Putting into question the unity usually taken for granted by ideologists, sociology may help to reveal those dimensions of collective action that are not visible at first sight. To understand how a

'social movement' succeeds or fails in *becoming a collective actor* is therefore a fundamental task of the sociologist.

Actors, of course, act under the practical necessity of having to hypostatize their action-in-the-making in order to be able to speak about it. So do the opponents and the observers, including the researcher. 'Objectification' is a basic feature of the operation of human cognition and also a means of cognitive economy employed in speaking about the world. Yet this does not release us, as researchers, to taking this reification for granted, as if the relational texture of social phenomena would thereby disappear. The task of analysis is precisely that of deconstructing this apparent reality and letting the plurality of relations and meanings appear.

This analytical task allows some distinction between collective identity as a constructive process and its objectified results: collective actors have always a 'public identity' (Johnston *et al.* 1994), they always act as 'historical actors' (Mueller 1994), in the same sense in which individuals present their self according to Goffman. But the concept of collective identity can help us precisely to question the surface and to reach the deep relational texture of the collective actor. How means and ends are interpreted by different groups of the movement? How are resources and constraints held together in the movement discourse? What kind of relation with the environment shapes the movement and how do its different groups interpret it? What kind of conflicts, tensions, and negotiations can be observed during the process of construction and maintenance of a movement as a unified empirical actor? These are some of the questions that can be derived from the concept of collective identity and that bring us closer to the beginnings of a different research practice. Chapter 20 will deal with the methodological consequences of this theoretical stance.

Identity and collective emotional experience

In conclusion to the preceding discussion, I want to briefly engage a level of analysis whose importance has often been underevaluated by sociologists. Smelser (1962) has already stressed the need for an analysis of collective behaviour which moves simultaneously on various levels and which combines, yet without confusing them, both psychological and sociological variables. Attempting to go beyond the simple juxtaposition of these two different points of view, I will address an analytical level which one might call *collective experience*, which involves people's feeling and emotions, and which should be neither confused with other dimensions of collective action nor generalized into an overall explanatory model. I believe it important for the understanding of the formation of collective action to complete an analysis of the meaning it assumes at the level of emotional dynamics. This is a complementary dimension which must be kept distinct from 'structural' analysis, but which nevertheless forms a constituent part of any analysis which takes seriously the task to understand 'action', not merely behaviour. Indeed, many misunderstandings and much pointless debate has been provoked by the confusion of these two levels. The analyst is caught between, on the one hand, the risk of an explanation using the categories of dynamic psychology, generalized at the level of structural explanation, and, on the other, the endeavour to use structural analysis also to explain processes which involve the motivations of individuals, the emotional meanings of action.

I shall attempt to make a step in the direction of overcoming this simple duality by indicating a possible level of analysis in terms of emotional experiential dynamics. Smelser has shown that collective action expresses both of the terms of the ambivalence (love/aggression) which characterizes relationships from an emotional point of view. This observation is echoed in Alberoni's theory of *statu nascenti* (Alberoni 1984), in which he formulates 'three principles of the dynamics' which regulate the relationship with the love-object: (i) ambivalence (love/hate); (ii) reciprocity of the energetic investments (love to those who love, hate to those who hate); (iii) tendency to reduce ambivalence.

Developing such a perspective, we can assume that, in terms of emotional investments, the objects of love are always affected by the love/hate ambivalence. It is difficult to endure the ambivalence and to accept its contradictory emotional content. If we hate those who we love we feel guilty. When the emotional charge of ambivalence reaches a threshold where it becomes unbearable for where it exceeds the actors' available energetic capacity, an attack on the enemy could constitute the defensive reaction reflecting the guilt of hating the loved one. Blaming the enemy projects onto him/her that part of aggressive tendencies towards the loved one which one cannot tolerate. By separating the terms of the ambivalence this enables both of them to be covered through investing the love-object only with eros and discharging aggression onto the enemy.

This model can be applied to what I call antagonist social conflicts. At the level of experiential dynamics, conflict takes the form of a reduction of ambivalence. Humankind's relationship with its own production is a relationship with objects imbued with an energetic positive charge (love-objects), for we identify ourselves with our products and always invest them with emotional and not just instrumental meaning. But love-objects are also those which enslave us and from which we become dependent. Hence the ambivalence towards our own production. In social conflicts, the struggle among adversaries for control over social production is a way of reducing this ambivalence. Each party reduces the ambivalence by one-sidedly projecting one of the poles onto the other; each one attributes to the adversary in a projective way the aggressiveness s/he feels towards her/his own love-object. Opposition towards the adversary who appropri-ates or threatens the love-object redirects aggressiveness onto him/her and resolves the ambivalence towards the loved one, who thus retains only pos-itive features.

This explanation applies to ongoing conflict but leaves its genesis unex-plained. It does not discuss, that is, how the situation arises in which the same object (social production) is contested by adversaries and in which each perceives a threat from the other. Reflection on the process whereby control over production is delegated in the process of division of labour and of social differentiation (the sociological reasons I have already addressed in chapter 2) may shed light on the matter. The distribution of control over the allocation of social production and the creation of imbal-ances of power among social positions involves a transfer of ambivalence. Those delegating power and control to others reassign onto the function delegated the ambivalence which characterized their relationship with the love-object. To delegate power is not only a relieving and facilitating expe-rience; it also implies a sense of loss and incapacity. Those delegating power invest the ones in power with aggressive emotions, in order to free their love-object (their own action) from any negative feeling. The recipients in the delegation experience the same situation of ambivalence *vis-à-vis* their mandators. To be invested by other people's mandate and expectations is a gratification and a honor but also a burden. The aggressive feelings are diverted towards the mandators, so that the action of those in power can be kept uncontaminated by negative emotions.

For both of the actors, the relationship marks out a situation of loss/conservation of the love-object. Those delegating power lose the direct control over their action, but through aggressiveness directed at the adver-sary can at least partially repair this sense of loss and preserve the positive-ness of their action. Those in power lose the unburdened freedom of not having to exert control and take care of others, but they can assign the blame to the mandators and channel towards them their aggressive feelings.

When there exists a situation of direct control over the delegation rela-tionship, a certain reciprocity of recognition prevails between the partners, for each of them accepts of receiving from the other something that is con-sidered equivalent to one's own investment. One accepts the burden of exerting the function delegated to her/him; in exchange, however, recogni-tion, deference, and gratification is received. One accepts to delegate power, but only to receive in exchange service, help, support, security. The situation can be interpreted as a type of relationship which permits reduction of ambivalence through a limited acceptance of the pain connected to partial loss, which is perceived as tolerable. Aggressiveness towards the other takes the form of subjugation by the delegator and that of service by her/him who exercises the control function. Reciprocal direct control and frequent face-to-face confrontations, as in small-group situations, allow continuous monitoring of the relationship, reduce the risk of an aggressive clash, and favour the possibility of making sense of the situation as a limited and acceptable loss, which is reciprocal (submission in exchange for service and responsibility, and vice versa).

But when, for the structural reasons we have already examined (differentiation of the system, increasing distance among social positions), the possibility of direct control over the delegation disappears, so too does the reciprocity of recognition break down. We may presume that the sense of an acceptable loss no longer predominates and aggressive feelings gain in prominence. Uncontrolled ambivalence emerges once again and triggers the mechanism whereby aggression is redirected onto the adversary. Thus is created the situation of conflict described above.

This brief outline provides one possible reading, in terms of collective emotional experience, of the 'structural' theory of conflict that I presented earlier. The opposition of the adversaries and the desire to appropriate social production between its different producers could thus be explained also in terms of the emotional investments that characterize social production and collective action.

Collective identity, the construction of a 'we', is then a necessity also for the emotional balance of social actors involved in conflicts. The possibility of referring to a love-object ('Us' against 'Them') is a strong and preliminary condition for collective action, as it continuously reduces ambivalence and fuels action with positive energies. Collective actors constantly need to draw on this emotional background in order to feed their action, to make sense of it, to calculate its costs and benefits. When facing changes, the necessity of renewing and possibly renegotiating the bond that ties individuals and groups together originates from this deep emotional commitment to a 'We' which must maintain its integrity in order to motivate action.

Collective identity in historical context

One could argue that the concepts proposed by my theoretical framework are historically related to a very specific wave of collective action, that of the movements which started to appear in the Western countries in the

1960s. It is indeed difficult to separate the analytical level from its historical sources which, in my case, were the movements which I started to analyse in the early 1970s. The concepts on which my work relies are certainly influenced by contemporary social movements; yet I have always seen it important to draw the distinction between the conceptual level and the empirical analysis of concrete social movements. The concept of collective identity is important for my work as it provides a way of addressing the question of how a collective becomes a collective, which is usually taken for granted. In other fields of sociology the situation may differ, but in the case of collective action the question itself is apparently raised by no one. We usually take the collective actors for granted and quasi-spontaneously attribute a kind of essentialist existence to them. The theoretical problem for us today is this unity, the creation of a collective subject of action as a process which needs to be subjected to explanation.

Of course, this question could probably not be raised for the movements of the past, not because these processes were inactive in earlier movements but because they were less important and less visible. Collective actors of the past were more deeply rooted in a specific social condition in which they were embedded, so that the question of the collective was already answered from the beginning through that social condition that accounted as such for the existence of a collective actor. A working-class movement is first of all the expression of a working class social background; it is already defined by the social conditions of that particular group. For the working-class militants it was extremely important that they belonged to a specific culture which was organized in structures of everyday life, in forms of solidarity which shaped the identity and grounded it in the material and cultural conditions of the everyday (Calhoun 1982; Fantasia 1998). This continuity between the structural location of the actor and the material and cultural world of its experience is what I mean by the class condition.

Today, as we are increasingly more dealing with movements which cannot be referred to any specific social condition, the question of how a collective becomes just that has become more prominent. In my work, I was able to raise this question as it was focusing precisely on such particular realities, but nevertheless the question in itself seems a reasonable scientific question which can be addressed also to other historical movements. Theoretically speaking, this question also could not be raised within another cultural and intellectual context, as there simply existed no social and conceptual space in which to advance thought in these terms. We are thus always proceeding within the circular relationship between concepts and objects, but if concepts prove heuristically effective once they are in place they can nevertheless find application beyond the historical context in which they were produced. They can help us to see differently objects in other historical contexts.

A final note could be added concerning the use of the notion of collective *identity*. As already stated, the term 'identity' is conceptually unsatisfactory: it conveys too strongly the idea of the permanence of a subject. At this moment, however, no other designation seems in possession of the capacity to replace it in its purpose. Thus, for the time being we must continue being trapped in the usage of the term in the near-contradictory situation where in order to bring to light the processual dimension of collective identity as an interactive construction, we inadvertently stress the reality and the permanence of the actor. What I am trying to do with this concept, however, is to bring it to its limits. Scientific enterprises proceed in this manner, through an increasing effort to 'use up' the relevant concepts until they reach their internal limits, to allow then the situation itself to affect a change in concepts when the older tools have proven useless and outdated themselves. To be sure, there exist even now notions that better stress the dynamic side of identity, but they seem partial successes as well. The term 'project', for instance, points out one dimension of identity: the capability of relating to the future, starting from the present. However, one has to be located somewhere in order to think of the future, to be rooted in an already established definition in order to have projects; otherwise one is left in the world of fantasies and images. A 'project' is possible only when a location somewhere in the present is established. It is the here and now, and this point of consistency provides the only possible starting point to think of the future. But the relation to the past is equal in importance to the projectual dimension in the definition of an identity (Halbwachs 1975; Namer 1987; Middleton and Edwards 1990). The relation with the past is necessary the same way as the capacity to make projects, and this has become particularly concrete and obvious against the backdrop of the dominant trends in our present culture. Ours is a culture which is making of speed and change its central values, and through them it creates new forms of power. There is a rhetoric of change and speed as values that reveals its belongingness to the dominant logic of big organizations, of production and circulation of goods, of the world media system; its consequence is the erasure of past and permanence.

More than in any previous culture identity today is in need of a relationship to the past. Such a relationship is created by the necessity of retaining something while changing, of maintaining roots, of reconstructing our history without which there is no possibility of progress. The whole notion of time is redefined with the new relationship to the past and the future: the present becomes a crucial dimension, not as a point-like, instantaneous dimension but rather as the possibility of forging in the here and now the connection between the past and the future, between memories and projects.

At the same time, however, the use of the notion of identity addresses and points out a contradictory situation which is important for collective actors. Every actor is faced with a two-sided problem. On the one hand, the actor must maintain a permanence which, on the other, must be produced continuously. This tension is always present, and probably the currency acquired by 'identity', the apparent paradox (speaking of the 'process of identity') it contains, captures something of it by signalling the contradictory necessity of permanence in the continuous constructive process. At any given time, when requested its identity, a collective actor (excluding the extreme, completely schizophrenic situation) is able to provide an answer through its many mouths in a definite way. Any such stable definition, however, is at the same time the outcome of constructive processes.

Ultimately, identity becomes a matter of the question that is asked and of the position taken by the observer. If one is interested in defining who the actor is at a given moment, identity provides a useful concept. Should one, however, be more interested in the constructive process behind its formation, then probably other concepts should be created that are more appropriate than identity for addressing this particular point of view and for account for the tension between maintenance and production of the definition that a collective actor gives of itself.

Having outlined our theoretical framework, analysis of 'movements' in complex societies may now begin.

PART II

Contemporary collective action

5

Conflicts of culture

The systemic field

Societies of mature capitalism; postindustrial, postmaterial, complex societies – none of these labels seems capable of capturing the substance of the transformations under way in the global society. Nor can they indicate to us the direction of the developments affecting the social system in which we live. That these labels, and many others, nevertheless seem unavoidable and have been adopted in diverse use is a sign of the fact that we do not really know, except in negative terms, what exactly it is we are talking about. In this situation, we should declare outright that we are trapped in an analytical and linguistical impasse which has left us wavering between, on the one hand, an outdated, if not wholly anachronistic, stockpile of terminology that we still employ in the absence of new cognitive tools, and, on the other hand, a set of allusive concepts bereft of any substantial analytical significance. For the fundamental transformations in the nature and physiognomy of social life have already made themselves manifest (Inglehart 1977, 1990): were it not for the qualitative changes and incoherences which resist definition in terms of industrial capitalism – the formative experience of modern society – there would have been no need to invent new names in the first place, with new data rather falling neatly in place within the old categories.

Recent debates on modernity and postmodernity are the most significant examples of this impasse. An increasing body of literature, is devoted, implicitly or explicitly, to answer the question of what kind of society we are living in. By reflecting on the legacy of modernity (Touraine 1994a; Giddens 1990, 1991; Taylor 1989; Bauman 1991, 1992), or by outlining the new coordinates of the postmodern world (Lyotard 1984; Featherstone 1988; Harvey 1989; Turner 1990; Nicholson 1990; Rose 1991; Jameson 1991; Lash and Friedman 1992; Seidman and Wagner 1992; Smart 1992;

Rosenau 1992) the question concerning the nature of contemporary society is addressed without openly declare its ambiguous nature. Even those who are trying to substantively analyse the transformation of present society are obliged to rely on images and metaphors to define it (Lash and Urry 1987, 1994; Crook *et al.* 1992; Beck 1992).

Those listed above and many others circulating in recent literature, however, are not concepts but allusive notions, whose very weakness indicates the need for a qualitative leap in our theoretical understanding of present society. If we need such an abundant panoply of prefixes and adjectives it is because we lack strong analytical categories. And this applies also to the notions such as postfordism (Lipietz 1992), which has been proposed as a singular improvement over that of complex society as conceptually more precise than it and possessing a greater capability of accounting for structural changes and new forms of social control in present society (Bartholomew and Mayer 1992; Mayer and Roth 1995). The point of the 'postfordist' analyses certainly calls attention, and makes a tangible contribution, towards a better knowledge of new forms of domination. However, they, along with a great host of others, continue being restrained in their conceptual capacity by their obstinate adherence to the whole class of residual and negative 'post' notions that fail to provide elements for the qualitative renewal of research practices; thus they rather risk doing nothing to thrust us out of the imprisonment within the framework of the old categories and the outdated thought.

The first step out of the impasse is then to acknowledge the scope of the problem behind the linguistic artifice; the weakness of our conceptual tools can become the starting point for new understandings and in time for its own improvement if it is addressed openly rather than kept out of sight. Only then will a space be opened up to accommodate new research questions and directions which, by eschewing global answers, can begin the work to build a new paradigm. At present, what needs to be realized is the extent of the crisis of both of the models that have nurtured the self-understanding of the modern society: the industrial and the capitalist. Industrialism and the market, technology and social classes, rationalization and exploitation represent the opposite and complimentary images of modernity we have inherited from the nineteenth century. Both, however, are ill suited to capture the nature of present change. The terms we must accept for use are precarious, and my intention is certainly no more than to merely indicate the existence of the dilemma, by inciting the inevitable collision of the old categorial frameworks with the sensation of new realities seeping into the consciousness. In the meantime, I have opted to proceeding with the working notions of complex society and information society, which, complementing each other, retain a degree of neutrality *vis-à-vis* the exhausted polarities of the old terms. As such, they still capture some of the key dimensions along which the changing society reveals its nature: the former indicates a type of structuration, the latter the core resource that is produced.

It is against this background that I want to advance a series of hypotheses concerning antagonist conflicts in complex systems. The situation is paradoxical and provisional: we cannot help but define our society, while knowing nevertheless that our definitions are working hypotheses whose purpose it is to only throw light on certain empirical phenomena. These hypotheses emerge as guidelines; they are not intended to contribute to the formation of a general theory but, rather, to serve as tools for analysis of those empirical phenomena which do not fit within the framework of old hypotheses. Observation and research may in turn provide confirmation and extension of the validity of these guidelines and lead to the first foundation of a theory, which, however, will always and by definition be a 'regional', middle-range theory. This circular path will not constitute a vicious circle if it helps us to reach the categorial limits of the present paradigm and opens up the way for the passage to a new one.

In complex systems, capacity for intervention in the symbolic order not only generalizes itself to comprehend the whole of society but now puts the individual at the centre of its focus as well. Whereas in the past social processes affected individuals principally as 'members-of' – that is, as defined by some form of membership – today the achievements of modernity, such as mass culture, the rising educational levels, and the generalization of citizenship rights, have turned the individual into a subject of action; but no less into the terminal point of the processes of regulation. Society acts on the system as a whole, just as it does on single individuals: on their symbolic capacities, on their personal resources for defining the meaning of their own actions.

Social intervention shifts to the domain of individual motivation and to the foundations of action in biological structure. The amount of investment reserved for the funding of research into basic biology, genetics, and the study of the brain is indicative of the directions at which contemporary systems are directing their capabilities to transform and control. There are those who have insisted on the prominent role of the molecular articulation of control within the fabric of daily life today, speaking of the microphysics of power (Foucault 1970, 1979, 1980a, 1980b). This image of omnipresent power is matched by a corresponding portrayal of conflict as the spontaneous and quasi-natural expression of deep-seated needs which resist manipulation, as it appears in some extensions of the Foucauldian argument (see Deleuze and Guattari 1977).

A similar idea has been put forward by several studies which read the changes observed in the welfare state in terms of the generalization of control (Offe 1984, 1985b). In them, forms of resistance and conflict are likewise treated as ultimately residual, as the expression of indelible natural needs. By emphasizing the dependence of modern welfare systems on dominant forces, one forgets that the actual functioning of a system is not just a product fashioned after the interests of its dominant logic (or, a mere restructuring of the form of capitalist rule through the welfare state mode); instead, it is a field where interests and social groups meet and clash under conditions created by the interaction of multiple forces. Without underestimating the significance of the emerging new forms of disequilibria and power, we should nevertheless bear in mind that the concrete workings of a system always reflect its *social* character as a product of a field of relations. Therefore, the dominant logic of a system cannot be disconnected from the behaviour and motives of its actors. In truth, there is no dominant logic imposing itself in a linear and coherent directionality; what we must examine are actions and relations that structure themselves according to certain patterns of imbalance and power; actions, however, which, to a variable extent depending on the nature of the constraints, always remain openended, plural, ambiguous, and often contradictory on account of the relational nature of the field.

Contemporary systems provide individuals with symbolic resources which heighten their potential for individuation – that is, their potential for autonomy and self-realization. The capacity of individuals to define what and who they are, and what it is that they are doing and wish to do, is enhanced by broadened access to education. We have witnessed the increasing importance of educational systems and their changing profile, from the caretakers of simple socialization and of the transmission of values and rules towards the overseers of the development of personal skills. Similarly, individual resources are today enhanced by increased political participation and extension of citizenship rights, and by the importance acquired by organizational and communications networks.

On the other hand, however, in order for highly differentiated systems to be able to guarantee their internal integration, it becomes necessary to extend the system's control over the symbolic levels of action, so as to include in its scope the spheres where the meanings and motives of behaviour are constituted. Control can no longer restrict itself to the external regulation of the production/appropriation of resources; it must also intervene in the internal processes of the formation of attitudes. For their proper functioning, complex societies need participatory input in social and organizational networks and require a high level of individual identification with the generative processes of social life. This, again, calls for an appropriate disposal of motivational and symbolic resources on the part of the individual elements of which these societies are composed.

On the one hand, then, complex societies distribute resources with which individuals can identify themselves as autonomous subjects of action; on the other, they ask the same individuals to 'identify-with' – to function as dependable and effective terminals in complex information circuits. Systemic demands are thus contradictory, since the same resources must be distributed *and* withdrawn, entrusted *and* then placed under control.

Hence it follows that analysis of complex systems cannot be conducted solely in terms of forms of power, regulation, and legitimation; it must also examine the social needs and orientations that feed those systems. While focusing on such orientations, however, the analyst should not forget that study of the differential access of various groups or categories to social resources will highlight the processes of discrimination and exclusion, the logic of compensation and substitution – in sum, the ways in which the system controls tensions and potential conflict through its differentiated distribution of social compensation among various groups and areas of intervention.

When individuals possess sufficient resources to think of themselves as individuals and act as such, they are able to construct their own identity as something not already given, and especially as something which is not given once and for all but depends on potentialities for which each of them feels at least partly responsible. New inequalities stem precisely from the way in which these potentialities are distributed. No longer merely material, these disparities concern the chances of individuals and groups to fulfil themselves as autonomous actors. Differences in access to these opportunities stem from potent forces excluding entire social groups and parts of the world. Within the central societies and in the periferies of the planet, new forms of inequality arise as cultural deprivation, as the destruction of traditional cultures replaced only by marginalization or by dependent consumption, and as the imposition of lifestyles which no longer provide individuals with the cultural bases for their self-identification.

Taking into account these new forms of inequality, my intention, however, is to examine here the needs and orientations that feed complex systems and identify contents and forms of action which clash with the established culture and the 'normal' image given of the needs that these systems are supposed to address through their organizations, services, welfare and communication agencies. One thinks, for example, of the issue of health, and also of the difficulties involved in defining the meaning of that which is simultaneously turning into a need, a right, and a system requirement, as we shall see shortly. The gist of the matter is the fact that complex systems now have to deal with human needs that are to an increasing degree cultural products.

In no human group, not even in those that most closely depend on natural constraints, has it ever been possible to analytically separate needs from the system of social relations and the capacity for symbolic representation: needs are invariably the result of social perception, of a symbolic mediation which enables their definition and representation on the basis of the conditions imposed by biological structure and the environment. Yet, while it is true that the definition of needs has to a certain extent always been the result of cultural processes, there is no doubt that in contemporary complex societies there has been a change, in a manner and to a degree incommensurable with any other society, in the capacity for the social perception of needs. Contemporary societies interfere massively with their natural environment and its processes (an interference, which now borders on creative destruction on the brink of a total annihilation through ecological and/or nuclear catastrophe). They seek to intervene in the very biological foundations of the human species and are beginning to inquire into (and act upon) the fragile and ambiguous borderline that separates the biological behavioural structure from meaningful action. How, then, could one fail to take notice of the fact that in such societies there is a concomitant increase in the capacity for perception of needs as a social product, as the outcome of symbolically mediated behaviour?

Consequently, no analysis of complex systems can afford to ignore the task of recognizing the full significance of the changed capacity to define and perceive those needs as they become issues for social debates – debates in which collective energies are brought into focus and whereby are addressed the deep-seated dilemmas, the critical choices on which a society concentrates its attention (Individual or Society? Culture or Nature? Difference or Integration? Past or Future? Quantity or Quality?). Such debates, however, must be approached as loci of misunderstanding, for what is at stake is never that which is overtly discussed; hence, they are only the outward symptoms of ongoing or nascent inner conflicts that affect the societal field, the elemental orientation of social resources. At the more visible level of the culture, such issues highlight problem areas which attract collective attention, and debates on these issues are sometimes followed by development of opposition of social groups and the formation of 'movements'.

In contemporary societies, the definition of needs is one such problem area, organized around two opposite poles. On the one hand, there is an appeal to Nature; on the other, a hypersocialized image of needs takes shape. 'Naturalization' and hypersocialization are the two extremes in a continuum along which can be arranged the whole spectrum of symbolic models present in postindustrial culture. Needs as the expression of a Nature which resists and rebels against the social; needs as the integral reflection of the system of relations of which the individual is part – these are the two basic representations of the formation of social demands in the culture of contemporary societies. The former model can be related to emergent movements in a rather straightforward fashion, and the latter to upwardly mobile technocratic groups. In the first case, the spontaneity of primary needs challenges the omnipresent social control; one recognizes here certain ideological features of the women's, ecological, and youth movements. In the latter case, the relational ideology of needs lies at the basis of the modernization of organizational systems, the updating of communication processes, and the grouping together of educational, psycho-social, and therapeutic services. Here there is no longer an individual dimension to behaviour or pathology; all problems are brought within the ambit of communicative processes for their solution. The individual can only be educated, cared for, and informed, all within the group, and s/he is thus integrated into a relational code of normality.

However, simply relating these two extreme cases to dominant and opposition groups is easily misleading. In fact, the definition of needs is a system of cultural representations which ramifies through the whole society, and which is appropriated by different social groups even in diametrically opposing ways. The appeal to Nature becomes a message of integration taken up and broadcast by the media. It feeds new markets and regulates lifestyles and patterns of consumption; it creates, that is, a new conformity. On the other hand, the social nature of needs becomes the watchword for opposition groups which mobilize themselves against the mechanisms of social marginalization, against the individualistic reduction and atomization with which weapons the system encounters social demands.

The symbolic field in complex societies is therefore never organized into the simple geometry of good and evil we can detect in the passing structure of the political parlance. It is, instead, a system of interweaving opposites, of ambivalences, of multiple meanings which actors seek to bend to their goals so as to lend meaning to their action.

This said, one must still acknowledge that the appeal to Nature has been a crucial battle cry in the formation of new conflictual demands. Nature is seen as apparently that which resists external pressures because it eludes instrumental rationality. It presents itself with the opacity and callousness of the already given, as repelling the forced socialization of identity prosecuted by the new forms of power. But as it has been utilized by collective actors (particularly women's, youth, and environmental movements), the very notion also contains within itself the suggestion that natural existence at the same time is a field of action, an object to be produced rather than a datum. Body, desire, biological identity, and sexuality as brought to the interest of the modern consciousness have all become issues at the heart of the new social needs. Treated as pure cultural (that is, socially produced) representations, as contested fields of interpretation, they betoken the incipient awareness of the fact that human nature can be created and transformed by social action; and this means that they can also be drawn on and mustered for purposes other than those imposed by dominant interests.

It is precisely here that the roots of all ambiguity in the relation of collective action to the resurrected Nature lie. Bearing the banner of spontaneity, purity, and immediacy of natural needs, contemporary movements move on challenge the social and its reduction of differences to systemic normality. But, at the same time, Nature becomes the ideological phantasm which nourishes the illusion that it is possible to cut oneself off from social relations. By retreating within themselves under the illusion of recreated spontaneous Nature, movements open the doors for their development into marginal countercultures displaying but a pathological refusal to face up to any of the problems associated with sociality: the scarcity of resources, the need for efficiency and effectiveness of action, the division of labour, and power.

The drive for liberation thus turns into an exaltation of the fantastic spontaneity of needs, the consecration of immediate experience as opposed to reflective awareness. As a consequence, the most distinctive feature of individual needs is suppressed: namely, the fact that they are the very point at which man's natural membership and social membership meet, a point which signals both a possibility and a limit. Both within and without us, Nature ceases to be the realm of obscure forces and is readied for conscious human action; but nevertheless it itself continues to set limits on that action, through the operation of biological and ecosystemic constraints and through the constant reminder of birth and death. The social, in turn, delimits Nature with its rules and its codes by transforming energy into information.

Any enslavement can be justified in the name of an abstract spontaneity of Nature. In complex societies, moreover, systems of control are being restructured in order to integrate the naturalness of needs into new models of conformity. There is no resisting this tendency if the tension between natural needs and the constraints of social existence is allowed to slacken. The Nature that we are discovering within ourselves, as the site of deep-seated needs and resistance to external pressures, has never retreated from the mold of the rules and rites of social behaviour.

A similar ambivalence is to be detected in the appeal to the sociality of needs. This ideological model serves as an instrument for the expansion of tightly-knit social control, when it is used as a justification for the interlacement of the individual into relational networks which impose conformity, and, another case in point, in the perennial fancy to deny the irreducibility of the human problem to the problem of the group. At the same time, however, the selfsame creed betrays the presence of communicative and relational needs which the atomized structure of mass society tends to deny. It also stresses the social origin of the demands made on welfare services, and the political nature of individual needs. Lastly, it resists the processes of reduction, of bureaucratic-administrative specialization, of the fragmentation that the system imposes in its mode of dealing with social needs.

We are living in a time when social and cultural objects are being redefined. Mind, body, health, sickness, needs, and desires are words which mask a void, precisely when they are at the centre of collective attention. Behind these words we can detect a plurality of meanings which correspond to the networks of oppositions and debates on the nature and sociality that constitute us. We no longer have unambiguously identifiable objects at our disposal; they have been finally replaced by a symbolic field, a system of social and cultural oppositions, within which needs for reappropriation of what people meaningfully produce through their action come into conflict with new impulses for integration. Movements interpret these tensions and make them manifest.

Contemporary social movements

Emergent movements in complex societies, arising around youth, urban, women's, ecological and pacifist, ethnic and cultural issues, have up to this point been interpreted in basically two ways. Firstly, such movements have been explained in terms of an economic crisis or of crisis *tout court*. This has been the approach used in interpreting, for example, certain youth phenomena; the relationship between unemployment, urban ghettoes, and protest; the position of women on the labour market; immigration and ethnic revival, and so forth. The second model of interpretation attributes protest to the deficiencies in political legitimation suffered by groups which find themselves excluded from institutions, and which therefore mobilize to gain access to the system in order to participate in it. This framework has been used to analyse campaigns waged against the obsoleteness and authoritarianism of various institutions in preparation for broader participation through redefinition of the rules of the game, the mechanisms of access to decision-making, and the forms of authority. Student movements of the late 1960s have been explained as mobilizations against the authoritarianism of the academic system; women's action has been interpreted as a struggle for equalization of rights; minorities seeking inclusion or political recognition have been seen as the major source of contemporary ethnic revival.

There do undoubtedly exist kinds of collective action which can be read as effects of marginalization, as reactions to crises, or as demands for legitimation advanced by social groups excluded from participation. These include phenomena of exclusion from the labour market, of the disintegration of social memberships, which require analysis of the classical functionalist, Durkheimian kind. When the rules governing social exchange break down or cease to function properly, processes of anomie and exclusion multiply and the foundations of identity formation are undermined. This type of explanation, however, tends to deny any antagonist quality to the demands that arise in complex societies, in the sense outlined in chapter 1. Marginality is defined solely in terms of exclusion or extraneousness to the system; it is only a reaction or an adaptation to imbalances and does not generate any collective oppositional behaviour.

This interpretation lends itself to two different ideological uses: on the one hand, by those who resort to it so as to provide for a justification of the prevailing social order; and on the other, by those who struggle to overthrow that same order. The former tend to reduce every kind of conflict to anomic reaction, to dismiss every form of opposition as a social pathology. The latter look at marginality to exalt every form of breakdown in the social order – including even those strictly anomic – as fostering genuine opposition and conflict. Yet the two forms of action are entirely different. A simple breakdown in norms, moreover, a crisis in the day-to-day fabric of social life, has always provoked loss of identity and reactive behaviour that are to be found at the basis of fascist movements.

Thus, on the one hand, an interpretation in terms of marginality reassures the ideology of the ruling order which seeks to reduce all antagonistic behaviour to deviance, and which would rather have conflict coincide with pathology only so as to be able to legitimate the repressive measures or 're-education' directed at the conflictual elements. On the other hand, when applied to support protest and opposition, this type of interpretation finishes up in analytical insignificance by conferring conflictual dignity to all forms of anomie.

Another explanation hinges upon the assumed closure of political institutions, and it is of particular importance for the understanding of the European New Left action and ideology in the 1970s. After '68, collective action in France, Germany, and Italy was confronted, to a different degree in each country, with the closedness of political institutions; this, then, is the factor that should be taken to account for the radicalization of social movements, for the prevalence of sectarian Marxist organization in the New Left, and even for the tragic turn towards terrorism. But the preaching of the revolutionary gospel, sometimes supported by the intellectuals of the Left, was often grounded in a reductionist analysis of the kind that was just discussed: it tended to dignify social disorder for its own sake and to confer a 'revolutionary' label to any kind of 'disruptive' behaviour.

This interpretation rather tended to mask some of the features of the phenomena it sought to clarify. It overlooked the presence of nonpolitical elements in emergent movements, elements which we shall examine in detail shortly. On the side of the defenders of the social order, the ideological effect amounted to the treatment of whatever was not directly political in nature as folklore, so that everything not reducible to the political was relegated to the obscure corners of social life as private escapism. On the side of those contesting that order, this interpretation, subsequently generalized in the New Left culture, underestimated the specificity of the emergent movements and channeled all collective demands within its scope into rigid forms of political organization of a Leninist type. Such an arbitrary 'politicization' of demands has been one reason for the failure of the New Left politics in the 1970s (for a detailed analysis of the Italian case as an example, see chapter 14).

Emergent collective phenomena in complex societies cannot be treated simply as reactions to crises, as mere effects of marginality or deviance, or purely as problems arising from exclusion from the political market. We must acknowledge that social movements in complex societies are also the symptoms of antagonist conflicts, even if this does not wholly exhaust their significance. In societies with high information density, production does not involve economic resources alone; it also concerns social relationships, symbols, identities, and individual needs. Control of social production does not coincide with its ownership by a recognizable social group. It instead shifts to the great apparatuses of technical and political decision-making. The development and management of complex systems is not secured by simply controlling the workforce and by transforming natural resources; more than that, it requires increasing intervention in the relational processes and symbolic systems on the social/cultural domain.

Never before in the history of the 'great transformations' have the changes under way been met with such a bewildering confusion as the one reigning among the analysts today. As already stated no agreement can be reached even on the working label for the society undergoing the transformations. In the global society – whether named tentatively as postindustrial, complex, postmaterialist, or otherwise – antagonist demands arise concerning the way development is conceived and identities and needs defined. Production no longer is identifiable with transforming natural and human resources into goods for exchange through the organization of the forms of production, division of labor, and its incorporation into the techno-human complex of the factory. Instead, it has come to mean controlling complex systems of information, symbols, and social relations (Gershuny and Miles 1983; Donzelot 1979, 1984). The operation and efficiency of economic mechanisms and technological apparatuses depend on the management and control of relational systems where cultural dimensions predominate over 'technical' variables. Nor does the market function simply to circulate material goods; it becomes increasingly a system in which symbols are exchanged (Tomlison 1990; Featherstone 1992; Shields 1992; Yiannis and Lang 1995).

In order to be able to produce and consume, social actors must recognize themselves in terms of an identity which they themselves can construct, or in terms of a definition imposed on them by the multiple social memberships and the systems of rules that govern their everyday life. A society of apparatuses imposes identity by defining the sense and direction of individual action through the tightly-woven networks that transmit its symbolic models. This signifies creation of molecular forms of identification, shaping of functional, viable identities that can easily adapt themselves to an ever-intensifying pace of change, while everyday life also becomes the space where individuals try to build meaning for their existence (Lalive d'Epinay 1983; De Certeau 1984; Shotter 1993a).

The distinction between production and reproduction becomes increasingly blurred. It still made sense during the phase of modern society we are now leaving behind and for a historicist model of knowledge. In a society that laboriously exerted itself so as to shake off the fetters of Nature, seeking to bend matter to the dictates of 'progress', the world of reproduction represented everything that resisted, but also encouraged, progress towards the glorious goals of history, towards the wealth of nations or towards Utopia. Reproduction both constrained and sustained the conquest of Nature, by offering to the Promethean project the support of natural forces (labour force being the principal of them, but also the necessary 'opaque' counterpart resisting to the 'dynamic' impulse of capital towards transformation).

Today, however, the terrain of reproduction is eroded by the broadening capacity to produce social life through knowledge, decision-making, organization, and economic investment; as a consequence, societies no longer reproduce themselves but maintain themselves in change.

Reproduction is subjected to social intervention, to the action that takes command over it: we are moving towards the paradoxical state of the production of reproduction. We may note, for example, the role of demographic policies in the eminently reproductive field of population renewal, or of policies of education or socialization addressing the elective areas for the transmission of the norms and values of a society. Social intervention in these areas turns them into fields of action rather than structures which conserve and transmit the 'hard' nucleus of society. Also sexuality and fertility become fields of intervention transforming human reproduction into an arena for scientific experiments, political decision-making and individual choice (Field 1988; Bonnicksen 1989; Strathern 1992). The height of the paradox is reached in today's tampering with the genetic code – the reproductive structure *par excellence* and the guarantor of the transmission of the biological basis of society. Here social intervention marks the passage to an absolutely new kind of a relationship between reproduction and production.

Conflicts thus shift towards the new goals of reappropriation and reversal of the meaning produced by distant and impersonal apparatuses. These large organizations operating across the borders of economic, political and cultural spheres adopt instrumental rationality as their 'rationale' and tend to impose on individuals an identification based on these instrumental criteria. Antagonist demands do not restrict themselves to challenging the productive process in the strict sense, but address time, space, personal relations, and individual selfhood. Demands arise that have to do with birth and death, health and sickness, and that focus on the relationship with Nature, sexual identity, communicative resources, and the biological and affective deep structure of individual behaviour. In these areas, intervention by the control apparatuses and manipulation increases, provoking, nevertheless, a manifest and widespread reaction against the heteronomous definition of identity; reappropriation demands are raised by which individuals claim back the right to become themselves.

The difficulty to clearly understand and define these processes is connected to the fact that we find ourselves today stranded at a pivotal moment: the embryo of the new is being born within the womb of the old. As it always happens in the history of collective processes, the new actors still speak the language of the old, for they have yet to create the new idiom. As the new movement emerges, it draws on the heritage of the ones that preceded it, rooting itself in memory and the symbols of the past. This paradoxical situation is the origin of all the ambiguity and the difficulties of an era of transition. But it should not be forgotten that the phenomena that form the matrix of the actors that emerge have little in common with the bases of the categorial and linguistic traditions that they utilize to define themselves.

Recent forms of collective action in contemporary societies share a number of prominent features which serve to highlight certain specific features of the emerging conflicts. One is struck, first of all, by *the heterogeneity and low negotiability* of the goals posted for the action. Diverse areas of social life have been the stage where the waves of mobilization and collective protest have taken place: we may think of student and youth movements, women's movements, gay and lesbian liberation, urban movements, ecological and peace campaigns, consumer and service user mobilizations, ethnic and linguistic minorities, neo-religious and communitarian movements, health action groups, and anti-segregation and anti-racist campaigns. For the reasons set out in chapter 1, not all of such forms of organized struggle share the same meaning, nor are they all the expression of antagonist conflicts. Yet they all signal the metamorphosis of collective action. In particular, they mobilize social groups around objectives of low negotiability, because, as social phenomena, they are not entirely reducible to political mediation. Only a portion of collective demands can be mediated and institutionalized through political representation and decision-making; a large share of them survive in nonnegotiable forms to reappear again during a new wave of mobilization, frequently carried on by different actors.

Here we are brought to a second feature, one that has been pointed out by numerous observers: recent forms of collective action largely *ignore the political system* and generally *display disinterest towards the idea of seizing power*. It appears that the traditional goals of taking political power and gaining control over the state apparatus have given way to a desire for immediate control over the conditions of existence and to claims to independence from the system. This feature – often cited as a 'political weakness' of contemporary movements – certainly raises questions about the relationships between movements and political systems, which shall be discussed in the remaining part of this book.

A third notable feature of the contemporary movements relates to the fact that they *challenge the modern separation between the public and the private*. Public and political relationships are subjected to demands centreing on the affective, biological, and sexual identity of individuals. The 'private' spheres, where affective exchange traditionally took place and where individual rewards or recompense were dispensed, have been invaded by the media and have become arenas for the mobilization and augmentation of conflict (see D'Emilio 1983, 1992; D'Emilio and Friedmann 1988; Adam 1987). The great stages of the 'private' life-cycle – birth, adolescence, adulthood, love, old age, death – become crucial nodes of sensibility for collective action; they enter the 'public' domain and become fields of human experience to be reappropriated (Levinson *et al.*1978; Thorson 1995; Prior 1989; Clark 1993; Field 1989).

A further feature concerns a certain *overlap between deviance and social movements*. Forms of control propagate themselves and permeate daily life and existential choices. They thus render the empirical distinction between protest and marginality more difficult to draw. The silent majority is no longer a phantasm evoked by authoritarian politics, but a reality that threatens the democratic character of complex societies. The system breeds forms of 'treatment' for handling all kinds of opposition through their reduction to deviance and social pathology. Dissent becomes sickness, struggle is relegated to the sphere of conduct to be 'cured' by behavioural therapy and repression. Opposition is thus swiftly turned into deviance, and all the more so as the requisite stigmata are readily at hand: oppositional action always involves a minority, it tends to reject any mediation regulated by the system, and has no access to information control that enables the apparatus to brand all conflictual behaviour by blurring the distinction between it and pathology. The mental health system becomes one of the most critical areas where the distinction between rehabilitation and control is made increasingly difficult (Busfield 1989; Luske 1990; Braden Johnson 1990; Fancher 1994).

Particularism seems to be the appropriate form of resistance to a power that generalizes itself. *Solidarity as an objective* for action is yet another feature shared by contemporary movements. The search for a communal identity, the revival of primary memberships (gender, age, locality, ethnicity) build resistance against changes instituted from above. Struggle always has instrumental goals, but more important than those is the strengthening of group solidarity, the search for symbolic and affective exchange. The group centres on its identity and resists the 'rationality' of decisions and goals imposed by a distant and impersonal power.

The *quest for participation and direct action*, the rejection of representation, is a final characteristic shared by contemporary movements. Mediation tends to reproduce the control mechanisms they fight against. Rejection of every kind of proxy gives rise to non-negotiable, unflinching opposition to decisions and goals imposed by the apparatuses. Appeal to spontaneity, anti-authoritarianism, and anti-hierarchism seem to be common to many recent forms of collective action. Hence the fragmentation, the weak organization, and the incoherence which persistently plague such forms of action, and which have been promptly pointed out by their critics. Together with the suspicion of political mediation, these tendencies constitute the central problem of emergent movements, which I will examine more closely below. Identification of the problem, however, should not induce us to ignore the specificity of the phenomenon; even less should it serve as a pretext for a denial of the conflictual potential that the movements express.

The above characteristics assume various forms in the empirically observable contemporary movements. To complete the descriptive framework set out thus far, which has concentrated on the form of collective action, I shall now turn briefly to its contents. Over and above the issues relating to the specific areas of social life in which such action develops, there seem to be a number of recurrent themes in contemporary movements which play a key role in their action.

Many movements are characterized by their *regressive Utopianism*, which is directly or indirectly religious in character. This is a feature that has been invariably present at the birth of social movements. Many historical examples show that, as the group forms, it defines its identity in terms of the past, drawing on a totalizing myth of rebirth which is often at least quasi-religious in content. Yet the present phenomenon also has a specific character which, I believe, has to do with the nature of modern movements. Demands tied to identity and daily life are progressively less 'political'. The secularization of social life means that the legitimation of the order is no longer sacral in character (Beckford 1989), but is based more and more on evaluation in accordance with the criteria of instrumental rationality. In this situation, a Utopian appeal with religious connotations becomes one of the principal contents of collective action.

This is a 'religion' divested of the ritual and organizational apparatus of the churches. It is therefore more a quest for 'transcendence' from the social order than a liturgical practice. As such, it can simply feed a new spiritual search and a moral commitment to a better and more human social life (Wilson 1990a). The 'religious' content may become a cultural form of resistance against the instrumental rationality of dominant apparatuses. But very often spiritual search can turn into a totalizing myth on which to base identity (Bromley and Hammond 1987; Robbins 1988; Smith 1991b). Totalizing monism is the central distinguishing feature of regressive Utopianism: the reduction of reality to the unity of one all-embracing principle; the negation of the existence of different levels and different tools of analysis; the identification of the whole of society with the sacral solidarity of the group. The reappropriation of identity is translated into the language and symbols of an escapist myth of rebirth. On account of the defensive nature of the process, movements in which the 'religious' element predominates show greater susceptibility to manipulation by the power structure: they face marginalization as sects and/or transformation into a fashion, to be offered for sale in the marketplace as a soother of mind. Contestation dissolves into individual flight and a mythical quest for the Lost Paradise, or it crystallizes into fanatic fundamentalism..

Another feature is the *primacy given to Nature*. As was stated, the notion of Nature is reintroduced into complex societies as a cultural definition of needs, as that which escapes the control of the power apparatuses. It is conceived as a sort of 'non-social' raw material which stands opposed to the omnipresent 'social'. Yet this is always a cultural definition of needs; it is the form given by postindustrial culture to demands created by the changed structure of social production. The appeal to Nature is one of the modes of representation by which the individual resists control and rationalization. The return to Nature is therefore the awareness of the fact that our 'Nature' belongs to us and that it is not external to social action; hence it can be ordered in ways that run counter to the stipulations and desiderata of the apparatuses. This gives rise to a profound ambivalence which is constantly present in contemporary movements, and to which I shall return below.

A final aspect concerns *the role of the individual*. Collective demands increasingly refer to the individual, to her/his internal experience, needs, and 'unconscious' existence. The problems of the individual have become collective problems precisely because they involve, on the one hand, the manipulation of individual identity by the power structure, and the cultural representation of needs as an individual concern on the other. Analysis of the increasing 'socialization' of the individual dimension and, conversely, of the 'individualization' of social problems is made more difficult by the dominant apparatuses' simultaneous attempt to counter and offset this very tendency. There is a push towards de-differentiation, to the reduction of all problems to the level of the individual taken as an atomized entity. Forms of power are transformed, and one witnesses an attempt at psychologization and generalized medicalization of society, with the purpose of absorbing every potential collective conflict that arises around the problems of identity by reducing them to the individualistic dimension. The construction of personal identity becomes a potentially conflictual process in which definitions imposed by external powers clash with the self-realization needs of individuals. But if the sphere of identity is confined within pure psychological or medical categories and submitted to the treatment of specialized apparatuses, its conflictual potential is reduced to a psychological or medical problem. It is often the case with intimate relations and sexuality (Foucault 1980; Giddens 1992) as particularly evident in the case of the social treatment of AIDS (Watney 1987; Gamson 1989; Aggleton *et al.*

1990). Or, on the other hand, when individual needs for self-realization and for an autonomous construction of identity are successfully manipulated to accommodate mass production and the media market (commodities and messages), they are effortlessly domesticated in forms of narcissistic behaviour and individualistic search for self-affirmation and instant gratification.

Movements, for their part, by their very existence testify to a profound change in the status of the individual and her/his problems. Through their action, movements affirm the necessity for addressing the individual dimension of social life as the level where new forms of social control are exerted and where social action originates. They claim for real the bogus priority the day-to-day experience, affective relations, and the deep motivations of individual behaviour have received in a society that intervenes in the very roots of individual life. These areas of human experience thus become the terrain in which are bred crucial social conflicts, in which new powers and new forms of resistance and opposition confront each other.

Analysis conducted from this perspective has to cross many of the frontiers that still divide the traditional disciplines (biology, psychology, anthropology, sociology) if it is to come up with a new, more adequate definition of its subject matter and fashion tools appropriate for the understanding of the change taking place. 'Socialization of the individual' and 'individualization of the social' are not just provocative *jeux-de-mots*, but indications of the limit reached by our linear way of thinking. When social power penetrates the roots of individual life and when the individual is socially bestowed with the resources to become an autonomous subject of action, the borderline between the individual and the social becomes blurred and the dualistic language and disciplinary cleavages we have inherited from modernity reach their limits. To be able to indicate the problem is the first step beyond the linear paradigm of modernity. Social movements, by their very action, have started opening the way out.

Antagonist action?

In complex societies, power has become impersonal; it is dispatched though the great apparatuses of planning and decision making, through the administrative management of all aspects of social life. Antagonist movements emerge and break down, dispersing amidst the action of social groups more readily than ever susceptible to manipulation from above. It is the field of opposition that remains constant, not the actors. Analysis must begin with what is at stake in conflicts; only then will it be able to identify the actors involved. Some levels of conflict in complex societies continue to focus on the production, the appropriation, and the allocation of social resources. The actors engaged in the conflicts are mutable, and it is the task of empirical analysis to single them out and specify their identity. A change of approach in the study of conflicts is therefore necessary. The analyst must begin with the systemic field, with its logic, with the processes that enable it to reproduce and change. It is at this level of generality that the crucial issues and the vital resources that provoke conflict may be identified. Specifying the actors becomes a problem for empirical analysis, which must explain why in a certain period certain social groups mobilize themselves for antagonist conflicts. Theory can no longer *a priori* ascertain the presence of a 'historical subject'.

The variable and provisional nature of the actors drawn into antagonist conflicts is particularly evident in protest movements, although to a certain extent it is also a feature of the life and times of the dominant groups. The latter, to be sure, exhibit greater stability, greater integration, and greater coincidence between the actors and the system's mechanisms. But even the analysis of the power structure must take account of its mutability. This of course holds more at the systemic level and may not always be the case in actual national societies, where both the crystallization of elites and the historical continuity of movements may be stronger.

The analytical perspective emerging from the discussion thus far yields three observations:

(a) Conflictual social actors do not exhaust themselves in the conflicts in which they are engaged. Whether measured in terms of its duration or in terms of the multiple roles performed by a specific social group (for example youth, women, ethnic groups) in different subsystems, involvement in an antagonist conflict does not cover the entire range of action available to, or performed by, the given actor. Therefore, no actor can be defined solely or even principally by its engagement in an antagonist conflict (hence the futility of any attempt to compare the features of the actors in contemporary movements with those of the working class in industrial conflict).

(b) Contemporary conflicts are, in their concrete features, temporary and short-term. They are provoked by specific issues and mobilize variable actors. Yet they are destined to reproduce themselves with a certain facility and, once institutionalized, tend to shift, or spread, to other related areas.

(c) The actors in antagonist conflicts become such when they activate the mobilization. One might say that certain elements in a social group's condition collide with the system's logic, making manifest the forms of domination and power that are brought to bear on that group, thereby revealing to the group itself the availability of resources and opportunities for taking action. Actors test and utilize the available potential for action, while at the same time they are subjected to forms of power which prevent them from actually enjoying the available options.

Only empirical analysis can give an exhaustive specification of the intersection of a particular social condition pertaining to a group with the dominant logic of the system (and tell us, for example, why young people and women become at a certain point actors in antagonist conflicts, why certain groups get involved in environmental or peace mobilizations in a given context at a given time, why an ethnic minority becomes a conflictual actor). Social actors are not conflictual 'by essence'; they become antagonist actors in a specific conjuncture at which domination is made visible, the clash between the system's logic and the expectations and resources available to the group revealed, and specific opportunities for action provided.

To a far greater degree than any other society in the past, the one in which we live has the capacity of subjecting its environment to purposeful action, extending thereby its area of operation to its own natural bases in biological substructures with the means of science and technology: it 'socializes' its own action at the same rate as it brings 'natural' constraints under social control. The self-appropriation of social action is made possible by a higher reflexive (symbolic) potential of the action itself. Identity thus may be defined as the reflexive capacity to produce an awareness of action (that is, a symbolic representation of it) above its specific content. Identity becomes formal reflexivity, pure symbolic capacity, acknowledgement of the production of meaning in action, within the limits set at any given moment by the environment and the biological structure. In societies which closely depend on Nature, social action is made visible by its products. When, as has happened in contemporary societies, capacity for action on the social and natural environment outstrips any such capacity in the past, action is no longer appropriated in the form of its results. Recognition of capacity for action becomes relatively independent of its products; it becomes the ability of the actors to recognize themselves as such, the ability to recognize their capacity to produce action.

From this point of view, one might say that complex societies concern themselves with the production of what Habermas has called 'inner nature' (Habermas 1976). In action terms, this signifies the ability to control the capacity for action and the production of meaning. Identity is no longer a 'given', a fact of Nature; nor is it simply the content of a tradition with which individuals identify. It is no longer founded solely on the sense of belonging to 'normatively regulated associations' (states, parties, organizations). With their action, individuals and groups participate in the shaping of identity, which is the result of decisions and plans, as well as of conditionings and constraints. There is an increase in life chances – as the possibilities for personal development and self-realization made socially available. These opportunities are increasingly cultural in nature, and they form what has been called a 'cultural surplus', an openness to the possible but also to the indeterminate.

The unprecedented expansion of learning, socialization, and communication processes demonstrates the scope of this transformation. Human societies are not only able to learn; they are increasingly more characterized by their reflexive capacity: they learn to learn. One may, therefore, say that whereas the definition of identity in previous social structures was given – mainly through membership in groups or classes, and in any case through an identification with socially stable and circumscribed collectivities – in the highly complex mass societies the social identity that enables participation in collective processes like education, consumption, and politics itself, tends more and more to coincide with the constructed condition of being a social actor *tout court*.

The control of 'inner nature' is a scarce resource, and new conflicts arise over its appropriation. On the one hand, individuals are asked to participate in the shaping of their own identity, in the constitution of their capacity for action; on the other hand, their identity is denied and their capacity for action is circumscribed through the ramified intervention of the apparatuses of control and regulation which define the conditions, forms, and goals of individual and collective action. The reappropriation of the meaning of action, of the very capacity for action, generates new conflicts. It is as if, beyond the more specific objects of contestation, what is at stake in the emergent conflicts is the possibility for reappropriating the meaning and motivation of action.

Individuals are able to participate in the process of shaping their own identities as a 'social' process of production and learning. The system avails chances to intervene in the production of the capacity for action, in the case of both the individual and the society as a whole. But, at the same time, this opportunity is withheld by the vast and dense processes of identity manipulation, which the apparatuses set in motion in order to ensure the management and control of complex systems under their jurisdiction.

On the one hand, thus, there is a greater potential for end-directed action, in other words, for the reflexive ability to produce meaning and motivation for human action. It is no longer external nature which is transformed by social action, but the action itself in its motivational roots as the outcome of social relationships. This increasing 'socialization' simultaneously results in a heightened potential for 'individuation', for an individual appropriation of the meaning of action on a scale previously unseen in history. On the other hand, there is the imperative for extending and intensifying control over the processes of the formation and transformation of identity, an erosion of the margins of individual independence from the system, a 'social' regulation of behaviour down to the level where its meaning is shaped.

The rationality of the apparatuses is instrumental rationality – its operation is oriented according to the systemic needs calling for the maintenance of balance and control of tensions, and it is evaluated according to the efficacy and efficiency in reaching these goals. Simply in order to operate, these apparatuses produce and nurture needs and individual motives which nevertheless have to be kept within the limits of systemic normality. The conflicts that arise are therefore formed in opposition to the functional requirements of the apparatuses. The latter, in order to fulfil their purpose, must manipulate 'from within' the meaning and motivation of action in order to maintain balance against the conflictual demands of social actors, who strive to reappropriate the meaning of their own action and to control the processes of the formation and transformation of their identity.

Above, I referred to the control over inner nature as a scarce resource. In fact, social investments must concentrate on the production of identity, and the instrumental, decisional, and normative resources required to achieve this end must be accumulated. Moreover, the potential for social transformation must be oriented towards ends that are no longer given by tradition but must be decided by society itself. Therein, a field of cultural behaviour and social relations is mapped which embraces the ends and means of human action in complex societies. It is within this field – or, better, in order to define this field – that the actors in new conflicts join the battle. Educational and training processes, interference in the bio-psychic structure, the regulation of interpersonal behaviour, the creation and transmission of information – these are some of the areas where the 'normalizing' rationality of the apparatuses clashes with the collective demands for the right to autonomous definition of identity. Normality and pathology, health and sickness, have become issues that now transcend the traditional confines of medical or psychiatric knowledge to affect the meaning of action itself.

This situation creates a two-fold demand for the analysis. First of all, it shifts the conflict to a terrain which is apparently far removed from the level of collective action. We are, in fact, witnessing processes which encourage individualization of the capacity for social action. The ability to produce sense and recognition migrates from the prerogatives of a group to the individual actor. This gives rise to the apparent paradox of the increasing individualization of collective conflicts. Secondly, the cultural representation of the social processes concerned with the production and appropriation of identity takes the form of an appeal to Nature. These features not only make interpretation of emergent conflicts difficult; they also entail the redefinition of collective action with respect to the past and the actors, now profoundly different from the images of the unified historical subjects as the standard-bearers of Revolution, presented by the modern mythology of social movements.

On the one hand, then, the terrain where collective identity is fashioned shrinks progressively into the individual endowed with a capacity for action. Such identity is no longer dictated or imposed by belongingness through membership but comes into being constructed by the individual in her/his capacity as a social actor. One should note, however, that this is always a *social* capacity. Thus the paradox that social conflict – which always relates to human sociability and to social relationships – forms at the level of the single individual, and evinces a demand for the reappropriation of individual capacity for action. On the other hand, resistance against the finely woven socialization of the processes of regulation and control takes the form of recourse to Nature. Reappropriation of identity is culturally represented as a rediscovery of the nonsocial (biological structure, the body, sexuality, primary affiliation).

The difficulties for analysis generated by this dual meaning of contemporary collective demands are therefore quite evident. There is the permanent, almost physiological, risk of an atomization, of the fragmentation of collective conflicts and their capacities for mobilization and struggle. Movements dissolve into thousand particles as they strive for the immediate reappropriation of a primary identity, apparently dissolving the object of study along with them. On the other hand, the collective definition of the conflicts and of the stakes involved in them retreats to the pre-social terrain of the defence of 'Nature', to the exaltation of a quasi-biological particularism, the conservation of the existent.

Herein lies all the ambiguity of contemporary movements. As they reject a 'society' that to an unprecedented degree has become subject to the pressures of normalization, to the straitjacketing of behaviour, to tightly woven control, they open up the way for a flight into the myth of identity, for an escapist withdrawal into the illusion of an individual and a Nature magically freed from the constraints of social behaviour. By claiming the right to life, to desire, to being before having, movements in fact reaffirm the meaning of social action as the capacity for a consciously produced human existence and relationships. But, at a single strike, they also fall victim to the illusion of being able to evade the constraints of social action. They dream of a magical rebirth, of a spontaneous unity freed from the difficult interplay of differences, from the imbalances created by the division of labour and by power relationships, from the limitations imposed by instrumental calculation. In reality, such 'naturalistic' attitude, however, cannot release the movements from their dependence on scarce resources, free them from the obligation to subscribe to a form of rationality geared to the assessment of the relationship between ends and means, or protect them against the imbalances and divisions created by the forms of power required to govern complexity.

The ambivalence lies in the fact that the 'individualistic' and 'naturalistic' ways of defining collective identity simultaneously embrace the entire potential of emergent conflicts for antagonism and innovation. They indicate new areas where conflict may arise, and they introduce unpredictable forms of aggregation and expression of collective action. From this point of view, the chief problems of the emergent movements are how to escape from an 'individualistic' reductionism and from a 'natural' definition of identity, how to acknowledge the social character of conflict, and how to tie the specificity of individual demands for reappropriated identity to collective action without canceling out either. If collective action is unable to achieve this social and political capacity, it will lapse into the presocial and withdraw into the sect, the small group, the celebration of primary identity.

There are two consequences for theory to be drawn from the analysis I have presented. Firstly, change in complex societies is evolving out of a linear, cumulative, global (if it ever was such in the first place) process into a discontinuous, fragmented, and differentiated one. A system never undergoes change at all its levels at the same time and in the same way. Specific mechanisms govern the regional transformations of a system. The political system performs a central role in the refashioning of a complex society. It reduces uncertainty by producing decisions and representing interests. It is the only level of a system that can exploit the potential for transformation that conflicts express.

Secondly, collective demands do not assume a political form. Hence, they may easily splinter or veer off into violent outbursts, marginal sects or market fashions. Only political representation can prevent collective demands from being dissipated into mere folklore, individual escapism, or aimless violence. At the same time, however, these demands are irreducible to representation through the functions of the political system, because they traverse different areas of social production to reemerge in other sectors of society, outside the official channels of representation submitted to rationalization and control by the planned intervention of apparatuses.

The relationship between movements and the systems of representation and decision-making is a critical node in complex societies. The creation of 'political' forms, or forms of representation that can convey the collective demands expressed by movements and transform them into decisions without undermining their autonomous character; the formation of movements capable of assuming forms of action and organization which are amenable to political mediation without yet becoming identifiable with it – these constitute the challenges which, if met, will begin to transfigure conflicts into an engine of change. There are, however, no assurances that such a resolution will be possible. More than ever before, societies rely on their dramatically increased ability to decide and to act for their functioning. Authoritarian rationalization or ungovernable crisis remain thus not just figments of the imagination. The hard fact makes the responsibility of choice even more burdensome, especially for those living in relatively open systems and able to design the future of the ones who still today are deprived of a voice.

Networks in the everyday

Apart from the novelty of their actors and contents, contemporary conflicts are characterized by their particular relationship with political systems and with the traditional forms of representation. Contemporary movements, whether youth, feminist, environmentalist, ethno-nationalist, or pacifist, have not only generated conflictual actors, forms of action, and issues extraneous to the tradition of struggle prevalent in the societies of industrial capitalism; they have also brought to light the ineffectiveness of the traditional institutions of political representation as a vehicle for these new demands. Collective mobilization assumes forms – organizational forms in particular – which do not fit into the traditional categories, and which make evident a distinct *analytical* discontinuity between contemporary movements and those of the past, especially as regards the workers' movement. Various observers have pointed out, from their first embryonic appearance in the late 1960s and 1970s (Gerlach and Hine 1970, 1973; Freeman 1983), the segmented, reticular, multi-faceted structure of the so-called 'new social movements'. This structure has been confirmed by later developments even if the actors and issues have changed over time. A movement consists of diversified and autonomous units which devote a large part of their available resources to the construction and maintenance of internal solidarity. A communication and exchange network keeps the separate, quasiautonomous cells in contact with each other. Information, individuals, and patterns of behaviour circulate through this network, passing from one unit to another, and bringing a degree of homogeneity to the whole. Leadership is not concentrated but diffuse, and it restricts itself to specific goals. Different individuals may, on occasion, become leaders with specific functions to perform. This structure – which is to be found in the youth, feminist, environmentalist, pacifist, ethnic and cultural groups of various countries – makes it extremely difficult to actually specify the collective actor. Contemporary movements resemble an amorphous nebula of indistinct shape and with variable density. Also, because of its scant division of labour and the inevitable duplication of functions among its various components, the kind of organizational model found in the movements seems hardly capable of ensuring efficient and effective collective action. Yet research shows that strong incentives for solidarity and direct participation as the condition for action do create considerable cohesion among the components; cohesion which even persists through troughs in the cycle of collective mobilization. It has also been noted that the apparent 'dysfunctionality' resulting from the duplication of functions and roles is often a resource with which to counteract possible defections, to cope with organizational crises or with repression aimed at particular sectors of the movement, and to penetrate deeply into certain areas of the social in order to marshal support and consensus necessary for the movement's directional action.

In the 1960s and early 1970s, these new demands were still embedded within the culture of Leftist movements and within the legacy of Marxist forms of organization. Particularly in Europe, where this tradition was stronger, the forced hyperpoliticization of non-political issues accompanying it distorted collective action, dissolving it into atomized escapism and aimless violence. The crisis of the movements splintered them into thousands of 'private' fragments, or terminated in the all-consuming self-escalation of the desperate activism of the terrorists or, at times, in extreme forms of individual self-destruction. This situation was interpreted by analysts almost universally in terms of a deep crisis of collective action. The elements of crisis were evident and we should not underevaluate them. The crisis made clear the dilemma faced by collective mobilizations which carried contents and meaning qualitatively discontinuous with the tradition of modern Leftist movements, and which still organized and framed the new issues within the framework of the structures and languages inherited from that tradition. Nevertheless, such a crisis could not prevent important transformations from taking place, particularly during the 1980s. Above all, from the pressures of movement action were born the processes that led to an unprecedented modernization of institutions (economic, political, cultural), as they were forced to gear themselves better to the tasks and issues pertaining to the predicament of a complex society; this took place through the incorporating of many of the themes and practices coming from movements action. In the late 1970s and 1980s, Western societies experienced a period of 'postmodernization', frequently under the auspices of conservative politics reacting to the previous wave of mobilizations: the differentiation and articulation of the interests within the major economic, political and cultural institutions; the globalization of the world economy; the establishment of a world media system; the transformation of the welfare state, particularly in the sphere of health; the enormous innovation of organizational and corporate culture; and, finally, the cultural change of everyday life, interpersonal relations (particularly gender relations), lifestyles and practices ('yuppification' of society and the 'culture of narcissism' being the extreme symptoms of these changes). Movements, for their part, underwent a transformation in their forms of collective action, reflecting the crisis of the hyperpolitical model, addressed new issues like environment, peace and cultural differences, and developed similar features in various countries (Stein 1985; Epstein 1990a; Larana *et al.* 1994). Movements were also responsible for a substantial modernization of public attitudes and thinking and collective action resulted in the emergence of a new generation of skilled personnel in the key communications media, advertising, and marketing sectors of the information society.

Movements in complex societies are hidden networks of groups, meeting points, and circuits of solidarity which differ profoundly from the image of the politically organized actor. There has been a thorough-going transformation in the organizational model, which now constitutes in itself a way of defining and addressing conflicts in highly complex societies: the very 'form' of action before its specific content is the expression of a conflictual, and sometimes antagonistic, orientation. Above all, as I have said, one notes the segmented, reticular, and multi-faceted structure of 'movements'. This is a hidden or, more correctly, latent structure; individual cells operate on their own entirely independently of the rest of the movement, although they maintain links to it through the circulation of information and persons. These links become explicit only during the transient periods of collective mobilization over issues which bring the latent network to the surface and then allow it to submerge again in the fabric of the daily life. The solidarity is cultural in character and is located in the terrain of symbolic production in the everyday life. To an increasing degree, problems of individual identity and collective action become meshed together: the solidarity of the group is inseparable from the personal quest and from the everyday affective and communicative needs of the participants in the network.

Bearing this in mind, we must distinguish between relatively permanent forms of network and specific moments of mobilization and struggle which are increasingly cyclical (Tarrow 1989b, 1993b; Brand 1990; Koopmans 1993). The former interweave closely with daily life, with the needs and identity of the movement's members; the latter transform a potential that has prepared and nourished itself in latency into visible collective action. The molecular change brought about by the hidden structure should not be seen as a 'private' and residual fact, but as a condition for possible mobilization. The mobilization, for its part, strengthens primary solidarity and protects the various cells from the effects of centrifugal forces threatening the movement's integrity. The aspects of the external forms of mobilization reflect the inner solidarity of the cells. These forms can be summarized as follows: Participation in mobilization is concentred, that is, it forms around a specific goal; it focuses on the present, and does not pursue distant, unattainable goals; it is possible only if there exists a certain coincidence between collective goals and the affective, communicative, and solidarity needs of its members; and, finally, it must guarantee its members an access to immediate and verifiable control of the goods pursued through collective action.

This structure of mobilization accounts for both the strength and weakness of the collective actors. Their strength derives from the mobilization of primary solidarities, which no complex organization could hold together on a stable basis; from their provision of flexibility, adaptibility, and immediacy, which more structured organizations cannot incorporate; from their provision of channels for the direct expression of conflictual demands and participative needs which otherwise would be hard to aggregate. Their weakness lies in their permanent risk of fragmentation; in their inability to pursue general goals over the long term; in their susceptibility to expressive escapism; in their uneasy handling of problems political in the strict sense, such as the complexity of decision-making and mediation, the problems of efficiency and effectiveness, and in general the constraints of a system in which a number of interests compete.

What, then, is the role left for the changing collective action in today's complex society? If what I have described is the physiological structure of movements, what are its implications for systems of representation and political organizations? First of all, it should be emphasized that the form of political organization as we know it (party, trade unions, interest associations) is unable to give adequate expression to collective demands, because it is structured to represent interests that are assumed to remain relatively stable, with a distinct geographical, occupational, or social base. Political organization is designed for pursuit of long-term goals through a progressive accumulation of results and resources. Moreover, it must ensure the continuity of the interests it represents, by mediating between short- and long-term goals. Today, when political organizations are faced with the task of representing a plurality of interests, they find that their traditional structures must be adjusted to accommodate more unstable and partial interests as well – hence the transformation of political organization into complex organizations, the growing emphasis on their organizational dynamics, and the parallel difficulty of unifying them by ideological appeals.

Secondly, precisely because of the fragmented and scattered nature of their action, movements in complex societies cannot operate without forms of political representation. Only the presence of channels of representation and institutional actors through which conflictual pressures can be translated into 'politics' can ensure that the antagonist issues will not become dissipated. The political effectiveness of movements depends on the openness, receptiveness, and efficiency of the available forms of representation. Yet precisely because of the character of the demands they convey, movements do not exhaust themselves in representation, and conflictual pressures persist and reproduce themselves outside the bounds of institutional mediation. We thus come up against a two-fold paradox. On the one hand, collective action is no longer separable from individual demands and needs, and it is therefore constantly threatened by trends towards atomization and privatization; and on the other, the conflictual pressure brought to bear on the logic of the system does not operate through politics. Nevertheless, and precisely for this reason, it cannot do without politics.

The evident paradox is difficult to handle analytically. It marks, however, the onset of the processes of the invention of the present which movements strive after and in which they involve the whole of society. In the rest of this part of the book, I will examine the general frame presented above with reference to specific fields of collective mobilization.

6

Invention of the present

Being young: choice or destiny?

Why is there a 'youth question'? Why has there developed a particular interest in studying young people? The answer, in terms of the sociology of knowledge, is relatively simple: young people are recurrently involved in forms of conflictual *action*, and for this reason an investigation of their *condition* is a frequent concern of sociologists, psychologists, anthropologists. In what follows, I want to challenge the line of analysis investigating a condition in order to explain an action. The way the issue of youth in contemporary societies is engaged exemplifies the procedure that is frequently used in addressing the theoretical problem of social movements in general. Once the presence of collective action has been ascertained, analysts move on to an examination of the social condition of a specific social category (in this case, young people) in order to deduce from this the causes of its action. Collective action is never studied on its own; it is discounted as a meaningful object of investigation, and related to the 'structural' or 'cultural' determinants of the social condition of the actor involved. The case of young people, like that of women, provides a good illustration of the procedure. Analysis of the condition of youth or women may be an important element in the description of contemporary social structure, but by itself it tells us nothing about their action.

Never before has it been as necessary as it is today to draw a methodological distinction between the analysis of a social condition and the analysis of collective action. The question implicitly present in the numerous studies of the condition of young people is, in fact, whether young people are potential actors in antagonist collective conflict. It is claimed, or hoped, that deeper understanding of the condition and culture of youth in metropolitan society will resolve the issue. This hope, however, is bound to become frustrated, as it will inevitably run against an insoluble problem we have already addressed: how does one move from condition to action? How does a particular movement of young actors take shape and develop out of a general condition?

The only way out of this *theoretical* impasse is to reverse the terms of the problematic. Since action is not deducible from social conditions, the sequence of the analytical procedure must be reversed. We must identify, at the systemic level, the issues that lie at the core of social conflicts, the arenas in which the struggle for control over crucial resources takes place. Only after this we can ask ourselves which are the elements in the youth condition that, under certain conjunctural circumstances, are liable to activate collective action; that is, what are the elements that are likely to turn this particular group into a conflictual actor. This raises a number of problems of empirical nature: which elements of a social condition facilitate or prevent conflictual action? Which categories within a given social group are most susceptible to conflictual mobilization?

Problems such as these can be resolved only by careful empirical study using all available information on the condition of the young. Such information is crucially important for a sociology of youth movements. Nevertheless, as stated, it must reverse its procedure so that the analyst moves from the field of conflicts to the actors, not the other way around. In this manner, analysis of the condition of young people should reveal how pressures for individuation and the processes by which identity is expropriated are rooted in the condition of the young people, and how, consequently, their mobilization takes place. In epistemological terms, this reversal of the analytical perspective is a research programme, and as such it lays down conditions and establishes categories that only empirical study can fill with content. Within the limits of the present context, however, it is only possible to single out those elements in the condition and culture of young people that are most likely to trigger conflict.

In complex societies, an autonomous life-space for the younger age categories is created through mass education. It is the mass schooling that delays entry into the adult roles by prolonging the period of non-work. It also creates the spatio-temporal conditions for the formation of a collective identity defined by needs, lifestyles, and private languages. The market intermeshes with these needs, both fostering them and offering symbols and a space for consumption practices (Yiannis and Lang 1995) separated off from those of adult people (clothes, music, leisure). The youthful condition, the phase *par excellence* of transition and suspension, is protracted and stabilized so that it becomes a mass condition which is no longer determined by biological age. The imbalances between school and the labour market swiftly add a note of stifling precariousness to the extended period of transition: delayed entry into the adult roles is not just freedom, but reflects also imposed and lived marginality, characterized by unemployment and lack of any real economic independence. In complex societies, the condition of the young – homogeneous in many respects, but also differentiated by social and geographical belonging – is marked by this stable precariousness, by this lack of limits, to such an extent that it turns into a void, a hiatus that is known to be bogus and controlled from outside.

Because of these features – as amply described by the sociological literature on youth culture (Hall and Jefferson 1979; Hebdige 1979; Chambers 1985, 1986; Willis 1990; Ziehe 1991; Mitterauer 1992; Fornas and Bolin 1995) – youth becomes a mirror held up for the whole of society, a paradigm for the crucial problems of the complex systems. It reflects the tension between the enhancement of life chances and diffuse control, between possibilities for individuation and external definitions of identity. Incompleteness, as openness to the possible, as the changeability and reversibility of choices, is transformed into destiny and becomes a social limbo for those who refuse to comply with the codes of normalcy. Young people therefore become actors in conflicts, since they speak the language of the possible; they root themselves in the incompleteness that defines them, and they call on the society at large to create its own existence rather than merely endure it. They demand the right to decide for themselves, and in doing so they demand it for everyone.

Youth culture gives manifest expression to several of the themes that define the field of contemporary conflicts. In this connection, we must above all consider silence, the repudiation of the word. In the world of words, images, and sounds, it seems that young people find coherent discourse impossible to assemble. They resort to fragmentary, disjointed stuttering, to the inarticulateness of spastic utterance, to an erratic combination of sounds and noises striking in rock or rap music (Chambers 1985; Frith and Goodwin 1990; Shusterman 1992): the faltering language of youth borders on aphasia. Yet in this word that is not the word and that can become a pure sign like in graffiti (Castleman 1982), in this incoherence and inconclusiveness that arouses the indignation or the sarcasm of the paragons of good sense, there is something more than the mere absence: There is the affirmation of a word that no longer wishes to be understood independently of the emotions; there is speech that seeks to root itself in being rather than in doing, so as to prepare for a return to the essentiality of emotional experience, to the discontinuity and uniqueness, to the ineffability of inner life.

Its antithesis is the formalized language of systems governed by instrumental rationality, of systems which preserve a rigid distinction between discourse and image on one side, and actual pleasure of the experience on the other. The cold rationality of the apparatuses makes no concessions to emotions; it banishes them to the isolated enclaves where alone regulated discharge of eros and outbreaks of frenzy are condoned under the system's supervision. The time and place of emotional, affective, and bodily experience is carefully circumscribed, rigidly demarcated apart from the sphere of 'rational' language and action.

The absence or the poverty of youthful discourse challenges the enforced compartmentalization of experience, the dichotomization of meaning. As a plea for rebuilding the human experience, as a search for an alternative voice and language, it acquires connotations of resistance, even of conflict, as it clashes with the canonical word of the apparatuses and with the monopoly they exercise over discourse.

There are those who promptly denounce the young for their apparent conformism, their indifference to power. Although such behaviour often eludes the grasp of the observer and shows itself bordering on marginality, it in fact disguises a radical change in attitudes to power and in the nature of conflicts: power, as the asymmetry which, in some form or other, is a characteristic of all social relations, is no longer denied but becomes openly acknowledged. By force of its own existence, youth behaviour symbolically addresses the constitution of (adult) authority, demonstrating where the foundation of authority lies and why imbalances tend to reappear even in the most egalitarian of relationships. Power is counterposed with responsibility, as the subject's autonomous capacity to respond. The opportunity to occupy an autonomous space in social relations without denying their disparities becomes a condition for action, for initiative and change. What youth culture asks is not that power disappear altogether, but that it should become visible and confrontable: young people make their distance from the adult world even more manifest, but they are not ready to accept authority as self-evident. They ask for a power capable of displaying its roots.

Thus, youth culture takes on antagonistic connotations in its relation with the systems of regulation and control that give power its increasingly invisible, impersonal, and aseptic character. In complex societies, the message is that, apparently, power does not really exist: to the public eye, it either resides at too great a remove from the everyday experience to seem noteworthy, or it is so finely interwoven within the structures of the daily life as to become practically imperceptible. In both cases, the call for the power to be rendered visible, for the asymmetry of social relationships to be laid bare, becomes thus charged with antagonistic tone.

This attitude towards power can account for an apparent contradiction in the features of youth culture that various observers have reported. In fact, youth culture simultaneously displays a susceptibility to integration and a tendency to segregate itself from public life and institutions. The paradox, however, is only apparent if one thinks of the pattern of distance/confrontation assumed by its relationship *vis-à-vis* power. Youth culture gives forceful expression to communicative needs, but it also claims the right to decide when, and with whom, to communicate. It is in this sense that the pattern of outward/inward, openness/closure, communication/loss of speech is the mirror image of the demand for power to be drawn out in the open. In complex societies, we are forced to communicate by the imperatives of the system which must multiply interactions and the relations for the exchange of information in order to perpetuate itself. Young people oppose this 'obligation to communicate' by claiming the right to silence, to isolation, to apartness. Parallel to the completion of the irresistible and ubiquitous circulation of information, however, the action of the system also atomizes personal relations, standardizes messages, and denies culturally and affectively rich communication. As a reaction, youth culture claims for itself the freedom of unrestricted communication and endeavours to exploit all the networks of sociality that make it possible, to explore all the expressive and communicative channels that society makes available. Thus the mirror of youthful experience indirectly reveals openness and closure, integration and separateness as profoundly individual and collective needs in complex societies, and, by the same token, as potential fields for conflict.

Another frequently noted feature of youth culture is the unplanned and provisional nature of its interests, aggregations, and choices. We spring from a culture which viewed history teleologically, as an end-directed grand design where the present stood for only a transitional point of passage. Present action acquired meaning with reference to its final outcome, its purpose projected in the future. This paradigm was common to both liberal theories of progress and Marxist theories of revolution. In complex societies, where change has become the routine condition of existence, the present, however, acquires an inestimable value. History, and therefore the possibility of change, is oriented not by final ends but by what is happening now. Youth culture directs society's attention to the value of the present as the sole yardstick of change; it demands that what should be relevant and meaningful is the here and now, and it claims for itself the right to provisionality, to the reversibility of choices, to the plurality and polycentrism of individual lives and collective values. For this reason it inevitably enters into conflict with the requirements of a system centred around the need for predictability, reduction of uncertainty, and standardization.

All the features of the youth culture I have described are highly ambivalent. They may act as triggers for conflict, but they may just as well serve to help integrate youth culture into the vast market of mass culture; or, alternatively, they may function as markers of an institutionalized marginality. This is a common feature of the emerging cultures (Coupland 1991; Nava 1992). Young people in themselves are not conflictual actors. Their mobilization can only be explained if analysis identifies a systemic field of conflict and the presence of conjunctural factors that facilitate the emergence of a critical situation; only then may the youth condition translate into antagonistic action. But when this happens, youth movements probe into the society's deep-rooted demands, problems, and tensions, and bring them to the surface. Within the time and space circumscribed by the conflict, young people do not speak for themselves alone. Being young is thus more than just destiny; it is a conscious decision to change and to direct one's own existence.

Time and the culture of the possible

Experience of time is a core issue in complexity (Melucci 1996), and young people, particularly the adolescents, are key actors in the ways in which time is lived and defined in our culture. The growing interest in this issue (for an overview, see Adam 1990; Hassard 1990) is a sign of the changes affecting the modern conception of time (Elias 1993; Luhmann 1987; Novotny 1992) and its social organization, governed by the standards of masculine rule and Western rationality (Zerubavel 1981; Fabian 1983; on women and time, see Davies 1989; Shelton 1992; on the logic of measurement in work and society, see Sirianni 1988; Young 1988).

Adolescence and youth, it is said, are the phases of life when time is suspended and the words to express the unfolding experience of change are so difficult to come by. Thus it had better be left for others to speak on behalf of the youth – adults, institutions, the media, advertising. Society seems ever more preoccupied with the question of the youth and, in an unprecedented fashion and force, brings to our everyday awareness the image and the voice of the troubled actors burdened by the intensity of their existential crisis.

Instead of becoming self-appointed experts claiming the privileged access to the knowledge of the young, adults should inquire into the changes themselves that have rendered the youthful experience problematic. Beyond the alarm of those safeguarding the outward calm of our streets and institutions from the unpredictability of the young actors, what adults share in common with young people is the experience of the wider changes occurring today. Young people are the primary subjects of dramatic transformations that affect contemporary society, and they also experience them most immediately. By listening to their sharp voice, adults can learn about themselves.

The fundamental question affecting individual and collective existence in today's society is given in the unrelenting interrogation directed at the self: 'Who am I?' In traditional societies the question of identity, most delicate and critical at the moment of passage from childhood to adolescence, was principally answered by others – the parents, the family, the community. What was involved in this was the adoption of a member of the society still without the effective characteristics of societal membership, and ensuring her/his transformation from a sort of natural residue within society – almost a biological accident – into a rightful social subject. The social life in the past contained a certain moment when children became effective members of the community upon completion of the predetermined passage between childhood and adolescence, acquiring thereby an identity through the affirming function of various tests or rites designated for the purpose ('rites of passage' or of initiation). Such tests, which were different for males and females, consisted of stern and sometimes very painful examinations through which were learned the basic skills and responsibilities pertaining to the adult life in the society in question. Having proved to themselves and to others that they were in fact able to exist as elementary parts of the group, the young were accepted into the community as its fully entitled members.

Today, some remains of the initiation rites can still be observed in rural societies (festivals, departure for military service) even if they have lost much of their previous social prominence. In the traditional peasant community, the distinct and uniform phases of passage were made possible by the relative stability of social positions: most individuals were born, grew up, and died in the same place, destined for a certain trade and family life. The future was in a certain sense already assigned: except for emigration, war, or epidemics, individual lives unfolded along relatively predictable paths without major changes affecting their course. A person, as it were, was channelled into a relatively stable trajectory, with clearly demarcated stages and fixed deadlines marking the organic transitions in life.

What distinguishes contemporary society is its multiplication of memberships. Individuals no longer belong to any single community that characterizes the acquisition of their identity and its substantive contents. We participate simultaneously in a number of areas of social life: we are consumers, we use services, we are members of associations and groups of various kinds. In each of these settings only a part of our selves, only certain dimensions of our personalities and experience are activated. A place of residence or a certain job no longer univocally avails in the definition of a person's individual identity. Contemporary societies are characterized by the frequency of their internal geographical migrations and by the self-recycling of great numbers of people into other professional and affective roles during a single life course. It thus becomes less easy for individuals to forecast their progress through life: no one can confidently predict even the basic events that will shape our futures far more open to the range of possible and unforeseeable outcomes than ever before in the past. While this cultural experience has today come to concern all social categories and all age groups in differing ways, it is the young people who are more immediately exposed than others to the pluralization of life opportunities.

There is, however, another general phenomenon affecting the younger generation in particular. Our society has enormously expanded the field of symbolic possibilities. The fact that we today relate to the entire world in a planet-wide interaction and that our culture is marked by an ever-increasing quantity of messages and information in flux translates into an explosion of symbolic opportunities for individual experience. Even the universe of those living in a remote rural village has by now been incorporated into a planetary system based on its constituent commonality of information, life models, and cultural referents. As a consequence, the life-horizons within which experience is constructed are no longer charted solely or even primarily by the material conditions of life, but also, and more significantly, by systems of signs, by the imaginative stimuli to which we have irreversibly become exposed. This is true of everyone, but it is manifested in particular in the life of young people, and for two reasons: because of their age, they have always shown the greatest receptivity to the imaginary, and today a specifically designed flow of messages is aimed at them by the media and the market which nourishes it.

Young people feel the effects of such widening of the range of possibilities in the most direct manner: the seemingly limitless expansion of the field of experience (everything can be learned, everything can be attempted); the provisional character of any choice (everything can be changed); the substitution of symbolic representations (images, computer-assisted communication, virtual reality) for the physical dimensions of experience (everything can be imagined) (on the expansion of these dimensions of experience, see Woolley 1992; Benedikt 1991; Featherstone and Burrows 1995). The opening up of the horizon of the possible, the potential of young people to be anything whatsoever seemingly at whim, is not an abstraction but affects experience in its full concreteness. The media, advertisers, and information engineers not only supply young people with the material with which to construct the image of their present and future, but also the languages with which they can design their experience in all of its aspects. Experience is overtaken by the symbolic appeal of possibility and new forms of suffering, the new pathologies of young people, are often tied to the risk of a dissolution of the temporal perspective. Presence, as the capacity to make sense of one's actions and to populate the temporal horizon with connections between different times and planes of experience, becomes fragile and threatened.

In such a cultural context, then, how does the passage to the adult world come about? In today's society, the clear-cut boundary line between childhood from adulthood has dissolved; either the passage from the one to the other takes place almost unnoticeably or the juvenile existence continues without a socially effective arrival at the end of childhood. Both cases are likely to be anchored in the reality of the situation of an entry without passage in the adult world. Youthfulness has ceased to express a biological condition and has become instead a cultural one. People are no longer young only because they are of certain age, but rather on account of their forms of adherence to common styles of consumption or codes of behaviour and dress. Adolescence is now prolonged far beyond its biological boundaries and commitments of the adult life are postponed past twenty-five or even thirty years of age. The lack of clear signals of passage indicating the transition from one condition to another has two kinds of effect: on the one hand, it prolongs the youthful condition even when the biological conditions for it no longer exist; on the other, it impedes actual entry into adulthood, which itself requires a relatively stable identity. The adult must be able to provide for her/himself some kind of a definite answer to the question 'Who am I?'; that is, s/he must be able to identify what work s/he does, who s/he lives with, describe the affective relationships and responsibilities towards others that characterize her/his personal life.

Today it is difficult in youthful experience to take one's measure against such obligatory passages; that is, to gauge one's own capabilities, what one is, what one is worth; for this means measuring oneself against the limit, and ultimately against the fundamental experience of being mortal. Initiation awakens the person from the juvenile dream of omnipotence and confronts him/her with the powerful experience of pain and suffering, even the possibility of death. Today's wide range of symbolic possibilities is not matched by concrete experiences that test individuals to their limits. The indeterminateness of choice, and the attempt in any case to postpone it as much as possible, keep young people in the amorphous, comfortable, and infantile situation of the maternal womb, where they can feel at ease with everything seemingly possible. Drug use allows one extreme way of perpetuating the need for omnipotent well-being: it removes the onus of having to really measure oneself against the limit, and constructs the dramatized, bogus experience of a mortal challenge, a deliberate gamble with death. Yet even when the experimentation with the substance, and other instances of comparable forms of risky behaviour, such as dangerous driving, turn into a very concrete threat to life, they provide but the possibility for a fake challenge which does nothing to modify the deep weakness of the personality and leaves intact the condition of indeterminateness – that is, the position of standing before the threshold of the test without entering into the world of the limits and risks of the adult life.

Youth as a mirror

If all this is true, how can we conceive of a passage to adult life which will not induce us to imagine an impossible return to a low-consumption society, to a society of abstinence and deprivation outside our horizon? It is here where the need to encounter the limit and to measure oneself against that part of human experience which shows us that we are not omnipotent attains its full importance. In a society which opens up the field of possibilities far beyond our actual capability for experiencing them, it is left up to us to recognize our limits. Those same limits which were perceived in the past as uniquely imposed by biology and the social structure can today become a matter of individual and collective responsibility.

First of all, we are brought up against the limit of pain and death, those enduring properties of human experience which we try to ignore and remove from the scenario of our everyday life. Our culture has indeed progressively eliminated the experience of pain by confining it to separate and, where possible, hidden enclaves where it disturbs no one. Maintaining contact with this part of human experience, however, is an important way of keeping the sense of the limit alive.

The second aspect confronting us with the factuality of the limit is the irreducibility of our situatedness in an ecosystem. Environmentalism represents not merely a fashion; it serves as a reminder of the finiteness of our capacity for action, of the natural limit that extends within and around us. The destruction of the forests of Amazonia and their inhabitants, for example, touches our human condition at its deepest level because it reminds us that we are not omnipotent, that respect for the surviving part of Nature and its custodians means respect for the Nature within ourselves – an acknowledgement of finitude of the powers of our technological society.

There is, finally, a third facet to the sense of limitation which affects our ability to choose: we encounter it in relationships. Today we are growing increasingly more aware of the fact that we are different individually and we belong to different and intersecting cultures. Thus, our communal living does not evolve as a spontaneous and automatic process; it has as its precondition our responsibility, the acceptance of the difference of others. The establishment of social relationships entails the experience of limitation in a society which must continue to be diversified, open to the widest possible range of personal realization, but which must nevertheless learn day by day to recognize the fact that we are not sufficient unto ourselves.

Youth, because of its biological and cultural condition, is the social group most directly exposed to these problems – the group which makes them visible for the society as a whole.

By addressing the problem of passages, the problem of choice, uncertainty, and risk, young people live for everyone, as sensitive receptors of our culture, the dilemmas of time in a complex society. By challenging the dominant definition of time the youth announces to the rest of the society that other dimensions of human experience are possible. In so doing, they moreover call the adult society to its responsibility – that of recognizing time as a social construction and of making visible the social power exerted over time. By reversing the adult definition of time, the adolescents launch a symbolical challenge to the dominant patterns of organization of time in society. They reveal the power which hides itself behind the technical neutrality of temporal regulation accomplished by society. Often at a great price of personal and collective suffering, they remind us that the time of too many possibilities can be a possibility without time, without limits, without choices.

It is as if society has appointed young people to live this global situation in the most intense and dramatic of forms. We are surrounded by change and in this unfolds the drama of the choice which must always sacrifice some possibilities in order to bring others into being. We know that we must choose, and we cannot not choose since even not choosing is by choice. Choice is our destiny; we are thus obliged to be free, we choose willingly or unwillingly. Choice has become a requirement we cannot avoid, yet we know that it is no longer necessarily once and for all, that it is partial and temporary. Keeping this awareness to oneself is not to shun reality but to know that other possibilities remain open if we pass entirely, consciously through the gauntlet of choice. We may therefore conceive of adult lives as a progress through various metamorphoses or changes of form. In adult life the need to transform one's personal situation into a question escalates, exposing identity to many risks: there is the terror of the definitive, but there is also the great consolation of the definitive that enwraps and soothes us.

Change means calling certainties into question, but people still continue to need what they recognize as ideals and hope, simply in order to act. To what motives, then, can we appeal to renew hope and passion, when we no longer can count on the force of the confident faith in that 'what is to become will be better than today', on the once great myth that has nourished the entire culture of modernity with its assurance of the future society that will sweep away the restrictions and injustices of the present one? In youth cultures we find the birth of a desire to experiment in the present with the possibility of change. The observable decline of political action of contemporary youth movements in the long term cannot be explained away as a reflux, an ebbing of energy; today they are rather altering the ways in which they express hope and passion to match them with the conditions in societies that differ from those in which the ideals of the egalitarian, classless, transparent society first sprang up. These ideals of the yesteryear postponed the fulfilment of everything to a postulated perfect future and thereby in effect sacrificed the present. Today, however, hope flows through different channels: there is a need for passion, but our hopes cannot be pinned on what is to come.

Hope, as a motivating force, must relate to the now-time: this is what young people affirm through their specific forms of action. All current forms of youth social and civil participation, of voluntary action, of cultural innovation, as they are born and grow, proclaim the following: We want to experience now what it is possible to accomplish and what we do must be meaningful in itself, not for some distant future; we want what we do, even if we act on the small scale in a circumscribed local context, to create meaning within a more general compass, as part of a global dimension. If goals are no longer projected into the future, then they are to be specified principally as the ability to adopt an authentic relation to oneself and to the others. Here it should be the task of adults to meet the young and recreate the space for initiation.

Where have all the flowers gone?

Collective action among the youth has apparently disappeared after the 1970s. Apart from some short waves of mobilizations in different countries during the 1980s and early 1990s, such as the anti-apartheid movement in the United States, the short waves of student mobilizations in France, Italy and Spain (Larana 1995) youth action seems to be in the process of transforming itself into exclusively expressive 'countercultures' (centred around music, dressing, creation of new languages, as with rappers, for instance). The question has been asked: crisis or transformation of youth aggregations?

By comparing the recent waves of youth and student mobilizations with the model from the 1960s and 1970s (Larana 1995; Flacks 1967; Fraser *et al.* 1988; Stryker 1994), analysis shows that the structure of youth mobilizations is significant at two levels:

1 The poverty of the instrumental outcomes of action conceals a metabolic richness of stimuli, relations, and exchanges. Mobilizing against racism, heroin, or the mafia in Italy, or marching for peace may not directly affect the phenomena themselves, but it promotes the creation of a solidarity network essential for the structuring of individual and collective experience of youth. The criteria of rationality operating in the political market are usable for this purpose only in part, since they can at best cover only some of the meanings embodied in the action.

2 The apparent fragmentation of today's youth as a collective phenomenon conceals the operation of a process structured around alternating phases of visibility and latency. All that is required for an effective, rapid, and wide-spread mobilization to take place is the propulsive role of some media internal to youth culture, of young opinion leaders who gain access to the general media, of participants of previous mobilizations now partially professionalized in the cultural or media market, often though their interaction with public institutions after the mobilization phase.

Precisely because effectiveness, rapidity, and extension are parameters which measure the organizational capacity in a mobilization process, to interpret youth action solely in terms of fragmentation is inappropriate: although segmentation, networking, diffuse forms of leadership may put into question the model of a youth movement as homogeneous actor, they also ensure the survival, sedimentation, and cyclical emergence of youth collective action.

Besides proceeding by campaign mobilizations, youth action integrates a manifold set of belongings, identities, and interests. Youth networks react to a highly differentiated system in their own fashion, apparently with a determination to play the game of complexity to its fullest extent, reserving the right to change its rules or not, according to circumstances. Young people respond to the multiplication of interests and identities, and to the acceleration of time, either by joining the system or by evading the spread of control through the constant redefinition and indistinctness of their choices of belonging. Being part of a youth network means keeping open the range of opportunities for recognition through symbolic exhibition of signs or through overt conflict. Interests are not ascribed, they do not pertain to a stable condition; they are a matter of decision – one is part of the 'movement' because one acts. One belongs to it out of choice.

The accelerating alternation of campaigns and apparent lack of collective action focuses mobilizations on mutable goals, whose priority depends on their practicability. The alternation sequence is also a way to address the problem of the multiplication of the loci of power and the difficulty to establish a permanent hierarchy of interests in society. Given the heterogeneity of the social basis for mobilization, the choice of increasingly more general goals enables the reticular fabric of the 'movement' to become effective. These goals, even if they are embodied in universalistic values (peace, human rights, poverty and so on), are pursued on a short-term basis and with reference to specific issues, allowing an immediate but equally transitory aggregation.

Should one then speak of one or different youth conditions? The social definition of 'youth' today comprises biological, cultural, and sociological dimensions. Although biological youth is a short-term condition, it still provides a strong foundation for the feeling of belonging to the youth as a social group. But it is increasingly substituted by a cultural definition of being young, chosen on the basis of symbolic identifications (ways of dressing, consuming, relating, behaving independently from the biological age). Sociological definitions of youth get therefore blurred and construct very often statistical categories, to which it is easier to attribute an 'objective' identity. The youth condition is then, on the one hand, an enduring primary datum based on biology, but, on the other, it increasingly patterns itself according to cultural choices (or even to statistical attributions, which are in fact institutional choices). The co-occurrence of these definitions with blurred features calls for an analysis of *several* possible conditions. The particular patterning and emergence of these diversities alter the features of youth collective action, which recover and adapt previous mobilization patterns, mixing themselves with models of collective action common to other social movements.

The forms of youth aggregations confirm their tendency towards heterogeneity and non-specificity. There are different components which converge in youth mobilizations: leisure and cultural centres partly connected to governmental and local policies directed towards emergent youth interests (music, theatre, expressive arts, international voluntary action, leisure and travel, radios); some of these agencies have a well-established relationship with the institutions or professionalized sectors of the market; houses occupied by squatters which act as local points of aggregation; subcultural bands with more or less distinct and stable territorial points of reference; students who find their immediate referent for aggregation in the school or university.

Each of these components comprises different actors. Very few identify themselves solely on the basis of an ideological choice or a clear-cut political commitment. House squatters, apart from their evidently instrumental objective, act to fulfil needs centring on integration and solidarity, which are particularly intense in the case of immigrants. Those who have found an occupational outlet through previous mobilizations thereby fulfil the need to lend continuity to their experience by combining an identity as 'opponents' with a choice of 'new professionalism'. Those who opt for image as the immediate referent of belonging find the meaning of action in the scrambling of the messages and symbols broadcast by the system. Those who act as students use the fact that they share the same structural ambit to gain a collective identity which legitimates their citizenship in the system.

The heterogeneity of these positions translates into differentiation of action, ranging from a ritualized inaction to professionalized action, from symbolic challenge to constant wavering between one objective and another, from one belonging to another.

Heterogeneity of condition and non-homogeneity of action shatter the unitary nature of young people's mobilizations but give greater specificity to their individual identities. Mobilization is not based on totalizing principles or values, which today cannot provide a sustainable youth identity; it is instead framed by the conjunction of global concerns and the ever narrower horizons close to individual everyday experience. The model that thus emerges appears congruent with the requirements of collective action in highly differentiated societies. It allows, on one hand, precise specification of the contradictions emerging in different areas of the system where young people experience their exposure to new resources and new forms of domination; it, further, allows rapid passage from one area to another. On the other hand, discontinuity of action and dependence of collective action on temporary interpersonal bonds are the risks that follow it.

Universalism of the issues and specificity of the grounds for action seem to facilitate the passage from latency to visibility in collective action. The most ideologized components seem increasingly destined to a marginal role; for the others, the option of public action is still open and bound to the contingent and external enabling factors. The criteria for this choice, which is not considered a necessary condition for the existence of the group culture, depends on constantly redefinable opportunities and on the nature of local and governmental policies towards youth.

7

The time of difference

Women's voices and silences

More than any other contemporary movement, the women's movement has interwoven reflection on the female condition with its conflictual role within society; and more than any other it has based its collective action on an appeal to difference. Because it is rooted in the ancestral experience and nature of the species, this difference is irreducible; and this is why it is so difficult to disentangle women's struggles from the history of womanhood itself – from the awareness of a subjugation imbibed into the most archaic memory of human societies. Be that as it may, we must again resort to the method outlined above: our analysis must distinguish between the female condition and the women's movement; it cannot deduce one from the other.

Women have for a long time struggled for the equality of opportunities, and this struggle based on the common biological and historical condition has also helped focusing collective energies against an external enemy (Evans 1980; Rupp and Taylor 1987). But from the 1970s on, the women's movement has moved on to follow different routes in pursuit of its goals (Freeman 1975; Buechler 1990; Ryan 1992); similarly, reflection on woman's condition has also concentrated on the plurality of the modes and meanings of being a woman (Chodorow 1978; Gilligan 1982; Fraser 1989; Skevington and Baker 1989; Lorber 1994). Mutated by time, diversified by social membership and life-course, the female condition is today even more strikingly marked by difference. The speed of change, the prolongation of the life-cycle, and the strains involved in the passage from one stage of the reproductive cycle to another heighten this potential for diversification. Naturally, fundamental features common to all women still persist. Their resistance against subordination and oppression – resistance expressed in forms that are not those of masculine struggle – continues. There is, furthermore, the necessity of women to come to terms with motherhood as the crucial node of the female condition. It can be received as destiny, accepted as a possibility, or sometimes rejected as an obstacle to independence; in any case, it constitutes a condition with which the female body must inevitably come to terms. Regarding each of these shared areas of experience, however, a more acute awareness of complexity is becoming increasingly evident among women.

Women are rediscovering the value and meaning of everyday resistance as their inheritance from the past. The family has always been, and for the most part still is, the arena of the commonplace. It sets the tempo most typical in the history of women, the one which follows the rhythms of birth and death, love and suffering – the slow and uniform repetitiveness of days and gestures, of many silences and few words. It is within this humdrum, this quasi-natural cadence that women are now beginning to discern the signs of its own antithesis: change and female action as the vehicles of meaning. They are discovering the origins of the female identity in silences which may become words, while daily routine is no longer just manipulation and oppression but at the same time becomes the locus of meaning as well. Women's collective action is nourished by these everyday experiences and does not express itself only through public mobilizations; it develops through the shared apprenticeship of difference and resistance in everyday times, spaces, and relationships.

Motherhood, for so long women's sole destiny, is now also marked by diversity: in the alternative arrangements among which to choose, in the subjective meaning of the experience, in the ways it can be lived physically and emotionally. The last thirty years have seen a rapid transformation of family models, and the growing importance of choice in love relationships has to a certain extent eliminated some forms of inequality. In the broader culture, however, the idea still persists that a woman can only express herself through her partner and her children. Probably the most pressing need today is the supersession of the fusional relationship imputed to the female condition, and seeking of personal identity in the difference. Although motherhood thus progressively loses its status as the female destiny and becomes a personal choice, there is still a long way to go before childbearing and child care are freed from the burden they impose on women and before relationships of care will not lend themselves to fusional experiences preventing the autonomous growth of both mother and child. The social practice of childbirth, entirely medicalized and managed by the male-dominated health system, still effectively prevents a woman from living the experience of life-giving as hers alone. But motherhood is not actualized in the act of giving a birth alone; it continues afterwards as a relational experience. The woman's relationship with her child raises the problem of fusion, as the difficulty of accepting and carrying forward difference. Her life-chances as an individual therefore seem to move through a series of separations and via the affirmation of multiple differences *vis-à-vis* the man she loves, the foetus she carries in her womb, the son or daughter who bears her image.

Analysis of the female condition finds that domestic work still occupies a central position in a woman's life: far from disappearing together with more traditional forms of discrimination, it has become laden with new functions and responsibilities (Smith 1988, 1990). Woman's work for the family is not just maintenance work, the daily chores of conserving and activating the family's various assets (domestic work in the strict sense). Today women perform an important function in the relationships with the welfare system, in obtaining the services the family requires; they are second-degree users, as they 'work' to get the services (health, education, assistance) and to adapt them to the specific needs of their beloved ones and relatives (children, teenagers, old people, sick persons). They are also the undertakers of the work of building the relationships which ensure the integration of the family nucleus, to absorb conflicts and maintain relations with the outside. In contemporary families all these functions are still performed principally by women, paying often a high emotional price (Mirowsky and Ross 1989). Their possible transformation into a different model of role distribution thus becomes a crucial gauge against which to measure the evolution of the family; in the near future, men-women relationships will be put to a severe test (Tronto 1987).

These features of the female condition and culture map out a field of limits and possibilities. The novelty of the women's movement lies in its capacity to address difference; and not only because it has taken the 'natural' difference between men and women to be one of the central foci of its struggle – a difference which has subsequently proved to underpin many other inequalities in the power structure, in role systems, and in forms of social organization – but also because it has called into question a number of the certainties and conquests of modern consciousness. It was thus with emancipation. The struggle for emancipation and the equalities that women, sometimes at a great sacrifice, have at least partially won, did not signify the end of their ambiguous position, torn as they were between the designated female world, which they rejected for its subjugated status, and a male world, in which a place was put aside for them but which they nevertheless found unacceptable. The women's movement affirms another kind of freedom: no longer a freedom from want but the freedom *to* want; no longer a struggle for equality but a struggle for difference; no longer a freedom to act but the freedom to be. The tradition of masculine rationality that has typified modernity seems to be totally incapable of bridging the rift, the void between the two types of freedom.

The dangers of such a radical appeal arising from women's action are as great as the challenges it directly poses to the structures of domination. Insisting on the private may steer towards isolation of the individual in an illusory enclave of the emotions; appealing to nature may pave the way for every form of irrationality and violence. Irrespective of these risks, however, women's collective action rejects the logic of instrumental rationality and marks the beginning of a new definition of collective action itself: it is as if its voice has spoken for everyone, as if it has declared that history will never be the same again because female history has transformed the coordinates of meaning (Gilligan 1982; Jacobus *et al.* 1990; Harding 1991). In this dramatic tension lies the strength and the weakness of the women's movement: It proclaims a wholesale change which equally entails a change of the self; it affirms the partiality of difference but does not renounce the validity of non-instrumental collective rationality.

Beset, even riven, by the ambiguity of this tension, the women's movement becomes an actor in conflicts which touch upon a central dilemma of complexity. Whether it is possible to be oneself without breaking the circle of communication and recognition conjoining us and the others – this is the issue the women's movement has announced to society as its field of action. The themes of identity and difference, as an assertion of the priority of the right to be before the right to do, and as a claim for a life-space in which to withdraw from the structures of social control, will never disappear from the sphere of social action. The women's movement has reawakened collective consciousness to the radical nature of needs which no 'politics' can ignore. And by doing so it has pointed the way to a different kind of politics – yet another difference.

Between condition and action

In highly differentiated societies, commuting between one social sphere and another is central to the processes whereby adult identity is defined. In the case of changing female identity, the process is particularly visible in the dual presence of women, commuting between the public sphere of work and politics and the private roles fulfilled in taking care of many family tasks, childbearing, and affective relationships (Abel and Nelson 1990).

Women's collective action is thus marked by phenomena of co-presence and the transition of individuals to different forms of movement with greater or lesser visibility and with different degrees of investment. The recent history of the women's movement exhibits cycles in which the emancipatory-claimant aspect and the production of new services alternate as the predominant characteristic in women's issues. This, however, does not rule out the co-presence of less visible forms of action and the commuting by actors from one form to the other. In terms of both cycles and co-presence, the women's movement is marked by the relationship between forms of manifest struggle, formalized collective production, demands for access to/pressure on the political market, and more finely-knit forms of aggregation, absence of mobilization, processes of self-reflection, and the development of new collective forms of behaviour.

This perspective entails superseding the equation of movement with demands, an equation according to which there can be no movement without demands, without the relative forms of struggle and pressure on the political market. Antagonism is not necessarily always demand-oriented. In a manner most marked in the women's movement (but noticeably in other movements as well), there appears the *offer* dimension in which models of new social rationality are being developed and anticipated. Antagonism exists, but it concerns cultural codes, not necessarily confrontation and conflict with the political system and the state apparatus. The growth of conflicts affecting gender roles, the use of group solidarity to support individual women faced with the contradictory nature of social requirements, upsets the univocal, masculine logic of the system and allows a reappropriation of the multiformity of roles.

Proposed in an analogous sense is the concept of resistance: the work of production and reproduction which involves women is not only functional to the reproductive imperatives of the system. In their everyday action women also elaborate strategies for survival, resistance, and change of dominant cultural patterns. In their everyday activity – and therefore also in the downward cycles of organized struggle – women both help to shape and resist the dominant social system.

Adult women engaged in reproduction play a central role in service work, for their very identity depends on their success or failure in providing services for their families. This social centrality of adult women, their autonomous role in defining personal needs, their constant mediatory relationship between the state (welfare, health, education) and the family, gives everyday female experience an antagonistic function and situates it along the continuum ranging from *survival* (action which enables difference to survive) to *resistance* (in the form of active defence, of the struggle for difference), to *innovation* or *change* (the creation of new arenas for action and culture which may be sometimes explicitly antagonistic in character). Various analysts of the political path of women in Western societies (Gelb 1987; Hellman 1987a; Jenson 1987) have emphasized the eclipse of protest and the decline of women's mobilization brought about by the redistribution of the political and social benefits that were won during the 1970s. Institutionalization of women's political action has been accompanied by an increased capacity for social and political bargaining, by graduation to a position of major importance in the market of ideas (cultural and academic roles, entrepreneurship, professional skills) (Mueller 1987; Martin 1990; Ferree and Martin 1994), and by development of cultural forms of antagonism constructed and expressed in the everyday lives of women (Morgen 1983; Evans and Boyte 1986; Steinem 1992). Although the latter forms a different level of analysis, it is not necessarily in contradiction with the previous ones.

However, the difference involved underscores the fact that the level of observation chosen must be specified: whether it is an examination of *feminism* as an overall historical phenomenon principally engaging the political system, or of the *women's movement* as it relates to female action and its orientations. In each case, the definition of the subject and content of women's collective action is different. And this entails differing evaluations of the impact of the change introduced into the system by the women's movement. In the former case, attention focuses entirely on the political effects of feminism, on its success or failure (Gelb 1987; Costain and Costain 1987; Costain 1992; Klein 1984, 1987; Katzenstein and Mueller 1987; Freeman 1987); in the latter case, on cultural codes and on the ability of female action to produce other meanings for society as a whole (Richardson and Taylor 1993).

This aspect of women's action creates an unstable and changing relationship between movement, professionalization, and social mobility of women. That relationship takes three different forms.

1 *Overproduction* in groups. Women's groups seem to devote themselves to a kind of symbolic waste (Cassell 1977). Their cultural production is not finalized in the achievement of an instrumental goal, and apparently ends up in the creation of a useless surplus. This, on the one hand, correlates with a surplus of education and intellectual capacities with respect to occupational placement and other social outlets (politics, for example); and, on the other hand, with the ideology of egalitarianism, of diffuse female culture which legitimates protected enclaves – outside the market in the group and in the movement – ranging from silence to the use of only proper names for collective texts, and to a difficult and affirmative re-entry into the market when the children have grown up.

But actually overproduction means non-formalized service work, a widespread, massive but invisible cultural training in new feminine skills. The movement acts as the locus of *antagonistic compensation* for the increasing distance between levels of education and intellectual resources on the one hand, and the possibility of utilizing them and having them recognized by the social organization on the other.

2 *The channelling of overproduction* towards retraining processes aimed at inserting women in the market and institutions. This tendency is particularly evident in the birth of new groups pursuing cultural and occupational goals for women, in the creation of new enterprises or cooperatives, agencies for job placement and training, women's cultural agencies, etc. (Brown 1992).

3 The directions in which female overproduction has been channelled coincide with the area of *new service occupations* in the advanced tertiary sector. The development of these occupations can be seen as the emergence of mobility strategies by the weaker component among the offspring of the higher social strata (namely women) and by the offspring of the middle social ranks. These are sectors such as journalism, radio broadcasting, cooperatives, therapy, welfare and so on. In this respect, therefore, one of the effects of female collective action has been the modernization of the system, through the expansion of innovative occupational sectors, the higher turnover of personnel in communications and welfare services.

Antagonism directed towards cultural codes and the modes of symbolic construction in society conjugates ambivalently with this modernizing innovation. These two facets, which interweave in the empirical reality of the movement, are destined to coexist and to enter into conflict, thereby generating new debate and new provisional equilibria.

The analysis of the empirical 'women's movement' concerns the passage from a condition (with its connotations of social discrimination, deprivation, suffering) to the collective action undertaken in order to change that condition. In other words, within the broad population of those sharing a condition, who are the subjects mobilizing themselves (social and, for women, above all generational profiles), for what reasons (sources of movements), and to achieve what ends?

Three principal explanations can be proposed for this passage:

(i)   The explanation which views the origin of the women's movement from the 1970s onwards as internal; that is, as the response by certain groups of women to the contradictory demands made on them by society through the collective redefinition and reconstruction of their identity: This is exemplified in the analyses of mass schooling and its effects, to which women gained open access after World War II. Participation in the movements of the 1960s and the New Left accelerated the process, by intensifying the exposition to contradictory demands (Evans 1980; Mueller 1994).

(ii) Which groups of women are most susceptible to contradictory social demands – such as the offer/demand of intellectual and occupational performance on a par with men in the educational system and the labour market, together with the maintenance/strengthening of demands for affective care, for nurturing, for service work, for the high levels of skill-specialization imposed by processes of reproduction in a complex society? They are the adult, educated women involved in the processes of mass intellectualization characteristic of the urban contexts in which the service culture has developed most strongly. These are women of a dual presence, a social group under pressure which shares particular conditions of privilege (high levels of school-ing, social centrality, emancipation, location in economically and socially advanced social contexts) and also of deprivation (the co-presence of both innovative and traditional expectations regarding them, the need to cope with extremely rapid structural and cultural changes).

(iii) The presence of various generations of women in the movement, and various generations of feminism: the forerunners of feminism, the sur-vivors from the groups of the New Left, and the younger generations that became involved in the 1980s and 1990s. Interweavings and con-flicts among these generations and the different forms of feminism marked the history of women's groups during the 1970s and 1980s (Whittier 1995). The youngest generation in the 1990s benefits from the gains in equality and emancipation achieved by previous mobiliza-tions. The youth condition in which young women participate is, more-over, markedly egalitarian: the school system is no longer selective (as regards gender criteria) and the labour market, still selectively open for women but much less so than in the past, is realistically viewed as the true laboratory test for parity. It is in fact in terms of parity and not of identity that feminism appears to be perceived and lived by the younger generations.

To make a difference

For women, their profound memory of subordination and entrapment in a body 'other' than that of the dominant culture makes a struggle for emancipation an important, and quantitatively perhaps the most signifi-cant, component of the movement's action. However, collective action by women is structured not only around the campaign for equal rights, but for the right to be different as well. The struggle against discrimination and for access to the economic and political market interweaves with, but is nevertheless distinct from, the struggle for difference. Being recognized as different, in fact, is perhaps one of the most crucial rights at stake in complex systems. Granting recognition to women entails accepting a different 'eye' on the world, the existence in a feminine body, a different way of establishing and taking care of relationships.

In societies which exert strong pressures towards conformity, the appeal to difference has an explosive impact on the dominant logic. By claiming difference, the movement addresses not just women but society as a whole. At the same time, the movement's action allows women access to political and cultural markets and contributes to their renewal. Success on the market transforms the movement into a pressure group, segments the network, bureaucratizes some groups and dissipates others. The movement's professionalization, however, does not affect its antagonistic nucleus but makes it more difficult to locate.

It shifts towards *the form* of communication. The self-reflective form of the small group – which was the core of the women's movement and preceded and fostered its public mobilization – already expresses its intention not to separate practice from meaning, action from the awareness of its significance and emotional content. The work done by the women in the movement speaks for all of us. It shows that one cannot act publicly and effectively without a stable component of reflectiveness which constantly questions the meaning of what is being done; and without communication that finds room not only for the instrumental logic of efficiency, but also for the feelings, uncertainties and affective conflicts that always nourish human action. But what does this privileged communication of the women's movement, so long engaged in and with such difficulty, actually express? In it, what is set forth is an effort to break the necessary tie between power and difference that masculine culture always contains. Women challenge masculine power and through their action they ask society whether a different form of communication is possible, one, more specifically, in which difference will not turn to power.

By questioning their relationships with men and increasingly their own internal differences, women interrogate the whole of society concerning the very roots of communication; they raise again the question whether humans can communicate without a necessary component of oppression in that relationship. This message, moreover, becomes antagonistic in content in the sense that the system, which multiplies communication and lives by it, knows only two kinds of communication: on the one hand identification denoting incorporation into dominant codes, fusion with the power that denies diversity, and on the other hand separateness which establishes difference as exclusion from all communication.

Other features of female communication reveal its antagonistic nature. The particular is not to be lost; the details are important as the whole; minute memories matter for the present; repetition, slowness, and cycles are not just boredom: all these requirements of female communication acquire a profoundly subversive significance when confronted with the dominant standards of our (masculine) culture – measurability, homogenization, and speed are the criteria that an information society exacts in order to make possible the generalization of its procedures.

Yet not all women mobilize themselves. The actors in the movement are those women who have experienced the contradiction between, on the one hand, promises of inclusion in the labour market and in the arena of political rights and equality, and, on the other, the social costs of being a woman restricted to the immutable roles of a mother, a wife, and a mistress. Women who mobilize are thus those who have experienced a surplus of resources within the narrow confines of the female condition. They are those with higher levels of schooling, those exposed to the contradictions of the welfare function, of which they are often the agents and the recipients. Besides emancipation struggles, women's action takes the above-mentioned form of the cultural overproduction, a symbolic wastefulness containing a profound ambivalence. 'Female' activities within the movement consist of apparently pointless meetings, of expressive activities for their own sake, not for the market (writing, arts, crafts, bodywork, self help), of time spent in ways incoherent with the logic of utility and efficiency (Simonds 1992). The cultivation of memory, the search for the margins, nuances, seams of experience (Davies 1989; Forman and Sowton 1989), the duplication of the same activities by a myriad of groups with complete disregard for economies of scale – all these are aspects that the dominant culture of the masculine can only judge as 'senseless'. Nevertheless, changes in everyday gender culture, the market and politics over the last thirty years show that it is precisely this waste that breeds innovation.

In fact, this at the same time is one of the ways in which the system controls uncertainty, a sort of an enclave where haphazard experiments in innovation are conducted. The system absorbs the results of these experiments by sifting out their essence in a kind of natural selection process. But the symbolic wastefulness of women's groups serves also as the expression of an irreducible difference, of what is 'valueless' because it is too minute or partial to enter the standardized circuits of the mass cultural market. The symbolic extravagance of female output introduces the value of the useless into the system, the inalienable right of the particular to exist, the irreducible significance of inner times which no History is able to record but by virtue of which individual experience nevertheless becomes the ultimate core of experience.

Besides equality, and besides access to the domain of male rights, women also speak of the right to see difference recognized. Today, it is still difficult to find the language for this right which would exist independently of the codes of the dominant language. The women's movement remains thus hazardously balanced between its role as a modernizing force, a role which it cannot refuse but which with seeming inevitability is transforming it into a pressure group, and its function as a symbolic appeal which reaches beyond the female condition. In its modernizing role, the movement helps to spread the political and cultural contents of feminism by now professionalized: small, residual fundamentalist groups resist institutionalization, while groups of intellectuals cultivate the memory of the movement.

Many layers coexist within the same collective action: the historical experiences of feminism; the memory of separatism, of the struggles for emancipation, and abortion; and, more recently, the many different paths that bring young women to a collective engagement through their personal life experiences and the contradictions of an emancipation that still burden women with the affective charge of caring for love relationships and family ties.

Women's groups reject the separateness of historical feminism (with some fundamentalist margins still surviving, see Taylor and Whittier 1992; Taylor and Rupp 1993), but also the pure and simple reduction of the women's movement to a process of emancipation in the professional and political field. While they decline the practice of consciousness-raising as a reflection purely centred on affective experiences, they equally refuse to transform themselves into a mere professionalized cultural agency. The work of the 'movement' consists in following a path of self-reflection on the differences of and between women, through the creation of a 'female' culture. The 'movement' is thus faced by the problem of the uneasy relationship between internal self-reflection and an external presence in issues concerning the women's condition and rights.

The many layers that compose the 'movement' express themselves in different internal cultures. Some groups consider solidarity between women the essential condition for individual and professional autonomy, but also for an action in society to express the feminine difference. Others are engaged in a cultural production based on the experience of women and intended to modify the perception of reality produced by the dominant (male) culture. For many women, the women's groups are the social and affective environment in which it is possible to find confirmation and support for one's life choices. The younger generations express through their engagement their need for self-fulfilment as distinct individuals, distinct also from other women.

These orientations find a point of convergence in the *form* of internal relationships: the major investment in the form of interpersonal relationships does not deprive the women's groups of the possibility of external mobilization, but it makes work on the self a condition for social interventions. The 'movement' is then a network of networks connecting the tensions between groups centred on the transparency of internal affective needs and the professional groups committed to conquering a public space for the feminine difference; between the groups producing female culture for internal consumption (writing, art, expressive body activities) and those engaged in the production of services for the broader society (communication, therapy, welfare, housing, health, education); between the groups centred on self-reflective activities and individual differences and those which put the accent on sorority and women's solidarity.

These various orientations are integrated by the high degree of flexibility of a very adaptable organizational form: the groups and the networks fulfil simultaneously *self-reflective* and *productive* functions (the main production is that of feminine cultural codes). The elasticity of interpersonal relationships allows an easy shift from one function to the other. This collective identity structure supports the public mobilization of women, and the 'movement' takes the characteristic double-level (visibility/latency) form. The submerged life of the networks and their self-reflective resources provide the energy for short-term and intense public campaigns, which in turn feed the groups with new members, train new skills, and redefine the issues.

In its confrontation with difference women's collective action has spread all over the world, crossing conditions and cultures and becoming a planetary phenomenon (see: for example, on black women, Hill Collins 1990; Hooks 1993; on Arab women, MacLeod 1991; Abu-Lughod 1990; on Latin American women, Massolo 1992; Vàldés and Winstein 1993; Jelin 1987a, 1990). As regards its symbolic appeal, in the long run the women's movement seems destined to deny itself as a specific social actor, becoming one pressure group among all the others. By giving everyone the chance to be different, it cancels out its own separateness. In their collective action, women seem to repropose in a paradoxical way the 'maternal' drama and symbol of femaleness, that of being for others, while being themselves.

8

Roots for today and for tomorrow

Ethnic and cultural identity

The rise of ethno-nationalist movements, territorial and cultural struggles in contemporary societies has drawn much attention on the role of ethnic identity and cultural differences in conflicts. Involved here is a composite phenomenon in which elements belonging to centuries-old traditions interweave with others peculiar to postindustrial conflicts. Ethnicity, territory, and cultural traditions have asserted themselves as criteria by which identity is defined in complex societies. What are, then, the contents and meanings of these struggles? In what ways are they akin to other emergent movements?

An ethnic group is defined by a set of common biological-hereditary features and a shared historical-cultural tradition, by certain physical and racial traits, by a culture and specific forms of organization of social relationships, and by the self-affirmation of these commonalities. From this point of view, the problem of ethnic identity, especially in European societies, dates back at least to the time of the nation-state formation and to the processes of forced integration that these states set in motion. Such being the case, why has a problem as old as this, one which in certain cases has been an incessant generator of forms of resistance and struggle, now moved back to the centre stage of political and analytical interest? An attempt to provide an answer may conveniently begin with the issues that have been drawn into the focus by ethno-nationalist mobilization in Western countries in the late 1960s and 1970s, to move on next to the factors responsible for the revival of ethnic and cultural conflicts in the late 1980s and 1990s. The range and severity that ethnic, territorial, and cultural conflicts have assumed over the last three decades precludes the possibility of their treatment merely as residual dimensions of development. The renewed conflicts triggered by the collapse of the Soviet empire and the events that towards the end of the 1980s culminated in turmoil in the countries of Eastern and Central Europe, with their consequences unsettled still today, have raised new questions and created new dilemmas. Ethnic, territorial, and cultural conflicts seem to be spreading far beyond their well-attended context in the Western societies and become a feature of the world situation as such. The available research material is still primarily gathered with the focus on the countries of the West, and my analysis will mainly draw on the descriptions of their particular experience, even when it is becoming increasingly evident that there is a necessity to broaden the conceptual framework to embrace a problem that already by now constitutes a transnational dimension of our planetary society (see e.g. Esman 1977; Touraine *et al* 1981; Smith 1981, 1991a; Johnston 1991; McCrone 1992; Cornell 1988; Jenson 1995; Melucci and Diani 1992).

Ethnic nationalism was first revived in the West in the period culminating in the late 1960s. The movements taking their issues from the repertoire of contents propagated through it arose as a particular form of social mobilization based on an appeal to a collective actor which possesses a specific ethnic and cultural identity and seeks to gain political control over a given territory. Ethnicity, first of all, has been the criterion about which the defence of material interests has been organized. Since World War II, the economic development of the centre with respect to the periphery has exacerbated traditional inequalities between geographical areas. The central regions have monopolized the exploitation of resources in outlying areas, condemning them to social as well as to economic marginality. Policies aimed at concentrating development around a restricted number of geographical poles have induced massive migrations of labour, which have further weakened the peripheral regions and established a relationship which some call 'internal colonialism' (Hechter 1975). The growth of the historical nation states created and consolidated the isolation of ethnic minorities in economically and socially peripheral areas. Postwar development has only confirmed and accentuated this coincidence between subordinate ethnic membership and economic discrimination. The 'ethnic' division of labour, of course, affects not only relationships among geographical areas, but extends to the distribution of occupational roles and income as well, even within the same social class. Such discrimination and the exploitative relationships imposed by the centre, above all on areas with local resources of their own, has provoked the majority of ethno-nationalist struggles.

The second salient feature of these struggles is their claim for, and defence of, cultural autonomy. The reaffirmation of a cultural heritage consisting of the language, customs, and traditions of an ethnic group has given minorities a weapon with which to oppose the cultural and linguistic monopoly of dominant groups and resist forced integration into the systems of symbolic codes imposed by the centre.

This latter feature links with a third: in order to preserve their cultural heritage, ethno-nationalist movements advance political claims for a different distribution of decision-making power among social groups and for political independence or, at least, substantial autonomy.

The movements of the 1960s and 1970s have displayed all these features: They have sought to safeguard national languages (by insisting on their use in politics, their inclusion in the school curriculum, and on the rediscovery and diffusion of cultural heritage); they have sought to gain control over their natural resources to so counter effects of economic discrimination; they have endeavoured to build independent nations, or at least to win broad margins of political autonomy.

How can we explain the fact that ethnicity has affirmed itself in advanced societies as an organizing principle for interests and collective solidarity? We must first examine the conjunctural factors that have encouraged the growth of the phenomenon. Far from facilitating integration, the accelerated processes of modernization have increased differentiation by intensifying communication, by exposing isolated sectors of the community to central models, and by slackening state-imposed constraints. Different 'ethnic'/identities – which have continued to exist and have never been entirely eliminated by the processes of state-building – are revitalized and thus aggravate centrifugal forces.

Nationalist pressures are further increased by the new forms of supranational cooperation and integration which, by incorporating marginal regions into broader economic and political markets, reveal both their dependence and their potential for autonomy. This accelerates the shift away from the central state, manifesting itself in demands for independence or strong autonomy. These pressures are reinforced by the weakening of the traditional centres of state power.

These features, however, which have often been stressed by analysts of the revival of ethnic nationalism, fail to give an adequate explanation of the phenomenon. Insistence on the continuity between of the 1960s and 1970s movements and the unresolved problems of nationalism in the past, problems which are revitalized by certain conjunctural conditions, only manages to capture part of the whole picture. What we should do, instead, is to explain what is *discontinous* in contemporary ethno-national mobilization. Academic literature tends to emphasize the links between the new nationalism and the classical nineteenth-century nationalism, and considers current events as the most recent stage in an enduring historical process (Gellner 1983, 1987; Greenfield 1992; Coakley 1992).

At issue here is not the plausibility or the utility of tracing back the historical roots of recent phenomena. Their specificity, however, is underestimated by a strictly diachronic approach which focuses almost entirely on the political dimension of the processes examined. The new feelings of ethnic belonging are not just inherited from a tradition rooted in the history of the nation state: they are the specific product of the changes currently taking place in complex societies. Ethnic solidarity under industrial capitalism found itself 'dislocated' by class solidarity, which at the time was more central (Lijphart 1977). Today this solidarity has re-emerged as an autonomous force. While other membership bonds have slackened or dissolved, ethnic solidarity responds to identity needs which operate not just at the material level but at the symbolic level as well. Identification with a particular difference – here 'ethnic' and linguistic – buttresses demands and needs typical of complex society, as if ethnic identity would provide a symbolic arena for the expression of conflictual forces that go well beyond the specific condition of the ethnic group concerned. This view is also supported by those analyses which maintain that ethnic identity is being progressively transformed into 'symbolic ethnicity' (Gans 1979) within systems where the 'material' connotations of ethnicity have been diluted in the great melting pot of mass society; a similar process takes place for national identity which is exposed to a progressive 'informalization' (Frykman 1995).

Ethno-nationalist struggles in their concrete form are the outcome of various different processes in interaction, processes which must be carefully distinguished. There is, first, a dimension of interstate conflict, when an ethnic group living in a border region aspires to independence or a union with another state. Further, there are situations of ethnic pluralism where groups of relatively equal size grapple with the problem of regulating their mutual relationships. Finally, there are groups with a distinct ethnic identity and traditional culture which claim autonomy or independence from a relatively homogeneous national state, and demand control over a geographical area. The movements discussed in the present section are primarily of the last type; it is these cases that show most clearly the process of grafting new demands onto the traditional problems of ethnicity and territory.

Empirical analysis of ethno-nationalist movements must therefore incorporate two of the classic themes of political science: intergroup relations in systems of segmented pluralism, and international relations among multiethnic systems. Only after these different levels of analysis have been distinguished can we address the problem of the manner in which ethnic identity may constitute the basis for the formation of conflicts in complex society. Many demands stem from a situation of relative deprivation, aimed at obtaining a more advantageous position within the system of resource allocation; this type of demand is most frequently expressed by the archaistically oriented fringes of the movement, those most committed to the defence and fortification of traditional identities and the communal culture. There may, further, be demands for greater autonomy or independence in national or supranational decision-making, advanced most commonly by the modernizing spearhead of the movement. Finally, there are also those anti-technocratic components of the struggle which resist, or oppose in the name of ethnic identity, the logic of rationalization furthered by the central apparatus.

As these various elements are intimately intertwined in a specific historical conjuncture, they restrict the autonomy of the movement's various components and expose it to the danger of a constant veering between a purely regressive ethnic appeal and the pursuit of short-term political and administrative advantages. None the less, they contain also an antagonistic dimension: on the periphery of the system and in the presence of an ethnic and nationalist tradition, the impact of postindustrial transformation has created a web of conflictual issues, actors, and forms of action that more properly belong to the central metropolitan society. Ethnic identity, with its solidarity networks and its historical heritage, shows it can provide the language, symbols, and organizational resources with which new conflicts can be voiced.

In the 1960s and 1970s ethno-nationalist conflicts were part of a broader wave of collective action which swept through all Western societies and involved diverse social groups. Nationalist mobilization often assumed an explicit 'leftist' connotation and it was often wedded to an anti-capitalist orientation which blamed the subordination of the ethnic group on a given social system, and no longer solely on a form of political organization represented by the centralized nation state. The younger generation of nationalist militants grafted cultural themes proper to postindustrial metropolitan society onto the stock of ethnic and territorial tradition. This established a further link with the praxis of symbolic antagonism present in the broader area of social movements.

In many situations, these forces waned during the 1980s, and in the West the nexus between ethnic nationalism and other movements appears weaker in the 1990s. Moreover, the claims forwarded by social categories or local communities that were threatened by marginalization or by economic decline, and which were previously closely associated with ethno-nationalist movements now increasingly assume the character of defensive mobilization in defence of group interests, rather than of struggles against internal colonialism or the central state. This changes may have resulted, among other factors, from the increased capacity of central governments to respond to the demands raised by their internal minorities. Ethnonationalist conflicts, however, have subsequently spread to other parts of the world as well (Eastern Europe, Latin America, Asia). In these areas their nature is complicated by their interlacement with the requirements and contradictions of rapid industrialization and by their clash with the weak nation state still in formation in the developing countries (McGrew and Lewis 1992).

A different level of analysis should consider, on the other hand, the overall incidence of *territorial conflicts* which are not necessarily related to ethnicity and which at the world scale have by no means diminished. Indeed, although territory has always been a central factor in the definition of interests and political identities, it has assumed a particularly important role during the last decade, in which the influence of supranational organizations has undoubtedly increased, and the interdependence of markets and policies has considerably strengthened. This has had the effect of both accelerating the exclusion of weak areas and of creating new channels for the allocation of resources, removed, at least in part, from the control of the various national states.

In the interpretation of recent forms of territorial mobilization one may first regard the territorial dimension as a permanent component of the political process, one which emerges with cyclical regularity as a factor in the aggregation of interests. Local territorial entities may in fact provide the focus for identification regardless of any ethnic specificity (Touraine *et al.* 1981). They may be defined on the basis of specific structural features having to do with the economy or services, or alternatively on the basis of specific administrative arrangements. These criteria constitute further potential sources of conflict within the more general cleavage between centre and periphery (Rokkan and Urwin 1982), by providing opportunities for interests and collective identification to constitute themselves. The rise of localism may therefore express the sense of relative deprivation felt by the inhabitants of a peripheral area affected by crisis. Alternatively, it may express the perception of inadequate political representation by an economically advantaged population. These attitudes are more likely to emerge in a situation like that of complex societies, in which the mobilizing potential of other cultural perspectives inspired by class or universalistic principles is weaker or in decline.

Secondly, the growth of localism may stem from a breakdown in the state's regulatory capacity, both in its welfare and neo-liberal versions (Keating 1988). Localism also manifests the slackening of identification with the state as the agent of national political unity and hence the weakening of that sense of belonging which surpasses local boundaries (Diani 1996). Compared with the traditional opposition between centre and periphery as the mainspring of conflictual mobilization, in this case it is the reaction and response to crisis which predominates.

Finally, mention should be made of the link between territorially-based mobilizations and a new wave of collective action committed to defence of the environment. A localist heritage with its historical roots in a particular territory, may incorporate the defensive components of recent environmentalist culture, for which the territory is the repository of a quasi-natural identity and its protection a guarantee of mankind's survival. A more explicit political connection may establish itself when the defence of the territory becomes part of a programme for the conservation of the natural resources of a region and for the maintenance of the quality of life.

A further distinction concerns the growing incidence of *conflicts among ethnic groups* whose principal purpose is not to gain control over specific territorial areas. These conflicts are typical of multiracial countries like the United States, but they also affect European countries with large-scale extra-European immigration such as Great Britain and more recently Italy, or with cycles of migratory flows (as France or Germany). The massive wave of immigrants from the Third World – and predictably already from the countries of East Europe – seem bound to bring substantial changes to interethnic relations in all Western countries. Today these problems increasingly affect the South Asian countries with an accelerated pace of development. The segmented structure of the labour market will certainly give rise to considerably violent tensions between the newcomers and the social groups which come most frequently into contact with them (Adams 1993). These latter may consider themselves threatened by the presence of a desperate and nonunionized labour force. Their resentment may, alternatively, be directed against immigrants on account of frustrations stemming from status inconsistency or a rapid rise in expectations followed by their equally rapid fall. Both of these phenomena may depend on variables internal to the country concerned, or else on the workings of the international market, without any direct connection with the new immigration. Finally, certain groups may react to what they imagine as the threat to their overall life-quality and status attributable to immigrants, taking the form, for example, of the degradation of the inner cities. In certain cases, the resentment of the host community has already spilled over into racism and the reaffirmation of ethnocentric identification with the nation or the state. These impulses have sometimes fed into the emergence of new right-wing formations and racist mobilizations (Kepel 1987; 1994, Donald and Rattansi 1992; Wiewiorka 1995). The minority groups, for their part, may mobilize in order to advance their claims for citizenship rights. However, these forms of struggle are different from the classic mobilizations by the working class for the extension of certain rights to subjects so far excluded from citizenship. In the case of immigrants, the demand is not voiced by a group which, in cultural terms, may be considered homogeneous with the dominant one. Instead, they are demands which derive from the assertion and defence of diversity. For this reason they do not involve the simple extension of citizenship rights to encompass the excluded group; they entail a redefinition of the representation system itself in order to safeguard diversity and to institute new relationships among groups.

Finally, analysis should refer to the explosion of *nationalist mobilizations* now sweeping through the countries of the former Soviet bloc (see Daragan 1991; Johnston 1993). Here the phenomenon once again assumes different features which, in many cases (from Latvia to Croatia and Bosnia), resemble outbreaks of nineteenth-century historical nationalism. Indeed, these phenomena have frequently been described in terms of 'Habsburgic' nationalism (Gellner 1983) in order to stress the relationship involved between oppressed nations and centralized imperial power. The collapse of the Iron Curtain and the growing economic and political interdependence between the Western and the Eastern Europe does not allow treatment of the collective phenomena in the former socialist countries as analytically separate objects of reflection or study. They should, instead, be viewed as belonging to the same field of inquiry with the phenomena that can be referred to the growing influence of the supranational dimension in shaping the development of ethnic and nationalist conflicts.

The break-up of the Soviet Union as a multi-ethnic empire and the recent events in the constituent parts of the former Yugoslavia demonstrate all the complexity of a painless transition to democracy in the presence of deeply rooted ethnic-territorial questions. The case of the Soviet Union is probably the most significant example of this complexity. To historical differences between the various areas and cultures, migrations and differing rates of population growth have added further reasons for tension. Under an authoritarian and centralized regime, restrictive ethnic policies and planned economic policy restrained potential tensions and postponed their explosion. The cautious liberalization introduced by *perestroika* allowed virulent ethnic-national questions to surface and become incorporated into the more general crisis of the regime (Arutyunyan 1990).

The weakness of the central power, the action of conservative forces exploiting ethnic protest to forestall democratization, the rise of radical leadership within ethnic-territorial cultures, and finally the explosion of ethnically based racism and the ensuing interethnic conflicts produced, in something akin to rapid temporal condensation, the explosive mixture of protest, defensive reaction, and breakdown in law and order that character-ized the last years of the USSR. The opening up of the political system (however minor it may have been in relative terms) produced a radical reac-tion (literally, re-actionary) and interethnic intolerance; but it also created an arena for new instances of democratic change. We should not forget, however, that these have been conflicts which intrinsically differ from each other: it is only for conjunctural reasons – the crisis and rapid collapse of the authoritarian order – that they have merged into protest and violence. This applies more generally to the transition from Communist regimes (for examples, see Touraine *et al.* 1982; Ost 1990; Pickvance 1995; Misztal 1995).

A first kind of conflict stems from the traditional cleavage between centre and periphery. Anti-centralist and markedly political movements have grown up in areas, such as the Baltic republics, in which there previously existed a relatively vigorous civil society of ethnic origin. A second type of conflict involves interethnic strife within a particular territory; strife pro-voked, as between Armenia and Azerbaijan, by historical disputes over borders, by centuries-old ethnic feuds, and by rigid social segregation. There are, further, forms of mobilization which seek to conquer cultural and linguistic autonomy and adequate representation rights (Jews, Tartars, Turks, Greeks). Finally, we find the reemergence of historical forms of extremist and reactionary nationalism, predominantly defensive in charac-ter, of which the Ukraine is a salient example.

The impact of changes in economic policies and of the opening-up of the political system has definitively compromised the system's previous ability to keep conflicts under control. Liberalization creates disequilibria, brings long-established inequalities to the surface and creates new ones. Groups and regions find their relative situations and their relationships with the central power suddenly exposed. Where these conditions encounter an urban middle class socialized to the modest liberalization of the 1960s, ethno-nationalist mobilization burgeons into a movement and achieves better results in terms of the democratization and modernization of civil society.

The wind from the East therefore warns Western societies of a historical legacy fraught with dangers, but at the same time advises them that not everything which appears archaic is actually so: at the heart of the most enduring problems of the disintegrating empire lies an enormous potential for innovation. But the East European crisis conveys a further message: the solution of dramatic ethnic-territorial problems depends on the ability of political systems to accept differences and to render them negotiable. Here lies the greatest weakness of those societies that, through the collapse of the political system into the state, were for too long prevented from turning political relations into an arena for the negotiated settlement of conflicts. It is on the reconstitution of a civil society worthy of the name, and of a political system able to regulate differences without annihilating them, that the fragile hopes for democracy in Eastern Europe depend.

Ethnicity, nation, territory

The processes outlined above (the revival of old nationalism in the West, the emergence of new territorially-based claims, new ethnic conflicts, the growth of nationalism in Eastern Europe and other parts of the world) have substantially altered, as well as complicated, the analytical framework for the analysis of ethnic and cultural conflicts. In the 1970s it was still easier to treat ethno-nationalist movements as phenomena empirically distinct from politics based on territorial interests, and from non-territorial ethnic conflict. The positioning of these movements within the area of the social movements of the 1960s and 1970s highlighted their specificity with respect to neighbouring phenomena, and even more so with respect to the still-dormant societies of Eastern Europe. Today, typological distinctions are much more difficult to draw, and there is an even greater need for the methodological criterion I have for long called for to govern analysis of collective phenomena, the one which also underpinned my own study of ethno-nationalist movements (Melucci and Diani 1992): namely, that it is impossible to treat collective phenomena as a unitary empirical datum, and that we must disassemble analytically what, in current discourse and in the perception of the actors themselves, is a monolithic reality. Adoption of this criterion is necessary if adequate account is to be given of the multiple processes that constitute the empirical field of nationalism, ethnicity, and territorial interests. These processes, although overlapping and intertwined, are qualitatively distinct, and understanding them requires a wide array of conceptual tools.

In our time, the cultural models of central societies impose themselves as self-evident and universal codes of behaviour and communication. They thus erase, along with all difference, also the very possibility for communication, which always has as its prerequisite equality just as it does diversity. The ethnic-territorial impulse bound up in age-old national questions together with the added burden of intricate and delicate political problems channels and conceals a new and crucial need among individuals and groups in the society of total communication: that of existing in diversity in order to coexist.

Ethnic and cultural conflicts embed their roots in the past, and they extend historical questions tied to modern state building into the present. But they also add elements of marked discontinuity to this legacy; elements which stem from the changes currently under way in contemporary societies. Without these roots, mobilizations would lose all social consistency and their followers; they would indeed dissolve into merely symbolic expressions herded into reservations as tourist attractions or consigned to museums as ethnic artifacts. Were they unable to count on the conflictual energies released by emerging needs, they would soon subside as regressive forms of resistance, archaic residues from a past tenaciously resistant to change.

There are theories which regard the ethnic revival as the reappearance of class solidarity in a different guise: the onset of modernization and the integration of the working class into the system of industrial relations shifts class conflict and exploitation to centre–periphery relationships. Although these analyses of present conflicts retain a certain validity as regards more economically backward contexts, they nevertheless tend to ignore the complexity of the elements involved in contemporary mobilizations: ethnic and cultural identity presents itself simultaneously as a revenge for old and recent forms of discrimination, as a lever applying pressure on the political market, and as a response to identity needs in highly differentiated societies; frequently at issue are also relationships among different ethnic groups in multi-ethnic societies, and conflicts among states over the definition of borders and the rights of their respective minorities. All these analytically distinct dimensions combine into concrete phenomena, but their theoretical and political significances should not be confused.

Many conflicts develop in order to protect a group's culture and to restore its vitality. The cultural dimension of ethnic conflicts has been frequently pointed out (Horowitz 1977) and it has been an important component of any national consciousness, even if it does not necessarily refer to a unified set of values and beliefs (Gellner 1987; Burke 1992; Billig 1995). A mobilization of this kind may be regressive and highly conservative, or else it may embed the needs of a society abandoning industrialism and moving towards planetary integration in a well-established historical heritage. A basis of cultural traditions is vital in order to create new symbolic systems in which the codes and languages of the past are used to express the needs and conflicts of complex societies: the need for independent identification outside the control and standardization of the dominant culture finds fertile terrain in ethnic cultures.

Ethnic and cultural issues also involve the distribution of social resources and opportunities by exposing old and new inequalities: those crystallized by social segregation and with an age-old history, and those which result from modernization and from development in conditions where the periphery depends on the centre. In the political arena, two problems crucial to complex societies are brought to the surface: that of new rights for all members of the collectivity, most notably the right to be different; and the right to autonomy, or to control over a specific life-space (which in many cases is also the territory in which the culture puts down its physical roots).

In terms of political action, this requires opening up of new channels of representation, granting of access to excluded interests, reformation of the decision-making processes and the rules of the political game. The focus of such change is the historical legacy of the nation state, but also the contemporary form of the state as the agent of rationalization policies aimed at reducing complexity. The contemporary state is radically different from its original model, and its internal combination of public intervention and private interests produces pressures for standardization which most of all affect minority groups. Ethnic and cultural mobilizations denounce the normalizing function of public policies and demand a different form of participation in their definition.

Again, in the political arena one should not forget that ethnic conflicts bring out problems tied to the political cohabitation of diverse groups and cultures within highly segmented societies. In these cases, the question raised simultaneously concerns the forms of political democracy and of distributive justice.

A final, crucial aspect of ethnic mobilizations as regards their territorial dimension concerns the relationships among states whose boundaries have been created without regard to cultures or peoples. This aspect clearly evidences the supranational or, as we shall see, transnational dimension of ethnic-national questions.

Within this multi-dimensional picture, the revival of regional and local conflict (as epitomized for example by the regional Leagues in Italy in the late 1980s, see Diani 1996) contribute to the increase in the combinatory and conjunctural character of the ethnic and cultural impulse: 'combinatory' since it merges a set of distinct elements into a societal vehicle fuelled by discontent directed against the central state; 'conjunctural' because this combination can only come about in the presence of precipitating factors (economic crisis, the failure of reformist policies, and so on) which generate various forms of discontent and fuse them together. Unless these diverse elements are kept analytically separate, and unless distinct and appropriate conceptual schemata are applied to them, discussion of territorial and culturally-based phenomena inevitably lapses into the stereotype and interminable debate about their 'Rightist' or 'Leftist' character.

Identity as problem

With their multiple and distinctive features, ethnic and cultural conflicts bring to light a new dimension of social identification processes. In the course of capitalist development, industrialization and urban concentration upset traditional social and territorial equilibria. Nevertheless, the new urban-industrial model still preserved a certain coherence between the positions occupied by the various social groups with respect to dominant production relations and the distinctive traits of these same groups. Corresponding to a segmented social order, with strong class distinctions, was a polarization of cultures with little interpenetration among them. Those born into the bourgeoisie and the working-class of Liverpool, Lyon, Milan, or Düsseldorf belonged to two different worlds, spoke different languages, dressed, ate and behaved in different ways. In the segmented and relatively stable social order of industrial capitalism, the subordinate classes and the marginal geographical areas within the national state continued to enjoy, paradoxically, relative cultural autonomy guaranteed by social distance and based on a lifestyle, behaviour and language at odds with those of the dominant culture. As in the relationships among classes, so in the relations between centre and periphery segmentation entailed isolation and dependence but also ensured a degree of cultural autonomy. The central state could impose its rules, its language and its policemen on ethnically based regions, but it could not exert its control over the deep-reaching texture of the culture and over the fine-spun yet highly resilient fabric of day-to-day living.

After the Second World War, all the Western societies underwent intense and rapid processes of modernization which reached their climax in the 1960s. These processes are now spreading at varying pace to other parts of the world: to Eastern Europe, Japan and East Asia, and Latin America. The modernization that progressively changes the face of capitalist industrial society – varyingly named as late capitalism, postindustrial society, complex society – has a direct influence on the social enclaves of minority cultures and drags them into the huge machine of a transnational society governed by information. The intensification of exchanges, the circulation of peoples, the diffusion of the messages and lifestyles that constitute mass culture destroy the autonomy and relative internal unity of separate cultures: the deep penetration of the standardized and increasingly visual language of the media, migrations, and mass tourism threaten specific cultures and drive them towards extinction (Featherstone 1990; Robertson 1992; Friedman 1994). The relative homogeneity and internal solidarity of ethnic groups, already weakened by industrialization, are shattered by the enormous differentiation produced by complex systems, and individuals find themselves enmeshed in networks of functional and fragmented relations that are instituted by the great organizations. It is these latter which assume many of the functions traditionally performed by solidarity based on ethnicity, and they extend their influence to embrace and regulate everyday social behaviour and even the meaning of individual action itself.

However, because of their very complexity, these new social relationships are vulnerable to a certain fragility, and they do not always secure for individuals and groups that stability of belonging and that certainty of identification which usually define social identity (see Chambers 1994; Melucci 1996). Because of the resources that they distribute, contemporary systems increase the need of individuals and groups for self-fulfilment, communication, and appropriation of the meaning of action, but they also expose them to the risk of fragmentation and smoothing into conformity. Faced with highly impersonal social relationships governed by the logic of organizations, traditional solidarity, ethnic identification, and the particularism of language may constitute a response to the need of individuals and groups to assert their difference; and they simultaneously ensure a unified identity which is not perceived as standardization.

For this reason, the ethnic, cultural and nationalist impulses are not solely, nor necessarily, triggered by discrimination or exploitation. Individuals and groups find themselves acting in situations of uncertainty bereft of stable reference criteria. Ethnicity, above all when referring to a real territory, to a 'motherland', is brought back to life as a source of identity because it corresponds to a collective need in information societies to lend certainty and meaningfulness to action. This criterion is selected among all those available, because, as we shall see, it is able to counteract the risk of disintegration inherent in a highly differentiated society: primary belonging and 'homeland' are *counterinformation* to be injected, as elements of resistance or even opposition, into the grand scenario of mass culture.

Ethic identity is losing its biological connotations, and its roots in cultural tradition are weakening. It has become a problem of cultural choice, a reservoir from which individuals and groups draw their identity. It is not that the biological features or cultural roots (primary socialization, language, tradition) that constitute ethnicity have disappeared; rather, for an enlargening proportion of the population today defined 'objectively' by ethnic traits these constitute an area of cultural choice in which self-identification can be grounded. For another sector of the population, however, they are the shrinking roots of a world onto which it holds with tenacious attachment. The two processes are certainly connected, for they take place within the same ethnic or ethnic-territorial group (Anderson 1991; Werbner and Anwar 1991; Gilroy 1987, 1993a, 1993b). But they should not be confused. Whereas the former is destined to succumb to the planetarization and cultural integration of a global society – while resorting to even violent forms of resistance – the latter may become the driving force behind a mobilization which asserts the right of peoples and cultures to the self-determination of their difference.

Identity is not something that is permanently given. Instead, it is a process of identity-formation which constructs and reconstructs itself in the life-course of individuals and groups and through their different faces, roles, and circumstances. How stability can be created in this process, how links and continuities to self-recognition are secured, is a further problem to be addressed by the social actors of complexity (Melucci 1996). Ethnic identity is thus a container which offers individuals and groups a high degree of certainty in an uncertain world – the certainty of uniqueness and stability, because calling oneself a Breton, an Armenian, Irish, African-American, Native American and so on marks both an irreducible uniqueness and a distinct and incontestable difference from others; and the certainty of memory, because the definition is imbued with the past and for this reason becomes enduring. Hence, although the traditional roots of ethnicity are fading away (under the impact of assimilation, migrations, mass culture), it may be chosen as a criterion for identification which ensures permanence and history to identity.

When territory is added to identity, one reaches to the most profound dimensions of human experience to be mobilized; the reptilian memory surviving in the limbic system of our brains is still the original source of our experience. A person's place of origin not only has the force of tradition on its side, it rests on an even deeper bond which fuses together biology and history. For this reason, the combination of ethnicity and territory has an explosive power which mobilizes the most recondite and enduring energies, those elements in a people and its individuals which remain non-negotiable. Account must be taken of this power before one can expect to explain the strength of that which may be considered a regressive attachment and to understand the dynamic impulse which utilizes all the energy of profundity to project it into the future. Both of these forces are operationalized in ethno-nationalist movements. When working against each other, they only produce aimless violence or cultural death; but when combined, a strong potential for change may be released.

The processes of rapidly accelerating development have emphasized differences and multiplied the channels of communication. Even peripheral areas have been exposed to 'central' models. Meanwhile, institutional constraints have slackened, and traditional social structures are no longer able to ensure group cohesion. Identity based on ethnicity and nationality as a cultural choice is a response to these processes. While other criteria of belonging relax their hold or recede into the background, ethnic solidarity responds to a need for what is principally a symbolic identity. It provides roots embedded in all the power of a language, a culture, and an ancient history for needs and conflictual pressures which transcend the specific conditions of the ethnic group. The 'innovative' component of ethnic identity reaches beyond the protest against discrimination and beyond demands for political rights: it has a cultural character in the strict sense of the term, for the ethnic and cultural impulses raise their challenge against complex society on such fundamental issues as the direction of change and the production of symbols and meaning. Rooted in a heritage of social relations and symbols, with its vital sap of language, difference finds its voice and speaks to the society as a whole of one of its fundamental dilemmas: of how to preserve the meaning of human behaviour and the richness of diversity in a global society (de Certeau 1986; Fabian 1983; Spivak 1987).

Multiculturalism is a notion that has recently entered in academic and political discussion to address the issue of cultural differences (for an overview, see Locke 1992; Taylor 1992). A self-reflexive attitude should however guide the usage of this notion from the very beginning: Why has multiculturalism become such an important issue, with both scholars and popular audiences today taking considerable interest in it? In terms of a sociology of knowledge, the growing interest in multiculturalism should be connected to the characteristics of a society constructed and shaped by information. The issue of multiculturalism has assumed its controversial character as, in fact, it is not an unified conceptual object but a field of cultural and political debates reflecting the deep changes which our society is undergoing at the world-scale. The discussion of multiculturalism is not by chance related to the discourse on racism and anti-racism. These discourses, implying in their background the dramatic reality of phenomena such as globalization, migrations, exclusion, intergroup conflicts, are never only academic, but increasingly political. They address critical issues of present society and strive to make sense of the many differences with which we are confronted in a world that has transformed itself into a single arena for cultural, political, and economic debates. The conflicting definitions of these notions are all symptoms of the fact that we are living in a society which is increasingly shaped by information and defined by its cultural dimensions; in it, the differences in cultures and the definition of cultures themselves become critical social and political issues wich affect economic and social policies (for example, on racist discourse, see van Dijk 1987, 1992; Wetherell and Potter 1992; on anti-racist movements, Peterson 1994). The notion of multiculturalism is not yet a concept, analytically clear and distinctively applicable. It is more of a stake in cultural and political debates. It can constitute a goal and a political objective for highly innovative cultural movements, but also, and equally likely, a banner for a new rhetoric open to manipulation by elites seeking to impose the functional ideology to support their position and agenda as ways of control over the increasingly differentiated social environment.

A dimension of conflicts which traverses all ethnic and cultural movements is entirely new and does not belong to these social actors alone as their privilege: it takes shape as a *conflict of nomination*, conflict over the meaning of words and things in a society in which the name to an increasing degree supplants reality. It is precisely because of this that language, through ethnic and linguistic identity, becomes so important: in today's information society, the manner in which we nominate things at once decides their very existence. The language component in ethnic conflicts is therefore not solely a claim for a traditional right. It raises the crucial question of whether it is possible today to *nominate differently*. Thus, the right to autonomy in the construction of the world is affirmed in the diversity of language. Different languages bring different worlds into being, and the bond with the mother tongue (another dimension of the womb!) enables the individual to name the world as she or he wishes, resisting or opposing the standardized lexicon imposed by the planetary centres of mass culture.

Traditional language adds the richness of its own semantic distinctiveness to this general linguistic function. Traditional language evokes the names of a disappearing world, poor in technology but rich in relationships with nature and driven by subtle forces external and internal to mankind. At the deepest layers of human culture, traditional language opposes the nuances of light and shade to the neutral functionalism of technological language, the newspeak of information technology and advertising, the formalization of fragmented human experience. The loss of this richness is nothing short of a loss of humanity itself. Ethnic and cultural movements speak for everyone – fortunately, still in their own language.

Culture is increasingly shaped by anonymous apparatuses imposing the names and the languages through which people should understand and relate to reality. Naming the world in a different way challenges this homogenization and the imposition of standardised codes. In this respect ethnic and cultural conflicts join other recent forms of collective action challenging the new powers, which tell people how to name reality. But difference represents only one side of human relations. Community, solidarity, communication are the other side. When difference alone becomes the watchword, the results can be paradoxical and possibly leading to dramatic forms of fundamentalism and violence. Fighting tribes can be an outcome (Maffesoli 1995) and political correctedness can result in a new prison (Berman 1992; Hugues 1993). The problem is never mere difference, but rather the parallel necessity to overcome it, to make the constant effort of listening and understanding each other. In a highly differentiated world, values no longer bear the seal of the absolute, and their only foundation lies in the human capacity for agreement. Ethnic and cultural movements have been the first announcement of this enormous cultural change already well on its way.

9

A search for ethics

Ecology and pacifism

The emergence of the environmental issue is primarily a manifestation of a systemic problem. It reveals, that is to say, the reality of the network of global interdependencies in which a modern society is inserted, and the society's fundamental inability to comprehend individual structures and processes of social life without taking into account the links between them. The sheer fact of the completed planetary interdependence makes it obvious that linear causality is no longer conceivable as a possible foundation of historical dynamic, and that we belong to systems where the circularity of causes entails the restructuring of cognitive patterns and of our expectations of reality. The environmental issue, moreover, brings the cultural dimension of human experience to the fore. It demonstrates that lying at the heart of the question of survival is no longer the problem of the expedient system of means (on which both goal-directed rationality and the calculus of political exchange are based), but the problem of ends – that is, of those cultural models which orient behaviour and on which daily life, production, exchange, and consumption structure themselves. No livable future can be imagined unless we change our social relations and the circulation of information before simply improving our technical apparatuses. Today, acting on things means acting on symbolic codes; effectively operating on things depends on the cultural models which organize our day-to-day social relations, political systems, and forms of production and consumption.

The problems of the environment involve individuals *qua* individuals, not as members of a group, a class, or a state, whereas earlier in the modern age, it was these forms of belonging that constituted the basis for interests and solidarity. That the survival of the species can only be ensured by preserving the balance between man and nature is today a problem that affects the life of each and every individual. Change, therefore, cannot be separated from individual action; direct and personal investment becomes the condition and resource for intervention in the system.

Lastly, the environmental question signals that the conflict is a physiological dimension of complex systems. The differentiation of interests and social memberships, the uncertainty that characterizes human action on the environment and on the society itself, creates a permanent quota of conflict. Acknowledging that conflict can only be managed, never eliminated, entails that we must redefine the criteria according to which communal life is governed, by undertaking to render differences transparent and negotiable.

There are environmental movements today in nearly all countries (for examples, see Capek 1993; Jahn 1993; Dalton 1994; Diani 1995; Szasz 1995; Yanitsky 1991). The electoral successes of the 'Green' representatives may indeed have been the result of processes internal to the electoral markets of various countries. Nevertheless, they would be incomprehensible were we to ignore the forceful impact on voters of the issues raised by the environmentalists (see e.g. Kitschelt 1989). Various interests and objectives converge in campaigns to defend the environment and to build a better-quality life: forms of mobilization and protest by communities threatened by development projects involving serious environmental risks (Walsh 1988); voluntary associations acting as national pressure groups and transformed by electoral successes into environmental lobbies; new elites with specific technical and cultural skills highly sought-after in the market, by the media, and for the political system; networks of a molecular environmentalism where alternative lifestyles form the basis for solidarity.

The political activism of the environmental movements is their most visible feature. But the performance of the various 'Greens' at the ballot boxes has also brought along with it the danger that previous political elites recycle themselves exploiting the new ecological issues on the agenda. This risk is heightened by the competition among political actors seeking to appropriate environmental problems into the party platforms so as to enlarge the consensus base on which they rely. Within the movements themselves, their political participation fosters the growth of elites equipped with better skills in the political market and able to interact with their competitors more effectively than militants recruited directly through goal-directed mobilization. Institutional action is thus detached from everyday networks and the mobilization is deprived of its cultural substratum.

Peace mobilizations, too, which have been often associated with environmental concerns, coagulate a submerged nebula and bring it to the surface by providing an external field of action with political effects for the various solidarity networks that operate in different areas of society (Rochon 1988; Marullo and Lofland 1990; Lofland 1993; Kleidman 1993; Flam 1994). What the networks have in common is the contractual and short-term nature of the mobilization, the close link between collective goals and individual change, their thrust as a symbolic challenge which poses the problem of ends, the impossibility of distinguishing between the instrumental and the expressive character of the action (Kriesi 1988; Schennik 1988; Klandermans 1994). Besides its effects on nuclear and military policies (Kitschelt 1986; Meyer 1990, 1993), pacifism has had transnational effects with a forceful impact on the general system of planetary relations (Hegedus 1988; Ekins 1992). Collective action for peace operates as a symbolic multiplier. By eschewing the logic of instrumental efficiency dear to the techno-military apparatus, pacifist action strikes at the very foundations of the powers that be. By forcing the apparatus to justify its deeds, it lays bare its weaknesses.

The message of peace movements for planetary consciousness is that, like individual life, the survival of systems is no longer guaranteed by a metasocial order or by the necessity of History registered in its laws. The fate of the species and of human society depends on the perilous decisions taken by the species itself.

In the culture of ecological and peace movements there are two, necessarily complementary roads towards the goal of a transformation of the relations between society and its survival. The first is a 'top-down' approach, embodied in the ideas of the new intellectual-political elite, whom the negative backwash of experience in the movements of the 1970s (such as ideological readings of reality, separatism and sectarianism) often prevents from keeping abreast with the changing terms of the conflict, of the front lines of struggle, and of the forms of action which the diffuseness and pervasiveness of power imposes in a complex society. This elite represents a generation still caught midway between the old and the new, and which in recent years has attempted to escape from the gilded but marginalizing ghetto in the intellectual avant-garde of the movement, beginning to offer experience and professionalism to politics and to the market and demanding recognition from these in return. It should be said, however, that one of the conditions for this recognition to be afforded resides in the capacity of these elites to provide, together with their ideas and intellectual output, also the tools with which the ideas can be put into practice; to provide, in other words, not just an alternative point of view, but also the means whereby it can be made practicable. This component of eco-pacifism and environmentalism, beyond its proposal of an antagonistic culture, is still not able to carry forward a political design which comprises instruments and models of transformation *compatible* with the historical, economic, and social context in which it operates. In the meantime, as it waits to move into the corridors of power, this generation of intellectuals and 'politicians' must content itself with weaving its 'new and other' knowledge into the interstices of official wisdom and power, shuttling constantly between non-recognition and integration, while the effects of its action at the systemic level reach no further than instigation of cultural innovation or institutional modernization.

On the other hand, there are groups ready to run the risk of integration, in the interest of achieving a possibility to carry out their plans. This is a 'bottom-up' and disenchanted approach, compared to the 'purist' tradition of Left militantism, and adopted by the younger generation. Bolstered by the knowledge that the ecologist movement and culture will have to wait some time before it moves into the 'room at the top', these groups act at their own specific level, aiming at precise, concrete, and unifying goals. For this core of the movement, the institutions and the market are not traps to be avoided but instruments to be utilized to the extent to which they enable the achievement of environmentalist goals. Better accustomed to wielding the same weapons as their adversaries, these actors may perform a modernizing role within the institution, while their behaviour towards the outside translates into institutional support or 'alternative' entrepreneurship.

At the level of the movement, a merger between these two components seems neither easy nor certain. It represents both the necessary synthesis and the dilemma of ecologist action ('think globally, act locally'). An increasing incorporation of the environmental and peace issues into politics and institutional life is likely to occur at the operational level. The moral dimension of these issues will, on the other hand, continue to fuel societal debates and future mobilizations.

Altruistic action

The emergence in complex societies of voluntary forms of action, especially in the areas relating to health and caring, has occurred at a time of an exacerbated crisis of the welfare models, when their decline is already evident even in the societies which first introduced them. These forms of action comprise a variety of heterogeneous components which are difficult to bring together under a single category. We should, however, realize that what we are also dealing with in this case is a type of collective action, here called 'altruistic action' – not the state or the market, nor private solidarity or interindividual exchange, even though all these dimensions combine to define the boundaries of the empirical field (see Kramer 1981; Alexander 1987; Wuthnow 1991a, 1991b; see also Verba *et al.* 1995).

What distinguishes altruistic action as a sociological category is the voluntary nature of the social constraint that governs it. A voluntary actor joins a form of collective solidarity of her/his own free will, and belongs to a network of relations by virtue of personal choice. Another feature is the gratuitous nature of the work supplied through altruistic action. This gratuitousness, however, does not simply lie in the fact that voluntary workers receive no direct economic rewards for their action. If, for example, a person voluntarily and without compensation provides assistance to her/his neighbour in gardening, this action is a form of private solidarity regulated by interpersonal exchange. In order for action to count as altruistic action, its gratuitousness must concern the relation that ties the actors involved together in the collective action. The distinctive feature of altruistic action is that economic benefits do not constitute the basis of the relationship among those involved, nor between them and the recipients in the performed action (unlike, for instance, the case of payment in a work relationship).

Altruistic action is therefore a form of action characterized by a voluntary bond of solidarity among those who participate in it, and by the fact that they do not derive any direct economic benefit from that participation. As regards other kinds of reward (symbolic advantages, prestige, self-esteem, power), such are present in altruistic action just as much as they are in any other form of social exchange. Altruistic action may also yield indirect economic benefits, insofar as the voluntary worker acquires special abilities, establishes networks of influence, or acquires leadership skills (for example, the volunteer may learn professional skills in a certain field, or establish professionally or politically advantageous relationships).

Implicit in what was just said are two further dimensions, which will serve to round out our definition of altruistic action. First, such action is undertaken in order to achieve objectives shared by all those involved, although there may also be a multiplicity of secondary objectives pursued by individuals and subgroups. Moreover, the action requires some form of organization for its prosecution, even when that organization will not coincide with an institutionalized associative structure.

The empirical reality addressed by altruistic action also has a distinctive character, which relates to the nature of its objectives. The action is, in fact, specifically aimed at producing benefits or advantages for subjects other than the volunteers, and it therefore takes the form of a service provided or a good distributed to others. Furthermore, its gratuitous nature lies not just in the work supplied by the volunteers, but in the free fruition of its product by the recipients. Self-help groups form a special case of this kind of orientation. While they seek to provide benefits to their participants, it is only by acting beyond her/his immediate interest that the participant can help the others and be helped in return. In general terms, altruistic action can be thus defined as a form of collective, purposive, and organized social altruism.

We may now ask ourselves why such a widespread willingness to engage in altruistic action has arisen in contemporary complex societies, and what are the individual and collective needs satisfied by it. To address these questions, we must single out from the phenomenon as a whole a number of profoundly different kinds of behaviour. First, it includes elements of traditional philanthropy, of lay or religious inspiration. The characteristic feature of traditional philanthropy is its paternalism; helping others or redistributing resources is an act of 'grace', the duty of the strong and the privileged towards the weak and the unfortunate. The Rich Man (formerly the King or the Nobleman) must concern himself with the 'poor' because he is responsible for them before God (or, in the lay version, before the moral law). Closely associated with philanthropy, but nevertheless distinct from it by virtue of certain significant analytical features, is populism. The behavioural orientation fundamental to populism is its dichotomous view of society, not in terms of relations but according to the high/low or, perhaps, centrality/marginality distinction. On the one hand stands Power, perceived as an abstract and alien Moloch; on the other, those who are excluded and in search of redemption. The cleavage so depicted is metaphysical in character, and cannot be represented as a relationship between social positions; the latter would involve the constitutive inclusion of interaction, exchange, conflict, and interdependence, which no dualistic conception can handle. Populism seeks to heal this rift detected in society by resorting to a totalizing vision, a 'religion of salvation', which may be couched in either strictly religious or lay language. Populism as a religion of salvation may assume the form of provision of care, and usually stands as an alternative to violence, the other head of the populist doctrine. The boundary between the two is often very fine, and populism almost always wavers between a pauperist-welfarist vocation and a radicalism that promptly becomes the energy of violence.

A third orientation of altruistic action links directly with the effects of modern welfare systems and their social policies. This is the reaction by individuals and groups against public measures designed to deal with a social need. Such a reaction may be markedly defensive in character, when it is triggered by overintrusive state intervention and seeks to defend those areas of experience deemed private and secured from the interference of the *res publica*. Alternatively, such action may denounce and seek to offset the culpable shortcomings of the welfare system. According to the national features of the welfare system and to the specific historical process of implementing the social policies, reactions against the excesses or absence of welfare provisions may fuse together due to the simultaneously deficient and intrusive nature of public welfare policies.

One orientation of action certainly not new to the tradition of the Anglo-Saxon democracies (but more recent in Latin countries, for example) is community activism. At work here is the desire that personal action manifest one's citizenship, and that its attendant right-cum-duty contribute to collective life, even in its everyday dimensions. Action is intended to create opportunities for participation; it expresses membership in a civil community, and it makes tangible people's sense of belonging and their feeling that they are bound by duty to work towards common goals (see Etzioni 1993 for an example of the recent communitarian appeal in the US).

Finally, there are orientations of altruistic action which belong to the analytical dimension of social movements, as I defined it in chapter 1. This is the dimension of symbolic challenge where conflictual forms of behaviour are directed against the processes by which dominant cultural codes are formed. It is through action itself that the power of the languages and signs of technical rationality are challenged. By its sheer existence, such action challenges power, upsets its logic, and constructs alternative meanings. Altruistic behaviour and a commitment to altruistic action contain this dimension of symbolic challenge, for it sets against the rationality of calculation and the efficiency of technique as a means-end relationship the gratuitousness of the gift, direct personal commitment to the here and now, and the desire for unmanipulated human communication. In sum, altruistic action indicates that the encounter with the 'other' is not reducible to the instrumental logic.

From these considerations we may deduce some of the functions performed by altruistic action in contemporary societies. First of all, new elites are recruited and trained. Altruistic action shapes and develops technical, professional, and political skills which can be subsequently traded on the market or used in public institutions. Secondly, participation in altruistic action has an expressive function for those involved. The psychological and social gratification that may derive from an altruistic act, the sense of belonging to a network of peers, the intense emotional experience of witnessing suffering first-hand – all these charge participation with a highly expressive content. Thirdly, altruistic action performs a distinct democratizing function: it institutes a process by which channels of participation are broadened, their flexibility is extended, and decision-making processes are disclosed. Put differently, altruistic action fosters the increasing autonomy of 'civil society' and its ability to exert pressure on the political institutions. Fourthly, altruistic action functions as a form of social control: it absorbs a certain amount of tension and potential unrest by occupying itself with the social outcasts that every society produces and which complex contemporary societies seem destined to generate in increasing numbers. Alongside their inability to dispose of the material rubbish of everyday life, complex societies appear unable to handle the social debris created by the processes of exclusion, discrimination, and pauperization that urban culture generates and reproduces. Altruistic action clears up urban waste and, at times, proceeds to recycle it. As harsh or even cynical as the statement might seem, it will still be necessary to recognize this particular function of altruistic action, over and above its subjective, ethical, or religious motivations. The 'salvational' urge that is often the motive force behind altruistic action thus blends with the structural requirements of complex systems to dispose of or recycle its social refuse.

Lastly, altruistic action discharges a change-inducing function, in which two aspects can be distinguished. The first of these is innovation. Altruistic action is the laboratory where cultural, organizational, and relational models subsequently transferred into the market or the institutions are developed. In operation here is also the recruitment of elites as discussed earlier. The second aspect concerns the prophetic function of altruistic action. Its very presence reveals and announces: it discloses the hidden existence of the great dilemmas ingrained in the constitution and operation of complex societies, and it announces the possibility of the otherness. Behind the formal neutrality of technical procedures, behind the 'objectivity' of scientific rationality, altruistic action signals the persistence of human needs and demands which cannot be reduced to routines. It reminds us of society's limited power over nature and over men, it declares to us that communication and relationships with the other are more than mere exchange.

By doing so, altruistic action calls into question the old dreams of power and glory and invites us to seek change and to assume responsibility. It brings to light, lays bare, and rescues from silence. And, for this reason, when it is not catering to psychological needs for self-esteem or serving in functions of social prosthesis, altruistic action becomes a vital component in the renewal process towards a 'civil society' that lives up to its name: a *civitas* both public and individual, and endowed with the ability to accommodate a space for difference and to reinforce solidarity.

The spiritual quest

Some of the collective phenomena examined in the preceding sections involve groups identifiable by a specific social condition. Others are much more intangible forms of mobilization or are identifiable principally in terms of the goals of their action. The collective processes which do not fall under any specific social category are those that make the cultural character of the conflict most directly explicit. But they are also those that are most obviously prone to fragmentation and liable to turn in on themselves, the ones most susceptible to evasive marginalization or, vice versa, to integration with the market and mass culture. An extreme example is provided by religious revivalism, which in recent years has proliferated in complex societies (Bromley 1987). There is no doubt that the chief characteristics of religious revivals are their escapism, their tendency to spawn sects, to transform themselves into 'churches' or multinational corporations selling 'holy commodities' perfectly attuned to the market (Robbins 1988, Wilson 1990). But it is equally clear that only an insensitive observer disposed to reductionism would be able to deny the collective urge that fuels such a renewed search for religious fulfilment.

The religious disenchantment of the contemporary world (Beckford 1989) has not only brought the death of the gods. Instrumental rationality has restored the world to mankind's scope of operation, but it also denies humanity all chances to transcend reality; it devalues everything that resists subsumption under the instrumental action. Society becomes a system of apparatuses identical with its own actions and intolerant of any diversity. The sacred thus reemerges as an appeal to a possible other, as the voice of what is not but could be. Divested of the ritual trappings of the churches, the sacred becomes a purely cultural form of resistance which counters the presumptions of power by affirming the right to desire – to hope that the world is more than what actually is. This projective, transcendent force is the antagonistic nucleus of the contemporary spiritual quest. It is a fragile nucleus, under attack from all sides as it is purely cultural. When this force takes physical form, it almost invariably turns into a church, a totalizing regressive Utopia, an appeal to the myth of rebirth. The totalizing integration of the sect or the 'mundanization' of an apparatus threatens the sacred more than ever before. The voice of the possible is soon reduced to silence.

Does spiritual experience convey conflictual contents? The answer may given in the affirmative, although such contents are expressed wholly at the symbolic level and concern specific groups only. The conflict, in fact, relates only to the control over the processes of the definition of meaning, as the capacity to give symbolic representation to action beyond its specific contents. If it is possible to speak of a 'challenge' raised by some groups engaging in spiritual practice, such a conflict is located precisely on this symbolic level and is not always openly critical of the social system. Its criticism is not directed against specific social structures and does not address the distribution of resources or of political power. It tends, instead, to be aimed at the production of meanings, values, behavioural models. Modern Western culture has given overwhelming priority to the material dimension of human experience, denying any relevance of the spiritual one. Some spiritual experiences reject massification and compliance with models of behaviour directed from outside, typical of a society that increasingly intervenes even in the tiniest spaces of everyday life.

Such criticism is also directed against the idea of global change, brought about by simply changing social structures. This idea encourages the flight from personal responsibilities, in the illusion that the positive effects of change will be automatically transferred to the individual. According to the tenets of many spiritual groups, change and understanding begin with oneself, and change should start from within the scope of one's own concrete experience and in minimal but real terms. One may not entertain aspirations as to the transformation of society and criticize its current workings without recognizing one's own responsibility for the present state of affairs, blaming that state instead on generic institutional apparatuses or structural mechanisms of the system in its entirety. Only under the condition of clarifying our minds and improving our consciousness can concrete changes be made in one's life.

It should be stressed that the potential antagonism of these forms of action lies entirely at the level of symbolic representations. Much more than hypothesizing an external modification of social relationships, the tendency exhibited by spiritual groups is to challenge the formal mechanisms of constitution of these relationships, their 'categorial' premises in our cognitive and affective ways of constructing them. This, however, does not mean repudiation of social action and commitment. If anything, it involves rejection of the meanings conventionally assigned to these concepts in the modern Western thought and a refusal to identify with them.

Transformation occurs through what may be called a cycle of death/rebirth. Transforming one's life entails a radical reassessment of one's approach to reality, a withdrawal from the dominant logic of representation of the social. The purpose of the endeavour, in fact, is not to add but take away something, to create space in which to operate. The moment of rebirth takes the form of a reconciliation with the world, for internal spiritual practice is not escapism from matters mundane. Indeed, it is the prerequisite for remaining in the world with greater awareness.

Altogether, therefore, the purpose of spiritual experience seems to be the learning of new interpretative codes of reality. The fact that the antagonism of a spiritually motivated group has purely cultural connotations, and that it is entirely without roots at the level of social organization or the political system, has various consequences on the possible outcomes and meanings of this kind of experience. First of all, the aspiration to unity and to the recasting of existence around a unifying principle may lead to a denial of the difference among the various ambits of life. At the same time, an exaggerated emphasis on inaction, on withdrawal from social relationships, may induce outright rejection of society as an autonomous and specific system, and it may encourage the search for a hypothetical presocial state of nature. Attitudes of this kind tend to fragment the antagonistic potential of the experience and push towards either individualism or communitarian integralism. In the former case, the priority given to the individual trans-formation generates reactions which oscillate between substantial accep-tance of dominant social relationships and isolated testimony to spiritual values. In the case of communitarian integralism, the group, but above all the cause with which it identifies itself, tends to become the only reference parameter. In both cases, the refusal to recognize the social nature of the experience encourages the manipulation and/or the commercialization of the message. It is of course also possible that this inner quest will not lead to the negation of the autonomous functioning of social relationships. The act of witness to spiritual values may in this case translate into group action on the terrain of cultural modernization, although it loses then its con-flictual nature. On the other hand, spiritual practice may lie at the basis of new forms of civil commitment by the individual.

In spiritual groups, different interpretations are given to the relationship between commitment to a spiritual message and forms of individual trans-formation. When an integralist point of view prevails, the nexus between these is almost automatic, for commitment to the message entails the dis-appearance of attitudes incompatible with it. From a less fundamentalist perspective, the causal relation is less linear.

A further difference concerns the type of relation hypothesized between individual spiritual experience and the testimonial act in society. The fundamentalist vision regards the continuum between the two phenomena as perfectly unbroken: the totalizing conception of religious experience entails restoring a global community and thinking of a society uniquely guided by spiritual values. In other groups, however, stress is placed on the difference of level between the spiritual message and the method of knowl-edge on the one hand, and the cultural and social form that spiritual expe-rience assumes on the other. It is acknowledged that the transposition of inner experience into a highly differentiated social reality raises real and largely unresolved problems. Fundamentalism not only affirms the primacy of the spiritual experience over the other spheres of life but also asserts the ambition and right of that religion to govern the functioning of the social system. Other spiritual groups acknowledge the complexity inherent in the relationship between religion and society and the autonomy of social and political processes.

According to the degree of prevalence of either an individualistic or a communitarian practice, fundamentalist attitudes can, respectively, lead to either an exaggerated individualization of experience or to a communitarian form of integralism. In other cases, a more 'lay' and desacralized spiritual practice is the frame of reference for action in society, and it can be expressed in an experiential form at the individual level or through a collective civil commitment, which may take the form of a direct intervention in society through cultural action or civil and political mobilization on specific issues like peace, environment, human rights (for an example on environmental issues, see Hornborg 1994).

Contemporary movements, and particularly those forms of action analysed in this chapter, tend to accentuate the cultural character of mobilizations, put forward by mutable actors. They are characterized by their desire to render actual what is only a possibility, to work for change in the here and now. The mobilization is rooted in a particular identity, in a difference, which becomes the fulcrum for a more general appeal, a lever with which to expose problems and stakes that go beyond the specific nature of the group. They bring to the surface the ethical dilemmas of our time (see Bauman 1993a, 1993b; Taylor 1992; Parfit 1984; Rorty 1989; Tronto 1987; Melucci 1996): the problems of identity, solidarity and responsibility, the links between humans and cosmos, our relationship to the invisible and the ineffable.

Contemporary movements are constantly exposed to the risk of being 'uprooted' from a symbolic universe incapable of influencing social relationships. Their function in conflict is to make power visible and force it to assume a shape. They thus give explicit form to conflicts and calls for change; they act as the engine of transformation and expose the lacunae, the contradictions and the silences that the dominant apparatuses seek to camouflage.

Latency and visibility are the conditions of the contemporary movements, which ceaselessly oscillate between them. As they do so, some actors disappear, others come to the fore. Processes of institutionalization and modernization gain in strength, but new problems arise and new areas of conflict open up. The cultural nature of movements raises the crucial problem of their relationships with political systems and the urgent question of developing structures for their representation and organization.

Before addressing these problems in part III and part IV, however, we need to pay further attention to the nature of power and domination in contemporary society.

10

Information, power, domination

Power and inequality

We are on the brink of transformations that will prove critical for our society. The quality and nature of information, as a cognitive and symbolic resource which is at the centre stage in the determination of the future, remains deeply ambivalent. The perspective inspired by Foucault (1970, 1979, 1980) tends to view the system as fully controlled through the manipulation by invisible power centres, which entirely organize our lives (see also Baudrillard 1975). Other authors, more inspired by Marxism, tend to see contemporary social movements as forms of opposition and resistance to a generalized capitalist power, which is taking over at the world scale (Castells 1983; Arrighi *et al.* 1989). The problem with these conceptions is that if power were a form of total control, collective action could not even be conceptualized in its conflictual capacity and it would be reduced to a pure *re*-action. But in social practice power itself is caught up in the same problem of the ambivalence of its own instruments, provided we are not to postulate a total system which is not only totalitarian, but a fully transparent society of pure domination, of which I frankly do not see any signs. In the symbolic realm, there is always ambivalence on both sides. Of course, imbalances, inequalities, and forms of domination persist, but since the emerging power is increasingly based not solely on material strength but on the production and circulation of information, it has today decisively exposed itself to its own weakness: where symbols enter the constitution of the field, they render it open to multiple interpretations and into something that is never under full control. What matters then is the construction of a sufficiently open arena of public spaces, where the conflicting nature of social issues can be expressed.

Under these circumstances, social scientists should be especially curious about all the situations where such ambiguity is manifested and appears at the surface. Whenever a new issue or dilemma is made visible through collective action, there appears a chance for redefining the public space. This happened when, for example, the gender issue was raised and openly addressed; in time, not only political life emerged affected but everyday lives, mental codes, and interpersonal relationships underwent transformations in the process. But as soon as the new theme is raised to the public sphere, it also creates new limits. Decision-making as a regulated and ordered mechanism is an elemental necessity of any political organization in performing a reduction of complexity without which contemporary systems cannot do, but for the very same reason it takes the shape of a selective process which excludes and suppresses some of the dynamic components of the issue. What has been excluded by the selection mechanisms of the political system remains nonetheless stubbornly alive in the society, facing the future of becoming either reduced to marginality or developing into a new voice for societal needs that can make itself heard.

One could argue that the symbolic dimension of collective action has been always present in social movements, and that, consequently, the effort invested in stressing the importance and the novelty of this aspect of the contemporary collective phenomena appears misguided by bias. Be that as it may, we have been today awakened to take a better notice of the symbolic thrust of collective action through our encounter in actual society with phenomena in which this particular level have become more dramatically salient. Starting from this new understanding, we can however proceed to apply the same question to other historical phenomena. Social movements of modern and premodern historical periods were deeply rooted in the material conditions of their environment, and their capacity for a symbolic elaboration and representation of this specific context was comparatively lower than it can be today. The capacity for symbolization and for cultural representation of social action evolves directly in proportion to the social capacity to produce symbolic resources. A society which is highly dependent on its material environment consequently possesses a lower capacity to produce an autonomous cultural sphere.

My work in this field of study has been accused of showing a tendency for cultural reductionism (Bartholomew and Mayer 1992). This criticism, however, is misconceived. Nowhere have I departed from the basic understanding that present social conflicts take the form of cultural confrontations precisely because of systemic reasons. Here we may consider the body, as an example of a sharply conflictual issue in our society (see Melucci 1989; Giddens 1992; Featherstone *et al.* 1991; Shilling 1993; Falk 1994) The body, up to now our objective anchor in nature, is currently undergoing a transformation into a domain of social intervention opened up for the enhancement of the individual capacity for self-definition and autonomy on the one hand, which, however, by the same token is readied for social manipulation by new forms of power (in fashion, advertising, medicine) on the other. Now, why these conflicts do not affect the whole of society but only certain areas or groups, is precisely what is to be explained. Sociological explanation of the levels of society being affected in each social conflict has to be 'structural'; but for this very reason it needs to incorporate in itself and conceptualize culture, which today has become the locus of production, power, and inequality.

Naturally, it would be extreme posturing to claim that membership in contemporary social movements is wholly 'cultural' and as such detached from a social condition. It is rather the case that the extent to which the constraints imposed on collective action by a social condition operate is variable. It is certainly difficult to separate the membership in a women's movement from the fact of being a woman. But the problem here is precisely how one defines such 'being a woman', or 'young', 'gay', or 'black'. Conditions such as these are to an ever-greater extent defined through cultural constructs which are only indirectly related to back their biological foundations and more and more connected to symbolic signs, lifestyles, and other personal choices. Today, who can decide whether a person in her/his thirties who dresses and behaves according to the associated style is part of the 'youth movement' or not?

The emphasis on the role of the symbolic dimension in societies based on information has been also criticized for under-evaluating the distinct role of material constraints, and particularly the significance of economic power in the determination of social action. Today, what we call material values or goods, however, are so overwhelmingly charged with symbolic investments and incorporate such a sophisticated quantity of information that it is difficult to evaluate them simply in economic terms. Through material goods people convey messages of themselves, their relationships, their gender position, their dreams of the future. Even money is no longer an objective medium, if it ever was, and today it is differentiated in a complex way which people increasingly invest with their own significance (Zelizer 1994). In other societies where the material constraints played a more direct and comprehensible role in the construction of people's lives, the language of material goods and natural forces was sufficient alone to allow people to make sense of their world.

The contemporary shift towards symbolic and informational resources bears thus on our definition of power and inequality as well. Inequality cannot be measured solely in terms of distribution and control of economic resources (Sen 1992); analysis of structural imbalances in society should refer more to a differentiation of positions which allots to some a greater and specific control over master codes, over those powerful symbolic resources that frame the information. There are organizers of information directing its flow which are more powerful, more stable than others: they 'inform' a wider portion of the field, they are keys to other information. The access to these primary codes is not distributed randomly and it corresponds to a distribution of social positions and power. But this is a new way of thinking about power and inequality, which, to reiterate, are still 'structural' in many ways but more temporary than in the past and more related to the production of nonmaterial resources. In order to detect these forms of power and inequality and to locate their site in a hierarchical arrangement in society we need a more comprehensive perspective which cannot simply draw on traditional theories – for example class analysis or the study of official elites in the political system (for a discussion of class analysis in contemporary society see Esping-Andersen 1993; Crompton 1993; and for class and collective action, Maheu 1995; Pakulski 1995; Eder 1993, 1995; for the role of symbolic resources in making inequalities, see Lamont and Fournier 1992). Whoever wants to research social movements and social conflicts should try to define the contested social field on both sides; not just analyse the forms of protest and popular mobilization but identify the new forms of power, locate the dominant discourse, and investigate the new elites.

What we already know provides us with many hints for an analysis of the new forms of power. The establishment of a world media system, which is a recent realization of the last ten years, operates basically as the manufacturer of master codes at the world scale. There are centres and people who decide the language to be used, the selection of information to be organized and broadcast throughout the world; the vast majority of people are simply users in the audience. There are decisions made about the popular culture market; there are centres controlling the languages of computers and the related information technologies; there are financial decision-making centres which move enormous amounts of economic resources through production and manipulation of information – all these are new forms of domination, whose power is based not on economic resources as such, nor on the fact that they exert influence or manipulate the local political system: the principal power is embedded in their capacity to organize the minds of people.

Master codes of this kind can be detected in different areas of society. Ideas enter the cultural and scientific debates not simply on account of their 'intrinsic' value, but according to the selection operated by scientific policies and institutions, by publishers and cultural markets. New centralities and marginalities are defined by this privileged contol of the production and diffusion of ideas.

Medical and mental health institutions set the standards of normal and pathological behaviour and diffuse them through prevention and information policies, mass screening processes, everyday medical practice. Even the so called 'alternative medicines' participate in the redefinition of medical standards that penetrate people's everyday behaviours (on medical power over the body see Turner 1992; Shorter 1992; on alternative medicines and their ambiguity, Salmon 1984; Sharma 1993; Wardwell 1994; Wolpe 1994)

The media system imposes at the world scale patterns of cognition and communication which work far beyond the specific contents diffused by the TV or the movies: the same soap operas seen in Australia, Alaska and Popular Republic of China do not convey only values or behavioural patterns, but structures of the mind and rules of emotional life.

The languages of computers are produced at the world scale by very few centres, that are increasingly shaping mental habits and physical skills: everywhere in the world people learn to 'open windows' and to compartimentalize their minds in 'files' and 'directories'; to work within the hidden boundaries imposed by programmes; to adapt their bodies to the constraints of screens and mouses.

Environmental expertise, partly issued from the environmental mobilization itself, creates the general criteria of a 'good' relation to nature and becomes the filter through which our 'natural' experience is perceived. We are already witnessing, for example, the first signs of potential conflicts between the 'rationalistic' environmentalism of Western experts and NGOs and the native cultures whose perception of nature and environmental concerns are not led by the same logic (for an example, see Hviding 1995).

The setting of political agenda is not just a matter internal to the political system (see chapter 12), but is increasingly organized by hidden priorities established by cultural and scientific codes: the choice among policies is already framed within these codes.

Consumption, sexuality, education and interpersonal relations are the realms where prescriptions of behaviour are continuously spread among the population through the packaging of merchandises, the production of manuals, the counselling activity of experts: here too, beyond the actual contents in terms of values or norms, what matters is the hidden operation of symbolic *forms*, patterning people's thoughts, emotions and feelings.

As mere consumers of information, people are excluded from the discussion on the logic that organizes this flow of information; they are there to only receive it and have no access to the power that shapes reality through the controlled ebb and flow of information. The 'structural' definition of differences is already incorporated in a system of meanings with no externalities. Even marginality or exclusion are increasingly defined in terms internal to the system, the 'without' is 'within', the difference is denied and the unbalance of power is made invisible. The master codes tend to include the deprived or the potential opponent as a dependent participant. The traditional ways of dealing with the 'other' consisted in refusing and expelling him/her or, alternatively, resorting to inclusion and assimilation. Today these strategies, still in operation, are losing their effectiveness and are substituted by a growing tendency to set the formal pre-conditions for any discourse and practice, where even the excluded is already incorporated.

Interestingly enough, what we are facing here is not a personal power, for the professionals working for the apparatuses of new power appropriately consider themselves in their large majority as employees of an organization. The emergent forms of power are apparently neutral and primarily functional in character, and one cannot readily address them as physical and as tangible entities of power, let alone personal. For this reason the problem has to be dealt simultaneously at both the cultural and the political level. By detecting master codes it is possible to think of forms of political control, which can render them visible and submit them to public confrontation, thus reducing their impact manifesting in inequalities, stabilization of privileges, and so forth. The more the public spaces are open, the more the codes can be appropriated in unpredictable ways and interpreted differently by the people and the more their ambivalence or polyvalence can be kept open. There is thus room created for negotiating different meanings and establishing the minimum agreement for living together on the shared planet.

The traditional Marxist analysis of ideology, its Gramscian development concerning cultural hegemony, and Althusser's analysis of ideological apparatuses could then be seen not so far apart from this kind of analysis of symbolic domination. In fact, ideology is the control exerted over the codes and languages, but it is conceived by Marx as the final and partly covered manifestation of a domination which starts rather in the deep material texture of the social structure. The Marxian idea of ideology as a superstructure corresponded to a dualistic view of a society where the material component of power and its organizational embodiment defined capitalist economy. This aspect was important and visible enough to, with culture as seemingly a residual dimension, provide Marx with elements to account for domination in a way that reduced the symbolic dimension to the status of a pure instrument of power. Already in the 1920s, however, Gramsci tried to correct this view and to accommodate a greater importance of the symbolic relationships between classes, and it was not by chance that his work coincided with the beginnings of mass society. It is precisely in a mass society shaped by information that the shift from the physical and organizational dimensions of power, through which it is embodied in structures, takes place towards the power of defining the sense of thoughts, behaviours, relations, and the action itself (on the role of the intellectuals in contemporary society see Eyerman 1994; Rootes 1995). But the Marxist legacy, even in Althusser's work on ideological appartuses, remains anchored to a dualistic view of social action and cannot but maintain a dichotomous opposition between culture and material structure, which today will no longer allow us to account for the cultural transformation of social production in complex society.

In the contemporary context, we can define exploitation as a form of dependent participation in the information flow, as the deprivation of control over the construction of meaning. The true exploitation is not the deprivation of information; even in the shantytowns of the cities of the Third World people are today widely exposed to the media, only they do not have any power to organize this information according to their own needs. Thus, the real domination is today the exclusion from the power of naming. It is the unreflected reception of the 'names' which frame human experiences, consumption, interpersonal relationships: the abiding by the rules implied in these names. To change such codes, it becomes necessary to reverse all the hidden rules upon which they are constructed. In the case of AIDS, for example, we have seen the difficulty for HIV positive persons, for gay people, for those who are ill and their families of introducing a human consideration of what at the beginning appeared a personal guilt and a moral scourge. Collective action, supported by scientists and doctors critical of the dominant medical paradigm, has succeeded in revealing the social and political nature of the definitions imposed by health apparatuses, and has to date achieved some significant results in changing public attitudes towards this very difficult human experience (Watney 1987; Gamson 1989).

Forms of resistance, withdrawal, and symbolic challenge

In the face of a hidden power which is channelled through information, elementary forms of resistance can express the need of escaping the excess of information that quickly turns into mere noise and experience of emptiness. There are spiritual components of the environmental cultures, of youth movements and new religious groups through which is expressed the new need to withdraw from social noise created by the overwhelming information flow. The risk involved here, however, is the transformation of spiritual needs into intolerant mysticism and the evolution of the movements themselves into sectarian organizations. It is very difficult to express such a need for withdrawal in pure cultural terms, and when it is transformed into social action it itself stands immediately in need of the support of an organization; and it is here that the form of the organization best equipped for effective resistance seems more often than not like a sectarian or escapist one.

However, beyond the outward appearance that may be assumed, it is important to understand that in a culture where communication becomes the means and content of domination, silence and retreat are forms of a resistance and express new needs through which alternative models of social life are experimented. Not to participate is the opposite of all the progressives' rhetoric of the nineteenth century ('Participate to have a voice!'). Today, however, we begin to see the other side to the call for inclusion and socialization – silence, retreat, and quasi-isolation as forms of resistance to the pervasive tendency of the system to exact participation, communication, the acceptance of one's assigned place in society as an effective processor of information. The pressure towards the required performance starts already in the kindergarten where, after the onset of the new pedagogic current stressing the importance of interaction, cooperation, and creativity, every instance of behaviour of the child who would rather prefer the calm of the corner to the incessant activity and clamour of the playroom is viewed with suspicion for pathological symptoms. This tendency is now generalized on a cultural level, with the values it propagates manifesting one of the dominant codes expressive of our society. Some movements are starting to bring to the surface and act towards the elaboration of precisely this neglected side of human experience: the need for silence and meaning.

The message of such movements is their action itself – not what they state for record or claim as its content, because they often do even not *ask* (for goods, advantages, reforms), they *bring* (make visible new meaning through their practice). This, then, represents a completely different way of challenging the institutional powers. Sometimes the movements, as it were, present the society with cultural gifts by their action: they reveal new possibilities, another face of reality. When they act, something has already been said by this very action; at once, the message has been incorporated into the social arena and the debates may commence. Whether or not the issues then become topics for political contestation depends on the extent to which they can be taken up by politically relevant agents or otherwise translated into political agendas for the public.

Here there is a conceptual gap to be filled that extends from the level of everyday experience to the level of collective action. Such continuum, however, can only be established through a change in the way we think about collectivity – no longer as a sum total of individuals but as a different relationship among individuals. In recent forms of collective action, starting with the culture of women's movements, there can be seen an effort to build a collective definition of the movement which strives to retain respect for individual differences. In contrast, the traditional way of defining the place of an individual in a working-class movement, for instance, was to conceive a militant committed to a collective ideal to which individuals themselves could legitimately be sacrificed. Self-sacrifice was elevated to the highest moral status, to an ethical value sanctioned by superior significance of the collectivity; the triumph of the working class as an abstract whole surpassed in importance any particular interest of the individual participant. But being an autonomous woman, or being a young person who opposes her/himself to the adult society, it is precisely the latter that in a new way becomes important for the individual in her/his own person – it matters no longer if the goals posted for the action will be reached in, say, twenty years if that action fails to change the person's life today.

There is, to be sure, a narcissistic side to this attitude, but the anti-narcissistic criticism of the new cultures under-evaluates the dimension of individual as fundamental for change; today, the dictum of those committed is, 'If I cannot become what I want to be starting today I will not be interested in that change.' The relationship of the individual to the others acting in the collectivity has today a different meaning, for a collectivity is something that everyone must build her/himself in togetherness with others, simultaneously answering to personal needs; without this fulfilment the involvement in the collectivity possesses no meaning. This attitude makes all the difference compared to the conflicts of the industrial age; it implies a different morality, a different set of values: one is not ready for a personal sacrifice in the interest of the collectivity unless it can be clearly seen to correspond to a motivating personal experience of change.

The high morality characterizing the recent movements has thus not encompassed within its standards the noble idea of self-sacrifice, of working hard today for a happy tomorrow. With it, a new problem is opened up within the movements' organizations, relating to the tension precisely between the necessity, or the hope, of safeguarding the individual identity on the one hand, and all the organizational constraints under which a collectivity must operate on the other. This has indeed become a typifying contradiction affecting the movement cultures, in which the effort to affirm the self, the individual autonomy, the respect for every person in her/his singularity clashes with the imperatives of the organizational setting that is being built to make possible coordinated and effective action towards common goals.

The effectiveness of symbolic action cannot then be assessed using the standards applied to other forms of action. Symbolic resources do not operate with the same logic as material or physical resources. The 'critical mass' has lost the weight it may have had in the past, as often the big changes are produced by small symbolic multipliers, through action carried by 'active minorities'(Moscovici 1979) evolving into major issues. In the case of many recent forms of collective action, their enormous impact simply cannot be explained with a focus on the political and practical organization. The effects of what is mainly such action of small 'active minorities' on a larger audience which could have been considered apathetic have at times been surprising; what actually happens is that these minorities prove capable of bringing about a change in the way people's experiences are perceived and named.

Of course, in order for an action of this kind to have any long-term and significant impact, structural changes must take place in society which create new resources and political channels for the institutional implementation of the effects of the action. Very often the negative outcomes of such transformations are due to the fact that no political institutions exist that are prepared to process and adapt to them. This paradox of small interventions producing big effects has to be incorporated in our understanding of how complex societies function. Proceeding in this direction, social sciences would draw closer to the new paradigm emerging in natural sciences, particularly manifest in system theory and quantum physics.

Are contemporary movements capable of bringing about social and political change or are they simply reducing collective action to expressive and 'narcissistic' celebration of the particularism of identities? In the passage from movements to institutions, in the transformation of collective action into new norms and new forms of social organization, there apparently occurs a loss which could be considered a waste of social resources. This is particularly true today with a change so frequent and rapid that not all of the capacity for change in society can be translated and transformed into political and institutional innovations. Contemporary movements are the bearers of the hidden potential for change; they are sensors of forming social needs and they announce new possibilities to the rest of the society. Not all of this work, however, is allowed the translation into actual change. On the one hand, one could thus point out and criticize this aspect of a waste in social resources, but, on the other, we should recognize in this a general cultural feature of our society. The potential for change is always far broader than our actual capacity for action. The gap between the vast prospects of possibilities open to the imaginative capacities, to the potential for projection and symbolic creation, and the actual chances for acting on them is one of the most striking features of our culture. It in fact becomes possible to construct in thought many alternative worlds, as a social construction fed by an enormous influx of information, images, and signs, while the life in the everyday continues unfolding within the limits of the given world where spatial and temporal constraints of reality must be reckoned with. How to manage this gap is the acute problem of today, a problem which for the new generations, as we have seen, goes beyond the simple repetition of the topical question of youth as to how to adapt to the adult world. Young people are the sensors of this societal dilemma, as it is they who most concretely disclose for the rest the enormity of the symbolic possibilities available at any moment, almost as if an embodiment of the insuperable gap between our increasing capacity to produce virtual worlds and our rootedness in natural and social constraints.

This hiatus opens a set of new questions about the institutionalization of social innovation. The aspect of waste fulfils a symbolic function in indicating the cultural potential embedded in an issue or in a specific social field. But, simultaneously, it opens up a new arena for innovation and change. How can the potential produced by societies which increasingly intervene on their own cultural foundations be translated into organizational settings, institutional rules, and political forms of representation and decision-making? How much cultural energy can be expended on 'waste' as a discharge of our creative potential without thereby promoting the dispersal of our capacity for change? These questions seem to me to pose a different way of addressing the problem of the institutionalization of the societal dynamics, one that is more appropriate to the scenario of a complex, global society than the simple reiteration of the interrogation as to whether or not social movements are politically effective.

'Identity politics'?

The stress on identity and the development of forms of collective action based on the affirmation and defence of one's identity has produced a paradoxical situation. One of the pathologies of what is commonly called 'identity politics' is competition among oppressed groups over whose claims to victimization should be privileged (for a discussion, see Calhoun 1994; Epstein 1987; Kauffman 1990). How is it possible for a movement to respect the value of the identity of its members without shattering the basis of a shared identity? How should one respond to the charge that identity politics can be harmful and divisive for social movements? For collective action to be effective and achieve political outcomes, is it not better to work together on the basis of a broader oppositional politics in which one does not worry about 'who we are' but chooses a common ground, on which many people can work together? Theoretically, the question is then whether and how it is possible to affirm both unity and difference simultaneously.

In order to answer this question, which moreover proves crucial for the theory of collective action, some methodological clarification is needed as the first step. It is very difficult, for instance, to draw a distinction between what here is called identity politics and interest groups, beyond the different uses to which the two actors involved put institutional means. According to the classic political science definition, an interest group is a collective actor striving to influence the political decision-making through institutional and sometimes partly noninstitutional means. The difference between institutional and noninstitutional means is merely a matter of empirical observation. It cannot be established in principle whether and when a group will employ for its purposes institutional means or perhaps extend its strategies of action to make use of demonstrations, petitions, sit-ins, and the like.

Here we run again into the problem of how to define that which is called a 'movement'. For many years, I have attempted to clarify the confusion by stressing the fact that a collective actor which empirically calls itself, or is called by observers, a 'movement', consists of a number of different analytical levels of social action, which are kept together in a historical and political setting under certain conditions. 'Identity politics' is a discursive way to refer to one kind of empirical actors, like the women's movement, the gay and lesbian movement, ethnic revivalism, and so on, in whose case the analytical distinction between the level of political interests and the definition of identity is particularly useful. The fact that in 'identity politics' these two levels are superimposed in a confused manner could be very consequential for political life.

A political actor interacts with political authorities, negotiates or is engaged in exchanges within the boundaries of the political arena. Once an issue is addressed politically, there, by definition, has already taken place a certain reduction of the multidimensionality of the issue, as it has entered the domain of the political system governed by a given set of rules. Even to change these rules, then, one is *de facto* forced to recognize such boundaries, if only to start interacting or negotiating with authorities. I define politics in such a narrow sense in order to stress the fact that not everything is political, that there are social and cultural dimensions of action which are never entirely translated into politics. The identity issues are certainly representative of precisely such a dimension of social life, and if they fail to find appropriate means of expression they can come in the way of the transformation of a collective actor into a political actor. Collective actors who address a political system need to find a common ground in order to produce political outcomes, and if they are not able to develop such a level of agreement, identity politics turns towards sectarian directions and potentially very dangerous for the functioning of the political system and ultimately for the actors themselves.

As said, there is always something in the identity issues that cannot be entirely translated into a political confrontation with authorities and which needs to be raised at a different level – as a more general question of how difference is dealt with in society. This general issue can never be treated within the framework of a particular political or organizational setting without a degree of reduction or some kind of negotiated agreement affecting the scope of the identity claims. But, on the other hand, if the identity claims are pushed too far, what follows is the inevitable fragmentation of the movement into self-assertive and closed sects; and this is the risk faced today by many groups involved in 'identity politics'. In their efforts to translate a dilemmatic social issue into a political rule they rapidly embark on a transformation turning them into intolerant preachers of just another sectarian Gospel. The issues they raise are inextricable from the problem of how difference can be accommodated in a differentiated society, in which both of the two horns of the dilemma must necessarily be kept together: a differentiated society can function only based on the acknowledgment and valuation of differences, but, at the same time, the increased differentiation of the system calls for a proportionate intensification in the operation of its mechanisms of integration. This dilemma affects every system from the smallest to society as a whole, and even the planetary-wide society in which they all come together. No final solution, however, exists in the situation; we can only make temporary arrangements which provide political or organizational answers in a given political conjuncture.

When gender, culture, sexual preferences, and ethnicity become political issues, the groups involved in their formulation risk thus transformation into sectarian groupings *vis-à-vis* the contradiction between the magnitude of the problem of difference and the inherent limitations of political decision-making never entirely capable of solving the problem. There always remains a hiatus between, on the one hand, what can be decided through political means and transformed into institutional rules and practices, and, on the other hand, the issue itself. After the conclusion of a political agreement, the issue will still persist in the absence of a final solution for the problem of how to practically arrange the handling of difference within the framework of complexity. People themselves can request for recognition of rights, for better institutional solutions, but these by definition always remain temporary. The refusal to accept them as such acts as a propellant in the transformation of issue-based action into orthodox sectarianism: the totalizing appeal of difference becomes a very divisive way of acting and thinking and it forgets that we are simultaneously living in a system whose defining characteristic is increasing interdependence.

A sect is a social organization which denies in its values, in its belief system, and in its actual organizational frame the interdependence of the social field. It thinks of itself as an actor capable of totalization, as an actor in possession of the control over the social field and thus apparently also of the ability to identify in negative terms, as non-actors or non-social, those who do not belong to the group. This basic belief of a sect is structured into the framework of the organization, where it is transformed from a principle into a social practice. The difference between a sect and a social movement lies then in the fact that a social movement operates in awareness of its commitment to a social field to which it belongs and with which it interacts. Even the most radical movements emerging around a conflictual position towards society share with the rest of the society a set of general issues they understand as something forming a common background with even their opponents. A sect simply breaks any such connection, accomplishing the rupture ideologically through a definition of the social field which creates an 'ontological' separation and a division that cannot be overcome.

Such risks of identity politics always remain considerable, and when they are not contained, the appeal to identity tends to cover up or deny a fundamental dilemma of social life in complex systems. The emergence and diffusion of identity issues in itself touches upon the dilemmatic situation in which complex systems must maintain themselves, and could be applied to the world situation as well. The problem we face at the planetary level concerns precisely the way to coexist and develop common goals while respecting the indelible differences. In order to act collectively at any given time, it is necessary to define a conception of a 'we'; however, this definition is not likely to be set once and for all, and it has to be agreed upon over and over again in a continual negotiation process. Even when referring to an 'objective' condition (as in the case of women's or ethnic issues), collective actors can never anticipate in principle which dimension they should stress in each case in order to achieve the necessary unity and to support the processes of mobilization. The dilemma constitutes a concrete problem whose settlement affects the whole existence of the movement: deciding for one side to focus on the difference and particularism of the actor, the movement may risk fragmentation out of existence; turning to the other side to stress the interdependence and the unity, it risks loss of support with people no longer recognizing themselves in a too general set of values. How to arrange for the way in between is never settled for good, but takes instead increasingly the shape of negotiated process, which itself has to be constructed through the actors' interaction, through an organizational structure, the role of leaders, the capacity for a unified and open-ended discourse.

In the context of any given political system, the capacity to create alliances, connections, and definitions of common goals becomes a central issue for collective action and its success. To be sure, this was also an issue for the working-class movements of the past, but probably in the context of the time it was easier to refer to some general common interest based on a shared condition. Today the common ground for collective action and for a successful political outcome has to be constructed through the awareness that it is impossible to reach one's goals without some support from others, without alliances and agreements. A radical form of 'identity politics' is not only dangerous for society in its intolerant fundamentalism; it is self-defeating.

The world system and the end of historicism

The idea we have inherited from the nineteenth-century thought – the conception of the last step in the historic development – was reserved two ways to materialize itself: Revolution or progress towards the wealth of nations was identified as the intermediate stages in the arrival of a final condition in which everything would be settled and everyone happy. Apart from its extreme utopian versions, this idea of a better society succeeding the present one makes sense only within a historicist paradigm. Today we are in the process of leaving behind this linear view of history, and begin to think more in terms of systemic interdependence, in terms of a planetary system which contains in its womb the seeds of no future: when time holds in reserve no further systems to totally and at once transcend the present one, we are left with only different ways of organizing, managing, and politically defining the existing world system from the inside. The present world system is entirely interdependent and has reached its boundaries both geographically and in temporal terms; in a provocative manner, we could state that there is no space nor time left outside the system (on the redefinition of space in our society, see Lefebvre 1991; Gregory and Urry 1985; Sennett 1993; Urry 1995; on temporal dimensions, Novotny 1992; Sirianni 1988; Young 1988). A new society, then, is not a society which will, or even could, succeed and wholly substitute the present one, but rather a different set of values and political goals which can be established through action to influence the ways of organizing the world system, its social structure, its political priorities, its transnational relations.

Contemporary social movements do not address the issue of a 'new society' in the historicist sense: on the one hand their action reveals the issues and dilemmas of a globally interdependent system, and on the other they address specific political goals, formulating temporary definitions of the problem at the level of single nation or the locality. An analytical distinction should always be maintained between this latter level of action and the global issues they address; for such issues can never be finally resolved through the movements' action, as there exists no final solution to problems such as the coexistence of differences, the relation between nature and technology, the split between material achievements and spiritual needs. These constitute dilemmas which are the property of a complex and fully interdependent system: to start with, we cannot choose technology over nature or vice versa, we can simply manage the coexistence of opposites; and political arrangements are the temporary forms through which we can keep the poles of the apparent opposition connected in a manageable relationship.

The analysis of contemporary movements must today take a systemic, global point of view, and it cannot be applied in a mechanistic way to the national or state level. Empirical social movements act within what the Marxist tradition used to call a 'social formation', within which layers of preindustrial or precapitalist 'modes of production' often remain extant and for which, therefore, the capitalist mode of production can still constitute a goal of the developmental orientations within the context of a particular nation state. But at the same time these societies are today inextricably inserted in a global system, participating in a shared world dominated by a set of central cultural models; they thus seem to exist at different stages of history simultaneously. They may often look to the industrial mode of production as a future achievement still to be instated in full, but all the same they remain a dependent party to the global world system where new powers and new forms of domination make their appearance. In what we call the Third World or 'developing' countries, the political level and the central issue of democracy form probably the point of conjunction between these two levels. In these countries, it is through the democratization of the nation state that the possibility of keeping the goals of industrialization and economic development together with a form of nondependent participation in the world system may be achieved.

It is not by chance that in these countries the issue of democracy has over the last ten years gained greater prominence than the issue of development, which contributed the core issue for the social movements and collective action of the 1960s and 1970s (on Latin America, see in particular O'Donnell and Schmitter 1986; Touraine 1988b; Calderon 1986; Avritzer 1994). The increasing body of literature on social movements, especially in

Latin America, clearly shows this shift which is comparable in countries as different as Mexico, Argentina or Brazil (see Slater 1985, 1994a, 1994b; Jelin 1987b, 1990; Escobar and Alvarez 1992; Foweraker and Craig 1990; Tarrés 1994; Ramirez Saiz 1995; Scherer-Warren 1993; Villasante 1994). The fact reflects not just a cultural current or a change in the political climate. The recognition of democracy as a central issue signifies acknowledgment of the fact that a country cannot develop regardless of the manner in which this development is reached. The way the state and the political system more generally are organized is relevant to the goal of development. The 'new society', which in many parts of the world still today means a society freed from hunger, poverty, striking inequalities, and suppression of political and civil rights, can be reached only if along with economic development it guarantees improved forms of political participation, equal rights, respect of civil and political freedom.

In the specific historical contexts, as in particular in the countries of the Third World, we thus discern a sociological mix which gives rise to a completely new set of questions and problems. Students familiar with the development literature of the 1960s realize how far we have come from that discourse, as regards both the functionalist and optimistic discourse on development and the oppositional discourse of Marxist theory of development. Our distance today from those images is owing to the global interdependence that erases the idea of the future. We have been confined, as it were, to a permanent present, and the dominance to be dealt with is that of a fundamentally synchronic system. The idea of development, in contrast, represents a diachronic idea: it is built around the transition from one society to the next, accomplished through Revolution, for example, or a decisive stage of economic growth. Now, however, if the dominant system is entirely synchronic, if it constitutes a global system, the change from one state to another calls for creative ways of using the resources of the system itself or reduction in the pressure of its constraints; otherwise change takes place as nothing more than a mere illusion and what one would call development in the given society is simply its increased participation and deeper enclosure in the dominated world system. Without democracy, 'developing' countries cannot conceive development in any meaningful sense. At the same time, however, the efforts to bring about the transition in them from one type of society to another must continue unabated, notwithstanding the particularly difficult conditions of the contemporary situation. For precisely this reason a change in the political framework of these countries becomes so important: it is a condition that will allow them to participate in the world system, not merely in a dependent position but with some capacity for exerting influence and engaging in dialogue and negotiation. By the same token, it is a condition also for making a contribution to a different democracy at the world scale.

In fact, the democratization process may thereby serve another purpose by drawing attention to a critical weakness of a global scale: the inadequacy of the world political system for the problems and issues facing us today. The current political system is based upon an old idea of international relations; the core actors of the world system are still nation states, allegedly independent and sovereign entities. Yet we have seen the emergence of other, far more powerful forces that operate at the world scale – megastates, transnational corporations, world media, transnational markets. Their rise has created a need for a transnational political system, which so far has not come to existence: the weakness of the United Nations in the main international issues of the end of this century is only the most striking example of the lack of mechanisms for effective political representation where transnational issues are concerned (Toulmin 1990; Falk 1992; McGrew and Lewis 1992; Laidi 1994). The Gulf War has showed how far can go the power of the media system (Wolton 1991; Smith 1992) and the necessity of passing beyond the simple debate on just and unjust wars (Walzer 1992). The problem at hand is how to translate a transnational social field which is already de facto established by economic, social, and cultural planetary interdependence into a similar political arena which is more than the globalization of politics (Luard 1994) and can no longer be made of and controlled by national states or blocs. This is an issue of fundamental importance that should be urgently addressed, considering the enormity of the hiatus between the changes in the social field and the actual capacity for representing them at the political level and for producing a new definition of human rights (Galtung 1994). If, for instance, one considers the fact that the United States is today the most powerful nation state in the world, and compares this political role with the degree of awareness of it, with the actual political debate in that country, and with the average level of information about the rest of the world, this gap becomes particularly perceptible.

This dramatically touches a deep problem of our time, and it is one of the roles of social movements to bring these issues to the fore. Is it not too optimistic to burden social movements with such expectations? My optimism or, better still, hope in this regard is based on the nature of the resources that lie at the core of present changes. Information is the crucial resource exploited by the world system, and it, literally, informs ('gives form to') all other kinds of resource, including those of economic nature. The significance of information here is that it does not follow a quantitative logic; unlike other forms of resource, its use and effects cannot be supervised by calculation alone. The diffusion and role of information have to be always measured at different levels: they show a multiplying effect which eludes quantification.

To take a dramatic example of the recent past, it would be difficult to explain the enormous and sudden changes in the East and Central European countries and in Russia, with all their contradictory nature, without referring to the invisible changes preceding the onset of the more sensational events. Below the surface of the Communist regimes, reticular changes had already taken place through the diffusion of new patterns of action, relations, and cultures carried by information whose circulation even the most repressive regime proved unable to prevent. In a similar way, we could cite the peace movements of the 1980s. A direct connection between the peace activism of that time and the recent changes in the military policies of a number of Western countries cannot be easily established, but it is nevertheless impossible to understand this turn from the past policies of escalation without considering the indirect effects of these forms of mobilization which in themselves, measured by the numbers involved and direct political impact, remained relatively minor events. Pacifist movements with their highly symbolic content have achieved much more in changing military policies and East–West relations than have decades of political negotiation.

Another example whose significance is becoming more and more notable in this context is the diffusion and role of telematic autonomous networks. In close relation to the present phase of the development of these information technologies, there is something going on which has not yet reached the form of a movement but could very well be the embryonic formation of a strong conflictual orientation, which, moreover, in light of its capacity for diffusion, may turn out to have important effects on a broader scale, even if the scale of the concrete phenomenon itself is today small and localized. One of the issues here, which has been raised among the professionals of the computer world but is beginning to develop far beyond its birth context into a general conflictual issue, concerns the control of programming languages and of the various media relating to computer assisted communication. On the one hand, there can be observed a concentration of power, with very few core centres that control the world in terms of the world-wide transmission and distribution of ideas, languages, programmes, and the like; on the other hand, we can see emerging symptoms of resistance to this trend, manifest in, for example, the action of hackers, information pirates, self-managed networks, and so on. The computer is becoming more and more common as everyday technology, and ever greater numbers of non-specialist people are learning the no longer unusual skills of the users of this media. Through this proliferation, there is therefore a possibility of a corresponding increase in the awareness of how novel forms of domination operate through the frames imposed on this newly emerged field of cultural activity through programming languages, through the organization of the computer markets, through the global standardization of software: as their consequence, margins of individual choice are effectively and in a tangible manner narrowed down where one becomes simply the recipient of pre-fabricated languages and rules whose later treatment consists merely of their application. In other words, one is de facto forced to submit to working within given frames which, moreover, have been produced else-where by those whose identity and motivations we do not even know. The prospects for opposition lie in the possibility that the user may realize here the fact that her/his mind is entirely framed within that particular world, and that processes of reflection may commence that lead to redefinition of the user's field. This, again, may develop into incipient forms of resistance and issue in demands for a different participation, for a more interactive way of building one's informational world. Conflictual signs such as these are not merely hypothetical; today we are witnessing different ways in which they are actually emerging in different countries around the world.

Given the dramatic and sometimes discouraging dimensions of today's problems, our only hope lies thus in addressing them not just within the framework of quantitative logic which measures the 'objective' weakness of democratic impulses against the strength of the enormous mega-appara-tuses. These apparatuses, namely, share in the very same weaknesses, pre-cisely because they too must necessarily rely on information for the achievement of their own objectives. Interdependence and the role of information allow a margin of ambiguity that renders seemingly weak and local forms of action potentially able to exert an enormous influence far beyond their actual size and immediate effect. In this situation, the change can be initiated by apparently minute phenomena, for in the information age their impact remains always unpredictable (and uncontrollable), given the rapid diffusion of ideas and the potential multiplication of any effect in a complex systemic setting dependent on the capability of its elements for advanced information processing – itself a resource growing progressively more ambivalent the more it is exacted. Invisible and outwardly modest forms of action, provided they find the proper channels, do sometimes extend to address the world to make the difference.

There is nevertheless another face to the ambiguity in the operation of information. Along with the possibilities of change increases the potential for catastophic outcomes. Today the risks putting our future at jeopardy have grown unprecedented as we can no longer be assured of a tomorrow with the confidence with which the industrial society still considered itself. Our problem has ceased to be the one of the right directions on which to work so as to move with awareness of the proper and efficient means for the achievement of what was promised already in the present. Today, we know that the future depends entirely on our choice, on our decisions, on nothing beyond our mundane capacity for creating political arrangements that alone can provide for our survival on this planet. There is, however, nothing that necessarily ensures that all will not end up in a catastrophe, whether ecological or nuclear or both. The future depends solely on our action purged of all teleological connotations. This is at once an exciting challenge and a scary scenario, for we do not know the ultimate outcomes of our choices and decisions.

The possibility of a catastrophe cannot be eliminated as such. From now on, it is a permanent part of the risks inherent in our life in a planetary society. The cultural situation of our society was fundamentally altered with the inauguration of the nuclear era, once the newly acquired capacity for creation and destruction had made its present dramatically known, as knowledge available to mankind; for the first time, human beings had come to possess the power to end their own existence as a species. But for the same reason they were given the power of building their future: they could recognize that power was not the prerogative of God, of the laws of history or any other force outside the society itself. As of that moment, however, be it a symbolic or a physical change in our real power of destruction, the risks and the possibility of failure in this enterprise are destined to remain undecided. We must settle with the bleak comfort of knowing that we can only work together towards its realization in a piecemeal fashion and to the best of our abilities, while nothing can guarantee that the final end will be successful.

We cannot expect that the possibility of reaching such a level of global awareness could be achieved in any linear process. It would be sheer naivete to imagine a progressive and gradual enlargement of our consciousness that could bring the gravity of the problems to the fore. In actual reality, it may well be that for the collective reception of these issues we shall have to pay the price of a major catastrophe. It would not necessarily be too far-fetched to expect here a series of dramatic processes, just as the Chernobyl accident acted as one of the main accelerators in the evolution of environmental consciousness and movements. To reach a transnational consciousness of problems, we may need the shock function of dramatic stages, and it remains uncertain whether, in our global society of interdependency and complexity, their effects can be safely contained within a limited scope. The risk of a planetary effect is real, and all the apocalyptic expectations at the end of the twentieth century are probably touching upon something real.

In the end, the salvation may after all be prepared in a Great Purgatory. In any case, we should remain aware of the prospect that we may realistically prove unable to avoid a high price for the required leap, provided we will be able to accomplish it at all.

Movements and the political system

It is impossible to address and analyse social movements as empirical phenomena without referring to concrete historical settings. At different empirical levels we must discriminate between the various movement organizations, the movement as a whole, and networks in everyday life. All these levels of analysis should be differentiated, and one should also make a distinction between the mobilization processes and the movement itself: mobilization presupposes a collective actor which does not exhaust its actions in the mobilization process. The actor exists also in the everyday networks and in the hidden solidarity circuits which feed its visible action. The working-class movement evolved long before the beginning of its public struggles, the women's movement had been active long before the issue of equality entered the political arena.

The intensity or the lack of mobilization waves has normally to do with the political cycle and the state of the political system. It cannot be explained at the general level which accounts for the formation of a conflictual field in contemporary society: this general level can only tell us that a phenomenon taking place in a specific historical context is related to certain societal processes. The presence or the absence of mobilization in national contexts should be explained with reference to the political system and the interaction among political actors and movements. This level of analysis is important for one wishing to explain a national case, but the risk cannot be ignored of becoming confined within the logic of the political system which does not exhaust the totality of social movements' action.

The role of the political system can vary according to different cases, and here one must seek to understand how the conflictual component raised by social movements is embodied in political actors. As a general trend, we are witnessing an increasing separation between cultural phenomena which bring an issue to the light on the one hand and the political actors who simply translate them in the political arena on the other: it is not one and the same actor who brings together a social issue and the capacity of acting politically on that particular issue. This trend can be expected to continue even sharper – cultural issues being brought by actors who in themselves are not political actors, and the translation of these issues into political action taking place as the work of completely different subjects.

The societies of the West, however, have not reached this point as yet, and the core issues of a society still continue being brought into the political arena through the political mediation of social conflicts. National societies organized around the nation state persist and the political translation of social issues, at least for the present, retains its central importance. Where there are no visible mobilizations addressing the political system, we see little or no changes taking place, whether really or apparently. The so-called 'new' social movements have been the first announcement of a qualitative leap in the nature of collective action: they have shown the possibility and the risk accompanying the progressive differentiation of social conflicts from political action. They have acted as catalysts in the debate and pushed towards the necessity of new conceptual frameworks.

If the above formulation of questions is correct at the analytical level, I do not find any contradiction between my position and that of the authors representing in this field of research what I have termed political reductionism (e.g., Tilly 1978, 1984; Tarrow 1989a, 1994; McAdam 1982, 1988). Here it is simply a question of a normal division of labour, in the sense that we are interested in answering different questions. Yet it is my impression that I understand the questions they are asking while they may not fully understand the questions I pursue in my work. These authors address a very important question concerning collective actors which can be summarized as follows: Given certain structural preconditions, how does a collective actor come to be able to act as a unified political subject, and how does that actor relate to a political opponent within a field of opportunities and constraints? The answers from the framework delimited to the dimension of political organizations have been highly interesting and detailed, and they provide a wealth of useful material and insights for any analysis of the functioning of modern political systems beyond their institutional action.

However, that perspective fails to address one basic question, namely, What is the meaning of the action for the people who get involved in it? No doubt not everyone should address the same questions, but here the problem concerns precisely the possibility of allowing for an analytical space for these questions to be asked. The reduction of social movements to their political dimension and the relegation of whatever does not fall neatly within that dimension to the realm of expressive action prevents the formulation of novel questions in the absence of precisely such a conceptual space.

Political reductionism in itself constitutes an entirely legitimate point of view provided one openly specifies the level of analysis chosen. All of us do, and have the right to, reduce reality to any one of its component levels for observation; otherwise no analysis were possible at all. Doing so explicitly in order to provide for a better understanding of the way an actor evolves in interaction with an opponent within a political field where, influencing and being influenced by that opponent, it uses these resources to construct itself and pursue its goals, this currently powerful analytical trend will legitimately put forth an interesting point of view. It contributes much to the understanding of social movements, in particular compared to the more conventional explanations couched in terms of collective behaviour or the traditional Marxist model.

The point here is, however, that there exist other levels of collective action which are present at the same time and which cannot be understood without posing new questions. This, moreover, is particularly true when addressing the recent forms of action, in which, for instance, the cultural dimension has demonstrated its great significance. Simply reducing these emergent phenomena to the political level proper, such dimensions and meanings that are not immediately identifiable as political become ignored and eliminated from the analysis. It is here that the point of view centred on identity formation, which as a concept takes into account the complexity and multiplicity of the levels of action, can help preserve an analytical space for a different understanding of what a collective actor does and what the meanings are that this actor produces.

Social movements theory is thus in need of a more systematic analysis of the relationships between movements and political systems. Until the mid-1980s, in fact, scant attention was paid to the relationship between the movement and its environment. In particular, few studies were conducted on the effects of movements on political systems, by which their behaviour is in turn modified. Adopting a multipolar approach will allow us to extend analysis beyond the confines of the logic embraced by the actors (institutional and otherwise), and permits understanding in systemic terms relating to the exchanges and conflicts taking place among the elements that make up a social field. By not restricting itself to an individual examination of the actors but treating their relationships instead as significant objects of theory and research, the focus of analysis has shifted to the systemic dimensions and reciprocal influence of the elements involved. This entails the redefinition of conventional concepts and methods, which will stimulate and enrich both the analysis of movements and the study of political systems.

By concentrating on empirical research and insisting on the importance of comparative analysis, Tarrow (1989a, 1994) has made a contribution to a 'field' approach of this kind by developing the concept of 'political opportunity structure' and an explanation of the relationship between cycles of protest and cycles of reform (1989b, 1993b, 1993c). According to

Tarrow, the political opportunity structure marks out the field of opportunities and constraints that delimits the actions of the two parties, as assessed by the cost-benefit calculations of collective actors. This opportunity system determines a movement's decision to mobilize, the outcomes of collective action, and its institutional effects – whether these will be reformist or result in more dramatic phenomena such as, for example, terrorist violence.

Subsequently, the shift of attention to the cyclical nature of protest and to the effects of these cycles on politics has two theoretical implications. First, it 'desacralizes' the analysis of collective phenomena by refusing to charge the appearance of protest with messianic aspirations and by refusing to consider its subsequent decline as the exhaustion of every conflictual impulse. Secondly, cyclicity signals that protest is a stable and 'normal' function of contemporary societies, in which it performs a propulsive role connected with the modernization of the political system (under specific conditions, that is, as Tarrow's empirical analysis clearly reveals).

The perspective offered by this type of analysis also makes possible an examination of the effects of institutional reaction on movements and their action: of institutionalization processes and of forms of political integration or, conversely, of the distortions produced by the inability of the political system to absorb protest through reform. This line of inquiry highlights the importance of an open civil society, of public spaces which provide an arena for the encounter between politics and the collective pressures applied by movements.

Tarrow's contribution is based on important empirical data which should lead the debate on the relation between collective action and the political system, suspending over the last thirty years, out of the dead end of conflicting ideological theories in which it has been trapped – namely, the contraposition between protest as the expression of marginal and violent minorities and protest as the expression of violently repressed revolutionary impulses. Tarrow provides empirical confirmation of the fact that what is at issue is a cycle of struggles involving multiple actors, goals, and forms of action. This is a thesis for which I myself have argued for many years (to little avail, to be sure, considering, for example, the debate on '68 which still advances global and summary interpretations of that cycle of struggle).

A second finding of Tarrow's analysis is that demands for the modernization of the political system and civil society were of central importance for the multiple and differentiated cycle of conflicts of the 1960s and 1970s. Such a demand never met with a satisfactory response and, above all, has been unable to find channels of representation that could translate conflict into institutional reform, organizational change, or renewal of civil society. On this point too I entirely agree with Tarrow, as it is the one that I have repeatedly brought up for a long time already and in part demonstrated empirically. In support of his thesis, Tarrow adds further confirmation from extensive and systematic research, although this evidence does not substantially alter what he earlier argued based on more limited empirical observation. In the case of Italy, for example, his data confirms that the cycle of struggles which began in the second half of the 1960s combined what I have called demands for modernization, stemming from the experience of problems relating to the passage of Italian society to postindustrial capitalism, with new antagonistic demands advanced by actors extraneous to the tradition of previous struggles and on a terrain unaffected by industrial strife. The question, of course, is how to distinguish analytically among these dimensions, and the relative proportion occupied by each of them of the whole. Tarrow gives only partial answers to these questions, but paves none the less way for further clarification of the topic of 'new movements'.

A third finding of Tarrow's analysis reinforces a conviction already well-established among scholars of collective action, namely, that violence is to a large extent a function of the system's response to conflictual demands and of the degree of the system's permeability and flexibility. Collective action in Italy, for example, has been blocked by the political system's adoption of three strategies which, in my terminology, I have referred to as restrictive reform (limited change within the old institutional structure by addition, never by replacement), repression, and countermobilization through the instrumental use of Right-wing violence. There is no denying in this context of the link between movements and terrorism: terrorism combines the residues of a process of distorted modernization, which produces fundamentalist fringes, with new demands which fail to find adequate channels of representation. Tarrow perhaps does not examine forms of representation as closely as he should, particularly as regards, on the one hand, the difficulties encountered by the traditional left in incorporating new conflictual thrusts in the course of the cycle; and, on the other, the pressure exerted by new left groups towards a hyperpoliticization of all demands, even when these themselves did not necessarily require organization in the form of the Leninist party (see chapter 14).

The problems left open by such an analysis concern, as I have already indicated, a number of topics of theoretical and methodological importance. They all relate to the problem of the 'new movements' and the purported centrality of the political dimension in analysis of contemporary collective action. Concerning the first aspect, Tarrow discovers that the 'new' movements are not in fact new, and that in the new cycle of struggles also more traditional categories have been recruited and already familiar repertoires of action resurrected, much more so than the revolutionary rhetoric would have had us believe. This strikes me as an empirical discovery of major significance, although its assertion in a certain sense breaks down a door that is already open and fails to eliminate the likelihood of misunderstanding inherent in the debate on the 'new movements'.

In order to clarify this misunderstanding, we may reiterate what by now should be clear to the reader: the research of the last twenty years on collective action and on the relationship between movements and political systems has crucially depended on the emergence of forms of action which have rendered both previous forms of organization and previous conceptual frameworks inadequate, highlighting their categorial and practical shortcomings. Interest in the emerging phenomena, above all during the second half of the 1970s, gave rise to a large body of studies, both theoretical and empirical, which implicitly or explicitly addressed the question of the 'newness' of contemporary conflicts. If, as I have argued above, contemporary phenomena combine in their empirical unity different orientations and meanings of action, debate on such newness cannot address movements as a general whole. It must, rather, examine aspects and dimensions of contemporary forms of action which cannot be accounted for by a paradigm of exchange or by reference to the strategic logic of a political system. Asking ourselves whether there are *dimensions* to contemporary collective action which belong to a system analytically different from industrial capitalism is not an irrelevant question, all the plethora of 'post-isms' now swamping us notwithstanding.

In my own research I have mapped out precisely such dimensions that resist reduction to political exchange, proceeding to demonstrate their nature as a symbolic challenge intended to overthrow the cultural codes that organize the meaning of action in complex systems. This brings us to my second criticism of Tarrow's contribution. A failure to pose the question set forth above, restricting analysis instead to the purely political dimensions of the observed phenomena (such as, for example, a clash with authority), equals yielding to a reductionism which ignores the specifically *social* dimensions of collective action and focuses exclusively on those more readily measurable features which, because of their high visibility, attract the attention of the media. One of course cannot reprove Tarrow, a political scientist, for plying his trade, but one can ask him to make more explicit the limits of his analysis as well as the circuit that ties together the reductionist option and the choice of method.

Indeed, although the research by Tarrow, Tilly, and their colleagues based on public sources that record the outbreaks of protest provides analysis with a quantitatively necessary and methodologically innovative basis, it cannot accomplish a sociological understanding of contemporary social movements. These movements do not exhaust their action in a more or less disruptive public confrontation against the authorities. Instead, their *modus operandi* is to fashion new meanings for social action and serve as vital engines of innovation. And this holds above all for the recent forms of the phenomena, in which the political dimension often represents nothing more than a residue. Analysis of the political dimensions of collective phenomena may help us to escape from global ideological explanations, and to this effect Tarrow presents a theory of social movements with an example of method and a wealth of material for serious reflection. But he risks reinforcing the ingrained tendency in many current analyses to take it for granted that politics comes before society and everyday culture, rather than intermeshing with them.

The importance that should thus be attached to the cultural dimension of contemporary social movements, however, does not lay the analysis wide open to the charge of naive culturalism. There is no cultural freedom without political freedom – without adequate rights and guarantees established and recognized by political institutions. The problem raised by contemporary movements rather concerns a redefinition of what democracy is, can be, and ought to be in a world where information becomes the central resource and where individuals and groups are offered the possibility of themselves constructing their identities instead of remaining simply recipients assigned them from the outside. What kind of political guarantees, what kind of representation channels are needed to answer the new demands issuing from individuals and groups? How can people make their choices more consciously and more at will than they usually do under the pressure of new forms of domination which manipulate information? How can people be enabled to make better use of their resources and to free themselves from material and other inequalities that prevent them from exerting their right to become autonomous subjects of action? These are all political problems, not just cultural; but, paradoxically, they can only be answered within a framework that assigns culture the central role it performs in today's social production. The traditional political science or market-oriented framework of analysis (political exchange theory, rational choice theory, and resource mobilization theory) remains impotent before the dimensions it is expected to address through such questions. With the conceptual tools their focus allows, the models it has advanced cannot account for demands affecting people's identities; they only explain how people calculate their advantages and losses in a political arena organized like a market. But this falls short of providing an explanation of the need for self-construction, self-determination, and self-reflection which forms the basis for new political rights. On the other hand, we have the post-modernist perspective which seems to empty politics of any importance and value, and tries to dissolve interests, social relations, and power in a pure game of signs.

We can only begin to ask new political questions when we are prepared to start from a different cultural standpoint; but it is precisely from this perspective that politics becomes important. No genuine change is possible without new political arrangements, without the establishment of new political boundaries, rules, and guarantees which ensure that needs become rights. Of course, the notion of rights should probably be more flexible, more temporary, and more mutable than it was in the past. But in any case every project of cultural freedom needs the institutions of a political setting for its embodiment and stabilization. Otherwise its prospects die out at the level of a rhetoric of new privileged elites who harness the discourse on it for the purposes of maintaining the established control over languages and codes and of camouflaging the exacerbation of old inequalities and the new that differentiate people in their access to that 'cultural freedom'. Cultural freedom becomes then more a frontier for new political rights, a stake around which we should expect social conflicts to appear.

PART III

The field of collective action

11

A society without a centre

Myths of totality

In its formative stage, a 'movement' always adopts the language of previous struggles. Still unable to define itself in terms of an identity of its own, the new collective actor uses the symbols, the organizational experience, and the forms of action of the movements that preceded it. Tradition can be used to convey new meanings (Burke 1969; Shils 1981; Hobsbawm and Ranger 1983) and this does not necessary imply that the collective actor is backward oriented, as some authors tend to think (see, for instance, Calhoun 1983). Thus the working-class movement spoke for longtime the language of the French Revolution before turning to socialism (Sewell 1980); in a similar way, the movements that arose in the 1960s drew on scholastic Marxism. While at that time Marxism itself was undergoing radical crisis, the movements' ideologues embarked on the doctrinaire revival of the most inflexible models of the Marxist vulgate. For example, the student movement of 1968 rediscovered Marxist doctrine, as preserved and reworked by the marginal cliques and the small sects that lay outside the mainstream of the Communist parties. The actors in new conflicts and movements resorted to an ironbound interpretation of doctrine and mechanically deduced rules of organization in order to define their identities and mark out their position with respect to their adversaries. Only in the 1970s did the women's movement introduce a language and a set of categories that broke with this reliance on simplified Marxism as a proxy for an as yet undeveloped independent identity (for a reconstruction of the New Left, see Breines 1982; Freeman 1983; Gitlin 1987; Katsiaficas 1987; on 1968, see Caute 1988; Fraser 1988; Flacks 1988; on the transformations that brought to new forms of collective action, see Epstein 1990a; Stein 1985; Evans 1980; Whalen and Flacks 1989).

Revolution, the workers' movement, and socialist society provided the ritual points of reference for the language of movements up until the late 1960s. Although these simplified certainties served to equip action with an ideology (for the purposes of mobilization, or of emotional reassurance, as the case may be), the knowledge that we now possess on the complexity of power and integration mechanisms in contemporary societies, on the ambivalent role of the mass parties, and on the risks of manipulated participation, has deprived these truisms of any substance.

What, in fact, does 'revolution' actually mean in a society entirely permeated by a microphysics of power? The notion dear to historicism was that of a transformation that moved outwards from the heart of the system to overturn its overall structure through the seizure of the control of the state apparatus. But the idea makes no sense when the whole of society has become one ramified and diversified apparatus. The problems we must deal with are not of the same nature as the ones engaged by modern thought, whose language and concepts we nevertheless continue using. The concept of 'revolution' itself entirely belongs to the linguistical universe of mechanistic physics, just as a 'movement' is a concept which is intimately related to the language of mechanics. In the era in which quantum physics has thoroughly changed our understanding of material, physical reality, the question poses itself: How can we conceive in non-mechanistic ways the relational nature of social action, and of the knowledge apprehending it in the first place? The system has no centre; it is a network of relations among differentiated and relatively autonomous structures which it must keep in balance. No change can simultaneously affect all the levels of a system when each of its various components functions according to its own logic – a law which admits of only two exceptions. One is the establishment of absolute power which ruthlessly eliminates all specificities and differences in the social system, building a community with the transparency of absolute violence. The second represents the other extreme in the continuum of possibilities: a nuclear or ecological catastrophe which annihilates complexity by crushing it flat in total destruction. These two limiting cases apart, transformations in complex systems only occur at specific levels, with each of them proceeding according to a particular logic of its own which cannot be automatically carried over from one level to another, and which thus can never simultaneously affect the system as a whole.

Thus, the concept of revolution belongs to a semantic and socio-political universe which no longer is ours. The mechanistic paradigm in which the concept was born (the term derives from the astronomic language developed for description of the movement of planets), and the historicist paradigm that inherited it, have both withered away before the historical transformations, only to be replaced by new patterns for the definition of the objects of knowledge. How, then, do complex systems change? What is the difference between modernization and structural change? What conditions of mobilization, what forms of representation ensure the closest control over the various processes of change? These are some of the questions that will guide my reflections on transformation processes in complex societies.

Change, as the constant requirement for a system (or systems) to adapt to environmental variations and to maintain its internal equilibrium, becomes the critical property of its normal status. The historicist notion of change as a global, homogeneous, and end-directed process has ceased to apply to the analysis of complex societies. History as a river endlessly flowing towards the sea of its fulfilment and constantly fed by its tributaries, the sun of the future lighting the path of our laborious ascent to a final goal – these are images that belong to a vision of the world now definitively superseded. Change in complex systems is always specific and cannot be directly transferred from one level or system to another. Every variation has effects on the whole, to be sure, but always in a mediated fashion.

The workers' movement has been another ritual reference point for collective action until the 1960s. The 'workers' movement' is nowadays a composite phenomenon which intermeshes and overlaps with occupational pressure groups and with solidly based, institutionally guaranteed bodies of representation. Claimant and political pressures still exist, but research has shown that these should be interpreted in the light of other variables (occupational status, gender roles, geographical location, position in the labour market), and that they cannot be related to the wage-earning condition as such. The working class performed an antagonistic role in capitalist development when the society's vital problems still arose centred around industrialization, the conquest of nature, and the subjugation of the workforce to the requirements of large-scale industrial production. But in societies that must confront the complexity of human systems, mass economic and political markets, and the equilibrium of the ecosystem, the image of a compact and homogeneous workers' movement assuming responsibility for global transformation (if, indeed, it would have ever been able to do so) belongs to the realm of ritual celebration.

Trade unionism and political organizations for worker representation have divested themselves of all mythology, and they have taken on all the characteristic problems of political actors in a modern system of representation. As they seek to maximize their goals by reforming power relationships – that is, by broadening their consensus base – they are forced to hold together and mediate a plurality of demands generated by the increasing heterogeneity of their memberships, and they are torn between the growing strength of the apparatus, increased organizational power, and pressures from the base for participation in decision-making.

To talk of a socialist society in this context is to conjure up another anachronistic myth. In complex societies which accumulate and invest more than ever before, the apparatuses of technical and political decision-making are centralized and tend to become invisible. Developmental decisions are mostly taken by specific groups, private or public. Complexity must be governed, and the concentration of forms of control seems destined to increase. How, then, can the illusion of a 'classless society' be sustained? The problems faced by complex societies are manifold: How can they reduce inequalities and status barriers towards a more equitable society? How can they make the formation of new forms of power more visible? How can they ensure that different interests are represented?

These are questions that were impossible to ask when the myth of the socialist society held sway. Even when confronted with the collapse of 'real socialism', Leftist ideology explained away the inequalities and the authoritarianism of socialist regimes as residues of capitalism, or as a relapse to capitalism in the form of 'state capitalism'. The main ideological preoccupation was to keep the myth of a classless society alive. Hence the manifest contradictions of 'socialist societies' were blamed on the enemy: the causes of the contradictions of 'real socialism' were something that still remained, or had been restored, of capitalism. Ideologues were thus relieved of the chore of inquiring into the specific reasons why power and inequality persisted in socialist societies. 'State capitalism' was the last ideological refuge for those who refused to ask themselves how power was created and maintained in these social structures, how surplus was extracted and allocated via the state and party apparatuses, how processes of accumulation and development were controlled, and how new relationships of international dependence on the 'socialist' imperialist powers had been created.

The demise of the totalizing vision of change has forced contemporary movements to accept the plurality of the levels and instruments of social transformation and their irreducible differences. This opens up an enormous field of action, for it is the real political openness of complex societies that ensures collective control (never transparent, always conflictual) over the goals, logic, and tools of a development that by now affects the social system as a whole. The invention of possible change passes through the political instruments of collective control, and through the guarantees of political democracy which govern the decision-making apparatuses responsible for development planning in complex societies. This creates a hiatus, one that is never entirely reparable, between the formation of needs and social demands on the one hand, and their organizational expression ('representative' in whatever way one cares to imagine) on the other. It thus gives rise to an undiminishable quota of conflicts, which only the political institutions can render into a creative force – that is, into a reservoir of transformative energies that can affect development without being dissipated in marginal violence or expressive revolt.

Autonomy and the limits of political action

Never before have political relations been as important as in complex systems; never before has it been as imperative to manage complexity by decisions, choices, and 'policies', and to ensure at the same time their frequency and diffusion in order to reduce the uncertainties inherent in systems mutating with astonishing speed. Complexity and change entail the necessity for decisions: highly differentiated systems create a plurality of variable interests incomparable with anything seen in the past, giving thus rise to a new need to handle multiple and changeable problems calling for solution. Urgent decisions must be made, which then need to be constantly verified and subjected to the constraints and the risks of consensus, as they attempt to cope with the rushing flux of change.

Political relations – the relations, that is, which are activated in order to reduce uncertainty and mediate among conflicting interests through decisions – become crucial to the workings of complex societies. At present, we are in fact witnessing a proliferation of political agents. In various areas of society, in institutions and organizations, processes are at work which are transforming into politics what in the past were authoritarian rules: that is, they are introducing systems of exchange and bargaining procedures which, by confronting and mediating interests, create decisions where the mechanisms for the repressive transmission of norms and power once used to operate. This is true not only of political systems in the strict sense, but has also now spread to numerous institutions (productive, educational, administrative) where – often through conflict – new instances of political decision-making, interest representation, and negotiation are being created. The process is a result of complexity, of the necessity to deal with a mutable environment, and of the increasingly urgent need to maintain equilibrium within the system. It is a problem which every complex system must confront and which no project for political reform can ignore. The specificity of decision-making processes and representation mechanisms, with their characteristic logics, cannot be neutralized by the cathartic power of struggle. This, however, is not to imply that the nature of the interests that enter the decision-making system is irrelevant, nor is it to claim that these interests are all of equal weight or that a system automatically guarantees the same chances of access to everyone; what it states is simply that specific decision-making processes are a necessary prerequisite for the functioning of complex systems.

Decision-making processes also work through representation and are ever-present in every kind of political organization. Representation inevitably opens up a chasm between those who represent and those represented, between their respective interests, between logics of action that may coincide but can also diverge, on account of the different positions occupied by those who are directly involved in the decision-making and those who only participate in it through their representatives. This chasm therefore signals that democratic political transformation, in whatever form, must be able to absorb the tension between the structures of representation and the demands or interests of those represented; and that it must devise social and political measures to reduce the distance that separates power from social demands, without, however, ideologically neutralizing the problem. The fact that simple command is replaced by representation, mediation, and the capacity to produce negotiated decisions does not amount in itself to democratic transformation in substantive terms, and the same process may result also in non-representative institutional arrangements (the old Soviet Union and Eastern European countries is a case in point and the breakdown of the Soviet empire opens up a process where the problem of democratization and the constitution of new forms of representation become the central issues for those societies); none the less, the multiplication and diffusion of political instances indicates that political relations fulfil a different role in the contemporary world.

We are passing from a totalizing vision of politics to a recognition of its specificity and its necessary function. This is a difficult transition, since it entails, for movements, all the disenchantment that invariably accompanies the desacralization and secularization of social life. The transition from a totalizing approach to the dimension of particularity is always accompanied by sacrifice; the natural urge to totality must always be renounced in order to recognize the limitations, but also the autonomy, of specific social processes. In complex societies, politics becomes the process of mediation between interests aimed at producing decisions. Politics does not represent the totality of social life, and this is so in two distinct senses. Firstly, there exists a level of society that, analytically, stands prior to politics, and which delimits and conditions it: the sphere of social relationships and interests which are translated and mediated through politics. We must resist the illusion of the transparency of pluralism, the presumption of society as a spontaneous and open plurality of demands and needs; and we must remember that the political game is never played on an open field with equal chances for all. But there is still another reason for renouncing the priority of politics as the representative for the entirety of social reality: there exist ambits and dimensions of human experience related to the inner life of individuals and their interpersonal relationships that fall wholly outside the realm of politics and cannot be subsumed to it.

A sign – perhaps an important one – of such a profound recasting of the status of politics is the disappearance of the conventional distinction between Right and Left, a distinction whose analytical vacuousness I pointed out fifteen years ago and has today become evident (Bobbio 1987, 1989, 1994; Giddens 1994; Hall and Jacques 1989; Flacks 1994). The sole function of that distinction was to provide empirical categories with which political actors in the Western historical tradition could be classified. But it tells us nothing about today's new conflictual actors, or about the direction of the present change. Traditionally, the term 'right' stood for an orientation towards the past, and 'left' for an orientation towards the future. Emerging movements have made us collectively aware that we live in a society bereft of a future – not merely because our future is in fact suspended on the brink of catastrophe, but due to the central problem that the complex systems must cope with maintaining equilibrium and that there is no final, perfect society awaiting for its patient believers. The 'anti-modern' character of movements lies in their declaration of the end of linear progress, and in their affirmation of the importance of acting for the present. The impossible task of forcing such a change in the attitudes towards the future of society into the conceptual straitjacket of the Left–Right distinction is another sign that the crisis of the old paradigm is definitively under way: 'Left' and 'Right' are no longer identifiable once and for all in any simple fashion, and if the distinction is to continue its existence it can do so only within the restricted domain of political jargon, with a possible descriptive function in the assessment of the nature of particular democratic policies.

The issues themselves remain controversial from this point of view; in isolation they can no longer be assigned simply to either Left or Right. The action in question must be placed within the historical and political framework of the given society or state in order to understand the direction of the conflict. Moreover, the whole constellation surrounding the issues can shift so that it may well be possible to observe the 'Rightist' of yesterday transforming into the 'Leftist' of tomorrow. Take, for example, the much-contested issue surrounding the abortion rights where 'progressive' claims have been challenged by anti-abortionist mobilizations (see Staggenborg 1991). In it, the focus has been set on the right to decide, with the dilemma sharpening around the individual decision in the reproductive sphere opening up to the state or community intervention in this most intimate realm of personal life. The fundamental problem is thus one that is truly controversial in our society and culture. The anti-abortionist position effectively raises the implicit problem of whether the public power has the right to interfere in such a private or personal matter. Furthermore, considering the so-called Third World countries where abortion has become a public policy offering means for controlling population growth as a method of birth control, one might quite well state that in that context an anti-abortionist movement would assume a progressive character: it could be viewed as a struggle against a public power striving to impose its own decisions on the most intimate sphere of individual life.

In this context are concepts such as liberation or emancipation still useful (for a discussion, see Nederveen Pieterse 1992)? The concept of emancipation still belongs to a culture that thinks of a future society. We are in need of a self-limiting concept of emancipation, one that is mindful of the dark side of the modern myths (of progress, liberation, revolution). For developing societies, future is still open to development, but at the same time they are thoroughly involved in the planetary system based on information. Thus it is at the political level that a project of 'emancipation' can be discussed. Free of all metaphysical assumptions, we can openly discuss our future, our hopes, and our limitations. In this civil debate social movements play a central role.

The life of movements depends on the workings of political systems: on the operation of all those instances through which the multiplicity of interests accedes via representation to the decision-making processes that allocate resources. These include the political levels which, as already mentioned, proliferate in complex societies extending beyond the national or local political system in the strict sense, within large organizations, institutions, administrative systems. The greater or lesser openness of the channels of representation, and the guarantees that these provide, constitute the sole condition that governs the emergence of dissent. Conflict can emerge and become visible only when the weaker interests can organize themselves, are not immediately repressed, and can make their voice heard in a public arena. Safeguards to protect the rights of minorities, the visibility and control of decision-making procedures, the extent to which electoral mechanisms are genuinely representative, the quality of the filters that regulate access to the political system and the amount of elasticity in the rules of the game, the restrictions placed on the action of the executive and of the repressive apparatuses, the freedom and the forms of political and associative organization, civil rights and the guarantees of the penal system – all these are indicators of the degree of openness of a political system.

Political institutions have two aspects which should not be considered in isolation from each other. They protect the advantage of certain interests, an advantage which is inscribed in the operation of formal guarantees never based purely on technical functionality. The equal right to vote, for instance, is formally guaranteed to every citizen; yet it is well known to everyone that wealth, education, and power can make a real difference in the actual exercise of this right. But, at the same time, political institutions create room for the expression of social demands. This, indeed, is the dual meaning of the term 'participation'. Formal guarantees open up, but also restrict, a field of participation compatible with the system. But these guarantees are specifically those that allow social demands to occupy the field of participation by transforming it into a collective opportunity for the real exercise of rights and the voicing of opposition.

Social movements fill the area of guarantees with content, they defend it against the erosion of power, they repeatedly redraw its boundaries, they push participation beyond the limits laid down by the political system, and they force it to change. Anything but linear, this process is constantly threatened by the tendency to centralization of power, by authoritarian backlash, by repression. It thus assumes the form of a game – a game which dominant interests seek to reduce to zero sum and which the movements seek to keep open. In complex systems, politics alternates between, on the one hand, the formal and, indeed, *de facto* authoritarian management of the political system by apparatuses which draw their power from manipulated consensus, and, on the other, the political system's propulsive energy generated by the dialectic between social conflicts and a power structure capable of innovation.

By reducing complexity, a democratic system of representation ensures that decisions are made. It assumes that there is an inevitable chasm between the interests of those who represent and those represented; it presumes that there is a more or less broad margin of consensus over the rules of the game and its procedures; it activates strategic behaviour designed to maximize the actor's advantage over its competitors. Naturally, these formal features, bound up with the logic of complex systems, assume different connotations according to the interests that gain access to representation and according to the particular nature of the rules and procedures. The distinction and the tension between institutional channels and movements, between systems for representation and decision-making on the one hand and the direct expression of social demands through collective action on the other, are indispensable for democracy in complex systems.

An open society is possible where political actors assume a non-totalizing role as mediators of demands, the formation and outcome of which they are not entirely able to control. Political actors must be aware of, and therefore manage, the duality that separates them from social movements. Systemic power can never be wholly transparent and it cannot be directed against itself. Whoever wields or seeks to wield power cannot at the same time represent the conflicts that challenge that same power. Guaranteed expression of antagonistic demands and conflicts in the society makes it possible for dominant social relationships to be challenged and partially modified, for the privilege enjoyed by the dominant interests to be disputed, for the decisions taken by the apparatuses to be subjected to assessment and challenge by collective needs. A society that can handle its internal conflicts is best equipped to avoid the spiral of violence or terrorism usually following the repression of conflicts, or the manipulated integration which characterizes societies where dissent has been reduced to silence, even under a formally democratic rule.

Contemporary movements by their very nature are ineffectual unless they work through the mediation of political actors. Constantly exposed to the twin risk of fading into folklore or terrorist desperation, they can only exist if their demands are interpreted by political actors capable of mediating them and rendering them effective *vis-à-vis* political decision-making. The demands themselves, however, at the same time continue to exist beyond political mediation and independently of its results, and thus to generate innovative energies. Successful mediation provides the yardstick for measuring democracy in systems for which the establishment of mass consensus no longer constitutes a serious problem, in societies which tend towards equilibrium (which may paradoxically be the equilibrium of crisis) and neutralize the question of ends in favour of the expedient choice of means and procedures. The dispersion, the fragmentation, the discontinuity of movements raises the problem of how they can find an adequate form of representation, one which preserves their specificity, valourizes their spatial and temporal limits, and withstands the cyclical trends of mobilization.

The myth of a movement able to assume power while preserving the transparency of the demands it conveys crumbled in the aftermath of the October Revolution. Power is a systemic requisite for the governance of complexity, and it is structurally distinct from conflicts. Collective action in complex societies, instead, keeps the system open, produces innovation, renews elites, brings into the area of the decidable that which has been excluded, and illuminates the regions of shadow and silence that complexity creates.

The dilemmas of complexity

Decision-making is a crucial process for controlling uncertainty. The rationality of complex societies, the way they operate, is based on information and grants priority to the technical choice of means in the decisions. The constitutive selectivity of every decision-making process also hides power relations behind its mode of operation and eliminates the problem of ends by concentrating on optimizing the means. Movements, in this context, create a space in which the profound dilemmas of complex systems rise to the surface. Numerous studies on the crisis of the welfare state, the problems of governability, pluralism, and political exchange in neo-corporatist systems have enriched analysis of the political effects of complexity by focusing on these dilemmas (Offe 1984, 1985b; Schmitter and Lembruch 1979; Streek and Schmitter 1985; Esping-Andersen 1993).

Firstly, such dilemma concerns the necessity for constant change accompanied by the need for a stable normative and prescriptive nucleus. On the one hand, account has to be taken of mutable interests, of the multiple locations of social actors, of the variability of their aggregations. On the other hand, guarantees must be created for the systems of rules and prescriptions that confer predictability to behaviour and procedures. I shall call this the dilemma of *excess variability*, for change always exceeds the arrangements established to institutionalize it and, simultaneously, change can become effective only through the establishment of institutional frames.

Secondly, complex systems display a high degree of fragmentation of power along with a parallel tendency towards its concentration. Interest groups capable of organizing themselves and able to gain advantages in political exchange proliferate. The decision-making structure fragments and expands, thereby giving rise to a multiplicity of partial, local, and participative forms of government. Correspondingly, however, one witnesses the consolidation of central apparatuses which monopolize the decisions concerning societal ends and effectively remove them outside the control of those affected, by concealing them behind the facade of the apparent neutrality of the issue of technical feasibility. The sites where the meaning of societal action is decided are made invisible and impermeable. I shall call this second dilemma the *undecidability of ends*; indeed too much is decided, but it becomes increasingly difficult to decide on the essential.

Lastly, in complex systems one observes a tendency towards the extension of citizenship and of participation, while the planning of social life through bureaucratic-administrative apparatuses becomes increasingly necessary. The broadening of the sphere of individual and collective rights entails planning, as coordination among the manifold interests and choices necessary to safeguard such rights. But every form of planning automatically entails no less the curtailment of participation and of effective rights by the centres of technocratic decision-making. Here we encounter what I shall call the dilemma of *dependent participation*.

These political dilemmas are closely bound up with the structural tension that strains complex systems. Variability and predictability, fragmentation and concentration, participation and planning designate polar aspects of the more general systemic problem, as it manifests itself within the operation of the political system. Complex societies are driven by the need to mobilize individual resources and to activate high-density, highly differentiated networks of organization, information, and decision-making. At the same time, individual action acquires an elective function as individuals are granted increasing opportunities to control and define the conditions of their own lives. The process of individuation – that is, the development of the individual's capacity to attribute meaning to social action – thus displays the twin facet of extended control through increased pressures of socialization on the individual on the one hand, and the demands by people for space, time, and meaning in their lives on the other. The risks of a fragmented and manipulated individualism are high (Dumont 1983; Bellah *et al.* 1985; Lasch 1978, 1984; Gans 1988), the impoverishment of the public arena and a destructive cynicism may be the outcome (Glendon 1991; Goldfarb 1991) and appealing to the community (Etzioni 1993) may not be sufficient to resist these tendencies. But the debate on individualism should not forget the dilemmatic nature of the issue and the fact that individuals are also becoming the core resources of complex systems.

Because of their close connection to the structural tensions of complex systems, the political dilemmas mentioned above can never be entirely settled by means of political decision-making. Any attempt to resolve them within the sphere of the political system alone must necessarily resort to technocratic rationalization, imposing a solution to either one or the other of the two horns of the dilemma as the 'one best way' to settle a social problem. An institutional regulation of the dilemmas of complexity should increasingly take into account the necessity of 'governing the commons' (Ostrom 1990), of creating common public spaces in which an agreement can be reached to share the responsibility for a whole social field beyond one part's interests or positions.

Public spaces, representation, and the role of knowledge

Those who believe that the nucleus of democracy in complex systems still consists of guaranteed competition among interests and the establishment of the rules which make such competition possible, have not grasped the dimensions of the changes taking place in today's society. A formal conception of democracy, however, is historically linked with the emergence of a social system based on the separation between state and civil society, in which it was the task of the state to translate the 'private' interests of civil society into 'public' institutions (Keane 1988a, 1988b; Arato and Cohen 1992).

Today that distinction on which the political experience of capitalism was founded is blurred. The state as the singular agent of action and intervention has faded away. It has been superseded by an overarching system of closely interdependent transnational relations, and its unity is split into a multiplicity of partial governments, with their own systems of representation and decision-making. The contemporary system of government is defined by an interlocking web of apparatuses which inextricably fuses the public and the private together. Civil society, too, has atrophied. The interests that used to define it no longer possess the permanence and the visibility of stable social groups unambiguously located within the gamut of positions. The unity and the homogeneity of interests explodes. Projected upwards, they take the form of general cultural and symbolic attitudes which cannot be attributed to any specific social group; projected downwards, they fragment into a multiplicity of 'quasi-natural' primary needs.

The distinction between state and civil society has given way to a more complex scenario. The differentiation and 'secularization' of the mass political parties has turned them into 'catch-all parties' institutionally incorporated into the apparatus of government. In a parallel manner, the parliamentary system has increased its role of selecting among social demands, and now performs a merely formal function in decision-making. At a different level, we witness the multiplication and the increasing autonomy of the systems of representation, with all the accompanying problems created by the plurality of decision-making centres – but also with the participative role of the proliferating decisional agents. Lastly, at yet another level, we can observe the formation of conflictual collective demands for the reappropriation of the motivation and meaning of action.

Under these circumstances, it would be mistaken to take the meaning of democracy to consist of little more than the competition for access to governmental resources. Democracy in complex societies can only mean the creation of conditions which allow social actors to recognize themselves and be recognized for what they are or want to be; conditions, that is, which lend themselves to the creation of recognition and autonomy. In this sense, democracy means freedom to belong, or, freedom to construct social spaces of recognition. Thus defined, democracy is also freedom of representation, freedom to express identity in systems of representation which preserve identity over time.

But such freedoms or rights always entail a certain degree of reciprocal tension. In order to perpetuate itself, collective identity needs the reassurance of a social space protected against control or from repression. This space, for the construction of which the collective actor is mobilized, can only be secured through institutionalized representation – that is, through the establishment of those processes (organization, leadership, ideology) which ensure the continuity of demands and allow confrontation and negotiation to go on with the outside. Freedom to belong, therefore, means freedom to be represented. Yet belonging does not equal being represented, indeed in a certain sense it is its opposite: Belonging is direct, representation is indirect; belonging is the immediate enjoyment of the good that is 'identity', representation is its delayed enjoyment. Due to the existence of this tension, a definition of democracy in a complex society must include two further freedoms: the freedom not to belong, as the right to withdraw from one's constituted identity in order to create a new one, and the freedom not to be represented, as the right to reject or modify the given conditions of representation. Nonauthoritarian democracy in complex societies can only be such if it succeeds in accommodating these dualisms: the right to belong or to refuse to belong; the right to make one's voice heard through representation or to modify the conditions in which it is heard. The condition for democracy thus understood to exist is the autonomy of the political space, itself a recent creation and a property specifically of complex societies. I shall call such a space the *public space of representation*. It is distinct from the institutions of government, from the party system, and from the state apparatuses; but it is part of the political system, in its analytical sense as the level of normative decision-making in a society (see chapter 12). Empirically, however, it extends beyond the political institutions proper, embracing systems of representation and decision-making diffused in society; relational systems which guarantee collective identity, allow it to persist, and encourage its crystallization into action; institutionalized systems which promote the acquisition of knowledge and the production of symbolic resources; and institutionalized systems for the circulation and control of information.

The public space of representation is characterized by its great variability. It may expand or shrink according to the degree of autonomy granted to it. It is, by definition, a flexible space, which only a creative relationship between collective action and the institutions can keep open. It is structurally ambivalent because it expresses the dual significance of the terms 'representation' and 'participation'. Representation is *presentative*; that is, it advances demands and promotes interests. But it is also *representative*: it embodies a reality which remains irreducibly different and often goes unnoticed to it. Similarly, participation signifies both *taking part*, or acting to promote an actor's interests and needs, and *being part*, as belonging to a system, identifying with the 'general interests' of the community. This insuperable ambivalence of 'the political' both threatens and empowers creative action.

Movements occupy the public space without losing their specificity. As the point of contact between political institutions and collective demands, between the functions of government and the representation of conflicts, this space is now beginning to take shape in complex societies as a specifically *political* space. The observers who make their case out of the historical record delineating the life and times of the bourgeois public space (Habermas is the first among them; see Habermas 1989) fail to notice the point due to their morphologically charged concerns. They turn their report of the relatively long history of the public space in the modern age into a critique of contemporary society, in which it is rendered vulnerable to the invasion of new forms of power and manipulation. But what they do not capture is the transformation of the public space into a conflictual arena: the public space becomes the arena for the contended definition of what is political, that is, of what belongs to the *polis*. Its chief function is to bring into the open discussion the issues raised by the movements and promote their collective conception – not to institutionalize movements, but to enable society as a whole to assume its inner dilemmas precisely as its own, to transform them into *politics* (literally, into something concerning the *polis*). In other words, it is in the public space that the issues are subjected to negotiation, forwarded for decision-making, and thus transformed into possibilities of change without, however, annulling the specificity and the autonomy of the conflictual actors in the process.

Whether the opposite poles of the above dilemmas can be kept in a sufficient state of equilibrium depends on the extension and strength of the public spaces of representation. Their locus on the internal and external borders of institutional dynamics makes them an ideal forum for openly addressing the central issues affecting the society – the great objectives and the great dilemmas that the collectivity must pronounce, as well as the exclusions and reduction to silence that complexity produces. As spaces for word, spaces for naming, they permit a new and different voice to be given to that which in society refuses to be reduced to the names that technical rationality imposes on the world. This perspective does not underestimate the risks of totalitarianism in complex societies (Arendt 1972; Touraine 1994b); nor it naively ignores the tendency of the dominant groups in any given society to establish a hegemonic control over the political mechanisms (Laclau and Mouffe 1985; Laclau 1990); but it stresses the role of conflicts *and* institutions in defining what democracy will become.

Political representation of conflictual demands is necessary in order to guarantee their endurance, to secure their mere survival and the sustained performance of their functions of contestation and innovation. But such representation and its organizational forms must take into account the specific nature of the demands in question. The organizational form most suited to the features of movements seems to be that of the campaign or a goal-directed mobilization.

The main characteristics of this organizational form are as follows: (i) The objectives set for the mobilization, its manifest aim of action, are general in character – that is, it concerns a problem that directly or indirectly affects the logic of the system, the way it defines development. The goal, however, also carries along with it a concrete referent, namely, reforming a particular policy; (ii) The mobilization involves present interests and benefits – those, that is, which are experienced directly, which belong to the space and time of the participants' daily lives; (iii) The mobilization is of short-term duration and expects loyalty to the goal, not identification with the organization. Militancy, from this point of view, is not a life choice but one stage in an individual's progress through collective life.

What are the organizational conditions for this kind of action? I shall simply enumerate some of these as they have emerged from the culture of movements: (i) A certain diffusion of cognitive and organizational resources among the members of the organization, and the absence of significant imbalances of power; (ii) a tendency to create spaces for self-reflexivity; (iii) self-management of economic resources; (iv) a 'transitional' mentality, which views the organization as a short-term means for achieving certain ends; (v) a tendency to experiment in the present with direct forms of control and alternativeness; and (vi) an ability to produce new skills, especially in the symbolic and communicative domains.

All these resources have to be deployed by an organization seeking to mobilize the potential enclosed in the latent structure of the movement. Only an organization of this kind, participative and vigilant over its own limitations (transitoriness, end-directedness, an inclusive non-totalizing structure), can provide channels of aggregation, representation, and efficiency for the demands of contemporary movements.

But these forms of transient and issue-centred mobilization must rely on the support of institutional actors, which bring along with them an historical continuity, an organizational memory, a praxis of efficiency as the relationship between means and ends, an ability to generalize and accumulate the results of action, and, lastly, access to institutional mediation and confrontation with political power. While the institutional actors draw on an inherited organizational tradition, short-term mobilizations require mobility, flexibility, efficiency, and non-authoritarian integration.

This structure of representation can bring notable benefits to the political system as a whole, since the two sides of it have a reciprocally useful function. The organization of permanent interests constantly runs the risk of corporative bureaucratization, while the organization of mutable interests is in danger of becoming dispersed and fragmented. Thus the one provides organizational continuity, memory, and capacity to generalize; the other continuously generates energies of antibureaucratic mobilization. The chief danger in the process, however, is that a stable division of labour and a hierarchy of importance of functions may assume a permanent and rigid shape. The autonomy of the intermediate space that I have called the public space of representation can facilitate the exchange and circulation of personnel and organizational resources.

Within movements, the provisional character of campaigns extends to stamp not only the mobilization in the narrow sense, but all the decision-making and representative agencies as well that arise in preparation of the mobilization, or that secure the withdrawal from it. Politics operates also through this network of participatory experiences, which already have all the prerequisites for political action arising from their status as training laboratories for political skills. From these experiences more stable forms of political organization and representation may develop, which subsequently transform themselves into institutions or else fade away as the problem that engendered them disappears.

The organizational forms born out of movements produce changes in the political culture by incorporating into their organizational practice symbolic and subjective contents traditionally extraneous to political action; by increasing the awareness of organizational dynamics which helps in treating the political organization as a complex organization and recognizes, furthermore, its specificity and autonomy; and by developing a culture of representation which entails renunciation of any totalizing urge and the recognition of the particular role of political actors.

Knowledge is a crucial resource for new conflictual actors, both because it is a focus of major conflicts (those over the appropriation and control of knowledge and information, and over the instruments of production and circulation of these), and because only in knowledge can the texture of social relationships be disclosed which lie behind the facade of neutrality that the dominant apparatuses seek to impose on social life. Opposition therefore becomes increasingly 'cultural' in character. Made up of antagonist languages and symbols, it is founded on a capacity to appropriate non-manipulated knowledge. In the past, ideology was an important component in the mobilization of the subordinate classes, a weapon with which to challenge the dominant ideology. Such ideology of the subservient was the expression of the separateness of a culture and of a way of life in some way perpetually antagonistic to the values, language, and symbols of the dominant class. In mass society, in which the rigid separation between cultures and ways of life is disappearing, ideology tends to become the principal channel of consensual manipulation. Escaping from ideology to the production of knowledge (of awareness, analytical capacity, communicative skills, self-reflexivity) becomes a key resource for collective action.

Analysis is different from action. It involves awareness of the distance that separates the actor from the achievement of the objectives of action and of the risks that ideology continuously creates for action. The sites where knowledge is produced are 'political' arenas where the demands by social actors and the exigencies of the system meet and clash; and so, too, are the places where information is processed and transmitted. They are part of that wider public domain where participation and the representation of collective identities takes place – provided that they remain open to the confrontation and negotiation of interests. Such openness is created when the autonomy of the function that the institutions producing knowledge perform is recognized; not, however, the defensive autonomy of the intellectual corporations, but, rather, the ability to carry forward critical analysis, research, and invention without merely mirroring social praxis. This autonomy can contribute to the transformation of the public spaces into points of contact and negotiation for the demands that arise within society.

Here, too, arises the possibility of a 'politics' which does not annihilate the specificity of movements but, instead, grasps their potential for innovation. Knowledge makes actors aware of their action. This does not, however, take place through any 'sacred' role performed by the intellectuals, whose task is to preserve the autonomy of their knowledge-forming function, while also recognizing the limits pertaining to it. The distance between knowledge and action is the recognition of the difference that is in the power of no voluntarism to overcome.

The intellectual has no new truths to bring into the world; these are all deeply embedded in people's own experiences and ways of defining their own worlds. The social scientist among them can only aid the actors in releasing the suppressed contents constituting their self-understanding – that is, their identity. Knowledge can contribute to the process of reaching a new level of awareness developed by the actor itself, resulting in that actor's restored ability to redefine the problem field. Thereby new resources may be discovered where it was thought only limits. In this, it is the responsibility of the intellectuals, of those whose profession involves production and dissemination of knowledge, to make distinctions, to separate what empirically is melded together, to contribute to the process of *naming* which is what in a society based on information makes all the difference in the people's lives. That difference is decided in the settlement between the options of being manipulated through the absorption of meanings simply imposed by external and invisible powers, and being able to autonomously produce and recognize meanings for individual and collective life.

Public discourse and the power of naming

The domain in which the word of movements can be heard is public discourse. Such a discourse is often regarded as an immediate product of the media, the latter understood as apparatuses impersonal and allegedly manipulative in nature (see Epstein 1973; Diamond 1975; Bennett 1988; Edelman 1988; Iyengar and Kinder 1987, 1991). There is no doubt about the capacity of the media system of manipulating news or transforming public and political life into a spectacle of worldwide proportions (see Comor 1994). The social existence of public discourse, to be sure, is not a given, but nor is it a product simple and plain. It is the outcome of a complex game of interactions, where indeed the goals and interests of power groups and political apparatuses play a part, but to which, however, the chief contribution is made by the communicators themselves through their professional skills and organizational dynamism, as it is, moreover, by the consumers of their output (Gamson 1988, 1992b; Hilgartner and Bosk 1988). Should one not wish to stick to the belief that professional communicators are nothing but mere agents of clandestine persuasion, it becomes necessary to grant the fact that this enormous, constantly growing sector in complex societies shapes public discourse through its skills, the autonomy of its language, and the complexity of the exchanges and organizational strategies that characterize it (Salmon 1989; McQuail 1992; Ferguson 1990). In the same way, the consumers of the products of communication participate in molding public discourse by filtering messages, activating everyday communicative networks, and by exercising their choice among the various media available for consumption (for example, see Modleski 1986; Chambers 1986; Fiske 1987; 1989, Miller 1988; Ryan 1991; Morley 1992). Not least, finally, collective action itself becomes a new medium and intervenes in the public discourse by its interaction with the media system (Molotch 1979; Gitlin 1980; Gamson 1990, 1992b; Schlesinger 1991).

This complex and multifaceted game makes up public discourse in its actual format. The world inhabited by us is irreversibly built of information. The ingenuous view that information mirrors a 'reality in itself' is a hangover from the past and must inevitably be shaken off. Information in its various forms *is* reality, at least in the sense that our experience is now wholly *mediated* (that is, by the *media*). The cognitive frames and the relations which enable us to *make experience* out of reality depend on the information available to us.

This dramatic change in the nature of social and individual life means that analysis of the ways in which information constructs reality becomes of unprecedented importance. But at the same time, it forces us to abandon the idea of an 'objective reality' which the media should reflect, and which they, in principle, could reflect more or less faithfully. Denunciations of, or protests against, manipulation by the media should not concern themselves with the gap between the representation and the supposed reality the media purportedly distorts; they should, instead, join the debate about the ways in which reality is constructed by it. The problem, instead of misreporting the reality, concerns the greater or lesser visibility of codes, the decision-making processes, and the construction of languages implicated in the production of that reality.

These processes, in varying ways and to different degrees, involve many actors. A world built of information cannot in fact be the result of the omnipotent will of a handful of manipulators (excluding the hypothetical totalitarian society of an Orwellian kind). It is the work of the constant adjustments of the cognitive frames, motivational choices, and learning processes of a large number of social actors, both individual and collective. Obviously, the imbalance of power and its inherent violence – more subtle and pervasive than physical – will not disappear; but it yields the analytical centre stage to the profound ambivalence of processes, and surrenders to a different notion of responsibility. In fact, the 'discourse' constructed by the media is also *our* discourse, but not in the sense of being simply imposed on us who facilely absorb it all like natural sponges to become one with it. It is ours because everyone (to varying extents and with different degrees of power and awareness) contributes to its creation.

We are all affected by the ambivalence of public discourse. Our attention wanders aimlessly in a world where too many messages circulate, and in which we can concentrate on only one object at a time. We are in fact forced to tie our decisions to emotively loaded images before the imperative to make decisions with ever-increasing frequency and always in a hurry.

Thereby the criteria of mere instrumental rationality cease to be adequate as basis for making decisions, and we become susceptible to the appeal of the emotions. Further, we suffer from the discordance between the immediate field of our daily experience and the symbolic reference frame conveyed by information, a frame which now encompasses the whole planet in its scope. We cannot help feeling impotent in the face of this hiatus, and in order to reduce the scope of that frame we repeatedly resort to more or less conscious processes of selection from the available information, to inevitable cycles of engagement and disengagement of attention and commitment. Should we wish to relentlessly follow the maxim 'I care', our psychophysical energies and our moral tension would be exhausted in no time.

The ambivalence of public discourse therefore involves us all, as intellectuals and professional communicators, as political actors, and as citizens and consumers of the messages of the media; and since individuals often occupy several of these roles, the ambivalence only multiplies.

If public discourse is an outcome, multidimensional and discontinuous, then one must examine the possibility of intervening in its construction as a set of processes irreducible to a unity. Dispensing with the myth of the transparency and the linearity of the linkages that hold public discourse together, we can start setting for ourselves a series of political, civil, and everyday objectives. We can aspire to greater visibility in the decision-making processes which govern the media and define the political agenda; we can act so that the controversial nature of the issues, the great debates that divide society, are not muffled and veiled behind the facade of formal neutrality and the apparent self-referentiality of technical questions. We can respect and encourage that part of the public discourse which is created in everyday networks, in hidden solidarities, in the consumption choices taken by citizens. Awareness of the constructed nature of public discourse, of its inevitable 'bias' which depends on the fact that every discourse is produced from a specific point of view in the field, should prevent us from under-evaluating any of its levels, or the relative and varying weight of each one of them in the formation, circulation, and assimilation of information.

Power is ever-present in this game, but not just as a great menace to be fended off. Power may simply mean dependence and manipulation, especially when we project it outside of ourselves and fail to recognize that we are also and always part of power relations. If, however, we instead take power to be constitutive of our human and social relationships, then addressing power means before all addressing our own power – the use that we can make of it, its limitations, the possibility of removing these limitations.

In a society where information has become the crucial resource, power too is a component of the symbolic field that encompasses us all. The relationship between David and Goliath can no longer be assessed by the sheer power of the wielding arm alone. In information societies, symbolic multipliers are at work which render the effects of communication unpredictable and disproportionate to the original impulse, as demonstrated, for example, by the allegedly 'weak' action of contemporary movements, which, however, have deeply influenced politics in critical areas of social life, such as gender, peace, and environment.

Action designed to change the ways in which public discourse is constructed is an open possibility, the effects of which do not depend principally on the 'material' force applied. The sling of David possesses today the force of language. The contemporary battles are fought entirely within language – but within one and the same language. In them, the lesser has at its disposal the power to reveal, through language, the distortion and the abuse to which that language is constantly subjected. Its reduction to signs can be rendered visible and therewith communicable; thus falls the elaborate mask which covers the gigantic weakness. The appearance and the comparison of meaning reveals the hollow force of the empty signs as being just that. The weakness of any power lies in the fact that no discourse can be wholly reduced to mere signs; even the evil needs meaning to be able to speak.

The 'power of the media' is not the power of a monolithic and treacherous Goliath. But even if it were so, at the vulnerable heart of the giant is its necessity to be understood. It speaks, and by the very fact of doing so creates meaning. Regardless of intentions, the word is thrown out in the open; the abused language is seized and rebounds back on the perpetrator, offering the fragile opponent a chance to prevail.

This said, there is, however, at least one condition that still must hold. The field must remain open, even when the game is not on equal terms. Therefore, in any game, above all else it becomes imperative to safeguard the rules. Once it is recognized that the power of information is essentially the *power of naming*, we can set out on the enormous task of redefining the 'right to the word' that is called for in the information age. In other words, we can start action to expand the intimations of public discourse into an authentic public space, into an arena of language where the meanings, priorities, and ends of communal life can be named and compared.

12

The political system

Political system and social relations

What is a political system? The present chapter is organized around this question and deals with both the relationship between the political system and the rest of the social structure, and the analysis of the internal mechanisms of such a system. One should note that everything I will say refers to the analytical levels of social reality, not to a concrete society. It is extremely important not to confuse a system, which is a conceptual construct and an analytical tool, with the empirical reality of a society, which comprises superimposed, multiple historical and geographical features within itself which are analytically distinct from one another. Therefore, when addressing a political system, what we refer to is an analytical structure and a specific type of social relations.

Analytically, I define a political system as that level of the social structure where normative decisions are made. These decisions can be divided into three categories. First, there are decisions over the norms and regulations that govern exchanges among different groups or specific interests in a society. Next, there is the drawing up and adaptation of the rules and procedures that guide the decision-making process itself. Finally, the political system produces decisions which guarantee the maintenance and adaptation of the mode of production and the distribution of social resources. The first type of decision tends to bear upon particular groups within society, the second affects mostly the actors within the political system itself, the third concerns the society as a whole and impacts forms of social power and domination.

Such a rigorous analytical definition of the political system, when adopted, can be applied to empirical units more limited in scope than a global society. In complex organizations and large structures for the production of goods or services (corporations, universities, research centres, hospitals, large administrations), the importance and autonomy of decision-making processes grow apace with their production processes or technical apparatuses. Similar transformations occur within large associational bodies, such as parties, unions, and special interest groups. The rules and exchanges within the organization depend less on technical constraints or the will of one power centre than on processes of 'political' bargaining, and they are the outcome of pressures and negotiations among different interest groups. Each organization creates within itself a 'political system' that is the institutional level at which decisions are made, and at which competing interests confront one another and are negotiated. Many large organizations, especially corporations and the academic and educational system, are presently experiencing a delicate phase of transformation, during which a transition is taking place from a rigid system of rules, handed down by a power hierarchy, towards the establishment of a 'political' system responsible for the creation of those rules through the competition, and even conflict, of the various interests represented within the organization. This process of transformation is far from painless, and it is complicated by the effects of the economic cycles and by interference of larger-scale conflicts. However, without an analysis which singles out and specifies the analytical level that I have called the 'political system,' many of the recent phenomena in today's complex organizations remain incomprehensible. One of the effects of the wave of conflicts which has shaken large institutions since the 1960s has been the development of a 'political' system within these institutions, a system which previously did not exist or was very weak, and which must produce decisions through the representation of different interests and negotiated mediation between them.

Having clarified this, we may return to the definition of a political system. North American political science, led by pluralist theories, has tended to view the political system as an open system of interactions where all of the active and legitimate groups of the population can make their voices heard at all stages of the decision-making process. This apologistic optimism contrasts with the traditional Marxist view of the state and the political system, which regards them as simply the executive committee for the interests of the ruling class. The two conflicting views have prevented careful analysis both of the autonomous internal functioning of the political system *and* of its possible dependence on other social relations (e.g. class, race, gender); they have effectively assigned the analysis of institutions to a residual role within the theory of the capitalist state, but also *de facto* denied any possible contribution of sociology to political science. Today there is a lively debate on the relationship between the state and civil society (Keane 1988a, 1988b; Arato and Cohen 1992), and it is time for critical reconsideration of what exactly is specific to political system. To this end, I shall attempt, on the one hand, to analyse the connection between the political system and other social relations, and, on the other hand, to give a more precise definition to the internal functioning of the system itself.

The classic Group Theory proposed by authors such as Bentley and Truman, in its theoretical foundations, provides the basis for the pluralist approach: according to it, the plurality of interests that are formed at the micro-level in the deep fabric of individual needs are represented in a transparent manner by the political system. A critical analysis in terms of social relations undermines both of the premises implicit in this assumption. First, interests are not the sum of individual needs; they are already structured by the relations among individuals, and particularly by the relationships involved in the production and appropriation of resources. Thus there is no microscopic and atomized level at which interests are formed; rather, they are structured according to social relations (class, race, gender and the like) and the roles through which such relations are activated in people's everyday life. Secondly, the representation of these interests within the political system is not realized through their transparent replication, but, instead, it is implemented within the boundaries and constraints imposed by the dominant social relationships of the given society. The free play of transaction and the overt confrontation of competing demands become ideological imagery masking the reality of a system of domination and imbalances, unless one specifically takes into account the limitations of the political game. Dominant social relationships set the boundaries and determine the possibility and the limits of action in a political system. Yet political power is obviously also the result of consensus and interaction, and performs a specific function in the allocation of shared values, as the pluralist view would suggest. Hidden, however, is the fact that the coercive character of political decisions is not simply a functional necessity founded on consensus, but also the way in which dominant social relations manifest themselves in the political system.

This system of domination imposes a double limitation on the political decision-making processes. First, it determines the structural limits defining the scope of decision-making, by a priori establishing the areas of decidability as well as the areas which remain non-negotiable. In every type of society these confines guarantee the reproduction of fundamental social relationships and tend to ensure the basis of domination. Such structural limits are not necessarily explicit; nevertheless, traces of them can be detected in the society's legal institutions and apparatuses, especially in its constitution. These limits, furthermore, become distinctly apparent during critical periods of transformation, when new interests and emerging demands tend to thematize them in public discussion, and when the action of new groups within the political system begins to strain the limits of its habitual functioning. The confines of the system are thus revealed in a negative way, through the repressive response of the state. We shall return to this problematic later in chapter 13.

The second limitation is the result of the direct intervention of dominant social relationships in the internal functioning of the political system. The opportunities for access to the system and its utilization are not distributed equally, but are, instead, allocated so as to ensure an advantage for dominant interests. Political competition is 'imperfect competition', structurally organized to effectively favor the interests of the dominant social groups. Whether in the opportunities for political organization, in the use of electoral mechanisms, in the access to the apparatus of the state and the media system, or in the influencing of legislative decision-making, the political forces which represent the dominant interests enjoy structural advantages within the political game, which can vary according to the specific functioning of the political institutions, as we shall see in due course.

Given these two forms of limitation, one may define a political system as that level of society where decision-making processes take place through a representative procedure of some kind as follows:

(i)   The political system is above all an open system surrounded by a changing environment (the environment is constituted by the other systems within the society and by other societies);

(ii)   the political system receives input from the environment in the form of demands, resources, and limitations;

(iii)   output from the system takes the form of normative decisions;

(iv)   the process whereby demands are transformed into decisions takes place within the system through the competitive action (pressure or influence) of numerous actors who tend to maximize their own advantage in the decisions arrived at;

(v)   the actors are representative of social interests or demands;

(vi)   the actors operate according to shared rules and proceed through strategic action which calculates costs and benefits, taking into account the multiplicity of interests represented within the system;

(vii)   modification of the environment, as a result of decisions produced by the system, involves a modification of input; the system has some feedback mechanism which transmits information on the effects of its decisions and which it uses to regulate its functioning.

We must now analyse each of these components of the political system, in an attempt to demonstrate the effects of the double limitation described above. But first there is a need to clarify three important points.

First, what is meant by 'political power'? The term power has many meanings in current usage, and the fact that in our case we need to use an adjective 'political' demonstrates its multiple senses. Students of political processes would agree to define 'political' power as the capacity of certain groups: (a) to exert privileged control over the processes of political decision-making; (b) to take normative decisions in the name of society as a whole; (c) to enforce these decisions, where necessary, through the use of coercion. Such a capacity implies a variable combination of consensus (legitimation) and coercion. In order to handle the generality of the term 'power' when referring to the political system, I propose to retrieve Gramsci's concept of hegemony so as to be able to encompass the three analytical components outlined above. Although in Gramsci's theory the concept of hegemony clearly was given a wider meaning covering class domination, I suggest to restrict it to the political system. Hegemony, then, denotes the degree of dependence of the system on dominant social relations, and the way in which the dominant interests are expressed in normative decisions through the action of the political forces that represent them. While the concept of power encompasses the exercise of social domination of any kind through the legitimation of the political system (but also through other forms of social relations and cultural processes), the concept of hegemony is well suited to indicate the interplay of autonomy and dependence (of legitimation and domination) that characterize political processes and the exercise of power *within* the political system.

The second point to be clarified is the distinction between the political system and the state. Although in current usage these two notions are often interchangeable, it is important to differentiate between the two on an analytical level. The political system, as I have stressed, is not an empirical unit; it is rather an analytical level of the social structure. The state, on the other hand, is an historical and territorial unit, in which coexist various analytical components. It could be said that a concrete society, a collective historical entity defined in space and time, *has* a political system (or, often, several political systems), while it *is* a state, at least in the modern era.

The third question concerns the use of the notion of class. As my thinking in this area has developed, I have gradually felt it desirable to abandon the concept of class relationships that still featured prominently at an earlier stage of my work. The concept of a 'class' appears inseparably linked to capitalist industrial society; yet I thought myself able to put it to productive use as an analytical tool with which to define a system of conflictual relationships within which social resources are produced and appropriated (e.g. Melucci 1980). The notion of *class relationships* served as a temporary tool aiding in the analysis of systemic conflicts and forms of domination in complex societies. Thus, a traditional category was employed so as to enable focusing on the relational and conflictual dimension of the production of the basic orientations of a society. But in contemporary systems, where classes as real social groups are withering away, more appropriate concepts are required – and this can be said without still ignoring the theoretical problem that the category of class relationships has left behind as its legacy: the problem of knowing what relations and which conflicts are involved in the production of the crucial resources of a particular system. Addressing this question (as does, for example, Eder 1994; see also Pakulski 1995, Esping-Andersen 1993) is critical for the understanding of the dual articulation of autonomy and dependence that characterizes the political system and the relationship between movements and processes of representation and decision-making. And the concept of class relationship can still matter for the analysis of a specific historical society. However, when what we are dealing with is an historical 'social formation' (say, Italy, Germany, Peru, or the United States of 1993 or 1963), we are always confronted with a mixture, a compound made of many historical layers. Class relationships, then, can certainly have their place in understanding the nature of a particular compound formation. But it seems that this concept no longer is useful for the understanding of the nature and direction of systemic conflicts at the planetary scale. Such conflicts are the expression of new social relationships that 'inform' every single part of the global system, transforming thereby the role and the meaning of previous forms of domination and conflict.

After this clarification we can now turn to the internal processes of the political system.

Political demands

A political demand could be said to consist of any request for a normative decision that is addressed to the political system. Such admittedly quite wide a definition includes a number of different empirical phenomena ranging from the action of parties to the requests by pressure groups, trade union demands, and direct action of social movements. But, on an analytical level, what constitutes a political demand? We could designate it as a request which (a) accepts, at least in part, the rules and procedures of the political system; (b) aims at securing a normative decision, that is, an intervention which is binding to the entire collective entity; and (c) is expressed by a group which, at least partially, has a legitimate access to the political system.

These three conditions make it immediately clear that not every 'need' or 'interest' present in a society acquires the form of a political demand, as the simple equation of pluralist theory would rather have it. Within a system, there exists a vast area of non-demand, of excluded interests repressed or kept to the margins, which do not reach the point of expression or organization and which are deprived of access to the political system as they are not recognized as legitimate. There are also demands which concern society as a whole and seek to alter the configuration of dominant social relations. These, at least initially, are not made manifest within the confines of the political system, or are deficient in recognized legitimacy and are therefore denied access. These demands can become manifest only through the action of social movements, or, alternatively, they may terminate in self-perpetuating expressive violence, according to the degree of elasticity of the political system and the capacity for adaptation of the social order. Over time, such demands tend to be translated, at least in part, into political demands, becoming thereby submitted to treatment within the limits of the system.

Political demands can be more or less general in nature. To simplify the matter, we could reduce them to the three categories already indicated, in the order of increasing generality: (i) demands regarding the regulation of exchange between particular groups within the society; (ii) demands that call for the modification or adaptation of the rules of the political system, so as to widen or restrict access to it; (iii) demands regarding the maintenance or adaptation of the mode of production and distribution of social resources.

If one refuses to treat a political demand as an original datum, considering it, instead, as a phenomenon which expresses interests formed outside the political system, it becomes necessary to pose the question of how and under what conditions a political demand is constituted. On the one hand, there are structural conditions caused by the imbalances and tensions in a social system, as provoked by the system's need for adaptation to the environment, or by contradictions arising from competition among groups or social conflicts. On the other hand, these potential sources of demand must be set against the degree of permeability of the political system at the specific time and place in which the demand is produced. The joint effect arising from these two conditions accounts for the sum total of the political demands actually present within a system.

A political system filters demands and selects those of them that can be dealt with through the decision-making process. The criteria governing this selection relate to the dual limitation discussed above. There are, however, also demands which are not expressed as such, or which, if expressed, are repressed on account of the perceived threat they pose as potentially undermining the very structure of domination in the society. Further, there are demands which face exclusion because they call into question the advantage of the particular dominant interests in utilizing political processes (they question the hegemony of certain groups over the political system). In spite of this, the force of certain demands may alter the balance of the political system, and cause the criteria for selection to be widened. Social groups excluded from the political system can thus gain access to it, without the system's structural limits being thereby affected. On the other hand, a frontal transgression of these limits would entail a general transformation of the political system and of society at large.

Within the boundaries of the dual limitation mentioned above, a political system's ability to deal with a demand depends upon the resources it has at its disposal. All the factors either favoring or limiting a system's ability to act can be seen as resources or constraints. The features of the natural and social environment, the economic and technological conjuncture, the international situation and relations with other societies constitute some of the conditions upon which the capacity of the political system to deal with a demand is based; these may be conditions that impose constraints, but also factors that provide inputs to the political system and fuel it with new resources. An important example of the mobilization of resources by the political system is the recruiting of political personnel. The channels and methods of political recruitment condition the functioning of the system, its capacity to deal with demands and produce decisions.

As regards the filtering of political demands, the resources available to the system, or the limits imposed on it, orient and specify the selection processes the system has at its disposal, by determining the applicable criteria for such operation. The concept of political demand must therefore be used with analytical precision, bearing in mind what has been stated concerning it so far. I suggest a self-restraining use of the term which would indicate a specific component of the political system as its central reference, so that the range of meaning covered will not extend to include every request or claim arising within the social system. To delimit the parameters defining the field of political demand means rejecting the premise of transparency and recognizing that a portion, larger or smaller, of social processes always escapes the attention of the political system and, consequently, treatment by it. Exclusion and silence often occupy a much larger area than do the problems rendered visible within a political system.

The production of decisions

After an analysis of the relationship between the political system and that part of social reality which stands prior to and beyond it, we can now turn our focus onto the internal relations that engender the decision-making process. That process is made up of four essential components: (1) The reduction of demands; (2) competition and negotiation among demands; (3) the articulation of solutions; and (4) the decision itself. These are phenomena which directly express the logic of the functioning of the political system, as well as its autonomy as a system constituted of specific relations. I will consider these components separately.

1. A political system must shape demands according to its actual capacity to deal with them, which again depends on the constraints on the system and the resources available to it. Thus the quantity and the type of demands that the system can handle do not depend on purely functional factors; nor are they neutral effects of technical limits, since to a certain extent they always relate to dominant social relations. The actual ability of the system to respond to demands by making decisions is always a variable combination of technical and functional limits and constraints imposed by the dominant social relations. Thus the system must work through processes for the reduction of demands, both in terms of quantity and variety, so that it can avoid a situation where input surpasses its capacity to deal with it. The political system contains within itself internal selection mechanisms which establish barriers at different levels of the decision-making process, such as, for example, the work of committees in parliamentary systems, or the work of the party apparatus or the bureaucracy in easing or blocking the path of various legislative proposals. Demands which have gained access to the political system, that is, which have passed through its external filters, are again subjected to a selection process inside the system, and can advance or be blocked in the decision-making process. They must be organized according to a hierarchy of priorities, and the order in which the agenda is set may exert an influence on the outcome of decisions. Finally, there is the process of aggregation, or combination, of demands, through which the diversity or particularity of interests is organized into more general proposals or formulae. This is one of the basic tasks of parties and other political organizations.

Internal selection, the regulation of the flow of demands over time, and the aggregation of demands are not neutral processes, designed simply to enable the efficient functioning of the political system. They involve imbalances between conflicting interests and an unequal distribution of advantage among the forces competing for a decision. However, it is equally true that, in purely functional terms, the incapacity of the political system to guarantee a certain reduction of demand can lead to the paralysis or crisis in the decision-making process. The infinite subdivision of legislative output, the proliferation of laws with particularistic targets, is the most visible sign of the inability of a political system to make decisions of general scope and applicability. A result of these phenomena we see a substantial immobility of the system.

2. Demands which manage to enter the political system engage in a competition against each other, seeking to maximize their own advantage in the decisions. In spite of reductive processes (and even internally to them), the competition arises between the different demands that resist reduction and aggregation. The extent and intensity of such competition depends on the extent of divergence and incompatibility found among the various demands. Differing demands may prove concurrent, allowing the conflict to be resolved in an alliance or a merger. Divergent demands may or may not be wholly incompatible, in the sense that the system may possess sufficient resources to satisfy, at least in part, both of them at once. When a favourable decision regarding one particular demand entails the certain defeat or exclusion of another, the maximum of incompatibility and the maximum of competition prevail. The degree of incompatibility between different demands also determines the prospects for negotiation between political forces. One should always remember that political competition takes place within a system of rules which limit the actions of competitors and permit the exchange of information. Each competitor can venture to predict the behaviour of the others and transmit messages designed to influence their expected conduct. As these interactions progress, either irreconcilable differences emerge or alliances are formed; and attempts may be made to maintain 'shadow zones' that mask the actual nature of competition and leave open the way to a variety of solutions.

3. In order for demands to be decidable, they must be translated into the language of the political system. In other words, they must become 'problems' or 'issues' that the political system can deal with and for which it must find 'solutions' or 'answers.' The representation of interests within the political system consists above all of the elaboration of solutions submitted to the decision-making process for adoption. The task of political actors, and especially of the parties, is to intervene in the decision-making in order to render the demands they represent easier to handle, and this takes place by proposing solutions. The political actors perform this role entirely within the political system, since they have no alternative but to respect the system's logic and language – a role which often conflicts with the pressures arising from a demand formed outside the system, which the political actors must in any case take into consideration. Those seeking to articulate solutions must be positioned inside the system and have available to them the largest possible quantity of information obtainable within that system.

They must be in a position to carefully assess the power relationships, the constraints and resources offered by the system. Similarly, they must have the capacity to predict the behaviour of the adversary, the effects that certain decisions may have upon the system and upon the actors themselves. They should be able to devise strategies and to anticipate the advantages or disadvantages of chosen courses of action.

4. The decision is a way of reducing uncertainty. A choice between alternatives is born of incomplete information about the status of the system and about the predictable effects of an action. Such indeterminacy means that the decision-making process is a real process of choice and not simply the mechanical result of a series of limiting conditions. The more open the system is and the greater its receptivity to stimuli from the environment, the greater the degree of uncertainty and the more urgent the need for decisions. It is this situation that characterizes the complex organizational systems of contemporary societies, and that incurs the need for a 'political system' within large organizations. It also explains why a political system is never merely a replicate assembly of the interests of any established ruling class but, instead, a functional whole operating with a high degree of autonomy.

Domination, except in the case of a (hypothetical) full-fledged totalitarian society, cannot secure control over all the variables of the system and does not encompass all of the information to be found within it. Thus there always remain wide areas of uncertainty which even the strongest dominant groups must seek to reduce. In one sense, the political system meets an essential structural need of the dominant groups, that of reducing uncertainty so as to increase the effectiveness of their control. At the same time, however, the reduction of uncertainty must be accomplished through decision-making processes in the political system, and here other interests and other demands find their opportunity intervene to complicate and obstruct the way towards the position of intended control.

Such uncertainty concerns, first of all, the present of the system with its incomplete information, and, then, the effects that certain choices will have on the system itself. It is difficult to establish any definitive priority of objectives, to calculate exactly the sum total of advantages or disadvantages, or to anticipate all the possible repercussions of a decision. Every decision thus carries with it a more or less wide margin of discretion and elements of risk. The range of possible choices varies according to the conditions in which the decision takes place: the more direct the impact of a decision on dominant interests, the narrower the range of choices. In every case, a decision calls for the calculation of risks and an attempt to reduce them to a minimum. One way for political actors to seek the reduction of the risk involved in a decision is to secure for themselves a preventive consensus through the use of propaganda and ideological manipulation.

A fundamental role in the decision-making process is played by the pressure or influence exercised by the different interest groups on each other. A decision is not only the result of an abstract calculation; it also reflects of a play of mutually influential forces. The 'rationality' of a decision cannot be evaluated in isolation from the consideration of the play of pressures. The political actor is not a decision-maker programmed with the logic of a computer; such an actor is always part of a network of exchanges, influences, negotiations. The decision resulting from the process is an outcome of the interaction of such a field of forces, not an issue of an abstract definition of interests. The need for political actors to take this play of influences into account may even lead to decisions that at first sight appear to contradict the interests of the particular actor in question.

The autonomy of the political process, especially with respect to the articulation of solutions and the actual decision-making, is well illustrated by the role of communist parties in Western democracies. In Italy, for instance, research has shown that most decisions and provisions, since the second half of the 1960s, have been taken at the committee level, with the participation and contribution of the communist members of parliament (Blackmer and Tarrow 1975; Berger 1981). This has been described as a 'negative integration' of the communist party into the Italian political system. The need to make certain demands easier to process within the political system and the desire to influence effectively the decision-making process together increased the gap between the public image of the party, which presented itself as the champion of class opposition, and the parliamentary practice of an actor operating entirely within the logic of the political system. This dual posture has damaged the communist party on both sides, weakening its traditional constituency in the working class on the one hand and preventing it from joining the government as a legitimated partner on the other.

The effects of the political system

The decisions by the political system affect the rest of the social structure in so far as their outcome is enforced. The implementation of decisions is not a problem external to the political system, but continues to be subject to the play of pressures and influences. A decision may be implemented only partially, not at all, or in a distorted fashion, according to the practical effect of the forces and the interests intervening in the implementation process. Passive resistance, bureaucratic inertia, and direct pressure on administrative bodies can also be used to distort the process or render a decision ineffective, or to secure an advantageous application of the new ruling.

The implementation of decisions always involves the administrative and repressive apparatus of the state (as discussed in the following chapter). In any case, implementation would be impossible without mobilization of consensus. The execution of a decision requires the mobilization of both the apparatus of the state and a sufficient quota of political consensus. The variable relationship between these two components determines the degree of legitimization of the decision. The role of political parties and interest groups acquires importance in the process of legitimation (or delegitimation), since they have the capability to mobilize consensus or resistance to the application of the new regulations.

Thus the political process continues to be a process of pressures, of negotiations, of power relationships, even during the phase of the implementation of decisions. The influence or the regulatory efficacy of a decision cannot be assessed in abstract, on the basis of formal legal criteria or of the technical quality of a law. It must be evaluated as part of the concrete relationship between forces and interests. Adaptation of the rule always takes place according to the actual power relationships and to the capacity of the various interests to influence the implementation process.

The implementation of decisions produces certain effects on the state of the system and its environment, or other systems, thereby changing the conditions for the making of future decisions. A political system has a limited capacity of collecting information regarding the results of its completed actions, thus allowing it to modify its operation in the light of that data. A decision can have direct effects upon the subject of the decision itself, but it may also have indirect consequences on the rest of the social structure, which are far more difficult to control over the short term. Moreover, certain tensions within the system may either be mitigated or increased as a result of a decision. This explains the growing importance of information in modern political systems, and the weight assigned to tools designed to make accurate forecast or to monitor feedback. The role of the social sciences in this situation is of ever-increasing importance: they make it possible to predict behaviour, and thus expose themselves to new risks in proportion to their conceivable uses as instruments of manipulation, as preventive techniques for the control of conflict and the creation of consensus.

The political system modifies its functioning according to the information it receives. These modifications take place within the structural boundaries of a given social system and its dominant social relations. A system will not overstep these limits except in the case of a general conflict involving the mode of production and appropriation of social resources. But within these confines, significant changes to the rules of the political game and to the institutional structure may take place; such cases can be characterized as changes of regime (for example, transition from an authoritarian regime to a parliamentary system, in which the capitalist foundation of the mode of production remains unaffected). Alternatively, adaptation may assume a more limited nature and form; these cases we can denominate as instances of 'political modernization'. In such reforms, a system can modify the filters which regulate the input of demands so as to increase their elasticity; it can widen the base of participation by recognizing as legitimate previously excluded social groups; it can step up the mobilization of resources, increasing its exchanges with the other systems within society; or it can increase the circulation of information and the efficiency of the decision-making process. These forms of adaptation are driven by the need to remain within the confines cited above at the times the pressures exerted by excluded social groups strive to call them into question. Dealing with problems of change always takes place within a concrete and historical structure, the *state*. It is not the political system alone that changes, but the state as a composite historical and territorial unit comprising different analytical levels, which we shall discuss in the chapter that follows.

13

The state and the distribution of social resources

The political system and the state

North American pluralist theories have provided a definition of the political system which supersedes the simplistic assertion of a direct point-by-point correspondence between the system of domination and the political system. At the same time, however, these theories have their basis on distinct ideological assumptions: the classic idea of a system in which all the active and legitimate groups can make their voice heard at any stage during the decision-making process, the idea of a disparate plurality of social groups capable of exerting influence in diverse sectors and all endowed with a generalized capacity, if not to determine decisions, at least to reject those that are undesirable. This idea seems to be associated closely with the ideological image that the system seeks to produce of itself, and to under-evaluate the force of the limits of the representative mechanisms and decision-making processes in reality.

In the Marxist tradition, on the other hand, there has been a tendency to ratify an image of a closed and monolithic political system in which the state performs the role of the direct executor of the dominant class's interest, as an agent of domination with no genuine autonomy of its own. Even if Marxist perspective has changed over time (Miliband 1973, 1989), the result has been to render incomprehensible a set of phenomena in which the relative autonomy of the political system plays a role of crucial importance; principal among these are the conquest of certain institutional arenas by the subordinate groups, the complex phenomenon of reformism, and the ambivalent behaviour of the public bureaucracy.

In order to steer clear from the impasse contained in the choice between the two alternative frameworks, our categories should take account, on the one hand, of the existence and weight of the system of domination and, on the other, of the autonomy and complexity of the political as an instance or level that is irreducible to that system. Secondly, the analysis needs to be freed from a conceptual confusion which has marred it from the beginning. The definition of the political system lumps together two different qualitative notions which should, instead, be kept separate. On the one hand, there is a conceptualization of the system which elaborates the rules governing the social organization; on the other, the definition also includes the institutional structures of the state and the political organizations. Thus, an analytical level is confused with institutions and organizations; in particular, the decision-making system and the state are melded together. The political system as a decision-making system should be treated rather as an analytical concept whose features we already analysed in chapter 12: thus characterized it constitutes a level of analysis, not a 'social place'. It is distinct from the state, which is instead a complex reality in which, as we shall see, an institutional system of rule elaboration unites with an apparatus of organizational management and an agent role endowed with specific autonomy in historical action. Thus clarified, the concept of 'political system' enables us to identify a level of analysis which is distinct both from the system of domination and from the workings of the social organization and the life-world. However, it is necessary to specify that this is a distinction, not a 'separation'. The concept of the political system as an open game of transactions between actors, as a relatively free encounter of competing strategies, remains an ideological construct if one forgets that the system of domination shapes and restricts this field of interactions. We encounter, in fact, the twofold limitation mentioned in chapter 12 which the pluralist tradition invariably seems to have underestimated. To be sure, it does not ignore the existence of power relationships and the coercive aspects of the political system; but it conceives these relationships as the outcome of consensual interactions; they are, that is, presented as specifically functional in the allocation of socially recognized values. But the coercive aspect of political relationships is not a just a functional necessity that derives from consensus on values; it is also the manner in which domination is inscribed in power relationships at the political level.

Thus, the openness of the field of political negotiations and transactions suffers from a double constraint. First, dominant social relations set the field's structural limits. They define beforehand what may be subject to decision-making and bargaining and what again is non-negotiable. In no society can everything be decided, and the limits of possible transactions are fixed in structures which translate and crystallize domination while ensuring its permanence: they thus preserve the 'reproduction of production relationships' on which the system rests. These limits obviously vary according to the type of society in question, but they have a basic feature in common – they guarantee the bases of power and prevent the calling into question of those bases. The second limitation of the political system is set through a process of rule elaboration. Not only is the field of strategies and transactions structurally limited, but, internally to it, the institutional game is not played on an equal footing. In the political market where the social forces confront one another, some groups are constantly handicapped, and their disadvantage is enduring because the field is constituted so as to favour other groups. Opportunities to exert influence are unequally distributed. Furthermore, dominant relations try to maintain themselves and to reestablish such inequality in new forms whenever collective action forms to redress or diminish the imbalance.

The political system, as I have defined it here, is therefore an input–output system limited both externally and internally through the control exercised by the system of domination, in such manner that the quantity and quality of input and output are specifically determined through this control mechanism. The political system, therefore, is never wholly open: it is always conditioned in the twofold sense I elaborated above. Nor, though, is it ever wholly closed, in the sense that it never transcribes social domination directly on a point-by-point basis. Having thus defined the range of our conceptual field, we may proceed to focus on certain aspects of the problem of the state.

The unity of the state

By examining the political system as an analytical level distinct from the rest of the social structure, I have wished to emphasize the specific kind of relations that constitute it in order to demonstrate the increasing importance of political decision-making processes in both complex organizations and, more particularly, in complex societies in general. Turning next to the state, a different kind of analysis is required, one which takes into account the empirical form of modern 'social formations', their historical evolution, and their developmental models. The notion of 'social formation' is to my knowledge the closest to the idea of an historical society comprising simultaneously different layers of its evolution. Such analysis, which would greatly aid in understanding the contemporary transformations in the nature and role of the modern state, lies however beyond the scope of the present discussion, and would require a specific and separate treatment. Therefore, I shall confine my remarks to a mere observation of the methodological difference between a synchronic, or structural, approach to the political system and a diachronic, change-oriented approach to the problems of the state.

The state is a composite historical and territorial unit, in which it is possible to distinguish three analytical components: (a) the state as a historical agent unifying a 'social formation'; (b) the state as political agent of an institutional decision-making system; (c) the state as functional agent of organizational bureaucratic apparatuses. I shall examine each of these separately.

The state is a complex reality at once narrower and broader than that subsumed by the notion of political system – 'narrower' in the sense that, as an institution or sum of institutions, the state lies at the empirical level of an historical society and can be conceptually circumscribed by descriptive categories (territory, nation, and so on); 'broader', because, although it comprises a system of decision-making, the state simultaneously amounts to something more than that. In fact, it comprises both a level of organizational management and functioning (the state apparatus) and a capacity for autonomous action as an agent endowed with its own unity.

This distinction in reality subordinates the other elements (decision-making processes and state apparatus) to the unity of the state agent. In any given society, which always is a complex historical society with many historical layers, the state takes the form of a specific unity which performs the essential function of giving cohesion to the various levels of the social formation. Subordinate to this cohesive function performed by the complex and unitary structure of the state are both the political system in the strict sense and the state apparatus. Because concrete analysis always operates at the level of a given social formation, we are entitled to speak of the state as an agent endowed with unity, in spite of the distinctions introduced at the analytical level.

A 'social formation' is a concrete society comprising differing historical modes of production and therefore different forms of appropriation of social resources. The state unifies these multiple components by organizing them around a predominant pattern which is the factor of cohesion of a social formation. Capitalist mode of production has been the dominant pattern of the modern age. The state's role as a unifying agent calls forth both decision-making processes and an administrative and repressive apparatus. What, then, are the ways in which this cohesive function is manifested? First, there is the state's capacity for an autonomous action affecting the mode of production itself. This capacity encompasses society as a whole: the transformation of society, the action of society on itself, may be assumed by the state as an independent agent, beyond the immediate interests of the ruling classes but never outside the limits on which domination is grounded. For example, the state may take responsibility for industrialization or development, if the elites are weak or hesitant. The state promotes and maintains the bases for the reproduction and development of the basic pattern, even over and above the immediate and conjunctural interests of the ruling groups. The forms assumed by this kind of intervention have been profoundly modified by the passage from a liberal society to monopolistic capitalism (Tilly 1975, 1984, 1990; Giddens 1985; Bright and Harding 1984; Evans *et al.* 1985) and, further, to 'postindustrial' or 'post-fordist' forms of the state (Offe 1984, 1985b, Lipietz 1992). What has been reinforced is the state's capacity for direct and autonomous action by intervening in economic, labour, and social policies in order to guarantee economic development and social integration.

In its role as a cohesive agent, the state also intervenes to protect the structural limits of the political decision-making process that were analysed earlier in this chapter. The structural limits on the field of political decision-making discussed earlier are manifest in the unitary structure of the state, particularly in its juridical structure, which sanctions the limits of the non-negotiable and defines the arena within which political bargaining may take place. Inscribed in the very structure of codes and laws is the defence of the intangible foundations of the system: these codes and laws establish the boundaries beyond which negotiation is no longer possible because the structure of domination would be attacked in its vital bases. The cohesive function of the state is accomplished through the legal structure, which determines the confines of political decision-making and sets the rules defining what may or may not constitute a demand for a political decision, and what on the other hand is not negotiable, inasmuch as it forms part of the dominant pattern of social relations. Above all, however, the state steps in to protect these limits by means of concrete intervention of its repressive apparatus whenever their unity is endangered by the actions of the subordinate groups. When political participation begins to expand beyond the limits of the institutional confines, when demands attempt to break the rules of the political game, repressive intervention is launched to reestablish the limits of the system, habitually with no excuses as to its blunt manner. Through various means, the state favours political action which confirms and reinforces these limits, and tends to obstruct or repress the organization and political participation of interests that call those limits into question.

Nevertheless, the state's action to maintain institutional confines must pass through the filter of the political system, that is, through the processes of mediation analysed above. Dominant interests must confront and negotiate with other interests and, particularly in parliamentary systems, with the political representatives of the subordinate groups. This means that the pressure applied by the weaker interests may achieve some success, albeit never beyond a given threshold. State action moves in two opposing but complementary directions: reform and repression. Pressure from the subordinate groups for widened access to the political system may cause a reduction in the filtering and selection of demands, and modify the executive apparatus. No state intervention can ever be completely and solely repressive, and reform, institutional change, the opening up of channels for the regulated management of conflict, and hence an improvement in the relative position of the weaker groups are the reverse and necessarily complementary side of state action.

The third component is the state apparatus, the organizational bureaucratic system whose task it is to give cohesion to a historical social formation by providing operational tools and procedures for the implementation and enforcement of normative decisions. The state apparatus is therefore, on the one hand, a political instrument which transfers the advantage of the dominant interests, filtered in the form of normative decisions, to the concrete body of the society. Apparatuses of social control (the police, armed forces, the judiciary) ensure that the decisions safeguarding the advantage of dominant interests remain in force. This function, however, is not solely reserved for the more artless forms of repressive action; its proper performance is complemented through control of the cultural and educational apparatuses (schools, media) and through the compensatory actions of the welfare structures.

On the other hand, however, the state apparatus is never merely a docile, monolithic instrument in the hands of the dominant groups; its operation also reflects the degree of autonomy of the political system. This, moreover, creates tensions between different forces and interests within the state organizational bodies. The further these apparatuses stray away from the classical model of bureaucracy as a rigidly regimented hierarchical order, the more frequently will such tensions arise. When forms of 'political' decision-making find their entrance into the bureaucracy itself, spaces for conflict and negotiation open up within it. One should, however, not forget that the state apparatus is a complex organization, which acts according to the functional logic of technical requirements common to such organizations. This widens the margins of autonomy with respect to the dominant interests, and can account for the radicalization emerging now and then in certain sections of the public bureaucracy, for the conflicts that oppose different sections of bureaucracy to each other, and for the resistance to certain policies and support for others.

The state apparatus is necessarily ambivalent. On one hand, it is the political mechanism whereby dominant interests filtered through political decisions are transmitted to, and implemented in, the concrete social arena;

it is the guarantor for the operationality of these interests. The repressive apparatuses of the state (police, army, judiciary) give concrete form to this function, although it operates not only at the purely repressive level but also by exercising control over the socialization and cultural apparatuses. Conversely, however, the state apparatus is also exposed to the effects of the autonomy of the political system and manifests internal incoherences, imbalances, and tensions which render it receptive to reform in response to demands advanced by excluded social groups. Administrative decentralization, the broadening of representative channels, change in electoral mechanisms and procedures, and democratization of the personnel recruitment and culture are all examples of such an influence of the political system on state apparatuses. Moreover, the state apparatus, as an administrative system, exhibits the same features as all modern complex organizations: autonomization of internal relationships and the increasing role of specific professional identities.

In complex societies important transformations are taking place in different sectors of the state apparatuses. From the schools to the judicial system, to the police and the armed forces, the pressures of societal changes and the increasing autonomization of the political system have produced a widespread crisis in the traditional functioning of bureaucratic institutions. Radicalization and conflict of interests have also made inroads into the state apparatus, which has become an explicitly 'political' entity. The rejection of false neutrality, which often hid the instrumental subordination of the bureaucracy to the dominant interests, is reflected in a new demand for recognition of the professional substance and organizational autonomy of the administrative apparatus.

Social organization or difficult integration

To conclude this chapter, we can now turn to the question of how social resources are distributed. The existence of role systems regulated by norms, of social positions bound by reciprocal expectations of behaviour, is the aspect of social differentiation that functionalist sociology has helped us to understand. But what was ignored by this tradition is the fact that domination is inscribed, following its mediation by the political system, in the social power which establishes the limits of what is permitted and what is prohibited, which assigns positions and decides their rewards, and which ensures its own reproduction through the transmission of norms. At the same time, forms of conflict and resistance are always made manifest within concrete organizations; they assume the form of economic demands, of organizational claims, of resistance to integration or of rejection of norms.

Here, too, the analyst must never forget the dependence and the autonomy of social levels. Within an organization, interpreting authority as a purely technical function is tantamount to forgetting that 'functional' power also embodies and realizes, on the concrete site of social performances, the exigencies of domination. Conversely, to treat authority as nothing more than the pure transcription of domination is to ignore the organization's requirements of internal integration and coherence, its need to adapt to a changing environment – in sum, the existence of the organization's more specifically functional problems for which the authority role ensures some sort of solution.

Likewise, on the side of the subordinates, there is no form of conflictual behaviour within the organization that is analysable solely in terms of maladjustment, of resistance to change, of anomie, or of deviance. Conflict, a challenge to the basic mechanisms of power, is to a certain extent always present in the demands of subordinates. But there also exist forms of action located more directly within the organizational framework which seek to improve the actors' relative positions on a consensual scale of values, and which call for a more functional integration of the organizational complex and its more flexible adaptation to the environment.

Here, again, a mere functionalist approach tends to obscure the existence of conflictual or even antagonist relationships. Functionalist theory has seen social norms as the transcription of values, and roles as a system of exchange regulated by shared norms. Values govern norms which, in turn, govern roles. Thus, the social organization and the specific institutions are treated as operational systems erected on a shared set of values. Authority roles ensure the coherence and internal functionality of the organization, while enabling it to adapt to the environment and grow: there are certain crucial functional requirements which, in every organization, guarantee the realization and permanence of values.

The values-norms-roles sequence underpins the classic Parsonian concept of institution, the sense of which certainly comes closest to what I have called an 'organization'. For Parsons, institutions are systems of reciprocal expectations of institutionalized behaviour. In other words, the process of institutionalization involves the passage from values through norms to roles, or the transcription of general cultural and shared elements into norms and, further, into reciprocal expectations of behaviour. Institutions therefore perform a two-fold function. On the one hand, they fulfil the task of *specification*, of translating values into specific and articulated social functions. On the other, they perform an essential function of *integration*, ensuring the unity of values in diverse contexts and enabling them to give coherent organization to the presocial material provided by the environment, such as, for instance, the biological needs. An institution is therefore the site of social mediation between a cultural totality (values), which is specified, and a presocial multiplicity (Nature, needs), which is integrated. It renders values 'operational' by lending them normative efficacy: it articulates them into specific systems of sanctions and rewards, which impose systematicity and coherence on the multiplicity of impulses, biological urges, and demands from the environment.

The limit of this Parsonian inheritance lies in its assumption that society depends on a values system, of which the structures of the organizations are purely functional transcriptions. This obscures the existence of structures of domination and conflictual relationships. The unity and integration of the social organization around values do not stem simply from a generalized consensus, but also from the influence exerted by the dominant interests (which of course varies from one society to another). No organization can fulfil its fundamental functional requirements without the intervention of a power, at once integrative and repressive, which subordinates the instrumental apparatus to those interests. The role system, far from being a simple market of consensual exchanges among legitimate expectations and performances, is the channel through which social power establishes and maintains itself.

From this point of view, the more recent sociology of organizations also shows itself to be forgetful of the presence of relationships of domination. In reaction to the Weberian model of bureaucratic organization, contemporary organizational sociology stresses the adaptive complexity of large-scale organizations, their progressive self-structuring according to mutable goals, their ever greater need to replace a rigid formal structure with mechanisms open to negotiation and transaction. The image that emerges is one of increasingly more flexible organizations which can constantly redefine their tasks and inner structures, and which do not contain tensions but manage them as a permanent component in their growth. The emphasis placed on the openness of organizations corresponds to deep changes in the present organizational life. It neglects, however, the fact that adaptive strategies and a flexible definition of goals cannot call the fundamental mechanisms of power into question; they operate wholly within the field defined by given dominant interests.

What has been said about the political system also holds for complex organizations insofar as they are endowed with mechanisms for decision-making. However open and flexible, however capable of absorbing change and producing decisions which are the outcome of inter-actor transactions, organizations cannot define their action outside, or contrary to, the limits imposed by dominant interests. Profit is still the goal of the large contemporary firm, and no adaptive strategy can release it from that obligation. A degree of socialization into the dominant value system is one of the functions assigned to the school system, and no form of modernization will eliminate this role.

However, analysis of organizations as if they were immediately and mechanically dependent on dominant social relationships precludes any understanding of the internal dynamics and the complex relationships which characterize the life of organizations. Against this reductionism, functionalist sociology, the sociology of work, and the modern sociology of the organization remind us of the importance of the functional mechanisms, of the integrative and adaptive problems, of the complex autonomies of every social organization.

An organization is the meeting point between a social power and a technical system endowed with a certain functional autonomy. Power subordinates the technical and human apparatus to its own purposes, but to a certain extent it must come to terms with the organization's internal exigencies and technical constraints. Technology and organization are therefore instrumental apparatuses subjected to a power which gears them towards the achievement of goals fixed by the dominant social relations; yet this control is never total, and an area of social relationships appears which is endowed with its own autonomy. The techno-human complex of an organization is also the site in which meaning is produced and forms of solidarity ripen.

Originally, capitalism regarded the technical and human complex which constituted the factory as substantially a business concern, purely as an instrument for the realization of profit. The control exercised by profit was still external to working conditions and manifested itself instead as the appropriation of a product which was then placed on the market in order to realize a profit. This situation was distinguished by the maximum autonomy of the factory on the one hand, and its maximum subordination on the other. On one side, in fact, the organization of work was still largely independent of the control of capital, and the professional autonomy of the worker intervened directly to define the work process. On the other side, however, the instrumental reduction of the work process and the extraneousness of the entrepreneur to the concrete conditions of production prevented the factory from constituting itself as an organization governed by its own internal dynamics, by its own laws, by specific relations among its members. The factory was still an aggregate of individual producers and of technical means, subordinate to the power of the owner in an individual relationship of dependence. The workforce, moreover, directly bore all the factory's labour costs (accidents, sanitary conditions) and the industrialists refused to take responsibility for the situation. Owner power, which refused to intervene and which indeed ignored the technical conditions of production, imposed the rigid unity of its goals on the disjointed social body of the factory, integrated the techno-human instrument and focused it on the realization of the owner interests.

However, the closer one approaches the great mechanized factory and the fordist model, the more this situation is reversed. On the one hand, the control exercised by capital on labour conditions becomes increasingly direct: it intervenes to provide an ever more precise definition of the technical modes of production, and surplus value is extracted by the progressive rationalization of the productive process. In these conditions, the professional autonomy of the worker is gradually reduced and the subordination of the factory to the objectives of the dominant class extends to the interior of the technical process of work. Simultaneously, however, the factory develops into an integrated and differentiated complex in which a set of mechanisms and social relationships typical of a complex organization is produced. The internal dynamics of the organization tends to become an area of social relationships which are relatively independent of the exigencies and the orientations imposed by the dominant power; the factory acquires a unity which now derives from the network of its internal relations and no longer solely from the intervention of a repressive and integrative power.

Capitalist power in its post-fordist stage discovers that it must control a set of organizational dynamics that progressively eludes its grasp. The introduction of psycho-social techniques of intervention in interpersonal relationships and the management's growing interest in analysis of organizational systems reveal within the organization a set of relationships governed by autonomous mechanisms and resistant to immediate subordination to dominant interests.

Every organization is thus ambivalent. On the one hand, an organization must coordinate and create coherence to a set of technical and human means in ways which are functional to the general goals set by dominant interests. From this point of view, norms define only the forms in which power is exercised within the organization: they are the set of rules imposed on the technical and human apparatus so that it can achieve the goals determined for it, and in order to sanction its instrumental subordination. Here, therefore, the rationality imposed on the organization is the rationality of domination, and operational rules embody the dominant relationships – by now crystallized into a code of behaviour – which social power permits or sanctions.

The power which sets limits on what is permitted and what is prohibited through norms and which fixes the rules for membership of, or exclusion from, the organization, must by necessity inhibit or restrict intrinsic conflictuality within the narrow confines of a preestablished code of behaviour. In one respect, therefore, and to a decisive extent, norms express the exigencies of domination inscribed in a body of rules, compliance with which is the necessary condition for membership in the organization. This renders the observation of such norms always dubious and always partial: conflict constantly spills over the preestablished confines of acceptable behaviour and manifests itself as rejection, marginalization, and deviance, or as an active response which advances claims and protest assaulting the power base.

On the other hand, however, norms also express the organization's need for internal coherence and functionality; they provide the linkage between means and ends, and they, to some extent, embody the formal rationality of purposive action. Hence, in this respect, norms tend to constitute the organization as an autonomous entity with its own requirements of coherence and its functional rules. But the functionality of the organization, which is obtained through an analytical distinction, is in reality always intertwined with submission to a power and can never be realized without referring to it. From this dense interweaving of elements, which can only be disentangled analytically, derives the necessary ambivalence of norms, which are always both the expression of power and the rules of functioning, the outcome of imposition and of imbalance but requiring consensus, both observed and questioned.

Finally, we should briefly address the problem of change in organizations. Whether one adopts the organizational perspective, or whether one considers society to constitute an integrated system of roles (which it to some extent always is, in as much as the ruling groups succeed in imposing their interests and goals as generally shared values, thereby constituting social exchange as a system of reciprocal expectations of behaviour), there is no doubt that one can observe constant quantitative changes and processes of differentiation/integration like those analysed by the sociology of modernization. Modernization therefore describes changes internal to role systems. These transformations, however, are never fully independent; they are subordinate to a system of domination and to social relationships which determine their nature and direction. Once again, to ignore this dimension is to go nowhere beyond the mere 'appearance' of organizational change. When Dahrendorf, in stressing the role of conflict in change, reduced such change to turnover in the authority roles internal to the organization, he stopped at precisely at this level. Such a change is important in the organizational life but, by definition, it does not call the organization's rules into question; it simply redistributes their power. The existence of antagonist relationships instead entails the presence of actors who contest the norms and the social role of an organization, and who struggle for change which necessarily spills over its 'technical' limits.

Classes or stratification?

When discussing social organization, one must not forget the significance of stratification within it, nor confuse or cause to overlap the concept of class with that of stratification.

In the best European tradition, classes are portrayed as those social groups which struggle to gain control over the productive capacity of a society. It is therefore at the very heart of the *productive process*, defined materially and culturally, that the concept of class relationships was analytically constituted.

Stratification, on the other hand, is a typically functional concept which rests on incontrovertible empirical evidence: in any society there exists a differential *distribution* of resources, a nonegalitarian allocation of goods and values between different social groups. There also exists apparent consensus over the fundamental criteria underpinning this distributive pattern: actors do not question the existence of differences as such, they merely claim different access to goods, measure in comparative terms possible inconsistencies in their position, or acquire or lose their status through processes of upward or downward mobility. On this evidence of the practical functioning of social life, well described by the classic functionalist theory of stratification, this same theory also performs an ideological role similar to the one that, more than a century ago, Marx denounced in the classic political economy. Like the classical economists, we are confronted by an assumption of 'appearance,' of the system's visible manner of functioning, which mask the deep-lying social relationships behind its surface. The empirical evidence for stratification is assumed as a theoretical criterion and legitimated as such: just as classical economics enshrined the workings of capitalist production relations in theory, without investigating their social structure, so can the sociology of stratification promptly turn into the pure legitimation of inequality, its assumptions left unexamined.

From this point of view, it is of no importance whether inequality is deemed just or unjust, whether stratification analysis is conducted by 'conservatives' or by 'progressives.' The apparently neutral use of the concept of stratification which does not address the ambiguity of social inequalities precludes the possibility of determining the limits of this conceptual framework.

We should therefore take a look at the ways in which the functionalist framework provides a *de facto* theoretical justification for stratification. Drawing on a celebrated work (Davis and Moore 1945) – much discussed but never superseded – the theory could be summarized as follows: Every society whose basic functional needs remain those enunciated by Parsons (adaptation, goal attainment, pattern maintenance, integration) by necessity contains within itself some social positions which are more important than others – functionally more important in the sense that they more than others ensure the fulfilment of the fundamental functional needs. It is inevitable that a society will allocate to these positions those individuals from its necessarily scarce human resources who are best fitted to occupy them. The mechanism ensuring the optimal allocation of resources to the functionally most important positions is the system of differential rewards. In other words, society motivates the individuals best suited to occupy certain positions by deploying a system of nonegalitarian rewards in terms of income, prestige, and power. It is for this reason that individuals undergo the training and the sacrifices necessary to achieve certain positions. Stratification, therefore, is a necessary requirement of every system with a complex organization which wishes to ensure a differentiated structure of roles and their integration.

Although the theory, in the version propounded by Davis and Moore, has been widely criticised, none of the functionalists have really doubted its basic premises (with the possible exception of Tumin (1967), who discusses the concept of functional importance but does not draw the full consequences from his own discussion). The problem, in fact, does not consist in showing whether stratification is more or less just, or whether differential rewards recompense effective capacities or acquired skills; it consists, rather, in conducting a critical examination of the presupposition of functional importance on which the entire theory pivots.

The existence of functionally more important positions is assumed, in fact, as a theoretical premise in a conventional operation whereby appearance is consecrated and elevated to a canonical status. There is no denying that in any particular society there are some positions which are 'functionally' more important than others; but, we must ask, functionally with respect to what? To this, the theory replies by citing the fundamental functional needs of the system. But this is a reply which, in fact, reads 'functional to a certain system of the division of labour'; that is, to the interests dominant in that particular society and to the maintenance of certain social relationships. For instance it is true that in capitalist society certain positions are rewarded better than others on account of their great functional importance. But it is also because they perform a more central role in safeguarding some interests and a certain structuring of the division of labour that they receive greater recompense.

Extending the argument a little, we may then assert that stratification and its criteria are not independent of dominant social relationships. It is these relationships which fix the distribution of rewards in an order which ensures their maintenance. But stratification simultaneously performs a functional task by permitting the optimal allocation of resources (optimal in terms of the given interests) and the integration of the social organization.

Once again it is necessary to distinguish between, but not to separate, production relationships and stratification. It is the former which govern the stratification of a society, although within the differentiation of positions there is a manifest margin, small or large, of functional autonomy within the social system.

We may thus contend that stratification in a society is based on shared values, but only as long as we bear in mind that these values are also the expression of the dominant interests; indeed, the rejection of the criteria by which a society stratifies itself is an enduring phenomenon, testifying to the fact that there is not just consensus but also conflict over the ways in which resources are distributed.

On the other hand, it is also true that actors often operate according to a logic analysable in terms of stratification and mobility, and that concepts such as 'status inconsistency' or 'relative deprivation' can explain a wide range of behaviour. In a stratified system of roles, reciprocal expectations of behaviour may display certain mismatches or disequilibria. The actor perceives inconsistencies among the various components of her/his status (for example, between the income and the power or prestige that s/he enjoys), or s/he may be frustrated by a drop in her/his status compared with other positions in the distributive hierarchy. Action in these cases does not necessarily have an antagonistic content but is a reaction against certain dysfunctions in the status system, which, for its own part, is not questioned as such. Conversely, the presence of antagonist contents is measured by the extent to which claimant behaviour contests the very criteria of stratification.

We thus find the principles of dependence and autonomy repeatedly enunciated. The problem of the empirical transcription of these criteria is still very much open. The foregoing analysis has sought only to indicate analytical criteria. It is certain that, as regards organizations in particular, theoretical clarification may have major repercussions on social practices. In a period in which institutional analysis and intervention assume increasing importance, we must hold firmly to the two principles put forth here. Institutional analysis and practice must not be restricted to the confines of the organization, confines which to some extent always preserve social imbalances; at the same time, the existence of properly organizational dynamics must not be annulled, but instead recognized in its autonomy.

14

Modernization, crisis and conflicts: the case of Italy

Demands for modernization

In this chapter, I shall consider the analytical frame developed in the fore-going chapters against the context of contemporary Italy. That country, with the vigour of its cultural and social development and the often dramatic display of the complexity of its political life, has attracted the attention of different observers, whether political, academic, or journalistic in intent. Government instability, innovative dynamism and recurrent economic recession, creative cultural life and terrorism, conservative elites and traditionally the strongest communist party in the West now caught in a profound identity change – these represent some of the characteristic problems of Italian society that make it an attractive object of investigation, and not the least so for those interested in analysing the crises and the transformation of social movements since the 1970s. In what follows, I want to participate in the discussion on the Italian case by proceeding to apply the theoretical hypotheses advanced in the previous chapters to an analysis of a concrete socio-political context. But in this, my analysis is not limited to a mere demonstration of the viability of an analytical framework; it, I believe, will moreover shed light on a general question that occupies the mind of the critical analyst today: What has become of the Left politics in our time?

Italy has witnessed the growth of antagonist movements in the situation of structural distortions of development and a blocked process of social and political modernization. The hypothesis connecting the rise of movements to their socio-political context of origin, to be sure, may seem too general to provide an explanation for the appearance of the full range of the forms of collective action that have made their appearance in Italian society since the 1960s. It, however, does not deny the specificity of the causes of the various kinds of mobilization and protest in the country, but merely suggests a key to interpretation of what was common to them and persisted beyond conjunctural variations. In Italy, the year 1968 marked the beginning of the conjunction between the country's large-scale modernization and the emergence of antagonist movements typical of complex societies. The innovative pressures destined to accelerate Italy's change into a postindustrial society clashed with the archaism of the social structure and with a political system paralyzed by the impossible task of mediating between traditional interests and the necessity for reforms in a complex society.

The mention of 1968, of course, refers to the set of political and social phenomena that that year symbolizes, in particular the cycle of struggles directed against the universities first, companies next, and then spreading to numerous other institutions (the urban, educational, health and welfare systems, the Catholic Church, total institutions such as prisons and asylums, apparatuses of social control like the army, police, judicial system). The students' movement, initially in conflict with the authorities and campaigning for reform of the universities (protest reached its climax in the spring of 1968), rapidly turned political in character and anticapitalist in content. Workers' struggles took shape as a response to transformations of the productive system and to the rationalization of industry during the 1960s, with the latter manifesting itself more as cuts aimed at the cost of labour and as changes in the production conditions than as growth in the investment rate. The most intense moments of labour mobilization were experienced during the so-called 'hot autumn' of 1969, but the cycle of struggles continued up until 1972. Civil life emerged profoundly altered (one thinks chiefly of the laws on divorce and abortion).

In order to understand the impact of these struggles on Italian society and the country's political system, we must remember that its prevailing model of development – based on exports and cheap manpower – added new imbalances (territorial, sectoral, between city and countryside) on the effects of its old North–South divide. The main function of the political system was to cushion the disequilibria produced by the accelerated and chaotically realized industrialization and urbanization without, however, allowing the guiding logic of the system change in that process. Special intervention under the pressure of particularist demands; the clientelistic management of power; compromise with traditional elites and with speculative and parasitical interests; the unabashed spending of public funds for electoral purposes (especially in the South and in agriculture); the feudalization of publicly owned industry, of the state economic agencies, of the banking system by the political parties; the partisan control of information (radio and television in particular) – these are among the features emphasized by observers when describing the management of the political system in Italy until the 1960s.

The failure of the reformist policies introduced by the Socialist Party and the Centre–Left governments of the early 1960s rendered even more intolerable the already existing gulf between an urban-industrial society geared to mass consumption on the one hand and the archaism of political, educational, welfare, and religious institutions still largely precapitalist in nature, on the other. The predominance of particularist interests smothered any attempt at economic planning, and the reforms themselves only grafted the new onto the old, merely swelling the bureaucracy rather than rationalizing it (Berger 1981; Salvati 1981).

The profound transformation of Italian society followed the urban-industrial pattern already evident in other capitalist countries, but wit certain significant differences. The 1960s saw an intensifying internationalization of the Italian economy which increased its dependence on others. The state-controlled sector, subordinate to the interests of the governing majority, grew in size. Firms, for their part, became increasingly dependent on the banking system, which, too, was tied to the majority party. In the social sphere, the distinctive features of this period were the widening of the North–South gap and the aggravation of new territorial and sectoral imbalances; the abnormal growth of tertiary towns, especially in the South; the ballooning of the public administration (the number of civil servants doubled between 1951 and 1971); the persistence of small peasant landowners and small shopkeepers, which were far more numerous than in other advanced industrialized countries (for years these two social groups provided the government parties with their reservoir of votes); finally, the apparently 'anomalous' presence of a large share of small-scale industry – in part innovative, in part marginal – which created strong divisions in the working class (between workers in central sectors and marginal labour, between innovative firms and those in decline, and so on).

The Centre–Left policies, beginning as of 1962 and lasting for a decade, thus brought no substantial change to the balance of forces and remained unable to significantly influence the social development of the country. Of the many reforms included in the agenda (school, university, urban, health, and welfare reforms, renovation of the public administration), all that was achieved was the introduction of the unified secondary school and the nationalization of the electrical power industry (in 1962, with a net loss to the Italian state, which had to compensate the former trusts). We may consider as 'delayed effects' of the Centre–Left policies the creation of administrative regions as envisaged in the Constitution (1970) – a long-standing objective for the Socialists, but also a response to the demands for participation voiced in the struggles of 1968–69 – and the Workers' Charter which introduced a modern industrial relations system; this, too, represented an old socialist proposal which became a law under pressure from the workers' struggle of 1969.

The paralysis of the Italian political system has been well described by observers: the overload of particularist demands forcing the parliament to issue an excessive quantity of minor particularistic laws instead of laying down general legislative guidelines; the instability of governments; the poor credibility of the political leaders of the majority, implicated in numerous scandals but practically irremovable; finally, the purely negative vetoing function performed for many years by the Communist Party, trapped in opposition with neither the chance nor the will to exercise a positive effect on reformist policy. Italians use the term 'imperfect two-party system' to describe the situation: the majority cannot move to the opposition, for the control over the resources of government, in particular public funds, is the condition for the Christian Democrat Party's very existence; the opposition cannot join the government so long as the Communist Party insists on its role as an 'anti-system party.' For many years, this has excluded the working class from the benefits of development and has prevented it from effectively furthering the democratization of the country.

Bearing these features in mind, it is understandable that the chief feature of the cycle of struggles which began in the 1960s was the pressure for the modernization of all institutions and organizations from the university to the firm, from the administration to the political system as a whole (see Tarrow 1989a; Crouch and Pizzorno 1978; Lumley 1990). Innovation was introduced partly as a result of these struggles, while the elites at the same time sought to contain the latters' effects and to limit their range.

In the years following 1968, a number of major changes occurred in Italian social and political life which can be considered as providing further examples of the ongoing process of modernization and its simultaneous 'containment'. The universities – inflexible structures which performed the function of elite selection using frequently authoritarian teaching methods and antiquated curricula – were forced to increase their intake of students and to modify their mechanisms of representation as well as their teaching facilities. After a 1969 law relaxed the university entrance requirements, student numbers increased enormously without, however, parallel and adequate provisions being made to cope with the multiplied attendance. As a consequence, the university system lost in efficiency and effectiveness. Some sectors of it became often no more than a 'parking lot' for unemployed intellectuals, remaining unable to convert the modernizing impulse into a factor of development.

The workers' struggles of 1968–72 managed to achieve a transformation in Italy's system of industrial relations which brought the country in that respect to the level of the other advanced industrial countries. By harnessing energies first expressed in the factory-based committees, the trade unions – traditionally weak inside the factories and distant from the decision-making centres of economic policy – created a new system of representation (factory councils and workers' delegates), boosted their numbers, began a process of unification, and became a recognized partner in negotiations at the level both of the company and national economic policy. The Workers' Charter of 1970 ratified the trade unions' presence within the factory and guaranteed workers' individual and trade union rights. After 1972, the revival of the confederations' control over the most combative unions (metal workers, chemical workers), the changed economic situation which pushed job protection at the top of the agenda, and the confederations' assumption of responsibility – and sometimes of substitute functions – on the political market turned the trade unions into instruments of political pressure, while the base structures of representation tended to become incorporated into their organizational structure (Crouch and Pizzorno 1978).

In the large cities, a rank-and-file movement began experiments in neighbourhood participation and urban decentralization. By the mid-1970s, however, these were institutionalized and mostly became administrative offshoots of local government. In the secondary schools, democratic students and parents experimented with forms of direct participation in decision-making. Here, too, participation was regulated by complex formal mechanisms which institutionalized electoral rules and representative bodies.

Struggles were waged in other sectors, especially against the prevailing health care system, the judicial apparatus, psychiatric services, and the media. Groups arose which mobilized themselves for the democratization of various institutions (Democratic Judges, Democratic Psychiatrists, and others) and which clashed with the more conservative elements of the various professional bodies concerned. These associations pushing for modernization often introduced important innovations into archaic and atrophied social structures and professional corporations. Movements for democratization also arose in the army and the police force, which succeeded in achieving a modest degree of institutional change in these apparatuses. Even the Church was affected by the conflicts manifesting themselves in society at large. An important current of 'Catholic dissent' gave rise, from 1969 onwards, to a rich experience of base communities (see Tarrow 1988a), which combined a return to the evangelical spirit with distinct elements of anticapitalist struggle and criticized the ecclesiastical hierarchy compromised, especially in Italy, by its dealings with temporal power (in 1973, following the Chilean example, was born a movement of 'Christians for Socialism'). Finally, also civil life and customs underwent profound transformations, the chief symptoms of which were the struggles for divorce and abortion. In 1974, after a referendum which incited widespread popular mobilization, the divorce law was effectively enacted, having first been approved in 1970. In the case of abortion, too, the call for a referendum (1975) forced the parties to approve the law that legalized it (which was confirmed by a further referendum in 1981).

This set of processes serves as so many indicators of the relationships between the struggles and the institutional and social modernization (Tarrow 1989b). As shown by numerous cases, these processes impacted upon the political system both as demands for representation and participation, and as demands for reform. The greatest advantages from this modernizing pressure were drawn by the Italian Communist Party, which presented itself as the interpreter best able to render it effective (see Lange *et al.* 1989; Hellman 1988). Electoral returns from 1968 through 1976 show that the Communist Party was the catalyst for expectations of change, and that it had managed to garner the most immediate effects of the student and workers' movements. The party increased its votes and membership, gained control of numerous local and regional administrations, renewed its cadres with personnel trained in the student and workers' struggles, and recruited new supporters from among the urban communities and young people. These represent some of the achievements that testify to the new role expectations set to the Communist Party – albeit, in the long run, it was unable to capitalize on its success, sliding into a progressive decline in the 1980s.

The intersection between crisis and emerging conflicts

The heterogeneous block of interests mobilized around the Christian Democratic Party could be kept intact only if the contradictory logic of Italy's postwar model of development (North–South imbalances, the alliance between traditional and modernizing ruling groups, the role of the Catholic Church, and so on) was never called into question. At the same time, it became necessary to respond piecemeal to the demands that, little by little, were created by the dualistic and contradictory development. Hence the failure of reformist policies and the uneffectiveness of the multitude of specific and particularistic legislative provisions. Reducing demand was not possible, as it would have compromised the very basis of the consensus upon which the hegemony was founded. Over the long term, however, this state of affairs has caused congestion and clogs in the political system. Susceptibility to particularistic demands weakens the political system's capacity for generalization, and, as a consequence, the fragmented distribution of resources through clientelistic channels and corruption, as well as the apportioning of public resources among the party apparatuses have become the system's principal forms of response.

Alongside the sharpening pressures for modernization, collective demands surfaced within the cycle of struggles that began in the mid-1960s which contained the embryo of antagonist movements: demands which pressed for an improvement in the quality of life, which rejected a distant and impersonal authority, and which experimented with new forms of solidarity. These were the contents of antagonist conflicts which appeared in all the advanced societies and subsequently spread and were diversified into the women's, youth, environmentalist, and pacifist movements.

In Italy, resistance against the process of modernization, which had lost its initial impulse, infused these new demands with all the contradictions of a society undergoing postindustrial transformation but unable to free itself of the inherited baggage of a dualistic and dependent model. The formation of these movements was therefore marked by the specific conditions that obtained at the time. Interwoven with pressures for modernization, and forced to confront the closure of the political system, antagonist forces were progressively diverted into a fight against repression, a struggle for the openness of the institutions, and resistance against right-wing violence and Fascist plots.

In this connection, we must examine more closely the system's response to the emergence of new collective demands. In order to do so, I shall focus primarily on the *capacity to govern*, by which I mean the quantity and quality of the outputs delivered by a political system. These in turn are contingent, on the one hand, on the function of legislation, and, on the other, are made manifest through the action of the system's decision-making, executive, and administrative organs in response to the demands addressed to it. Three principal kinds of response can be identified in the Italian case: *restricted reforms, repression,* and the *instrumental use of Right-wing violence.*

1 I have already examined the first type of response in the previous section. Institutional change and the reforms implemented by the political system are always the effect of strong conflictual forces, not the result of an autonomous dynamic of innovation. Reforms are conceded only as a last resort, and even then they are as restricted as possible in scope. This creates a discontinuous, haphazard pattern to processes of modernization, which

largely fail to attack the underlying logic of the institutions against which they are directed. This reductive use of reforms often produces an overlap between new and old institutions which aggravates problems rather than solves them.

2 Repression seems to be the political system's most habitual response, especially in the formative stage of collective demands. The indiscriminate and obtuse use of the police to break up demonstrations (in accordance with a long-standing tradition of the Italian state) meant that street fighting was a recurrent phenomenon in the years following 1968. Street violence is almost always a self-fulfilling prophecy, as sociological studies of riots have shown. Repression always triggers a spiral of violence that becomes more and more difficult to control and which dramatically conditions the subsequent history of the conflict.

3 The other method to control protest is recourse to Right-wing violence. The instrumental use of Fascist terrorism by the Italian state, and the strategy that aimed at an authoritarian takeover in the climate of tension and fear created by terrorist attacks, had its roots in sectors of the armed forces, the police, the secret services, and the upper echelons of the state administration. Christian Democratic governments and the moderate parties believed they could use Fascist violence, especially in the period 1969–74, as an instrument of countermobilization which would control social struggles. The state apparatus and the government covered up, supported, and connived with Right-wing violence in ways that only long years of mobilization and the courage of a handful of investigating magistrates have brought to light.

In any case, Right-wing violence, steered or condoned by the organs of the state, marked political life and conditioned the growth of social conflicts in Italy after 1968. Locked in a defensive posture and restricted to the struggle against the closure of the institutions and against the paralysis of the political system, the innovative importance of the movements emerging at the time went unrecognized, and the movements themselves were relegated to the status of residual phenomena.

To complete the picture of the system's response to collective demands, one must also consider the potential for representation offered to emergent demands by the political parties in the opposition, which could – and should – have served as their vehicles. Here I refer to the political parties' *capacity to represent* – that is, to the quantity and quality of the institutional channels provided by a political system to deal with specific demands and to translate them into effects on that system itself. In the case of Italy, the responses of the system can be summarized by pointing out to *underrepresentation* and *hyperpoliticization*, as regards the ability, respectively, of the Communist Party and the 'New Left' to play such a mediating role.

The political culture of the opposition in Italy has proven poorly equipped to handle the emerging collective phenomena and, where it nevertheless has managed to do so, to capture the specificity that marks them off from their historical precedents. For many years, the Communist Party closed its ranks from any form of conflict which might encroach on its monopoly of the function of opposition. The New Left, for its own part, was caught in a permanent oscillation between Leninist theory and practice on the one hand and the glorification of spontaneity and wildcat action on the other. It was thus possible to at once relegate movements into the secondary products of the crisis and, then again, exalt any form of marginality as a genuine revolutionary force. The degradation of collective action during the second half of the 1970s must be viewed in part against the government responses, but it was also the result of this theoretical and political inability of the opposition parties to grasp the conflictual importance and the specific role of the movements. This explains the opposition forces' inability to adapt their strategy and their forms of action and organization to the situation involving new conflictual actors, and move beyond the mechanical parroting of orthodox Leninism or pure empiricism.

As regards political representation – that is, the system's capacity to absorb demands and translate them into institutional change – the overall dilemma can be described by the two features mentioned above. On the one hand there was underrepresentation, particularly by the political opposition embodied in the Communist Party, which first ignored the innovative potential of the new conflictual actors (which had already expressed itself in the swing to the left in the elections of 1968), and then set out to gather the fruits from the revitalization of the political atmosphere in primarily instrumental fashion – still refusing, however, to grant recognition and legitimacy to the actors and contents involved in the new conflicts. On the other hand, the organizations of the New Left – which had been the only channel of direct representation for the new demands – still coerced these demands into an organizational and ideological framework which took overthrowing the state to be the prime objective of struggle. Hyperpoliticization meant in this context the programmatic transcription of demands in rigidly political (Leninist) terms, even when they were rooted in the problems of 'civil society' and everyday life.

This two-fold limitation in the process of modernization and in the formation of movements is a crucial key to any understanding of the outcomes of collective processes in Italy. During the 1970s, the situation was exacerbated by the crisis that hit all the Western countries. It was a crisis that found fertile ground in Italy, and its disruptive effects were multiplied. The Movement of 1977, which had its centres in the universities of Rome, Bologna, Padua, and Milan, provides a typical example of the process of grafting new, identity-based demands of young people onto the problems created by the economic crisis, the disequilibria between school and the labour market, the rising unemployment among the youth and the university graduates, and the 'parking lot' role of the universities. The movement was split between, on the one hand, a quest for personal creativity and, on the other hand, the students' awareness of their social marginality, with few job opportunities to be expected when and if they graduated. The Movement of '77 provoked a predominantly repressive reaction by the state, with violent police interventions in major popular manifestations, strict control over youth centres, and policing of the universities as the means at its disposal for immediate counteraction. In response, again, the degeneration of collective action into violence and the triumph of the most extremist groups were to take place as one result of the crude measures opted for by the state.

One of the main outcomes of the process of modernization that began in the 1960s was the progressive integration of the Italian Communist Party into the institutional framework of representation, and the incorporation of the trade unions into a 'mature' system of industrial relations, which turned them into an institutional partner in negotiations over company policies and – at least to some extent – over the economic policy of the country. These institutionalization processes reproduced phenomena already observed in other advanced societies; but in Italy they had the contradictory result of triggering a wave of collective mobilization. This situation had two specific effects. Among political actors of the left, it produced a tendency to monopolize representation of the conflicts that had made the institutional outcome possible in the first place. Involved here – in particular as regards the Communist Party, but also the trade unions to a certain extent – was a tendency to preserve the charismatic (global, almost religious) character of the political organization instead of developing its 'lay' (specific and differentiated) function of representing interests within the political system. Ideology tended to deny the limited and realistic character of the change achieved: the legitimization of interests and demands previously excluded from representation. The expectation of global transformation was thus perpetuated, although the vision of violent revolution began to fade.

In other words, the institutionalization that resulted from a vigorously opposed process of collective mobilization made it more difficult for political actors to occupy their restricted role as representatives of interests within a political system. One may speak in this case of difficulties in the process of secularization of political life – in the passage, that is, from 'sacred' globalism to the differentiation of the functions and levels of action.

Among the social actors that made this institutionalization possible, residues were inevitably created. The expectations mobilized during the phase of struggle were left unsatisfied by their 'realistic' confinement to institutional channels. Inevitably, therefore, fringe groups of disillusioned militants developed which extolled the original purity of the movement and fought against what they regarded as the 'betrayal' of its aims. This was a phenomenon that typified all the large-scale movements as they underwent the process of institutionalization, and the formation of fundamentalist sects vowing to uphold the original 'truth' of the movement was therefore a matter of course.

Autonomia (a loose federation of rank-and-file collectives) certainly represented the grafting of minority fundamentalist sects onto the crisis of the Movement of '77 that for its part was induced by the system's repressive response. The residues from the Marxist-Leninist organizations of the sixties (chiefly Potere Operaio), small extremist fringe groups which had abandoned the allegedly over-moderate organizations of the New Left (Lotta Continua in particular), found a new social base among the young people of the great urban hinterlands, among unemployed intellectuals, and among the movements' ex-militants. Violence was given theoretical legitimacy as the only effective means available. Armed clashes with the state apparatus during demonstrations, physical violence directed against adversaries (especially against the 'traitors' of the Communist Party) became routine from 1977 onwards (especially in Rome, Padua, Bologna, and Milan) and for many young people constituted their first step towards terrorism.

The distorted effects of modernization and institutionalization, political closure and the economic crisis therefore pushed collective action towards violence and its final outcome of terrorism. Due to the hyperpoliticization of movements, even when their action was not specifically directed against the political system, every demand was deflected into an attack on the state.

The systematic use of violence up to the desperate extreme of terrorism was the result of the disintegration of the movements, which had been prevented from expressing themselves on their own ground and were progressively forced to deal with the contradictions of a society in paralysis. As long as there were margins of elasticity in the system, movements continued to function as channels for the expression of demands. The 'revolutionary' intentions of their actors apart, they helped to mobilize the innovative energies present in society. But their ability to absorb conflictual pressures, without inducing changes in the political system, was limited, and this triggered a degenerative process difficult to control.

One section of the '77 movement sought to save the specific content of the new demands tied to identity, expression, and personal creativity. But in doing so it was pushed towards the privatization and fragmentation of collective impulses, which were rapidly reduced to marginal experiences of expressive counterculture. This was the road of the 'personal' in the form of a search for a purely personal and atomized identity in small religious groups or, more dramatically, through recourse to drugs and even suicide. On the other hand, the need for practical and political effectiveness yielded legitimacy and space to the minority fundamentalist sects. These residual fringes of the process of institutionalization were thus able to draw on the disillusion and impotence of the '77 movement, and on the areas of marginality created by the crisis.

In the history of movements, fundamentalist sects have not necessarily shown any particular proneness to violence, and in many cases they have developed by simply accentuating their doctrinaire nature. In those cases, they may thus become circles of theologians, which grow and subsequently pass away peacefully. But in the specific circumstances of Italy in the 1970s, the choice of armed struggle was determined by the degree of social breakdown, the closure and rigidity of the political system, and the potential for violence that this situation actualized. The fundamentalist sects flourished on this terrain and they became the nuclei of the first terrorist organizations (see Wagner-Pacifici 1988; Della Porta 1988, 1992a).

Terrorism paradoxically represents both the most radical outcome of emergent movements and their antithesis. On the one hand, terrorism is the product of a distorting process which forces movements to deny their own nature and to shift conflict into the arena imposed by repression and the political system's lack of response. On the other, the ideology and practice of the terrorist groups are the antithesis of the emerging contents of new conflicts. They reproduce the inevitable sclerosis, the doctrinaire celebration of models and forms of organization tied to the sectarian tradition, to inflexible Leninist principles, to the dogmatic use of Marxism. There is nothing in common between the Movement of 1977's slogan 'Take back our life!' and a lucid determination to murder one's opponents as a means to fight against capitalism and accelerate the revolution.

Terrorist groups display all the features of a fundamentalist sect: their sectarian organization quite obviously, but most importantly the symbolic universe that structures the personalities of their members (on terrorism, see more generally Della Porta 1992b; Gurr 1988; Slater and Stohl

1988;Wiewiorka 1988). A totalizing, radically 'integralist' vision of reality makes it difficult to grasp the differences among the various levels, processes, and instruments of action. It is a vision that allows the terrorist to strike equally at the political leader and the humblest of his followers; a vision which no longer defines the adversary in terms of social relations, but as an anonymous Moloch to whom all are more or less subservient – apart from the small band of the self-appointed elect. The 'Imperialist State of the Multinationals' is the enemy to fight against, and every act, from a mugging to assassination, is committed as a direct attack on the centres of capitalist power. All the apparatuses of the state, of production, and of information are articulations of this power and therefore potential targets.

Integralism is the inability of a social actor to distinguish among levels of action and to adopt instruments appropriate to the pursuit of differentiated goals. A 'physiological' integralism always characterizes the formative stage of a movement, when it relies on simplified symbols to strengthen its identity in formation. Furthermore, there is a 'regressive' integralism which is instead tied to the crisis of collective identity and to the attempt to keep it alive by the forced reduction of complexity, by returning to primitive and simplified phases of action, and by appealing to the purity of origins.

Terrorist groups cannot define even themselves in terms of social relations, because only the attribution of a charismatic role of purification and general salvation enables them to legitimate their action and to seek consensus, moral more than political. The reduction of reality to a handful of simple truisms guarantees the group's identity, strengthens its faith, masks its objective weaknesses, and makes its action subjectively effective.

The tragic balance sheet of terror is eloquent: it shows quite clearly the link between the crisis of movements and the expansion of minority violence. The year 1977 was pivotal, for it witnessed the first manifest coincidence between the paralysis of collective action and the intensification of terrorist activity. Bred by fundamentalist sects within the mainstream of the Left, terrorism shed its 'Marxist' origins after that year. Survival, the pure and simple affirmation of the existence of the group, a paradoxical search for 'expressive' identity with no further 'instrumental' objectives of political or social change – these seem to be the principal motivations for the terrorist groups whose remains were still active in the early 1990s. The weight of individual histories most directly mark their members' identities, while their political roots become more and more indistinct.

The predominantly expressive character of terrorism highlights a dimension that extends beyond the specifically Italian situation. Complex societies are witnessing the appearance of an integralism which seeks to control uncertainty by an assertion of a select principle of unity. The difficulty of undertaking global and instantaneous change, and the sense of impotence in the face of the bulk and strength of the apparatuses, favour totalizing urges and facilitate recourse to violence as the symbolic instrument for the expression of identity. Terrorism in complex societies therefore becomes a desperate indicator of the flashpoints of conflict. It cannot be explained solely in terms of crisis. Even societies in which the crisis was less severe than in Italy saw the formation of terrorist groups. 'Outlaw' behaviour is a deviant response to the rationalization and diffusion of administrative control by the apparatuses. In complex societies, which tend to normalize every diversity, violence and minority action become recurrent and 'symptomatic' signals of conflicts. Such kinds of behaviour must be considered very carefully, for they indicate with tragic clarity the issues on which conflictual demands are focused. Complex societies are destined to live with a certain amount of outlaw violence, and only properly functioning political institutions can minimize their effects.

Recourse to an integralist model of action and to a totalizing symbolic universe therefore involves a variety of meanings. I have already referred to integralism as a necessary stage in the history of movements which they leave behind as they reach maturity. But there always remains a residual integralism, a certain 'fixation' of fringes of the movement in its primitive phases. Analogously with the psychoanalytical term, 'fixation' here indicates arrestation in a particular stage of development and the difficulty of adapting beyond it. We may talk of regression in the same way, as a return to primitive stages of development. Terrorism in Italy combines an integralism of 'postindustrial' demands and needs in formation (distorted in the Italian case, for the reasons already outlined) with the reactionary integralism of 'fixation-regression' which an archaic Marxist language serves to conceal.

The transformation of collective action

The 'collective' response to the breakdown of movements in the form of terrorism is matched by an individual and atomized response which expresses itself in disengagement from collective action and disillusionment.

Religious groups drawing their inspiration mainly from the East have sprung up, especially since 1977, and count many ex-militants among their numbers. They cover a wide range of cult beliefs, and are chiefly located in the large cities with some rural communities linked to the centre. Communes, meditation centres, cultural centres claim to provide a solution to the numerous problems of human existence. There is much concern for man's relationship with nature, and many of these groups have an ecological, 'back-to-nature', dietary orientation. They are often animated by a spirit of cultural innovation and spiritual quest. But their totalizing communitarian structure also functions as a reservoir which dispenses security to their members. The sacral recognition of the charisma of the leader encourages the emergence of authoritarian personalities and fosters a herd mentality among their followers. The search for spiritual, mystical, or corporeal well-being in these religious groups may assume the character of an individual flight from militancy and from collective engagement; but it also comprises a genuinely spiritual impulse which responds to the need for cultural and social innovation. It must therefore be viewed as an ambivalent phenomenon, especially if one ignores the most introverted sects and looks at the more open-minded communities. In these latter cases we sometimes come across novel approaches to the search for identity, rather than reactions to crisis. Many Catholic communitarian experiments since 1977 also display this feature.

Drug use and suicide constitute the most dramatic examples of the process of automization that followed the crisis of movements. They are the individual's final response to a situation of frustration and isolation, to the disappointment of her/his every collective hope, to the impossibility of finding outlets for the needs of identity and communication. Statistics clearly show a connection between the crisis of collective action and the spread of drugs – even though the phenomenon as a whole has many causes. Drug use has increased among young people, that is, among those belonging to the age class and the geographical areas most directly affected by mobilization and the crisis of movements. While, given the paucity of the available data, it is impossible to prove a statistical correlation between the two phenomena, one can nevertheless document the general direction of the trend. Drugs have spread in the same cultural and social area that previously fuelled militancy. After 1977, the international drug trade was able to establish that Italy was a market in expansion, and massively invested in the country. For many ex-militants, after the crisis of collective action, drugs were a desperate last resort in the search for selfhood to which the political organization had been unable to respond. Many personal histories confirm this link between the crisis of militancy and the descent into the inferno of addiction.

Suicide is even more conspicuously an individual pheomenon, one that is difficult to link, at the macrosocial level, with the crisis of movements. In this case, too, however, there are elements which strongly suggest a connection, and for the purposes of analysis will suffice to simply note its probable existence suggested by much empirical material, such as personal letters and oral reports by the victims and those who survived. The search for identity, which found no outlet in collective action and was unable to create other forms of expression for personal needs, has also taken the road of no return that is suicide. But this gesture – as witness the numerous letters left behind by ex-militants who have opted for this road – is a message screamed aloud that collective action is impossible. It is at the same time a sign of the inability of the movements of the seventies to respond to the profound needs of their militants.

The breakdown of collective action, however, has not impeded its transformation, which has moved in two main directions: institutionalization, with a change of personnel and the renewal of the political culture of the Left, and disenchantment with antagonistic behaviour and the finding of new forms of collective expression.

The 1970s and 1980s saw a considerable renewal of personnel and political culture within the Italian Communist Party and the trade unions. The inflow of militants and cadres from the movement brought a stock of energies and experience to the traditional organizations of the Left that stimulated innovation, accelerated the decline of their traditional culture, and introduced modern styles of management. This genuine form of modernization was not extraneous to the subsequent crisis of the Communist Party. The selection of a modernizing political class was an outcome very distant from the ideological image that the party had given of itself, but it certainly corresponded to the systemic effects of collective mobilization. Indeed, one may say that terrrorism, especially in its original form, was a paradoxical and distorted aspect of this process. It was, that is, a perverse effect of the system's inadequacy of response: a new potential political elite, such as that which constituted the first terrorist organizations, was diverted into armed struggle because it was unable to find adequate channels of expression within the political system. Of all the dramatic aspects of terrorism this waste of political resources is certainly not the least important: the Italian political system was unable to absorb protest and harness its modernizing thrust. It therefore had to pay the tragic price of violence – not only the social effects of terrorism and the battle against it, but also the wasted opportunities to innovate with political personnel and the resources of leadership.

The second direction of transformation in collective action was the disenchantment of antagonistic attitudes subsequently expressed by the women's, environmental, and peace movements. Collective action moved closer to personal demands without, however, relinquishing its pressure for social change. The roots of this action were often related to previous forms of commitment (Hellman 1987a 1987b).

In conclusion, we may gather together the strands of the interpretative model proposed in this analysis. My guiding hypothesis has been that the cycle of struggles that began in 1968, extending its effects up to the 1980s, was triggered by the demands for modernization that accompanied Italian society's progress towards the postindustrial model, and by antagonistic demands arising from the embryonic formation of conflicts typical of complex societies.

In terms of the capacity to govern, the response by the Italian political system consisted of the introduction of restricted reform and of a resort on the other hand to repression and countermobilization. In terms of the capacity to represent, the reaction took the form of hyperpoliticization and underrepresentation. The effects of this system of relationships included distorted modernization, and the breakdown and transformation of collective action. As outcomes of such breakdown, I have pointed out terrorism on the one hand, and neomysticism, drug abuse, and suicide on the other. Collective action has been transformed by institutionalization, in particular the selection and renewal of modernizing political personnel in the organizations of the Left, and by the disenchantment of new antagonistic demands.

This model underlines two premises of my analysis: first, that it is impossible to understand the evolution of collective action in Italy without hypothesizing the presence of antagonistic demands; and, second, that systemic relations, not mere sequences of events, must be analysed in order to uncover the nexuses that bind demands, responses, and systemic effects together.

Winds from the Right

In Italy, the general processes of transformation which have led to the emergence of a 'postindustrial' planetary society have been grafted onto the historical distortions in that country's pattern of development and onto a clogged process of social and political modernization. Throughout the 1970s and 1980s, demands for institutional modernization accompanied the passage of Italian society towards the postindustrial model, whereas the cultural and social processes typical of that model – the birth of an information society, the appearance of new conflicts, integration with the world system, the crisis of the welfare state – continued at an accelerated pace.

The political system responded to these changes by keeping reforms within the narrowest confines possible, by encouraging further fragmentation of interests, by penetrating public life through the operation and apparatuses of the political parties and turning it into an arena of clientelism and corruption.

The innovative thrust of the processes activated towards the end of the 1960s was limited and thwarted in a manner that ultimately produced terrorist forms of deviance and the decay of civic culture as its upshot. The restructuring of the productive system and of industrial relations, the decentralization of the state, as well as the formation of the new needs and the new actors typifying the postindustrial society took place in a limited manner which produced neither effective modernization nor a real democratization of the institutions.

The changes that began in the late 1960s contained in them a cultural and social aspect that was, and remains, irreducible to politics as such. Youth, women's, pacifist, and environmentalist mobilizations, the transformation of lifestyles, the changed role of the media, the growth of voluntary action, new identity demands – all these contributed to a profound change in the Italian culture, mental categories, and everyday relationships.

Yet these significant features have been largely underestimated and, especially in the culture of the Left, attention has rather been focused on the political dimension, on electoral outcomes, on gains for the party. No notice was taken of the need for change from the point of view called for by the novel phenomena.

The electoral victory for the Right in the spring 1994 has not only upset long-standing political equilibria; it has exposed the reverse side of the impulse, the other face of these processes, which requires a reading that does not focus solely on the visible dimension of politics alone. Changes occurred in the 1970s and 1980s which affected the deep fabric of society: the quality of relations, the way in which individuals and groups perceive and construct themselves in their everyday lives. Although these changes were announced by the exemplary and symbolic action of movements, they were given development entirely within the political realm and hence their innovative contents were rendered practically invisible.

For twenty years, the main part of my work has taken shape as an effort to make explicit these contents in everyday experience, though not so as to minimize the impact and political importance of these phenomena but rather to show that the roots of politics were shifting elsewhere to a different domain, and that a wholly political reading of them would fail to capture the innovative and dynamic nature of that change. The confused phenomena of the 1970s and 1980s began to propel Italy beyond industrial society without an institutional modernization of the society at large having taken place. Italy was leaving the modern age and moving towards a society whose features were still not clear but which had already been contained in embryonic form in the events of the last thirty years. Manifest in these 'postmodern' demands were impulses towards individual self-fulfilment; different relational and communicative models were developed, the body asserted its role, and a new dimension of time and space proper to the shaping planetary society was discovered. I have also described the other side of this transformation, the reactionary response to innovation. Defensive behaviour is ever-present in contemporary collective phenomena; individuality and self-realization may swiftly turn into individualism and closure in the particular.

More than ten years ago (Melucci and Diani 1983, recently published in a new edition Melucci and Diani 1992), I felt it necessary to point out the importance of territorial identity and its defensive and reactionary components (see also Diani 1996). The endeavour to give rootedness to an identity which perceives itself threatened exhibits a great likelihood for a defensive closure. Identity no longer possesses any roots, as the social containers necessary for its transmission, preservation, and cultivation are no longer sufficiently stable and solid so as to act as its guarantors in a permanent fashion. Identity shifts towards the realm of individual construction, and this process tends to encourage a defensiveness posture. When people are forced to themselves assume responsibility for the creation their own identity, we encounter an incipient risk: the more pronounced is the sensation of vulnerability in the face of that task, the more prominent the tendency to close oneself off in a reassuring entity that can guarantee continuity and stability. Primary belongings, the need for immediate recognition, the homeland, origins, the group with which one most immediately identifies, may provide this security.

I pointed all this out in 1983, placing nevertheless more emphasis on its dynamic aspects, which I believed to be predominant in the long run. I pointed out the risks but underestimated the reactionary components, yet believing that such tendencies would in actual reality prove residual if only the political system succeeded in its project for modernization. However, the weakness of the Italian political system and all the gravity of its crisis have in the end created the ground for precisely such a defensive and reactionary dimension to prevail. The conservative and populist wave that shook the Italian political system in 1994, apart from the capacity to manipulate consensus that derived from its privileged use of the media, certainly stemmed at least in part from these 'postmodern' needs for individual self-realization and the assertion of difference. But it simultaneously offered the smoothly crafted reassurance of facile slogans mouthed with the same smiles and glossy images that used to sell products for personal hygiene and dog food.

All its sensationality notwithstanding, we should not allow ourselves to be dazzled one more time by the primacy of events on the political stage.

We should not perpetuate the tendency to underestimate or ignore the wealth of social phenomena that lie behind the electoral choices. The electoral success of the Right in 1994 has not eliminated the ambivalence of the processes that I have sought to describe, which manifest themselves in their defensive form as the need for reassurance, certainty, predictability, and yet also express the need to free individuals and groups from the control of the central state and traditional political apparatuses.

It should also be pointed out that the process that led to the political upset of 1994 still contains a sharp distinction between events in the political arena and events in the everyday realm of civil society. Despite the continuously growing risk of fragmentation and decay, Italian civil society is still much richer, much more variegated, much more able to articulate its vitality than its political – especially electoral – version is able to express (see Putnam 1993). This impossibility of reducing society to politics is typical of complexity in general. But in Italy, the primacy given to party-political struggle has thwarted the potential for innovation present in the society, it has paradoxically prevented the development of an autonomous civic culture, and a deeply-felt identification with the democratic institutions.

To refuse to reduce the social to mere politics, and in particular to the electoral process, means accepting that the translation of social phenomena into voting choices will produce outcomes that are much more temporary and unstable than has been the case in the past. An increasingly small proportion of the social will be translated directly into electoral choices and this will render political equilibria variable and provisional. For a country like Italy, with its tradition of political subcultures, of electoral choices which coincided for longtime with being born in a catholic or communist part of the country, this means a virtual revolution. But political representatives, whether on the Right or Left, must take account of the fact, for the consensus they enjoy will no longer be permanently guaranteed by a base with the social and territorial roots of the past.

The real danger lies in the decay of Italy's institutions and civil life. Institutional closure may spill over to provoke further damage to civil society, blocking any ongoing processes of transformation. For example, institutional measures which reduce guarantees, restrict rights, or interfere in the public role of information will augment old and new inequalities and may produce permanently deleterious effects in society. However, the game can still be decided either way, and the near future depends on the action of a number of different subjects. The Rightist solution is an unstable solution – in the chemical sense, on account of the elements of which it is composed, and in the political sense, owing to its inability to propose manageable solutions to the country's problems. Precisely for this reason, there is, therefore, a chance for different outcomes to the situation that has arisen since the spring 1994, thanks to the internal richness extant in civil society which has still to express all its potential.

This richness, however, may be also rapidly consumed, for the potential generated in the social sphere is fragile and, apparently, unable of developing an institutional form. Therein is manifested is the paradox of complex societies. It is as if the entire force of change resided in the invisible roots of civil society; but only if these roots manage to embody themselves in institutions will change come about. In the absence of such an institutional process, the potential will be dispersed. It will either degenerate into marginalization, as has been the case with youth phenomena and urban violence, or it will transform itself into forms of purely cultural innovation which, by passing through the mass media, will be reduced to discourse and image.

That every social innovation in Italy might be reduced to mere discourse depends in the first place on the role of television. In a country like Italy, in which religion for far too long has been an overarching institutional presence, the television preachers in the North American mold could never take hold. But their equivalent are the new Savonarolas, the lay preachers who minister to the collective conscience from the screen. Provocation and invective, like the fire and brimstone sermons of the past, can be directed towards any aspect of personal life, culture, and politics. This discourse – whose only purpose is to produce further discourse – may direct a frontal attack on the old, generically promise the new, and render all contents substitutable and interchangeable.

In the packaging of these new television preachers, mostly conservative, more attention is paid to the image and to the process than to content. Everything is exploited to hold the attention of the audience, discourse is deployed with great flexibility. There is no fear of contradiction and coherence no longer presents a value.

There is an instrumental purpose to this variability, but it is certainly also able, however superficially, to find correspondence to a widely felt need: the need to no longer commit oneself definitively to any one set of rigid values, which, once the choice has been made, must always be effectively adapted to the circumstances.

The political Left has long been an example of precisely such rigidity combined with pragmatic adjustment. Perhaps in this respect the heir of Catholic culture, the Italian Left has always been maximalist in principle and pragmatic in reality. This tradition has prevented the Left from acting effectively as a democratic opposition, a role which involves matching the adversary point by point, proposing alternatives on individual issues, informing the public, and mobilizing the interests affected by decisions. The

Italian Left has always acted in the name of the maximalism of principles – hence the anticapitalism, Revolution, the rejection of 'the system' – but, then again, it has been able to swiftly trim these principles wherever it has governed at the local level, or in its parliamentary behaviour. This adaptation, however, is a matter very different from the capacity for mediation required in any democratic system.

Some of its consequences in the 1980s have been to turn political action into short term compromise and even corruption, although the latter has certainly represented for the Communist Party an extreme and marginal phenomenon. The striking feature of the Left culture in the 1990s, especially its ex-Communist segments, is a kind of postmodern adaptation, a pragmatic assumption in their blandest form of the languages, styles, and theories that once represented the 'system' – that is, the adversary's territory. Accordingly, Marxism has been replaced by exchange theory, austere militancy by public relations; the carving up of a work order is pursued with the same off-handedness as the logic of show business. The 'yuppification' of leftist culture and practice risks to substitute superficial 'postmodernism' for the need for an effective capacity for channelling and institutionalizing the potential for innovation in Italian society. The new might be incorporated as discourse and image, without being converted into new institutions, the only positive outcome for innovative processes in a highly differentiated society.

In complex societies, the pressures and needs for change are rapidly institutionalized and give rise to new social models. Change is increasingly cultural, it involves transformation in mental and relational patterns, but it can survive only if it finds a political and institutional form. And it is precisely this that is lacking.

The shift to the Right in the 1994 elections displayed ambivalent features, but it also contained a clear component of outright reactionaryism. There are two aspects to this reaction, one cultural, the other politico-institutional. The cultural aspect concerns the inability to politically incorporate the new themes produced over the last thirty years – the great themes of change as they relate to difference, global interdependence, the crisis of the ecosystem, the relationship with time and space, the relationship with the body. There are very little traces of any of this in conservative culture, as the capacity to assimilate and process whatever society has produced. All that has been assimilated is the most superficial aspect, that of communication and image, together with certain languages which by now form a part of common culture but in fact often conceal a purely defensive traditionalism. It is as if only the outward form of these themes remains. The situation of women, the environment, and individual needs are transformed into pure image, a mere linguistic game, and enter the media market as hollow signs. This is the drift that I described earlier, and it represents the reactionary side of the process, as it empties everything that society produces of its innovative thrust.

The other reactionary aspect is political in nature and it concerns the contempt for the rules of the game, of the democratic game in particular. There is a deeply rooted element of fascism involved here which grows threatening in the context of our day: the more complex the system, the more essential become the rules. While it is important to render the rules flexible and substitutable, it is equally essential that they be enforced. If flexibility becomes the rejection or the flouting of the rules, the damage to the functioning of the institutions becomes incalculable.

Playing the institutional game and simultaneously denying it is the profoundly anti-democratic characteristic of this new Right. The rules of the game are the necessary condition for holding complexity together. They may be discussed and redefined as one goes along, but as long as they remain legitimate they must be respected; otherwise violence, in a subtle form, becomes the de facto rule. There is a latent and unknowingly fascist core to new Italian conservatism. It is represented in the reckless use of images and communication. It is less manifest in content or in verbal violence, but resides in the underlying conviction that there are no rules with which one necessarily needs to comply. The successes at the ballot box of this culture must mean that it draws on a groundswell of opinion and corresponds to attitudes widespread in society. It reflects in part the narcissism of contemporary culture and a certain impatience with the limit, which, as it stands, may become contempt for the rules.

Civic culture and democracy

In the strictly institutional sphere, Italy has embarked on a passage to complexity which seems intent on skipping the achievement of modernization. The country thus has to empty something (the 'old' institutions) which have not been really filled. Conservative culture rests on this weakness of the institutional fabric, on the weak identification with the civic culture, with the nation's founding values, with workings of the democratic institutions. The risk involved in such a case is serious, as the passage from modernization to postindustrial society might be simply mixing an appearance of hypermodernity with actual unaccomplishment of modernity. The risk is that behind the pyrotechnics, behind the change so proudly trumpeted, the actual outcome will amount to Italy's marginalization with respect to the rest of the Western countries.

The swing to the Right has created, paradoxically, the occasion for Italian progressive forces to commit themselves to the consolidation of democratic institutions and to their revitalization in a postindustrial society. The task of safeguarding and renewing democracy means playing the democratic game to its fullest extent, demanding that one's adversaries make their reasons public, ensuring that the rules are respected, struggling against the monopolization of information, matching government policies by credible alternatives. Autonomy must also be restored to civil society, not by collapsing it into the political dimension but by taking the trouble to respect its distance. But the culture of the Left is ill-prepared to undertake this task, as it has always sought to reduce everything produced in civil society to politics: if it served to win votes or strengthen the position of the party, it was encouraged; otherwise it was ignored. Today, we know that there is no longer linear link between electoral behaviour and social role, between the political choice and the position in society. People no longer cast their vote based on party loyalty but according to their shifting identities.

This fact increases the risks of manipulation and assigns a crucial role to information. Good arguments are not always those that win the televised debate, and people prefer reassurance to confrontation with problems. In a mass society, facile discourse, promoted through the simplistic slogans generalized by the media, is by definition easier than critical discourse based on reasons and arguments. But there is also need for meaningfulness, values, solidarity, and equity. Faced with the postmodern void, there is also a profound need for rootedness, for identity, for individual autonomy and for belief in the collective. There is still a yearning for justice which does not concern the distribution of material goods alone, but involves life-chances and the capacity to be individually autonomous, informed, and aware. It is only on this ground that the distinction between the Left and the Right can still become meaningful.

A perspective of openness and equity must be pursued through policies which reflect the great issues of planetary society, but do not simply address them *ad hoc* in reaction to periodic waves of concern or alarm; the environment, peace, immigration, the coexistence of differences – these are ever-present problems signalled by movements and cultural forces and translated through policies into institutional change. From this point of view, one policy is not equivalent to another. There are policies which are more democratic than others: those which can keep the great systemic problems visible, while seeking to solve them on the basis of equitable criteria. Other policies, instead, induce us to forget these problems by concealing them or by manipulating our perception of them. As a result, the problem is worsened, some parts of the population always pay a higher price than others, while the effects reverberate through the entire system.

There are policies which encourage the effective exercise of autonomy, of difference, policies which distribute life-chances more equally than others. There are policies which, instead, distribute the costs of the great problems confronting us onto the collectivity and favor particular interests. Certain of the prices to be paid for those representing the latter in complex systems will not be immediately visible and quantifiable; they can be assessed only in the long run, becoming manifest in personal distress, deviance, a deterioration in the quality of life. These, too, provide us with yardsticks with which the differences between policies can be measured.

PART IV

Acting collectively

15

Mobilization and political participation

Collective action as a social phenomenon

The preceding chapters on the internal functioning of the political system repeatedly presented the need for an analysis of interests and forms of action which are formed before and beyond the boundaries and the rules of the political game. Social movements and collective action are the constant reminder of the limits of politics; they remind society of the fact that social processes create demands for politics while occupying areas at the same time prior to and beyond politics. Collective action is fed by needs that originate in the social fabric of everyday life and are not comprehended by the political system or are excluded by its filters; but its emergence is no less encouraged by expectations and demands that are bypassed by the decision-making process – that is, by the negative or insufficient outcome of the political game.

In this chapter and the ones that follow it in part IV, specific attention will be drawn to the internal processes by which a 'movement' is formed and becomes a visible actor, sometimes as an organization participating, directly or indirectly, in the political system. Theoretical thought on the *social* dimension of social movements is much less developed than that regarding their role as *political* actors. In recent years, multiplication of forms of collective action has dramatically underlined this shortage of theory, making a new critical assessment necessary and calling for new analytical instruments. Both European thought, rooted mainly in Marxist legacy, and recent North American developments in social movements theory seem to share a common impasse and tend to undervalue the social dimension of social movements in favour of an increasing concentration on the political and organizational dimensions of collective action.

Traditional Marxist analysis, which has paid attention to the social dimensions of collective action beyond its more properly political expression (for instance, to the role of class struggles), has nevertheless ultimately reduced social movements to political action. Attempting to define the structural contradictions that could lead to a revolutionary transformation, Marxist analysis has not been attentive to the formative processes of collective action, to the multiple forms of the passage from 'objective' interests to the actual mobilization of people. This tendency has been aggravated in the predominant strands of leftist thought, which have elevated Leninist precepts to a general canon for every form of collective action aiming at social change. The party, as a rigid organization of professional revolutionaries, is the basic instrument, and the conquest of the apparatus of the state is the primary objective. Thus formulated, we are left with an approach which first underestimates and then excludes from the analysis all forms of action which cannot be reduced to the model, even implicit, of the party. When and if the party becomes the state, it is easy to consider, by definition, the new power as the direct and transparent translator of all collective demands, with the tragic consequences of totalitarianism that we have come to know by now. We also know, to be sure, that this has not represented the only line of thought within the Marxist tradition; but even when authors identifying with the Marxist idiom retain a critical distance from the Leninist model, they still subscribe to the primacy of politics and tend to reduce social movements to their political expression. Recent European theorists are still influenced by this inheritance of Marxism, at least as far as the structural conditions allowing for collective action are concerned (see Touraine, Habermas, Offe). Even those exhibiting great sensitivity to the social dimension of social movements (notably Touraine) incline to grant primacy to the forms of collective action that show capacity to manifest themselves in the political arena.

In North American sociology, social interactionism and functionalism have displayed keen awareness of the social dimension of social movements. None the less, they have also located the roots of collective action in some kind of dysfunction of the social system; consequently, collective behaviour has been separated from the ordinary, regulated, and 'rational' forms of behaviour. The recent critique of the collective behaviour tradition by resource mobilization theory, primarily in the United States, has correctly reestablished the role of rational calculation, intermediate networks, and entrepreneurial leadership in the mobilization of the people. This critique, in my opinion, has rightly brought to the fore the importance of the organizational level for any theory of collective action. But in spite or the good start, the stress on the organizational processes has in alike manner ended up in a new political reductionism. For resource mobilization theorists, social movements matter inasmuch as they bear upon the political system and are able to transform themselves into political actors – a new form of reversed Leninism surfacing in the recent American social movements theory? The important turn introduced by resource mobilization theory has been a healthy reminder of the necessity to pay attention to the internal processes of collective action. But, in the end, the success of the approach has emptied again the *social* dimension of the mobilization of resources it had first disclosed, by stressing the role of political mediators and entrepreneurs as the only factors capable of creating the preconditions of the meaning and effectiveness of the otherwise fragmented and insignificant collective action.

In this chapter and those that follow, I wish to point out the importance of the *social* processes through which a social movement becomes a collective actor, and for this purpose I will draw, among others, on the many contributions of the resource mobilization approach. At the same time, however, I will try to avoid the trap of political reductionism they exemplify and to concentrate the analysis, instead, on the ways people themselves construct and make sense of their action through socially organized investments. In this line of thought the political dimension of collective action is not given a special priority and there is no implicit assumption made as to which of the levels of collective action should be viewed more important than the others. It is impossible to know a priori whether or not a specific form of action will impact the political system; and even when it may do so, the fact itself does not attribute to that action any special value. The operation of one's analytical frame alone should explain how and why collective action has become political action in that particular case.

The formation of a movement

The current sociological term for the process by which a social movement is created and begins to take action is 'mobilization'. In a general sense, mobilization is the process by which a social unit assumes, with relative rapidity, control of resources which it did not control before (Etzioni 1968). With specific reference to social movements, we may say that mobilization is the process by which a collective actor gathers and organizes its resources for the pursuit of a shared objective against the resistance of groups opposing that objective. From the point of view of the ruling groups analysis could define the process in terms of social control and repression: the 'mobilization' takes place in order to preserve the social order against the threat of groups seeking to transform it.

But how does the process of mobilization come about? Current stereotypes tend to view with favour the idea that a social movement arises from the aggregation of the most severely disenfranchised members of a society. This point of view has been systematically put forward in the theory of mass society (Kornhauser 1959). Compared to traditional social system, mass society is seen as a system of atomized relations, in which the elite is more sensitive to the influence of the masses, but the masses are more easily manipulated by dominant groups. Individuals lose their ties with a primary order of groups, with the local community, with associative structures offering a sense of belonging and identification. Individuals are isolated, personal relations are increasingly tenuous, while public relationships become paramount; large, centralized bureaucratic institutions expand and all intermediate, locally based groups diminish in importance. These conditions generate standardized collective forms of conduct with strong emotional content, and totalitarian mass movements are liable to emerge. The mass society approach, therefore, assumes that mobilization becomes more likely the greater the influence of this process of disintegration of ties and community, and the weaker the network of associative inhibitors among individuals. Activists and militants in a movement will, therefore, tend to be those individuals with the shallowest roots or the weakest attachments, those who are most marginal and most excluded from participation in intermediate groups of an associative or community nature. Vice versa, belonging to a network of relationships and being integrated within a social fabric of groups would strengthen consensus, inhibit mobilization, and prevent the formation of movements.

The ideological implications of this theory, given its tendency to reduce collective action to deviance and manipulation, should not mask the fact that explanatory models of this kind are far more common in the interpretation of phenomena of collective mobilization than one would expect. When subjected to scrutiny, however, the theoretical premises of this approach prove very fragile. First of all, it adopts the postulate that belonging to a network – association or community-based – signifies the integration of an individual into society, and that conflicts will be contained and resolved at that level. To do so, however, is to neglect the fact that in strongly conflictual situations and in the absence of appropriate channels for the expression of claims, a group consolidated by ties of solidarity may become a resource which facilitates mobilization. Moreover, integration and belonging to intermediate groups can be open-ended and multiple, as is often the case in highly differentiated societies with intersecting and overlapping networks of affiliation. Alternatively, there may be strong segregation within structures which do not communicate to each other: each group is internally integrated but externally separated from the others by barriers of class, culture, race, and the like. It is clear that in the second case affiliation with associations or a community could become a conflictual resource of great importance, rather than an obstacle to mobilization. In the first case, the ease of individual mobility and the multiplicity of affiliations might operate in some measure as factors which prevent the focussing of conflict, and thus reduce the likelihood of mobilization (compare the exit-voice model by Hirschman, discussed in the following section). In brief, the theory of mass society, by reducing mobilization to a synonym for social disenfranchisement, ignores the ambivalent role of social networks and underevaluates the significance of institutional conditions that facilitate the formative processes of collective action: depending on whether the political system is open or closed, and whether or not there are institutional channels for the handling of demands, whether the stratification system is rigid or open to mobility, the role that associative or community affiliation can play in the launching of the mobilization process can vary greatly.

Another fairly common explanation for the process of mobilization centres on the common interests within the group that is mobilized. As already discussed in chapter 3 using the argument of Pizzorno against Olson, it is the affiliation with differentiated 'markets', or networks of relations within which the collective identity is formed in the reciprocal recognition between individuals, that creates a structure of rewards and sanctions; the necessity to maintain or rebuild this structure provides a strong incentive for mobilization and accounts for individuals' getting involved in movements of opposition or revolt.

Oberschall's theory of mobilization (Oberschall 1978, 1993) follows the same line of thought. In order for a protest movement to form, common sentiments of oppression or an identification of a common enemy will not suffice; there must also be a minimal organizational base and leadership. The probability that mobilization will occur hinges upon two conditions. First, there must be a network of pre-existing associational or community ties: a fabric of traditional affiliation, based on family ties, the village, race, or some other form of communal solidarity; or a network of secondary associations based on specific interests, whether occupational, economic, or political. These forms of social organization are not mutually exclusive within a concrete society; they produce a solidarity which constitutes a resource for the conflictual mobilization of the group.

The second condition under which mobilization becomes probable is the segmentation of society, that is, the amount of distance and the size of the barriers that separate social groupings. A society may be stratified but nevertheless permissive of a certain amount of mobility and exchange among social groups; alternatively, there may be more rigid separation and closure among different collective entities. The existence of these barriers facilitates mobilization. The hypothesis formulated by Oberschall is, therefore, that the higher the degree of segmentation, the denser the network of associational and/or community affiliation, and the more intense the collective participation in this network of relations, the more rapid and durable will be the mobilization of a movement.

The analysis up to this point permits the following reflections: (a) First, it seems clear that participation in collective action implies a prior network of affiliations. Participation does not take place by isolated individuals, but rather by individuals with some previous experience of it. Such networks form the foundation of the collective identity, in the sense that they make identification and recognition possible, as well as calculation and prediction of the effects of actions. (b) But in order for mobilization to occur, the adversary must also be identified. The existence of social barriers renders identification of the adversary much more immediate, and polarizes conflicting groups with greater rapidity. Without some kind of community- or association-based solidarity there will be no energy for action, but without an identification of the adversary the protest will peter out into the occasional explosion of discontent or become reduced to a kind of marginal deviance. (c) Previous affiliations are combined in the process of mobilization and give birth to a new collective identity. The different fragments joining together to form a movement are integrated into a new system of relations in which the original elements change their meanings. Mobilization is always a process of transfer of preexisting resources to the benefit of a new objective. During the process, a true 'mutation' takes place, the 'genetic code' of the group is restructured and allows the formation of a new social unit, capable of creating new resources. More generally, we could say that historical social movements, because they are situated in space and time in a concrete society, are always a point of conjunction between past and future, between old solidarities and new conflicts. A movement mobilizes because it has gathered the legacy and the resources of preexisting social structures and has oriented them towards new goals of transformation (see Marx and Useem 1971; Orum 1974; Klandermans 1993; Gerhards and Rucht 1992; Kriesi 1993; Hirsch 1990b; Tarrow 1993a; Schwartz and Shuva 1992).

Mobilizing factors

We can reformulate the discussion thus far by stating that in order for mobilization to occur, the following factors must be present: a collective identity, the identification of an adversary, the definition of a purpose, an object at stake in the conflict.

There must be, first, a kind of solidarity, a 'we' which is recognized and affirmed by all of its constituent subjects. This is why a preexisting affiliational structure is important as a condition for mobilization: it can provide the language and the material basis required for such a recognition to take place. Secondly, the collective actor must also be able to recognize its own temporal continuity, in such a way as to be able to calculate the costs and benefits and make predictions by comparison among successive situations. Finally, the effects of action must be attributed to the group, and there must be some claim of belonging or some will to appropriate the outcomes: this situation may be expressed, for example, in terms of performance/reward, or, in other words, what is socially due to the actor following a certain action recognized as having been performed by that actor.

Identification of the adversary must take place in the terms of the social system of which the actor is part, if conflictual action is to be possible. A generic situation of dissatisfaction or frustration is not enough to bring about the mobilization of a social movement. Without the identification of an adversary, of another social actor in conflict with the group for control of certain resources or values, discontent and protest will not engender a movement. The definition of a social actor as adversary is made in the ideological language of the movement, and it can be of greater or lesser precision; however, it will always refer, directly or indirectly, to the system of which the actor is part. Only under these conditions will it be possible for the group to undertake collective action and to avoid retroflection of its conflictual energy against itself or to project it on imaginary, unrealistically conceived antagonists.

Finally, there is the factor – more or less implicit according to the degree of ideological articulation of the movement – of definition of what is at stake in the conflict, of the object which is aimed at or of which the actors feel themselves to have been deprived. The more actors believe this object to be rightfully theirs and the stronger their desire to obtain the expected resource or value, the greater will be the intensity of this mobilization.

Thus far, we have considered the structural factors that operate as mobilizing agents. We must remember, however, that in analysing a concrete historical society, one is always dealing with a definite conjuncture, a specific combination of states of social structure, which can either favour or obstruct mobilization. Analyses of the political opportunity structure are good examples of such a perspective applied to the state of the political system. It will not be possible here to conduct an exhaustive analysis of conjunctural factors, for this would require detailed reference to a vast documentation of historical cases and empirical situations. I will therefore restrict my remarks to a presentation of a few general criteria, which will serve only as examples and do of course not represent the entire field of analytical possibilities.

The conditions which conjuncturally favor mobilization are all those that loosen the control of the dominant groups over the various systems that make up the social structure, or improve the resources available to the opponents: conflict within the dominant classes or ruling elites and/or economic development; a legitimation crisis within the political system and/or the availability of new representation channels; malfunctioning of the mechanisms of social integration and/or technological innovation. Thereby are created the society's critical focal points, consisting of problems raised but as yet unresolved, and against which it is possible to assess power relationships and estimate the weakness or incapacity of the adversary. Historically, this situation has arisen more often when periods of closure and repression by the dominant groups have been followed by a phase of reform, however cautious. Reform has great potential as a mobilizing agent as it loosens social control, widens the field of participation and increases expectations – without, however, affecting the fundamental interests of the dominant groups. It is in this light that one may interpret the collective conflicts which often follow closely the cautious (and frequently failed) attempts at reform on the part of previously authoritarian regimes. Unable to bring about structural transformations of any real significance under the constraints inherited by the past, the reformists widen the base of political participation and raise expectations, without at the same time providing effective outlet for the demands created in the process. Eastern European countries provide the most recent example of such a situation.

Reversely, one could argue that the creation of channels for individual mobility could, from a conjunctural point of view, be a factor which obstructs mobilization (here I shall ignore the situation of a highly repressive, authoritarian system, where mobilization is obstructed by a rigid control structure). In many cases, analysis of mobilization alternatives in terms of 'exit-voice', as in Hirschman's model (1975), may be useful. In this model, the actor either pursues her/his goals by resorting to an 'exit option', by changing her/his individual position within the system, or by entrusting the task of the achievement of the goals to the 'voice', that is, by taking action through collective protest and struggle for social change. When opportunities for individual pursuit of advantages is available, mobilization potential is likely to diminish.

However, this alternative seems applicable only to the conjunctural factors of mobilization. The opening of channels for individual mobility may certainly obstruct the formation of conflictual action, but only in the short run. Increased mobility does create rising expectations, which the system may not be able to satisfy without introducing other changes not always compatible with dominant interests. Hence the probability of barriers and blocks, which in the long run may recast the problem in terms of social struggle and trigger the need for collective mobilization.

Analysis of conjunctural factors also involves the consideration of time in mobilization processes. The most useful criterion for measuring the scope of mobilization and the degree of involvement of different groups in a temporal sequence is the ratio between risks and advantages. The highest level of participation by an individual or collective actor will occur at the moment bringing together minimum risk and maximum gain. These two elements combine to form a variable relationship during the mobilization process, and can be used to explain its progress. The reduction of risk and the maximization of advantage is a problem to be constantly addressed by a movement's leadership, should it wish to widen the base of participation.

In conclusion of this section, I shall turn for a moment to the other extreme of the mobilization process: the breakdown of a social movement. The factors that favour mobilization are the same that may eventually lead to the movement's disintegration. A movement is formed around the convergence and fusion of previous affiliations. But this multiplicity of components may also be a weakening factor, which means that movements face the constant problem of integration and maintenance of internal unity. Differing interests and competition for leadership may produce conflicts and tensions within the movement which must be dealt with at an organizational level. In the absence or weakness of permanent institutionalized procedures for the formation of decisions, and of a recognized system of regulations, each subgroup will tend to participate according to its own particular interests. Information circulates in limited quantities within the different circuits, thus accentuating the centrifugal forces. These pressures favouring withdrawal accompany the mobilization process and must be brought under control if the movement is to survive. The permanent risk of breakdown is, to a greater or lesser extent, kept under control by the creation of a central leadership, a permanent organization, and an ideological framework. In the following chapters, these features of a movement's structure shall be discussed more extensively.

Participation

I have stressed the fact that participants in social movements are not the disenfranchised, the outsiders or the excluded. Those who take part in a process of mobilization create a collective identity on the basis of previous networks of affiliation. The first to rebel are not the most repressed and emarginated of groups, but, instead, those who perceive an intolerable contradiction between an existing collective identity and the new social relationships imposed by change. These groups are more susceptible to mobilization because: (i) they are already experienced participants familiar with the procedures and methods of struggle; (ii) they already have their own leadership and some degree of organizational resources drawn from preexisting community or associational ties; (iii) they can utilize the extant communications networks to circulate new messages and passwords; (iv) it is easier for them to recognize common interests, in the sense discussed above.

Thus new movements are born within a structure of preexisting relations. The onset of mobilization is always the work of those who already collectively posses an identity and seek to defend it against the imminent threat from change. These actions can serve as catalysts for latent demands, and new groups are grafted onto the initial protest: through action, the newcomers try to define their own identity, at first by joining the mobilization of groups with a preexistent and more solid identity and later by proceeding to chart their own situation autonomously and in more precise terms. These new social groups may have no experience of participation, and no knowledge of the means and procedures for the pursuit of their interests. Even their language is inadequate for expressing their demands. In fact, as we shall see, the ideology of movements in formation often looks to the past for its points of reference or symbolic representations when it names new issues of conflict. The birth of a movement and the beginning stage of a mobilization are always characterized by the overlapping of different actors and the interweaving of multiple meanings of action. When the movement consolidates, a settling-down process begins and mobilization becomes cumulative.

Numerous empirical examples confirm this interpretative model. For a start, we might cite the origins of the labour movement. The first mobilization and early forms of organization were the creation of craftsmen and professional workers, still semiartisans, who fought against the new conditions imposed by capitalist production methods. They were relatively privileged workers, with still strong ties to the traditional corporation and a high level of professional skills. Only later was the struggle of the broad mass of factory workers added on to the defensive struggles of these craftsmen; a mass, furthermore, of unskilled or less skilled workers who were much more brutally exploited, with fewer professional skills and no experience of participation and struggle.

Significantly analogous to this classic process was the cycle of labour conflict in Europe (France, Italy) in the late 1960s (Crouch and Pizzorno

1978). The cycle was initiated by actors who already had experience of collective conflict, who already knew the techniques and procedures of struggle. The first to mobilize were the skilled workers, who possessed a tradition of trade union participation, were relatively privileged with respect to the mass of unskilled manpower who worked in automated factories or on assembly lines. The first strikes came about as the result of a decision on the part of those who already knew how to fight. This example encouraged the new workers who, until that point, had kept silent. When the first battles proved worthwhile, a widespread explosion of demands occurred, which at the beginning took place only on the inside of the factory and later moved beyond its walls, widening the gap between the unions and the constituency of new workers. In order to take over the leadership of the struggle, the unions were forced to modernize their strategy and organization. The significance of this cycle of struggles is, then, two-fold: alongside the characteristic features of a class movement there is also the institutional pressure which gives rise to an important modernization of the system of industrial relations, with the legitimization of union representation in the factory and a recognized partnership role for the union in the policy-making. But what interests us here is the pattern followed by labour mobilization at its early stages, and later exhibited by many other types of collective action.

Research on immigration, urban poverty, ghettos, and ethnic revolt shows that the recruitment of participants takes place among those who are active and integrated into the community. This disproves the common belief that mobilization is a phenomenon involving those who are the most affected by social disintegration and exclusion (immigrants, criminals, slum dwellers). Availability for mobilization is weak among such marginal and rootless groups, while those who do become participants in a movement generally have a more solid collective identity and closer ties to a network of social affiliations. In the case of the Civil Rights Movement, the importance of the network of interpersonal and group relations which preceded the movement has been emphasized. This network played an invisible role in the development and activities of the movement, providing a base for the recruiting of militants and enabling the movement to survive during periods of intense repression (on the civil right movement, see Barkan 1984; Chong 1991; Morris 1984; McAdam 1988).

The case of student movements is also of particular significance. The studies conducted on student mobilizations of the 1960s yielded an image of the participants as upper-middle-class youths of urban culture, with moreover a high level of academic achievement. Here again, it is the groups which are, relatively speaking, more privileged and better integrated that first perceive the contradictions of the system and are in possession of the resources with which to mobilize. Since the end of the 1960s, however, research has shown a change in student activism. Protest is no longer the activity or concern of groups who are central to the system, but has extended to include a wider range of students from a variety of social backgrounds and with more direct experience of the injustice of society.

We find many analogous situations in Europe (France, Germany, Italy, Spain). The origins of the student movement in the 1960s certainly reflected the mobilization of student groups among those who were relatively more privileged. Participation became progressively more widespread with the development of the mass university and the involvement of new social groups which tended to radicalize the movement and import egalitarian experiences to it. The waves of student mobilization in the late 1970s through the early 1980s confirmed this trend, aggravated by the crisis of the university structure. The mobilization was brought about by militant survivors from the crisis of the New Left, and it gradually spread to involve a broader mass of students and unemployed, for whom the university served as an academic parking lot, as it were. The crisis of the university as an institution, and the economic crisis in general, brought together a number of different processes within the movement: collective action was a catalyst for several strata of the unemployed youth in large cities and for violent revolt against the inertia of the political system.

One should not overlook the fact that, in the birth of the student movement and the New Left in general, a fundamental role was played by the experiences gained in earlier associations. Religious associationism, the experience of cultural groups, participation in leftist organizations or in students' representative bodies, were all sources of the frames of reference and the resources used by the new collective actors. The continuity/discontinuity of this process is a significant example of the pattern of mobilization discussed above. New movements inherit not only political personnel already experienced in participation and organization, but a language and jargon as well, which is transformed to take on new contents. Characteristic of the student movement has been its uncritical reappropriation of Marxist language and ideological sectarianism. This, however, reveals a continuity with previous affiliational experiences of militants who had participated in religious or leftist groups, but at the same time demonstrates the collective actor's difficulty in finding fresh language to describe new conflicts.

The women's movement provides another significant example of these processes. In the United States women participated in the civil rights and the peace movements of the first half of the 1960s in a subordinate role.

This experience of participation nevertheless nurtured a new women's consciousness. The initiators of the women's movement were to be precisely those women who had acquired their capacity for action and their organizational resources from involvement in these earlier movements, when they had experienced firsthand some of the contradictions inherent in their gender role. In Europe, women's movements developed during the 1970s as a result of women's participation in New Left groups and in the traditional organizations of the Left, the crisis of which had created the conflictual and organizational resources upon which the first mobilization of the women's movement was based. The subsequent expansion of the movement eventually involved much larger groups of women with no previous experience of mobilization.

Further evidence in support of this model can be found in the vast body of existing research on political participation. I will examine the heuristic value of this concept in a short while, and for the moment it may suffice to refer to a central finding in this branch of research which sums up the results of numerous studies and confirms the general hypotheses I have formulated so far: namely, evidence shows that the more closely the individual is integrated in a group, the greater will be the degree of her/his political participation. Political participation is an expression of belonging to a certain social group, and the more secure the affiliation is, the more intense also the participation.

Having so far examined the conditions that favour participation, we may now take a closer look at the processes of involvement which foster individual mobilization, seeking therewith to explain the differing degrees of participation. Regarding the former, we can single out the following features of the process: (a) The process of involvement is cumulative for those who mobilized during a movement's early phases. In other words, through experience of different forms of participation, the individual acquires the knowledge and resources than enable mobilization. (b) Affected by the stimulus and the tensions that set the conflict in motion, the individual evaluates her/his own position relative to that of the group to which s/he belongs, and any mobilization of the individual will be subject to assessment by the group. Thus the attitude of the group may either increase or hinder an individual's willingness to get mobilized. (c) In a similar fashion, an individual's involvement in a movement may be facilitated or obstructed by her/his relationship with secondary leaders, or the leaders of the various groups to which s/he belongs. In fact, one of the major concerns of the leaders of a movement is to obtain the consensus of the secondary leaders who control the various circuits of affiliation. (d) Willingness to invest personal resources and bear the costs of participation are proportional to the rewards expected (material advantage, prestige, fraternal bonding, emotional gratification). If, during the course of the mobilization process, assessment of the rewards becomes negative, individuals withdraw from the movement. One of the tasks of the leaders and the organizational structure is to maintain the balance between the investment and rewards of the various members; and one of the roles of ideology is to take the place of rewards when a negative balance threatens continued involvement. An ideological discourse furnishes new rewards or attempts to change expectations, so as to avoid the loss of the members' support or the prospects of their diminishing involvement.

These conditions, however, will still be not enough to explain the differing degrees of involvement of individuals in a social movement. That is, they do not explain why, under identical conditions, some individuals are mobilized while others are not, and why it is never an entire social group which is mobilized, even though all its members are affected by the same structural problems. I have already described the areas of a society in which the conditions for mobilization can be created, and the way in which the actual process unfolds. But if we wish to understand the mobilization of single individuals, we must introduce the dimension of deeper personal motivations, and consider collective experience also from the emotional point of view (see chapter 4). This kind of an analysis has been commonly set against the sociological approach, and has either been hailed by socio-psychological studies as the key to complete understanding or dismissed altogether as reductionist by 'structural' analyses.

It seems to me that the methodological misunderstanding stems from a failure to distinguish among the analytical levels to which the theory applies. Analysis of the conditions for mobilization must address the structure of social affiliations and conflicts. Examination of the differing degrees of individual participation takes place at the level of motivations. Every arbitrary extension of analysis beyond the level to which it pertains throws theory back into the domain of ideology. Thus, in order to explain differences of participation, we must examine the conditions which render a situation *subjectively* intolerable to certain individuals, along with the conditions under which these individuals recognize others like themselves and certain fundamental shared experiences acquired in the same or similar situation. Structural conditions provide the requisites for a common motivational structure with which particular individuals can identify and recognize each other, and on the basis of which they are mobilized. The biographies of participants in a movement often testify to the importance of such a *recognition* factor as a deeply emotional experience which brought about their participation and commitment to struggle. The joyful and encouraging discovery that other people are *living* the same experience is a strong support for individual commitment to collective action. Mutual affective recognition is not a post factum event but a central factor in the process of involvement. An integration – far from being accomplished today – of structural analysis and analysis of emotional experience along the lines given in chapter 4 could significantly improve our theoretical approach to the processes of mobilization.

Repression and social control

The first methodological criterion I have outlined above for the analysis of collective action is that it must be conducted in terms of social relations. Collective action always implies a relationship between at least two adversaries, and it can only be understood in terms of this relationship. Analysis habitually turns either on movements or on the response of the dominant system (political or otherwise), producing thus a great amount of distortion of understanding with respect to the relational nature of the phenomenon. This much should be clear by now. Instead, then, any analysis of collective action should take its lead from the examination of a relationship, even if we were to study only one of the many components of that action; for it is only by including in the account the actions of the adversary and of other actors in the field that the behaviour of the actor can become meaningful.

Therefore, in order to understand processes of mobilization, we must examine the ways in which the dominant system intervenes through the repressive apparatus of the state and the mechanisms of social control (Piven and Cloward 1971, 1977, 1992; Suttles and Zald 1985; Tilly 1990; Jenkins and Klandermans 1995). Mobilization does not take place in a vacuum: it must deal with the far more powerful counteraction of the adversary who strives to obstruct, contain, and repress collective protest (Oberschall 1978; Zald and Useem 1987; McCarthy *et al.* 1991; McCarthy and Wolfson 1992; Offe 1990; Meyer 1993). For the moment, we shall leave aside the structural advantages of the ruling groups, and the fact that their control is already embodied in the structure of society through socialization and the internalization of norms, through the codification of roles and the unequal distribution of resources. The repertoire of counteraction includes of course also direct intervention for the purposes of acquiring control over the mobilization process. We have already noted the manipulation of the structure of social rewards through individual mobility and the distribution of particular advantages. But the intervention may be directed at the political system as well, by means of widening the channels for participation and negotiated settlement of conflicts. Finally, recourse to institutional violence is possible through the repressive apparatus of the state. I shall examine these last two aspects more closely.

Whether the negotiated regulation of conflict is possible or not depends on the capacity of the dominant system to open political channels for the handling of collective demands, and on the willingness of the movements to invest part of their resources in institutional activities. Usually, the prospects for negotiations are higher when both of the adversaries expect greater short-term advantages than what they might gain from conflict. For negotiation to be possible, a minimum degree of mutual recognition must be present, although neither of the adversaries has necessarily relinquished other forms of action, kept in reserve for future repertoire of action in case the assessment of the situation points to a changed cost/benefit balance. To prevent this possibility from taking place, the adversaries must have mutually achieved a complete institutionalization of the conflict. In that case, however, we are no longer dealing with a social movement, but with an institutional actor located within the political system. A movement, to repeat, is always characterized by its dual orientation, operating both inside and outside of an institutional system. The action of those in power also vacillates between institutional largesse and repression.

Particular attention must be paid to the methods and instruments used to repress a movement. Direct confrontation always takes place with the agents of repression, such as the police, the armed forces, and so on; and the structural characteristics, social makeup, and behaviour of such agents is of great importance for analysis of collective action. In recent years there has been a growing interest in these institutional bodies of the state, in terms of research on, and political analysis of, their role in social conflicts. Yet not enough has been done to define the sociological features of the agents of social control, and still lesser are the achievements of the analysis of their conduct *vis-à-vis* the specific events of collective mobilization (for an example, see Morgan 1987). Changes in the culture of armed forces and the police in democratic countries during the recent years bear witness to a crisis in the traditional models of organization, to the impact of new cultures on the repressive bodies themselves, and to the composite, non-monolithic nature of the interests at work inside these organizations. Such changes stress the need for careful specification of the components, functions, and conduct of these bodies in striving to understand the role of the repressive agents in collective mobilization. The composition and internal relations of the agents of social control, their behaviour during concrete episodes of protest or revolt, and their techniques of information and repression are all elements through which valuable insights can be gained into movements and forms of social control.

Repressive agents play a key role above all in cases of collective violence. As many studies have shown and as we have learned from the experience in different countries, that movements will turn violent is a self-fulfilling prophecy. Intervention by the law enforcement agencies is justified in public as necessary to prevent possible violence, while in reality it is their very presence which frequently creates the conditions in which violent action erupts. In a great many cases, aggressive attitudes, control techniques, and the preventive or demonstrative violence of repressive agents have shown themselves to be factors which determine the course the collective processes subsequently takes and its possible violent outcome.

The spectre of violence too often serves as the pretext for repression, or for attempts to broaden the consensus in support of the system. It thus functions as an ideological instrument for social control. In fact, an organized collective actor, unless it is a small sectarian group, is seldom preoccupied with plans to engage in a direct confrontation with the forces of law; in the first place, its main concerns arise from the needs to maintain unity and increase its popular support in order to be able to pursue the movement's objectives. The prospects for gains from violence are never that lucrative, nor is the public image of the movement known to be improved by violent confrontations. Violence in itself guarantees no payoff. For this reason, movements organizations always have an internal structure designed for preventing random violence in public confrontations and for controlling its own factions most prone to violence. Often there are also consultations, negotiations, and preventive agreements with the institutional agents. Therefore the concrete forms assumed by the process of collective mobilization, violent or other, always depend on the way the action of the movement interacts or comes into conflict with the repressive agents.

On the concept of political participation

Finally, we should discuss the concept of political participation, which, in a number of senses, is often associated with processes of collective mobilization. Reflection on the heuristic limits of this concept and definition of its analytical contents may help in putting an end to the ambiguous, all-purpose use of the term 'participation'.

In North American sociology and political science, studies of political participation have discharged their energies in efforts to specify and measure the levels and forms of participation, so as to make possible comparative analysis and prediction regarding the actors, conditions, and ways of participation. This has given rise to a whole series of working definitions developed for 'participation', including references to types of political behaviour ranging from voting to the assumption of public office. Such definitions have made it possible to quantify the phenomena observed and to establish meaningful correlations among various kinds of behaviour (see Almond and Verba 1980; Barnes and Kaase 1979; Verba *et al.* 1995). The study of participation is thus reduced to recording observable behaviour, without any reference to the structure of interests behind this conduct, or to the limits within which the given types of behaviour are manifested. The premises of pluralist theory continue to guide the analysis of participation, in particular the idea of the direct transcription of interests into demands and political behaviour that lies at the basis of this approach. It is claimed, for instance, that political participation involves the activities of private citizens, aimed more or less directly at influencing the selection of government personnel and/or the actions of that personnel. Thus, what goes for participation is confined to that action which is effectively undertaken within the political system and has no relationship with 'non-participation', with those demands which are not evident within the system on account of their exclusion, discriminated treatment, or repression. Participation varies only in its level of intensity, from the minimum level of the vote to the maximum level of public office; no reference is made to the differing weights of interests represented in the political system, or to the difficulty or ease of access to the system by different demands. There are no obstacles or structural limits to participation, only various degrees of influence within the system.

The burden of these ideologically saturated premises of pluralist theories can be felt in the explanatory models and, further, in the variables they correlate with participation. In brief, the explanations advanced can be summed up in two models, one of which refers to the social status and personal characteristics of the individual and the other to her/his degree of organizational involvement (Verba). The first model could be defined as one of 'selection' or 'political propensity', and it claims that individuals are variably predisposed to participate in the political system according to their personal characteristics and attitudes. In particular, the model purports that there is a direct relation between social status and the degree of political participation. The higher the status, the higher the level of participation, because (i) the interests subject to political decision-making are more important – the stakes are higher; (ii) individuals of a higher social class have greater resources and capacity for relations, communication, and exchange; and (iii) they have easier access to channels of participation. Another element believed to stimulate political participation is the feeling of personal efficacy, or the expectation of success in influencing political decisions. Obviously, this variable too correlates with status. In sum, this model mantains that individual characteristics, in particular high social status and expectations of success, promote participation.

The second model, which we may call the model of 'mobilization', claims that the wider the range of an individual's affiliation with voluntary associations, the greater her/his political participation will be. Experience of participation in various social organizations allegedly increases the individual's propensity for political participation, since (i) participation in a group widens the sphere of an individual's interests and makes political problems more meaningful to her/him; (ii) interaction with other individuals, including those on other social levels, stimulates political activity; (iii) membership in an organization increases access to information and provides the resources and talents essential for political activity; (iv) participation in the group activities encourages acceptance of democratic processes; and (v) the members derive gratification from the group's activities, which becomes an incentive for political participation.

The first limitation of the explanations of this type stems from the very concept of political participation they utilize. Once participation is defined as the expression of activity within a *political* system, it will be no surprise that such a participation should mostly involve those with a higher position in the society. Access privileges are built into the structure of the political system, as described in chapter 12: the interests of differing social groups are not equally represented within the system. Secondly, a model which takes participation in voluntary organizations to constitute a variable corresponding to greater political participation seems to imply that inequities in the access to participation can be corrected through intensification of associative affiliations, that such voluntary organizations can engage the lower strata of society and thus introduce them into the political system. This assumption also contains within itself a similar ideological bias, as participation in such associations always reflects the unequal structure of the society. The possibility of creating and joining associations and thus entering the political system is not distributed equitably; rather, it reflects the imbalances established among the various social groups and interests. The associative sector is mainly institutionalized, and established associations tend to give stronger support to the interests of the dominant groups and to act more frequently in a defensive manner to safeguard the consolidated pattern of structural advantages. In fact, mobilization of the subordinate groups through associations is normally lesser in proportion, and more frequently excluded from institutionalized channels, and it must take place through non-institutional forms of collective action. Pizzorno in a classic essay (now in Pizzorno 1993b) has discussed the concept of political participation proposed by the

North American sociology, insisting on the relationship between social and economic interests which take form within the civil society and political action. I agree with his effort to demonstrate that participation can also be a vehicle for interests formed outside the political system, but I would argue that Pizzorno ends up with too broad a definition of political participation, presenting it as an action undertaken in solidarity with others, in the context of a state or of a class, and aimed at conserving or modifying the structure (and therefore the values) of the system of the dominant interests. This definition encompasses all forms of collective action and runs the risk of rendering the category of political participation too vague, allowing its use as a description of anything from the institutional actions of a political party to the struggles of a social movement.

I believe that, on the one hand, it is important not to surrender to the temptations of analytical clarity evident in the resort to a reductionist definition of the concept of participation, which, moreover, simply confers the status quo of Western political systems and the existing form of institutional action the aura of theoretical dignity. On the other hand, however, it is equally important to avoid the overextension of the concept, which jeopardizes its heuristic value. The term 'participation', in fact, has the two different meanings (already indicated in chapter 11). First, it consists of recognition of the fact that one belongs to a system, identification with the 'general interest' of the community, and action in the pursuit of shared objectives. Secondly, participation is the defence of particular interests in a competitive context, an attempt to exert influence on the distribution of power to the benefit of a specific group. Moreover, taking into account the reality of the imbalance of social relations, the two meanings of participation acquire quite specific connotations. In the first sense, participation is always, to a varying extent, the confirmation of dominant interests: identification with the system and the pursuit of shared objectives and general values are always governed by the consideration of the advantage of dominant interests. The political system, as we have seen, is subjected to the twin constraint imposed by a system of dominance anchored in social relationships: the confines determining the issues that can be submitted to the decision-making process are structurally set; partial control over the rules and mechanisms of decision-making are the privilege of the forces representing the dominant interests. Thus political participation of the subordinate groups must always take place under these conditions, and recognition of the confines and the rules is part of their subordinate position by definition. Or, one might say, political participation thus defined in effect amounts to some confirmation of the imbalance of dominant social relationships, even if it may modify that imbalance.

But political participation is also the defence of specific interests, an attempt to shift power relationships within the political system, to acquire influence over decisions. The problem is thus one of giving a precise definition to the parameters of political participation, bearing in mind that social relations influence such participation in the two directions. From the perspective of the ruling groups, political participation serves to confirm the priority of their own interests and to obtain the subordinated consensus of other social groups: participation takes place within the confines and rules determined by the dominant system, thus promoting, to a greater or lesser extent, the dominant interests. From the perspective of the subordinate groups, participation is a way to increase their influence in the decision-making process by altering institutional power relationships. But the interests of the subordinate groups, by definition, cannot be entirely represented and become full participants in the political system; they are always, to a greater or lesser extent, excluded from participation and manifest themselves through the non-institutional forms of collective action. The political demands of the subordinate groups receive their expression through participation within the political system depending on its degree of flexibility and permeability; but such demands will always overflow its confines to take the form of collective mobilization, which differs in nature from political participation.

In my view, therefore, any correct definition of political participation must restrict itself to institutional action, and must also include the constant influence of social relations beyond the political system. Thus I would define political participation as any action which takes place, at least in part, within the confines and rules of the political system, and which aims to maximize the advantages of the actor in political decisions. Hence, the concept of political participation can only be applied analytically to the internal processes of the political system. All phenomena which might empirically affect the political system, but threaten to disregard and infringe its system of rules or extend beyond its institutional boundaries, will instead be analysed as social movements, using analytical categories other than that of political participation. By contrast, any analysis of political participation which does not take limits and exclusions into account, or downplays the reduction of social demands that these imply, becomes pure apology for the existing situation.

Mobilization in contemporary movements

The specific features of the mobilizations of recent social movements are: (i) globality of the issues and particularism of goals; (ii) the formation of collective action both internally and externally to the political systems of representation; (iii) continuity between individual identity and collective identity. These features apparently reach back to preindustrial forms of social conflict as described in the literature of traditional peasant or religious movements which fused the globality of religious controversies with the particularism of local revolts. This, however, does not entitle us to to interpret them as regressive phenomena as several observers of contemporary movements have done. The revival of apparently 'premodern' elements of aggregation is, instead, the strategy adopted by these actors in order to operate in complex systems which, in contrast to past industrial capitalism, have today erased any clear distinction between change and conservation, between development and stagnation. Crisis management and system maintenance seem to have substituted the idea of linear development and the industrial myths of uninterrupted growth. The 'premodern' features of mobilization are ways of raising conflictual issues in a new context where traditional forms of class conflict are not effective in reaching the core logic of the system.

1 Affirming *globality* means – for these movements – raising issues that do not concern specific social groups only but, more generally, the system as such. Globality in its contemporary form, however, is not expressed in general ends, such as freedom or equality, but rather in effect replaces them with immediate and short-term actions, apparently centred on particularistic goals (local, group-centred, oriented towards immediate results). Having lost its absolute features, globality is focused on the present; it functions as a short-term aggregating factor; it is ever-renewable. In a symbolic fashion, it indicates general systemic issues through the particularism of the time and place of concrete social action. It fits and cohabits, moreover, with that system of multiple belongings engendered by complexity where actors pass from one association to another, from one network to a different one without committing themselves for good to a specific group or a specific issue.

Finally, it permits individuals to transform the promises for self-fulfilment offered by increasingly differentiated systems into practical opportunities for the self-planned integration of personal experience. Differentiation and complexity carry the risk of anomie and loss of identity. These risks are attenuated by collective actions whose internal and external effects can be immediately recognized. The differentiation of society imposes the need for recomposition strategies and its complexity entails the search for simplification. The small-group community restores an evident and shared unity which involves all the dimensions of the individual experience. This, however, remains only one of the many instances of belonging that individuals experience in their everyday action. It is not a totalizing commitment, one that demands a life-term involvement, but merely a temporary one, although symbolically very important and sometimes fundamental for individuals as it provides a major resource for the formation of meaning and integration of individual experience.

2 *Inside/outside the system of representation.* In complex systems it is increasingly difficult today to distinguish between centrality and exclusion. The mobilizations of recent decades have involved numerous marginal components which, in one way or another, have succeeded in wresting for themselves citizenship rights and a recognition of their interests. Moreover, the extension of welfare policies together with various forms of provisional and irregular participation in the labour market has altered the form and content of marginalization processes, transforming their subjective perception and increasing their temporary character. Insiders and ousiders are thus melded into each other and become at times indistinguishable. Mobilizations of social movements take some form of participation in the labour market and some basic democratic rights for granted. However, mobilization does not entail a position external to the political system but, rather, the recognition of its limits and its instrumental use to carry forward those demands (or elements of them) which participation in political exchange can satisfy. One may in this sense talk of the ubiquity and discretionality of these movements: they work to create channels of representation more congenial to their actors without eschewing official ones, and they thus stand both inside and outside the political system. As the occasion arises, they decide whether and how the representation of each individual demand should be handled, and thus bestow upon themselves broad discretionality regarding choice and action.

This tendency has been particularly marked in the debate within the environmentalist movement on the advisability of presenting green lists at the elections. Two options were examined: either submitting the movement's own lists, or, where possible, including the movement's candidates in the lists of the traditional parties. It should be stressed that these two options were compatible at the level of the movement as a whole and thus made it possible to exploit both the old and the new manner of doing politics. Common to both strategies, moreover, was a search for a form of representation whereby the candidate could only express her/his personal opinions and work solely for the specific purpose for which s/he had been selected.

Experimentation with new forms of action therefore does not rule out but combines with the utilization, in order to achieve *ad hoc* goals, of a system of representation which for its part operates in an increasingly selective manner. Action is not extraneous to the political system but distances itself from it, in an endeavour to secure those institutional advantages that disjointed and heterogeneous movements of this kind cannot forgo. Such confrontation at a distance provides the autonomy which gives viability to sporadic and loosely structured mobilizations.

3 The *continuity between individual and collective identity* is a further factor which characterizes recent forms of mobilization. Collective actors must take account of the multiple, mutable, and overlapping relations of belonging that articulate the base of a movement. They confront the difference that is not just a feature of the external differentiated society but penetrates the solidarity of the group itself. This patterning does not depend on the greater tolerance toward differences exhibited by the recent movements compared with earlier ones, but on the fact that it is well suited to express variable conflicts in societies which constantly redefine belongings, identities, and interests. On the other hand, these actors understand the enrichment to be gained from internal diversities. These they seek to integrate without ceasing to challenge the strategic-organizational constraints that collective action in mass societies involves. Sharing the same goal does not entail that equality must be searched for at every level. Through the renunciation of being equal on the basis of the same structural condition, these actors find that they share the same short-term interests, but they also accept the emergence of internal differences as opportune and also inevitable, as conveyed well by the slogan 'a movement of individuals'.

Taken together, these elements provide us with a basis for a number of hypotheses concerning mobilization as a dimension of collective action in complex societies:

(i)   In a situation in which 'crisis' has become a constant, it is impossible to make an *a priori* choice between crisis and development as the prime factor of facilitation; only analysis of a contingent situation can reveal their role. Empirical observation reveals that the groups that mobilize themselves into a movement are those that are central in some respects (educational level, geographical location, exposure to cultural messages) but marginal in others (position in the labour market, access to the political system, social recognition). The actors of mobilization are variable because the possible combinations of centrality and marginality, change and conservation, development and crisis are also variable.

(ii) The existence of channels for the transmission of political demands, the slack pressure applied by the agents of social control, as well as access to communication media reduce the costs of visible social action. On the other hand, the political system is only one of the possible arenas available. The movement-actors also assert their distance from the political system by advancing claims which the latter is unable to fulfil and by instrumentally using the institutional benefits it can provide. They also strive to ease the growing costs of organization by delegating to intermediate institutional bodies (public agencies, local administration) the task of providing some basic organizational resources, from meeting facilities to communication technology.

(iii) The existence of relational networks or of organizational experiences prior to mobilization attracts adherents. But, compared with previous social movements, these experiences ramify, overlap, and accelerate, so that their correlation with collective action is made less automatic and never univocal.

(iv) Small-group solidarity is a response to a power which conceals itself but nevertheless reaches into the person's innermost being. These solidarities, however, are not set once and for all: they are only some of the individual's possible belongings; they do not restrict the development of her/his experience, and they reduce the distance between individual and collective interests.

(v) The changing nature of commitment combines the dimension of collective action with that of personal fulfilment and blurs the distinction between leisure time and committed time. The continuity between leisure and commitment, by presupposing a close connection between self-fulfilment and participation, enhances the so-called 'expressive' resources and their utilizability in collective action.

(vi) The microrelational mechanisms which motivate subjects to join a movement remain of fundamental importance. The kinship networks, friendships, and acquaintanceships may reduce the cost of membership and induce the subjects involved in these relations to mobilize. However, such relations may subsequently trigger conflicts with the more formal aspect of the movement organization.

(vii) The low cost of entry into, and exit from, groups explains the tendency of participation to become temporary and short-term. As regards entry, the requirements for belonging are less stable and 'objective' than in the past, while exit is facilitated by the straightforward substitutability of the individual for the group and by the plurality of groups available for the individual. The sharing of short-term goals means that one and only one segment of individual experience is placed at stake. The dissolution of a group loses its connotations of failure, and individual exit from it the character of betrayal. The finiteness of goals and the surplus of collective resources allows the group to disappear with only minor consequences for the evolution and effectiveness of its network. On the other hand, leaving a group becomes less dramatic an event for the individual, as the range of all possible aggregations on offer expands with the increase in social differentiation.

16

The organization of movements

From revolt to organization

A social movement can survive over a period of time inasmuch as it is able
to resist its own centrifugal forces and withstand the actions of its adversaries. This becomes possible only if it can develop a relatively stable
organization and leadership. An organizational structure which unifies the
different components of a movement and is recognized by all of its
members is called for to institutionalize decision-making processes to a
necessary degree and to dedicate the movement's resources to the achievement of its goals. The organizational features vary greatly according to the
conditions of the social environment in which the movement operates and
the internal composition of the movement. Before proceeding to an analysis of these processes, however, some general criteria for the investigation
of the organizational dimension of social movements should be established.

A sociological tradition dating back to Weber and Michels considers
organization to be the inevitable cause of the institutionalization and
bureaucratization of collective action (Zald and Ash 1966). The passage
from spontaneous protest to organization always involves the emergence of
a bureaucratic structure, which transforms its objectives and blunts the
movement's initial conflictual thrust. Analytically, 'bureaucratization', or
the 'iron law of oligarchy', contains three distinct processes: (a) the substitution of objectives (or the distortion of ends); (b) the organization's tendency toward self-preservation; (c) the formation of an oligarchical
leadership. I shall examine these separately.

The substitution of objectives takes place through various processes: the
aims of the organization may be progressively adapted to the requirements
of the environment, as when their initial formulation has been proven unre-
alistic or impossible to achieve; they may be replaced by less specific, more

diffused objectives which allow the organization a wider field of action and make it more difficult for members to evaluate the success or failure of the movement; or the self-preservation of the organization may become an end in itself and grow in preponderance relative to the original goals.

The tendency toward mere self-preservation of the organization is then a particular form of the distortion of aims. The organizational apparatus develops specific interests of its own which do not necessarily coincide with the general interests of the movement, and tend to acquire relative priority. Preservation of the organizational structure, or of positions, rules, and procedures, becomes the principal goal of those who perform functional roles within the organization. This also tends to give rise to oligarchical leadership, or to the removal of decisions from collective control, insofar as the constituency might not show acceptance of the transformation of the organization's aims but moves, instead, to challenge the self-preservation of the apparatus.

This analytical perspective points up some of the central phenomena of the organizational process and demystifies the image which movement organizations tend to project of themselves through their ideology. This type of analysis reveals the rigidity and opaqueness of organizational processes and the logic of resistance and self-interest that they generate. However, the model according to which bureaucratization is the only and inevitable result of every organizational process oversimplifies the complexity of organizational phenomena and does not reflect the empirical reality of a great majority of actual movements. Thus it is necessary to place the analysis of social movement organizations in a wider theoretical context that can explain both bureaucratization and phenomena which move in different directions.

The organization of a social movement reproduces the dynamics of each complex organization. During the last twenty years, the sociology of organization has made a major contribution to analytical understanding of these phenomena, and a growing number of studies and research findings regularly add to a conceptual apparatus which is increasingly removed from Weber's model of bureaucratic organization. On the other hand, however, a social movement is a profoundly different kind of reality compared to the large corporations producing goods or services that have generally served as the original models for organizational theory. A social movement is an actor engaged in a conflict directly or indirectly affecting the distribution of power within a society. In this sense, movements are firmly committed to the building of their conflictual collective identities and cannot be simply defined by a system of roles and a network of exchanges. Moreover, they have to deal with the resistance, and often the repression, by adversaries possessing the monopoly over the instruments of social control. Consequently, the organization of a movement must take shape in very specific conditions, both internal and external. It must maintain a high level of unity and integration within itself, at the same time facing the challenges of a hostile environment. At the same time, it stands in need to reinforce and legitimize itself within the society at large.

Bearing these specific factors in mind, I will first outline my general approach to the subject and then enter into a more detailed discussion of them. An organization imposes on a multiplicity of groups and interests (the basis of the movement) the limits of a unitarian structure, gives it a central direction and establishes an agenda of shared objectives. But in order to be able to do so, it must also provide a series of incentives designed to build and secure the consensus and loyalty of its membership. Thus it must distribute resources and power within itself and develop the capability to control potential conflicts; at the same time, however, it must broaden its base of consensus within the overall society, competing against other organizations with partially conflicting aims. Analysis of these phenomena can proceed by distinguishing between internal and external processes of the organization.

To begin with, there must be an *internal system* for the allocation of resources and production of symbols (for a general frame, see Martin 1992; Agor 1989; Feldman 1990; Fineman 1993; Gherardi 1995; Stone 1990 Elster 1992; Douglas 1986; and specifically in reference to social movements, see Hirsch 1986; McCarthy 1987; Klandermans 1989b; Oliver and Marwell 1993). This includes (a) a system of roles and the division of labour; (b) mechanisms and criteria for the distribution of costs and benefits; and (c) a structure of incentives. A organizational structure is constituted primarily by a differentiated and specialized system of roles designed to guarantee the pursuit of objectives, adaptation to the environment, and the unity and self-preservation of the organization itself. The degree of internal differentiation and specialization depends both upon the specificity, or the degree of diffusedness, of the objectives of the movement, and on the conditions imposed by the environment in which the movement must operate. Every organization, in order to reach its objectives, must distribute costs and benefits among the roles and functions of which it is composed. Procedures, criteria, and variations in this delicate balance have a central role in the analysis of organizational processes. One particular component in the distribution of resources within an organization is the existence of a structure of incentives, that is, of rewards and sanctions which motivate individuals and groups to perform their functional roles.

All of these components are more or less directly connected to a system of power. The methods and criteria for the allocation of resources presuppose the existence of an authority structure within the organization. The power system itself includes the following dimensions: (a) a structure for the distribution of power itself; (b) processes for the aggregation of demands and the formation of decisions; (c) mechanisms that guarantee the succession of the leadership functions. The forms assumed by the distribution of power can vary within the organization. The leadership may be more or less centralized; the degree of autonomy of the different components of the movement may be greater or lesser; overlapping of influence can occur, or there can be areas entirely removed from control.

The distribution of power is also evident in the way the different demands arising within the movement enter the decision-making process, and, furthermore, in the characteristics of the decision-making process itself. A movement organization may comprise a variable quantity of filters and mediations for handling demands, and its decision-making processes can be more or less open to the participation and control of the various components. The norms of the organization guarantee integration, regulate the criteria for the distribution of rewards, and provide the critical point of reference for every process of transformation of the organizational structure. Finally, the organization controls the transfer and the redistribution of power through mechanisms of succession. The latter are extremely sensitive to processes of change and become frequently the subject of conflicts between the various components.

Thus internal analysis of the organization must identify the roles and specific mechanisms by which resources are allocated. Above all, it must show how each group intervenes in the decision-making process, controls resources, and competes for power. A major part of the analysis must be devoted to the conflicts which take place within the organization, both over the distribution of resources and over succession to leadership.

Moving next to the processes involved in the organization's *relationships with its environment* (Meyer and Scott 1992; Powell and Di Maggio 1991), one must first consider that a movement needs to gather the resources necessary for its survival in the context of the society of which it is a part. These obviously include material resources, but the hidden resource that conditions all others is support or consensus. A movement must broaden its mobilization base and secure ever-broadening support from the social groups it represents, but also from groups which, potentially, are not hostile to it.

An organization must gain consensus not only for its general aims but also for its particular objectives, and it must convince potential supporters to sustain the particular structure it possesses, rather than any other. When the collective demands which form the basis of the movement are organized, competition also arises among the different organizations purporting to represent the same demands; the ability of each of them to pursue its goals is closely tied to the forces which it is able to mobilize. Nevertheless, relations among such organizations are not based solely on competition: there are also various forms of cooperation and exchange, ranging from sharing of tasks to the formation of alliances and even fusion.

Finally, it should be remembered that one of the 'hidden' external variables which the organization must deal with in order to achieve its objectives, is the response of its adversary: the ruling groups or political authorities *de facto* establish the 'conditions of livability' of the social environment in which a movement organization operates. The degree of the openness or the closure of the political system and of tolerance or repression in contact with collective action exercise a significant influence on the characteristics of the organization: an open political system may favor a pluralism and competition of organizational forms, whereas a repressive one may foster the formation of centralized and sectarian organizations.

In the actual empirical situation, the analytical components enumerated should not be considered separately but in the context of their reciprocal interaction. The elements of the analytical model thus outlined must now be applied to a more detailed examination of the organization of social movements.

Internal processes of the organization

An organization of a movement is a complex structure in which the analytical components identified above interweave and overlap. I shall therefore proceed by singling out some of the internal processes of the organization that are central to the examination of the actual interweaving of these different components in the day-to-day operation of an organization.

The formation of norms. Norms are the point at which operational needs (the allocation of resources) come together with needs of integration and control (power). Every movement which organizes itself produces a constitutional system of norms, which are legitimized and institutionalized and determine the limits of discretion within which collective action can be developed. The degree of institutionalization depends on the relative complexity and importance of the organization, falling anywhere between a tacit or verbal agreement between members and a formal statute with written regulations. The elasticity or rigidity of these norms may vary in a similar fashion. What is important, however, is the fact that a system of norms is part of the foundation of every constitutional process of a movement organization. It is possible to identify at least four areas of normative regulation which govern the behaviour of the members of such an organization.

1 Firstly, exchange between members and the organization must be regulated. On the one hand, this means defining the degree of investment or involvement which the organization expects from each of its members. On the other, it is necessary to determine a structure of rewards and sanctions, based on which members can orient their conduct. The incentives provided by the organization for the loyalty and involvement of its members form part of the normative arrangement, but they may vary from one organization to another. Commitment to a movement by its members, at least in its initial phase, is based on solidarity and a strong identification with the goals of the organization. Material advantages expected are either nil or irrelevant; it is only later, when the organization consolidates, that these assume greater importance, at least for some of the members. Thus we can distinguish between (i) material or utilitarian incentives, or incentives which motivate individuals to perform organizational tasks by offering goods or resources of economic nature; (ii) incentives of solidarity, linked to the exchange or interaction between members, and offering prestige, recognition, and emotional gratification; and (iii) normative or value incentives, in which the reward consists of the achievement of goals or values with which the actor identifies.

2 Next, there is regulation of the relations among the different components of the organization. The tasks and responsibilities of the various units must be defined according to their functions, their geographical distribution, and their hierarchical order. From a situation of minimum differentiation and extensive overlapping of functions, a movement can develop into a national or transnational organizational structure with vertical, geographical, and functional divisions.

3 A movement mobilizes certain social groups and is thus directly tied to the society of which it is part. Constitutional norms must include a definition of the relationship between the organization and society, in particular of the relationship between the movement and the social group or groups that it represents. The actions of the movement are measured against the interests and objectives of a certain sector of the society (class, ethnic group, community, or the like).

4 Finally, the norms must specify the objectives and means of collective action. The general orientations of the movement must be articulated into specific objectives, and means to be used in achieving them must be specified so that the organization can mobilize its resources.

In the actual reality of a movement, the norms which form the structure of the organization are not rigidly codified. More so than in the case of other types of organizations, they are sensitive to the changes that take place within or without the organization. They are subject to tensions and conflicts to a greater degree than are such norms in other types of organization. For example, the incentive structure may change. The inability of Marxist-Leninist minority groups of the 1960s within the student movement to set realistic and effective objectives lead to their almost total reliance on incentives of solidarity; the self-preservation of the group and its solidarity became the sole reason for its existence, and also explains the limited influence the groups exercised in the outside world. Another example is the need of the organizations to react to new social groups and redefine the movement with respect to them. This is one of the most serious problems an organization may encounter. One might consider, for example, the impact of the 'women's issue' on Leftist organizations in the 1970s: an unavoidable demand advanced by a social group which had not previously been a point of reference for the organization, called the entire normative structure into question and generated extremely high levels of pressure for such redefinition. Crisis in one area of normative regulation may extend thoughout the entire organizational structure and challenge its objectives as well as means of action.

The recruitment and succession of leadership. Another process of great importance for the functioning of an organization is the selection of the leadership group and the mechanisms which guarantee its continuity or change. In the next chapter, I shall examine the normative basis upon which leadership is founded, and the relations between leaders and the group as a whole. Here I am concerned with mechanisms which are specifically organizational, and by which leadership is recruited and its succession regulated. An organization must select a governing group from amongst its membership or from the social groups part of the movement's constituency. In order to do this, it must offer rewards in exchange for the functions to be performed, valuable enough to appeal to skilled people able to fulfil these roles. Moreover, the organization must be able to alter such rewards when there are not enough available candidates so as to attract new aspirants. By means of these two general strategies and by an appropriate differentiation of rewards, the organization must recruit both the central leadership group and the rank-and-file cadres of the apparatus.

The actual selection of leadership takes place through three principal channels. (i) It can be entrusted to the social groups which make up the constituency of the movement. These groups can propose candidates or exercise their right of veto over an appointment. It is a rare case that direct selection is not filtered through the organization. More often than not, the

social groups of the constituency function as channels of political socialization for potential cadres in the organization, even if they do not directly
select the leadership personnel. (ii) The selection may occur through
delegation at the intermediate levels of the organization, both geographical
and functional. Whether or not this channel is used depends upon how
centralized the organization is. (iii) Finally, there is the possibility of
centralized selection, performed by the leadership itself by appointment.
These three recruitment models reflect different organizational logics, and,
again, they are a function of both the internal characteristics of the
organization and of the environmental conditions in which it operates.

Mechanisms for succession tend to be formalized through the institutionalization of certain channels of recruitment. But regardless of how
much the organization might seek to represent the succession of leadership
as merely a matter of efficiently achieving its goals, every change of personnel in the higher levels of an organization takes place under two conditions. Firstly, it reflects a certain balance of power relations between the
various components. Moreover, this change, to a greater or lesser extent,
always involves a discussion of the objectives and the means of the
organization; as a consequence, a reorganization can take place bringing a
new equilibrium, or, as we shall see, the organization can become subject to
conflicts and schisms. The formalization of procedures helps to forestall
such latter effects, but it does not detract from the political character of
every process of succession of leadership functions. Finally, it should be
noted that a movement organization can constitute an important channel
for social mobility through the recruitment and succession of its leadership.
When an organization is consolidated and, in particular, becomes a party
or a stable political organization, participation in the political system introduces the organization's leadership into the area of the political elites. The
leadership of a radical movement entering the political system is admitted
– albeit in a conflictual position – to the systems of exchange which
characterize other elites. Leaders from the lower classes change their status,
their relational network, and their cultural coordinates. This opportunity
for mobility can become one of the incentives by which an organization
obtains the loyalty of its members and recruits its cadres.

Conflicts and factions. The complexity of an organization by itself generates differing interests inside the organization, potentially giving rise to tensions and conflicts. These forms of contention may manifest themselves as
simple, occasional differences among groups, or they can create factions
within the organization or provoke actual schisms. The different components of an organization have specific tasks and interests, they compete for
power, and they respond in different ways to stimuli from the environment.

Tensions and conflicts can develop along different parameters of the organization, including functional specialization; differentiation of hierarchical roles; heterogeneity of the social groups that make up the organization; and heterogeneity of previous affiliations.

Such lines of differentiation may engender diversity of interests and demands that leads to conflicts. Conflicts, however, arise under particular conditions and on these depend the type and the degree of the tensions that appear in an organization as follows: (i) the quantity and fairness of the incentives that the organization offers to its various components create either satisfaction or a sense of deprivation among its members. An ability to maintain an even balance between performance and rewards for all the various components, an ability to replace incentives which have become unattractive or obsolete, and an ability to maintain or substitute the parameters which govern confrontation among groups – these are all conditions which help to control and minimize the risk of conflicts, (ii) the possibility that dissatisfaction may spread over different groups increases the probability of conflict. The quantity and quality of internal communications within the organization can facilitate or obstruct the aggregation of interests and demands. The more the information circulates, and the more there is information circulating, the greater the possibility of comparison among groups, that is, the possibility for evaluating the balance of incentives and recognizing the shared interests; (iii) the total quantity of resources available to the organization determines its capacity to satisfy different demands and interests. When there is a relative abundance of resources they can be used by the organization to pursue different but complementary strategies; when resources are scarce, a response to certain demands will necessarily exclude others; (iv) the organization's ability to articulate an ideology redefines its normative frame of reference and renders different interests and demands more or less compatible. The more the organization is able to adapt its ideology and to provide new ideological explanations for changes and decisions, the less likely conflict will be.

Internal conflict in an organization may appear randomly, or it may generate more substantial and stable formations which I shall call factions. A faction is a subgroup which pursues specific objectives within an organization and has the following characteristics: The presence of a leader or a restricted group of leaders, with some personal charisma; personal ties between members and these leaders, and often among members as well; its temporary character, inasmuch as it will either be reabsorbed into the organization or break off in a schism. A stable formation of subgroups appears in organizations which are relatively more institutionalized, such as national movement organizations; in such a case, it is more appropriate to speak of currents rather than factions. The appearance of factions seems to be governed by two fundamental conditions: the heterogeneity of the social base of the movement and the rigidity of the ideological apparatus. The more heterogeneous the constituency of the organization, the greater the probability that networks of affiliation and leadership resources already exist for the creation of subgroups. The more rigid the ideology, the greater the probability that differences in interpretation and application will be created and that orthodoxies and heresies will appear.

These two conditions are also fundamental factors in the development of schisms, in the parting of ways with the 'mother organization' in order to create a new one, formed usually in opposition to, and to compete with, the original organization. However, for the preconditions for a schism to exist, it must first be preceded by a formation of a transient faction which no longer finds room for action within the organization. This can come about in two principal ways, which in practice may also combine: On the one hand, the organization may not have sufficient resources or the capacity to respond to the demands of the subgroup. The group is thereby isolated and consolidates its deviant identity; at this point the question of whether the group is to be expelled or whether it should leave of its own accord is only a procedural matter. On the other hand, the organization may change its practices, paying but lip service to its original aims. Particular groups are then created that remain loyal to the original objectives of the organization, and a deviant identity is born; once again, expulsion or schism follows.

Finally, it should be remembered that the differentiation of groups and interest within an organization also plays a functional role in a movement's action. Different policies, never totally unified, diversify the image of the movement projected to various groups of potential supporters and thus create a broader audience. Differentiation can become an adverse factor only if it obstructs the achievement of goals, but does not necessarily need to be so as long as tensions and conflicts remain compatible with the structure of the organization.

The experience of the New Left of the late 1960s and early 1970s in different countries of the West contains instances of the phenomena described above. The tendency toward fragmentation and schisms has been greater in precisely those small Marxist-Leninist groups in which ideology was most dogmatic and which relied on a heterogeneous constituency of students, immigrants, and subproletarian classes. In larger organizations, schisms resulted in situations when pragmatic adaptation of policy took place hand in hand with a ritual reaffirmation of ideological principles. This gave rise to a number of fundamentalist sects, which insisted on the rigid, orthodox interpretation of the original aims, and set off along the road of terrorism and ungoverned action. A comparable trend can be found in the environmental movement in the 1980s: in different countries the formation of fundamentalist sects accompanied the decision of the major organizations to participate in the elections. A similar phenomenon could be observed in some of the minority fringes of the labour movement, when, after a wave of wildcat struggles, the unions regained control of collective action. In all of these instances there was a heterogeneous constituency of the movement (students and non-students, skilled workers and unskilled workers) and a central ideology, which radicalized the image of action beyond its factual contents. When, at a later date, the practice of the movement changed and moved towards more direct negotiations with the political system, fundamentalist sects arose demanding a return to the original purity of the movement and the break with the organizations' 'opportunism'. However, violence and terrorism are not the inevitable outcome of this type of process; they are rather the specific results from the rigidity of the political system and of its inability to respond to crucial demands (as the Italian and German cases during the 1970s show).

Relations between the organization and the environment

The environment of an organization is made up of the wider society in which the movement is situated and from which it draws its support base. From the point of view of a single organization, other organizations playing a part in the same movement are also part of the environment. In fact, a social movement is never identified with a single organization; rather, there are various organizations, and sometimes even parties, which claim to interpret and pursue the aims of the movement. The history of the labour movement provides a good example of such emergence of multiple organizations, as do the student movement, the women's movement, and the environmental and peace movements of the last decades. The possibilities for the mobilization of a movement depend, as we saw in the preceding chapter, on the conditions of the social structure. Segmentation and the existence of previous networks of affiliation, the openness or closure of the political system are factors that affect the creation of a support base for a movement. But in order to understand how a concrete organization procures support and consensus in a society, we must consider three principal variables: (i) the requisites for affiliation required by the organization; (ii) the attitudes of social groups which are not part of the movement's constituency; and (iii) the response of the opponents, or, concretely, the reaction of the political powers and the apparatuses of the state.

For the purpose of achieving its goals, an organization may require from its members the fulfilment of more or less rigid criteria for affiliation, a greater or lesser degree of commitment, or a greater or lesser ideological identification. The more elastic such requisites, the wider will be the support which the organization is able to mobilize. An organization of this type, however, is also more sensitive to the changes possibly occurring in society. The number of adherents and the quality of their commitment change much more easily following changes in the social environment; the presence of alternatives in the society, the proposal of values in competition with those of the movement, and the affiliation of some members with other social groups are all factors which can exert a direct influence on an organization with rather elastic requisites.

Another factor which can influence support for a movement organization is the attitude of social groups acting as, we might say, spectators to the conflict. The hostility, neutrality, or favour of these groups has a profound influence upon the conditions in which the movement must operate. They can provide indirect material or moral support, they can favourably influence the media or, on the contrary they can discourage the potential supporters or impede the recruitment of new members. Hence the desire of movements to obtain the consensus, or at least the neutrality, of a much wider segment of society than that which the movement has actually mobilized. As we will see in chapter 18, ideology plays a central role in this pursuit of consensus. The movement cannot offer direct advantages to the social groups which do not make up the base of its mobilization; therefore it will attempt to use ideological resources, to furnish a positive image of itself and a negative image of the adversary.

Finally, the response of the adversary, the tolerance or repression of collective action, constitutes the decisive factor in a movement's pursuit of its objectives. This variable also exerts a strong influence over the two factors just mentioned: when there is a repressive response, for example, the requirements for affiliation are tightened, and the probability of obtaining the consensus of groups which are not involved is reduced. Moreover, the response of the adversary also influences the results which the movement is able to achieve: the success or failure of a collective action in achieving its political goals can never be separated from the attitude of the adversary, although they do not depend solely upon this factor. An organization may fail to achieve its objectives for a great number of reasons, both internal and external; but, ultimately, the action (or inaction) of the adversary is always decisive, due to the relative or absolute advantage of its position in the power relationship.

Besides having to deal with the society as a whole, the organization also has to confront other organizations claiming to represent the movement in a broader field or arena of society (Garner and Zald 1985; Fernandez and McAdam 1989; Klandermans 1992). These organizations define the objectives of the movement and the means for collective action differently, and compete against each other for support by potential adherents. The competition may have a radicalizing influence on objectives and tactics. The dissatisfied support base of one organization may be successfully mobilized by another which proposes more radical objectives or tactics. This, in turn, may provoke a reaction from the first organization, which may now assume even more radical positions, or, vice versa, close in on itself in defence of its original identity. These observations are of great importance in disproving the inevitability of processes of bureaucratization in organizations, as asserted by the model derived from Weber and Michels. Organizations change following non-linear processes: bureaucratization is not an inevitable and irreversible outcome, and above all it does not necessarily accompany the adjustment of the radical aims of the organization. Organizations may also evolve into the direction of the radicalization of aims, and this process may coincide with either greater or lesser bureaucratization. The fundamentalist sects discussed above underwent a radicalization of their aims, but they also experienced accentuated bureaucratization and development of oligarchical leadership, as compared to more 'moderate' organizations. Competition on the left of the Italian Communist Party in the 1980s created more radical organizations which were relatively less bureaucratic (e.g. the Greens), but it also provoked important reactions within the party itself, bringing about its partial modernization. Grassroot or wildcat organizations of workers in Italy and France during the 1970s and 1980s have had an analogous effect on the unions' structure.

An organization does not, however, only comprise relationships of competition. Within a movement, there may also arise relationships of cooperation, either in order to resist the initiatives of the adversary, or because they bring common advantages. The forms of this interaction among organizations include actual cooperation, alliance, and fusion. Cooperation takes place when different organizations agree to a division of labor, with relatively specialized functions, in their pursuit of specific objectives. When collaboration becomes a regular occurrence an alliance is normally formed, in which resources are pooled and planning coordinated for medium- or long-term objectives. The organizations remain separate and distinct, but they intensify their reciprocal coordination. Sometimes an *ad hoc* organization is created to handle coordination functions, or else this role can be assigned to one of the allies. Finally, when fusion occurs, the preexisting organizational units disappear, and a new organizational structure is created. Fusion is always a delicate process. Previous identities may persist and make integration into the new structure difficult. Moreover, processes of fusion often entail losses for the extreme wings of the organization: fusion is always a compromise which leaves both the most moderate and the most radical groups dissatisfied.

In alliances and fusions, each of the parties concerned calculates the costs and benefits of the cooperation. This means that an organization is open to this type of process only under certain conditions. If its affiliation requirements are rigid, an organization will tend to safeguard its own identity and be less willing to establish relations with other organizations. Where ideological identification is more elastic, alliances and fusions are more probable. The necessity to defend the organization against the initiatives of the adversary, the presence of an indivisible objective, the prospects for broadening the support base – these are all factors which can facilitate such processes.

The forms of organization

The foregoing analyses might be used to classify the organizational forms of movement organizations. A typological analysis, however, is always conventional and can only serve as a preliminary orientation to the object. A second, more articulated, step is therefore necessary. Instead of thinking in *types of organizations*, one should use the dimensions relevant to the classification as *analytical tools* to make distinctions, to 'deconstruct' empirical unities, and to account for their complexity. In this respect, a number of classic categories of organizational analysis could be applied to social movement organizations and might provide a better understanding of the actual functioning of given empirical collective actors.

A first dimension, for example, concerns the organization's objectives. We can distinguish, analytically, between *expressive* and *instrumental* goals. The pursuit of the former are oriented towards the satisfaction of the social and psychological needs of the movement's members through participation and solidarity; the latter are achieved in the attainment of specific goods external to the organization. This distinction may be useful in operational terms, but should be applied with some caution to contemporary forms of action, for the reasons explained in chapter 1.

One may also refer to the requirements for affiliation as imposed by the organization, which can be divided into those that are *inclusive* and those that may be characterized as *exclusive*. The former do not imply rigid mechanisms for selecting members, and they expect a relatively low level of commitment; they do not require specific duties beyond the simple act of affiliation, and the ideological training is rather limited in scope. Exclusive forms of affiliation exercise a rigid control over the processes of affiliation and require intense ideological identification, a high level of commitment, and total discipline.

Organizations can also be analysed according to the incentives they offer to their membership. We have already distinguished *material incentives*, *solidarity incentives*, and *value incentives*. The first are economic goods or resources; the second ones are independent from the aims of the organization and derive from participation for its own sake, from the sense of belonging, from the relations established among members; the last are bound up with the aims of the organization and their realization.

Another dimension concerns the organization's relationship with the environment, and in particular with other organizations. One could consider the *isolation* from other networks of affiliation or communities, or, alternatively, the *integration* into a fabric of organizations with multiple affiliations and shared or connected leadership. Internally, the *homogeneity* or *heterogeneity* of the membership may be related to the social base of the organization, but also to its members' affiliations with other associations or communities.

Finally, one may also refer to the manner in which power is wielded, distinguishing between *authoritarian* and *participatory* forms, according to the extent to which members are allowed to intervene in the fundamental decision-making processes. Another aspect is the style of leadership, in which we can distinguish between orientations toward *mobilization* or toward *articulation*. In the former case the goal of leadership is to obtain membership loyalty and commitment to the organization. In the latter, leadership tends to establish relations with other organizations in society. These two functions are often present simultaneously in one organization, creating a potential for conflicts: one accentuates the role of participation, of propaganda and ideology; the other places emphasis on negotiation and mediation.

These analytical dimensions can be combined to provide an articulated frame for the analysis of organizational forms of social movements. Such a catalogue would be far from exhaustive; yet it provides more than a simple classification of types, allowing for a deconstruction of empirical unities. The actual organizational pattern of a given 'movement', its proper *form*, lies at the intersection of these various analytical dimensions.

With the same purpose in mind, discoveries of recent studies on nascent organizations can be applied to social movements. The results obtained in them support the idea that when social movements are formed their organizational structure does not correspond to an abstract model of rationality; nevertheless, it has shown itself to be suitable for carrying out the fundamental functions for collective action. As movements are born, the emergent structure takes shape as a network of different groups or cells, linked by multiple, overlapping ties and a number of leaders in competing with one another. These leaders are often associated with a specific function or situation and do not hold any definitive kind of a mandate. Such an organizational structure, which multiplies functions and causes roles to overlap, is nevertheless well suited for fostering the fragile early growth of a movement, precisely because it permits maximum adaptation of the organization to the environment and enables it to resist the initiatives of the adversary. Moreover, it increases the organization's capacity to penetrate and proselytize audiences in a variety of environments. Promoting experimentation through a process of trial and error, it selects the most solid and effective nucleus for the movement. In this way, the organization grows and consolidates in a hostile environment. Later on, more organic forms of division of labour and functional specialization may come into play, with the more specific definition of leadership and a system of norms.

This organizational form is common to numerous movements in the formative phase, and can be seen in the origins of the labour movement, as well as in the movements of the last few decades in complex capitalist societies. Sometimes a rapid entry into the political sphere obliges new movements to promptly assume the centralized structure of political organizations, but it is possible to observe these characteristics in the early phases of almost any movement. This structure is maintained for a longer period of time in the less 'political' area of recent movements (such as, for instance, some sectors of women's collective action, youth groups, and religious groups).

These observations, like those made above in this chapter, emphasize again the plurality of models and organizational forms, and the absence of any kind of linear logic or determinism in the development of organizations. The passage from protest to organization uses a variety of possible courses, and the organization changes in response to stimuli and limits deriving from both its internal structure and the environment in which it operates.

Self-reflective organizations

Contemporary movements maintain a degree of separation from the dominant cultural codes through the constitution and operation of organizational forms which prefigure the goals they pursue, and through their activity of visibly signalling the societal problems addressed by it. Hence derives the prophetic character of these forms of collective action, and hence arises their character as a challenge. The greater the emphasis on challenge and the more prominent such prefiguration, the lesser the risk that organizational forms will be assimilated or co-opted.

All this means that, in the movements' networks, a large quantity of resources are allocated to the creation and maintenance of a specific identity rather than to the pursuit of external objectives. In contrast to traditional collective actors, there has been a substantial shift from investment for the purposes of political action to an allocation of resources for the maintenance of an internal market for symbolic goods. Such a market prepares forms of future professionalization in innovative sectors of social life and of the external market (like music, advertising, the media).

The various groups of the network rely for the formulation and conveying of their collective identity on those organizations and groups most directly engaged in the production, processing, and broadcasting of information. The former become their customers by buying their symbolic goods. This, obviously, places a certain amount of control in the hands of the latter; control which is exercised indirectly in the selective broadcasting of information and in the mediation of demands advanced by the various groups. In this exchange, the grassroot groups themselves participate in bargaining and in the formation of the movement's culture. And they contribute to the concrete management of its action by exercising reciprocal control, by coordinating, by ensuring that initiatives do not overlap, by restricting competition, and by utilizing the information broadcast by each of them through these internal media.

In individual groups, a division of labour based on formal rules is a rare case. Instead, tasks are allocated in an informal manner, and mainly according to the skills that each member shows to be able and willing to contribute to the activities pursued. The more recent forms of collective action have brought with them a development of various types of difference, leading, in a certain sense, to a general recognition of the inevitability of power relationships – combined, however, with the attempt to keep that power under constant control and to continuously render it visible. In other words, there is an awareness of the fact that power exists; indeed, it is recognized as an inescapable condition, although relational forms can be constructed in which power may assume greater visibility and greater control (see for example Gerlach and Hine 1970; Brown 1992; Ferree and Martin 1994; Martin 1990).

This gives rise to a specific relationship between efficacy and the search for satisfactory internal relations. External time diminishes in importance and is replaced by the group's own internal time, according to which its action is measured. Control over strategic resources is repaid with greater commitment; this in turn is legitimately recompensed with greater power or greater material advantages. Differences among individuals are therefore accepted: the fact that commitment is viewed as a practical day-to-day goal and not as a long-term undertaking also provides justification for differentiated control over resources.

In the reticular configuration of the networks, one also finds a division of labour and roles among the various groups. Along with the horizontal specialization of the activities of the various nuclei, one can also discern a vertical division of roles within the individual networks. The associative forms which handle crucial resources like information, possess, as we have seen, a greater capacity to intervene in the production and negotiation of collective identity. These groups formulate the proposals which are broadcast through the internal media to the other groups, which, in turn, rebroadcast them and report the results of the discussion. This process ensures that the latter type of nucleus provides a flow of resources, among which is the capacity for control and aggregation, to the former. The organizations which process and broadcast information thus become the representatives of the members and users of the networks, while some core individuals belonging to the other nuclei perform a kind of an intermediate representational function. This structure tends to result into a diffusion of themes and a circulation of militants which characterizes today's movements (McAdam and Rucht 1993; Meyer and Whittier 1994).

Membership of the various groups in the movement networks is not atomized. Individuals never join the movement on a individual basis alone but almost always through relational channels (friends, kin, neighbours, associations) providing a connection to those already part of the network. This form of membership actually ensures access to information concerning the field about to be invested in, thus placing the aspiring member in a better position compared to an isolated individual, with regard to the possibilities to intervene in the bargaining of collective identity. On the other hand, these modalities are also the mechanisms by which individuals can more easily be kept under control within small relational circles. Another model is that of friendship circles. These are rather common in the movement networks and seem to perform the function of enabling simultaneous investment in two fields (friendship and commitment), thereby restricting possible losses. For this reason, the friendship-based group is rather common, especially where professional or cultural skills are weaker. The disadvantages are that it requires considerably greater control over the individual and her/his exchanges (even those established externally to the group) and that it raises stronger barriers against those who are not bound by bonds of friendship with the group's members.

A final consideration is that actors rarely make a profound personal investment at the moment of joining the group. Instead, one finds that their investment increases (as long as valid opportunities present themselves) as their knowledge of the field in which they have come to operate expands. Such investment will progressively strengthen the member's bond with the group or the organization, making withdrawal increasingly difficult. In this process, simple users may become professionalized producers of culture. However, if they have not made a longer-term investment they may not commit themselves deeply but simply utilize a short-term and more easily controllable exchange. This increases the risk of fragmentation and discontinuity of collective action, but it is offset by mechanisms which create a cultural and symbolic investment that is deeper and more binding and outlives the actual mobilization phase, even the actual period of participation in a movement.

Organizational forms of contemporary movements therefore seem to mutate towards informality and into groups of primary foundation. This, however, is not a regression to ascriptive forms of belonging, for the groups in the networks display a manifest element of artificiality, even in their definitions of apparently ascriptive elements of identification such as sex or age. These forms of collective action act on the basis of short-term projects, the coherence of which lies primarily not in their contents but in the self-reflective capacity which ensures them the quality of direct participation and which defines their divergence from the dominant social codes. This, therefore, brings out the distinct form of the relation. The movements propose through their organizational forms a cultural pluralism based on the possibility of qualitative participation which respects individual differences and needs.

This qualitative pluralism is the culture which underpins identity and which unifies the incongruities that organizations and actions contain within themselves. The challenge against the system is thus raised through the proposal of forms of action which are highly self-reflective. However, the networks must simultaneously be able to cope with instrumental needs directed both internally and externally if they are to avoid sectarian solutions or outright marginalization. They therefore raise the challenge by proposing to hold instrumentality and quality together. Regardless of its outcome, of the lacerations and exhaustion that it may sustain, this model opens a symbolic space that in itself is a cultural alternative.

17

Leadership in social movements

The leader-constituency relationship

Processes of mobilization and the organizational structure of a movement are fuelled by the action of the movement's leaders. It is the leadership which promotes the pursuit of goals, develops strategies and tactics for action, and formulates an ideology. The penetration of the movement in the society, the loyalty and involvement of its members, and the consensus of different social groups all depend upon the leaders' actions.

Contributions to a theory of leadership in social movements have remained extremely sketchy. Studies on the topic have been conducted mainly by social psychologists analysing small groups and interpersonal relations, or by sociologists of organizations and researchers specializing on management (for a synthesis of recent developments, see Hunt 1991; Sims and Lorenzi 1992; Bryman 1992). The organizational models developed in these contexts have been subsequently applied in political sociology, through the analysis of leadership in political parties. The processes of leadership are frequently addressed in studies of social movements but systematic elaboration of this dimension is, however, still limited (see, for example, Downton 1973; Paige 1977; Loye 1977). The aim of the present chapter is to take a step in this direction, utilizing the available findings and attempting to apply them specifically to the theme of movements. The focus of my analysis will be on processes of formation of leadership and the relations between the leadership and the support base, the components of the action of the leadership, and its integrative and innovative role.

A long tradition reaching back to Weber and the notion of charisma sees the foundation of leadership as being the personal qualities of the chief and the need for dependence of his subordinates. This charismatic theory of leadership has a number of versions, both psychological and sociological, ranging from the analysis of the exceptional personality traits of the leader to the theory of mass society, which portrays the leader as someone endowed with a capability to manipulate a formless aggregate of atomized individuals. The need for security and stability among individuals is considered to create the basis for their loyalty to the leader. Thus, behind these approaches there lies a more or less explicitly stated negative assumption of human nature which ends up by de facto rejecting the very point of departure of sociological analysis: the consideration of leadership as a *social* (that is, interactive) relationship. But it is from this observation that every analysis of leadership must begin. If the phenomenon is reduced to a series of individual qualities or 'natural' needs, we are denied at the very outset any possibility of understanding it, and will proceed nowhere beyond mere assumptions that, for that matter, are doomed to remain quite openly ideological. Participants in collective action are thereby described as deviant personalities, as social outsiders who willy-nilly submit to the charisma and power of a minority of individuals gifted in the art of manipulation. It is evident that the ideological legacy of the theories of 'crowd psychology' is still alive and well today, and participates in the production of an interpretation of social movements which adheres to the stereotypes and rhetoric of the dominant groups.

The foundation of leadership should be sought not in the qualities of the leader or in the dependency of his followers, but *in the relationship*, the type of relations, that link the actors together. Leadership is a form of interaction, in which each of the actors involved makes a specific investment, therewith achieving specific advantages. The relationship persists because both partners continue to find it mutually advantageous. The charismatic stereotype of leadership, with all its ideological baggage, forgets that the formation of leadership and its continuity depend upon this strategic rapport between the leader and his constituents. Leaders of movements cannot rely on an institutional structure; they must deal with the initiatives of their opponents and compete with potential rivals. More than in other kinds of organization, their position depends on their ability to maintain a balanced exchange with the support base that furnishes them with legitimacy and loyalty. The relationship between leader and constituency is based on the reciprocal benefits accruing to each from this exchange: as long as the leader pursues the goals of the group and satisfies the expectations of its members, s/he can rely on them for support and loyalty. In order to secure the commitment and mobilization of the members, the leader must reduce the risks from collective action and at the same time oversee the distribution of adequate compensation. The objective of the leadership, upon which its survival depends, is thus to render this balance as favorable as possible, and receive in exchange the increasing involvement and support of the members.

Continuous transactions thus take place between the leader and the support base. Leaders act as representatives of the group, guiding its members toward the pursuit of goals and thus providing them with specific advantages. The members endow the leader with status, prestige, and power, and invest their own resources in the collective action. Both partners to this relationship have expectations concerning the behaviour of the other which must be satisfied in order for the exchange to be able to be considered fair and equal. If one or both of the parties feel that the exchange is not equitable, there will be an attempt to restore the balance or to break off the relationship. This said, we may proceed to review the components of this exchange, the way it is regulated, the bases on which its balance or imbalance is assessed, and the ways in which the parties to it negotiate the transaction.

The leader must satisfy the expectations of the members by facilitating the pursuit of objectives, representing the group in its dealings with the outside world, and coordinating and integrating internal activities. These tasks require skills and resources which can be positively evaluated within the group and which constitute a specific contribution to its functioning. In exchange, the leader receives a reward in the form of support for his actions and specific advantages linked to his position. The rules of the exchange call not only for compensations but also for sanctions, or negative transactions. If objectives are not achieved, or if a request for investment is met with an insufficient response, the leader incurs the disapproval of the group and loss of support. The leader may also impose sanctions on members when their conduct is in breach of the 'rules of the game' of the organization and fails to respect the terms of the transaction and the organizational norms.

Each partner seeks to optimize the cost/benefit ratio as the exchange proceeds. Thus relations between the leader and the constituency are regulated in a constant bargaining process in which each party seeks to reduce its own costs and maximize the benefits. The leader engages in this bargaining from an advantaged position as s/he controls the resources which are in short supply – this, as we shall see, in fact constitutes the basis of the leader's power. More precisely, that position depends on the measure to which the leader succeeds in maintaining her/his role as the supplier of resources which others do not possess, which cannot be exchanged in terms of absolute reciprocity, and which are in demand among the members. Recognition of this advantage is expressed by assigning benefits to the leader that differ from those of the members. Nevertheless, the existence of this advantage is always subject to its determination by the group and, as I have stated, if objectives are not achieved or demands not satisfied, the leadership may be challenged (the less institutionalized the organizational structure, the more often this will occur).

The delicate balance between costs and benefits in the exchange governs not only the leader's ability to maintain her/his position, but also the action of the movement and the continuity of the organization. Apart from the general objectives of the organization, the leader thus has to pursue two specific objectives: s/he must act in such a way that the members can consider the exchange equitable, remaining satisfied with the resources they receive; and s/he must intervene whenever this equilibrium is threatened. These objectives involve constant rearrangement of the organization; above all, however, it is ideology which plays the central role. Ideology indicates to the members of the movement their position within it, and the commensurability between ends and means on the one hand and investments and rewards on the other. Hence the continuous efforts by the leadership to adapt that representation to changes in reality.

Leaders are the agents of mobilization of a movement and the promoters of its organizational structure. Therefore they are more than ordinary members exposed to the risk of having to pay high costs for their commitment, both in their relations with external society as well as in their internal relations with members of the movement. For these reasons, leadership is a rare commodity, and its creation and further development depend on the operational conditions of the movement. What was said of mobilization in chapter 15 is also applicable to leadership. The existence of a network of associations or community facilitates the emergence of a leadership. This is both because a network of affiliation and socialization can provide a training ground where the skills necessary for the exercise of leadership can be learned, and because the network issues rewards in the form of solidarity and values, which encourage the leader to assume the risks associated with her/his position.

Secondly, a strongly segmented social structure, with limits and barriers between different groups, encourages leadership formation both because the costs arising from the assumption of a leadership role may be judged to be less than those associated with the social segregation of the group, and because these social barriers make alternative, less risky forms of action impossible. When, on the other hand, there exist channels for individual mobility, resources will probably be invested in the pursuit of particular advantages rather than in the mobilization of a movement.

Charismatic leadership

According to Weber, the charismatic leader is recognized as being such by virtue of the extraordinary qualities that ensure her/him a mass following. Such personal qualities are the foundation and hallmark of the 'mission' or 'vocation' that he is called upon to fulfil in the world, and which make her/him the promoter and builder of change in values. In a 'disenchanted' history with no *telos*, charisma remains a dynamic force of development, the only impulse capable of stirring up in the masses the positive energy necessary for change. Because s/he is the interpreter of the profound needs of the people, the leader offers an answer and a direction by calling on his followers to 'convert' themselves (*metanoia* is the Greek word for religious conversion that implies a deep change of mind): the leader points out the ends and offers her-/himself as the one who knows the way to attain them. An extraordinary phenomenon, destined to be absorbed into the everyday routine of the institutions, charisma is necessarily ephemeral, limited in time, and fragile. None the less, its presence, today profaned through its transfer from the religious arena to the sphere of politics, is a central component in the great transformations of modern societies.

Few would object to the interest and usefulness of the concept of charisma and of a theory of charismatic leadership. But when compared against the insights gathered from contemporary research into leadership, on which topic there is by now a vast body of literature (for a review, see Sims and Lorenzi 1992), the Weberian theory leaves itself open to a number of criticisms. First of all, the nature of the social relationship of leadership tends to become blurred, because one of the terms of the relation, the masses, is annulled as an actor. Weber shared with the bourgeois thought of his time a view of the masses as an anonymous aggregate, vulnerable to contagion by irrational impulses and ready to accept the emotional guidance of a leader (for a penetrating analysis of this phenomenon, see Moscovici 1981). The presuppositions of elite theories and of 'crowd psychology' are also those expounded by Weber. A pessimistic naturalism which received its foundation in Freud's theory deprives the collective action of the masses of every social feature and reduces it to the expression of primal instincts. In the 1960s, these assumptions were again taken over by the theory of mass society. It required the richness of the research by Smelser or Goffman to show a way out from this unshakeable naturalism and to make the discovery that even in the most anonymous and amassed behaviour there are in operation relational networks and universes of 'meaning' which regulate conduct. A 'psychology of crowds' could not have been written in the 1980s without beginning from the realization that wherever there are relations (including mass relations) there exist systems of exchange, of communication, of meaning (see Gusfield 1963, 1981, 1995).

A theory of leadership as a social relation is therefore forced to treat charismatic leadership as a particular type of exchange between two parties to a relationship. Leadership is a relation between a chief and his followers in which each party gives and receives certain goods or values. For the support and prestige that s/he enjoys, in exchange for the power that s/he wields, the leader allocates to the base certain material or symbolic goods, ranging from the achievement of the group's concrete objectives to its integration. From this point of view charismatic leadership is a specific type of exchange in which predominates, with respect to other dimensions, affective identification with the extraordinary qualities of the leader and the enhancement of the followers' individual and collective identity. Of course, an exchange of this kind requires exceptional circumstances, specific conjunctures, and it is exposed to the ephemerality which I have already discussed.

It should not be forgotten, however, that this exchange is subject to the general conditions that govern every leadership relation. Both of the actors concerned must keep the costs/benefits ratio of its action carefully in balance; the amount of advantages obtained by the followers in exchange for their support cannot fall below a certain threshold, lest the leader be subjected to impeachment. A large proportion of the leader's energies must therefore be devoted to maintaining this equilibrium, or at least to creating a positive perception of it; consequently, the distribution of symbols of identification and recourse to ideology are always crucial resources of leadership.

Without detracting from Weber's contribution, a relational theory of leadership must place charisma alongside other types of resources, thereby accounting for both the role performed by individual qualities and the manifold relationships that tie the leader and her/his followers together. Of major importance for such a theory are, of course, the particular conditions which favour charismatic leadership over other types of exchange.

This line of research and reflection has been further strengthened by the findings of social psychologists investigating the topic of *influence*. A large number of studies, most notably those by Moscovici, have convincingly demonstrated that influence is a widespread resource within groups and that it should be treated above all as a relational resource (Moscovici 1979; Moscovici *et al.* 1985; Mugny and Perez 1991; Moscovici and Doise 1994). For long, it was believed that influence operated in a single direction, from the leader towards her/his followers, on account of the leader's conformity with the values of the group. But this, in truth, is not the case. In reality, in a complex network of exchanges, influence circulates as a variously distributed resource and becomes also a property of minorities with the ability to assert themselves and to bring about innovation.

As it has been presented, the theory of charismatic leadership fuses together two processes which should instead be kept distinct: First, innovative counterleaders and agents of change always arise from the breakdown of conformity and from a change in the direction of processes of influence within a group or society; and, on the other hand, the institutionalization of consensus, even in the case of a charismatic leader, is rather founded on her/his capacity to interpret the values of the group in the most conformist way.

Having said this, reflection on charismatic leadership and on the conditions for its emergence strikes me as a necessary step in analysing totalitarian movements. The populist dimension is present in all the great contemporary totalitarian movements, and its specific content is the union of past and future; more precisely, it is the mobilization of the past against the present in order to shape a different future. The religious and totalizing dimension of charisma, even though desacralized, ensures this mobilization of the sacred past (the people, the land, the nation, the race) in order to overcome resistances to change.

Much less convincing, it seems to me, are arguments that use the model of charismatic leadership to account for the role of great individuals in collective processes. These arguments put forward by conservative critics of modernity contrast the exceptional accomplishments of individual leaders to what is seen as a general trend towards the destruction of the individual in contemporary mass societies (for a discussion, see Lasch 1991). The role of exceptional individuals can only be denied by an obtuse, hyperstructuralist vision of collective processes, a perspective that is unable to distinguish between the multiplicity of levels within it. Indeed, a position of this kind is vulgar enough not to warrant further discussion. To be sure, though, to simply state that great individuals are the engine of collective processes is not satisfactory either. For theory to develop further, it is necessary to undertake more systematic analysis of the mechanisms that link individual action and collective action together. This, I believe, is becoming one of the central issues of contemporary research, and in various respects the present book, too, highlights its importance.

The argument that stresses such a dissolution of individuality as one of the causes of the contemporary crisis is far from convincing. In contemporary movements, the increasingly close linkage between collective demands and individual needs, the desire not to separate the goals of social change from those of individual self-realization, and the appeal for respect for differences have been forcefully asserted. Conflicts have shifted to the terrain of personal identity, and by so doing they signal a crucial change in the nature of domination and in the operation of the forces of resistance.

The role of leadership

In its action, the first task of leadership is to *define objectives*, which implies the ability not only to formulate aims for the movement but also to establish a system of priorities and adapt them to the changing conditions. It is possible to distinguish between two categories of objectives: general aims, which represent the final results predicted from the movement's action; and specific goals, which are more immediate and represent the means with which to achieve the more general objectives. In reaction to the pressure of internal and external change, the leadership must constantly adapt these goals to the conditions of the environment and the expectations of the members. The coordination of objectives and the choice of priorities always require an ideology to legitimize these operations.

Secondly, leaders must *provide the means for action*: they must, that is, gather and organize the available resources and direct them towards the realization of the movement's objectives. This function involves two distinct activities. Within the movement itself, the leader must facilitate the division and articulation of tasks, and make the best possible use of the different talents available to the movement; externally, he must procure the maximum amount of resources available in the environment by entering into relations with other groups and organizations and with the society at large.

Yet another task of the leader is to *maintain the structure* of the movement. He must guarantee interaction and cohesion among members, and in order to do so, s/he must counteract the influence of the centrifugal forces emanating from the action of the adversary as well as from internal conflicts. Far from presenting itself as a homogeneous, unified reality, a movement is, as we have seen, charged with tensions and conflictual tendencies which are aggravated by the destructive actions of the adversary. The maintenance of cohesion is a major undertaking for the leadership and can be achieved by using a variety of means from ideology to discipline. Here the circulation of information is crucially important. Communication serves to inform and motivate the membership. For the leadership of a movement, with relatively scarce resources and under pressure from a more powerful adversary, channels of communication are a vital need. The cohesion of the organization can be maintained through control of these channels. Information on demands and conflicts is a precondition for the mediation of tensions and their settlement. The changes which, one by one, threaten the unity of the organization can be kept under control through the adjustment of the balance between the aims and the rewards. Stimuli from outside can be filtered and selected in such a way as to control their effects on the group. In the same way, information transmitted by the group to the outside world can be monitored.

The leadership of a movement must then *mobilize the support base* in pursuit of its goals. It must preserve its constituency's consensus over objectives and attract growing investments from members. This role is particularly closely related to the management of a system of rewards, and to the leadership's ability to bring about the membership's ideological identification with goals. Closely bound up with mobilization there is also (as we saw in the previous chapter) the function of articulation, or the ability to enter into relationships with other components of the environment (organizations and social groups) in order to obtain support and consensus. This entails a capacity to receive stimuli from the environment and to adapt the organization to changes in it.

Finally, the leader must *maintain and reinforce the identity* of the group. He must furnish incentives of solidarity, projecting an image of the group with which members can identify and from which they extract affective gratification. The intensity of exchanges and interaction consolidates collective identity, since participation itself becomes a reward. The 'expressive' function of the leader is her/his ability to offer symbolic objects for identification, around which the solidarity of the members and their individual identities coagulate.

These various components of leadership action are interconnected, and in the concrete reality of a movement they become intertwined. Often the needs to which the leader must respond are mutually exclusive and necessitate a choice between alternatives. Thus the fulcrum for leadership action is the *decision*, that is, the capacity to choose between alternatives and reduce uncertainties. A decision implies that the leader be able to correctly assess his own position in the exchange, along with the benefits which he is able to offer, and to evaluate demands by members and estimate and prevent breakdown in the exchange ratio.

It is possible to construct various typologies from the different components of the action of a leader accounted for above. The literature on leadership is replete with such exercises (yielding to us, for example, directive or participative leadership, goal-oriented or interaction-oriented leadership, and others). However, typological attempts are of little of no real use, except for routine tasks of classification. It is more useful, I argue, to keep in mind the complexity of the actions of a leader and demonstrate the components involved in the process in each case.

To complete the analysis of the role of the leader, I should specify the principal forms of legitimization of leadership, the fundamental criteria governing the exchange between leader and support base, and the foundation of the leader's power. To this end, we can analytically distinguish between at least five types of power: (i) power of reward; (ii) power of coercion; (iii) power of conformity; (iv) power of identification; and (v) power of competence. The power of reward is based on the recognition that the leader is able to furnish benefits to members and to help them obtain the advantages they seek. This recognition involves establishing contractual relations and forms of negotiation between the leader and the support base. The power of coercion is based on the leader's capacity to discipline and punish the members of the group who fail to conform to the stated objectives. Loyalty and involvement may be obtained by using the threat of sanctions or losses, but in such a case the exchange relationship is more liable to become a source of tensions and conflicts, and give rise to the formation of factions. The power of conformity is based on internalization of the norms and values of the group. The leader possesses power because her/his conduct is in keeping with the norms and expectations of the members of the group, according to the legitimized definition of her/his role. As we will see in the next section, a dichotomy arises between conformity and innovation in the behaviour of the leader. The power of identification is based on the membership's identification with the leader, on the respect and acceptance s/he enjoys, and on the emotional gratification s/he is able to provide. As we have seen, the capacity of the leader to furnish symbols for identification and to reinforce collective identity is of great importance, since in this way s/he also reinforces the psychological structure of individual members. Finally, the power of competence signifies a recognition of the specific talents of the leader with respect to the aims of the movement. Success or failure in achieving the movement's objectives is the major point of reference in evaluating the leader's effectiveness.

The legitimization of the leader is always founded on multiple factors, and as exchange relations widen in scope, the leader can replace resources that are in short supply or no longer legitimate. Here again, we are not dealing with types, but with conceptual tools that can be used to detect the presence of various analytical components, the prevalance of one over another, and the variations which may occur in concrete situations.

Conformity and innovation

At this point, a central question poses itself: does the foundation of leadership consist in an ability to respond to the expectations of the group and to conform with its norms? If so, how can we explain innovation and change within a movement?

The thesis of conformity to the expectations of the group has pre-dominated in the study of leadership. This point of view has been developed mainly by socio-psychological studies. The mandate for leadership, it is claimed, results from recognition of personal capacities and specific skills in achieving the objectives of the group, but above all it is the ability to conform with the expectations of the group that is decisive in bringing about this. These expectations relate to norms and roles; the more closely the leader's behaviour conforms to such expectations and contributes to the pursuit of the group's objectives, the more positive the evaluation of his performance and the greater the certainty that he enjoys the consensual acceptance of the membership. Nevertheless, the leader also has an 'idiosyncrasy credit', by which I mean an accepted margin of deviation from the norms of the group (for this classic model, see Hollander 1964, 1978). The more the leader accrues positive evaluations and consensual approval by conforming to the norms, the greater such allowed margin permitting occasional deviation from the norms without incurred sanctions. These violations, however, must not affect the core norms and must not exceed the limits of the 'credit' the leader has accumulated by conforming.

The whole functionalist literature on leadership embraces this view. Groups develop norms which define the behaviour expected of the members. Once these norms have been established, there are strong pressures for conformity, which increase in force in proportion to the degree of cohesion of the group; those who persistently deviate will be expelled sooner or later. Becoming a leader requires internalization of these group values and norms, and those who take over leadership tend to represent and defend this normative arrangement. Indirect confirmation of the validity of this approach, which, as said, is predominantly socio-psychological, comes from sociological research on participation, discussed earlier in chapter 15. Rank-and-file leaders are the intermediate link between central leadership and grassroot militants. Research shows that rank-and-file participation in collective action presupposes strong attachment to the identity of the group to which the participant belongs, and strong identification with its values and norms.

Socio-psychological literature emphasizes the relatively greater conformity and commitment of the leader with respect to the objectives of the group, and this characteristic also seems to come across in the results of sociological research on the differences between the ideology of the leaders and the support base in political parties and movements. According to the prevailing wisdom, the leaders are always more conservative or more progressive than the average member of the support base, depending on the political orientation of the organization to which they belong.

Thus the model of conformity assigns to leadership a role that is chiefly the reduction of uncertainty: embodying the norms of the group and representing them by setting an example, leaders eliminate indeterminacy of behaviour and choices and guarantee the integration and unity of the whole. But this approach leaves the problem of innovation unresolved. There are, however, alternative directions of research which suggest some possible solutions. Studies on influence tend to consider this variable a resource distributed throughout the group and controlled to a different extent by each member. Thus the conduct of the group does not depend solely on the leader, but rather on the greater or lesser influence exercised by each of its members. Research into innovative group processes has revealed the importance of nonconformist behaviour. A minority that does not behave according to the expectations of the group, but which nevertheless provides a stable and coherent model of behaviour, can change the norms of the majority. If this conduct is seen to be consistent, or as having unity, continuity, and credibility, it can exert innovative influence on the choices of the group (Moscovici *et al.* 1985; Mugny and Perez 1991).

The contradiction which emerges from these two analytical approaches is not irreconcilable, as long as neither model is taken to constitute alone a general explanation. In reality, conformity and innovation correspond to two different analytical stages. If we consider the period of the formation of leadership, the establishment of an exchange relationship with the support base does not appear to be necessarily linked to conformity. On the contrary, a capacity for innovation can be an important resource in the ratification of the leader's mandate. An innovative proposal must, however, be backed by coherent and stable conduct, from which it derives its position of influence, even if it is put forward by a minority. The time of a movement's constitution is, as we have seen, a moment of continuity and of rupture. The leader who innovates and breaks with the past must also display a consistent style of conduct based on a strong identity. Therefore, a capacity for innovation should not be confused with the status of a social outsider. The leader does not stand outside the group mobilized by the movement; her/his social identity is strongly rooted in the identity of the group. The leadership status, however, gains legitimacy not simply as a continuation of this identity but also as a break with the past, and as an innovation. The passage to collective action requires the proposal of innovative models of behaviour and the ability to divert existing resources towards new objectives. The skill and effectiveness of the movement's leader consist precisely in this capacity to mobilize the past (that is, the values, norms, and resources of the group) for the objectives of change.

If one instead considers the time when a movement is already established and has consolidated into an organization, one can accept the idea that the principal function of the leader is to guarantee the cohesion and unity of the group and the pursuit of objectives. The leader moves within the organizational limits and is subject to control by the membership: under these conditions, the model of conformity, with its variant of 'idiosyncracy credit', or of tolerated deviation, better expresses the leadership situation. Nevertheless, influence is still a resource distributed widely among the members of the group, and even within highly organized groups innovation may be intermittent.

If a dissenting minority proposes consistent models of action, they may be able to modify the norms of the majority. Thus, 'counterleaders' may emerge whose actions go against expectations of conformity. These individuals or groups anticipate real demands and problems present within the movement, and thus enter into competition with the actual leadership. Their action may bring innovations without replacing the leadership; or it may result in a rearrangement in the old leadership, leading to the integration of the new members; or, finally, a structural change may ensue that leads to the formation of a new organization. Thus conformity and innovation are but two aspects of the action of the leader. It is important to distinguish between them analytically, but also to notice how they interact and are interwoven in practice in a movement on its way towards transformation into an organization.

Network leaders

Movements today still largely correspond to the description provided of them by Gerlach and Hine (1970): they are segmented, reticular, polycephalous networks. The formal role of leadership within an organizational structure in recent movements has been at least partially delegitimized. It is difficult to identify once and for all a set of stable leadership functions, which would concentrate themselves into a single entity, whether this be an individual or one organization within a broader movement. It is apparently not the individual leaders who define and subsequently perform these functions. Within contemporary movements, power relationships have many facets which can be only partially grasped using an approach based on analysis of personal qualities or group dynamics.

Instead, each specific relational context defines its own internal structuration and its own operational mechanisms, and, in consequence, also the relative importance of the various functions within it. It establishes, that is, a situational order of priority. The apparent importance assigned by the networks to the quality of their internal relations as compared with their objectives of social change is a striking indicator of this general orientation. The public dimension of action tends indeed to coincide with the outward proposal of cultural models elaborated and lived in near-invisible networks submerged in everyday life. The search for internal communication and everyday-life solidarity are a precondition for public anatagonistic practice. However, this does not mean that the function of solidarity maintenance takes priority as such. Various specific functions assume differing weights according to the context. Nevertheless, the unequal distribution of the resources pertinent to each given context gives rise to asymmetrical positions, still not definable in formal terms and variable over time. The functions of decision-making and representation are also present within recent movements but their range has been reduced and their modes of operation altered. Short-term mobilizations require decision-making processes that are less formalized and representatives that are more temporary. Moreover, the permanence of the same individuals in these functions has been challenged and often substituted by mechanisms of rotation of representatives, spokespersons, organizers.

Contemporary movements face a deep internal dilemma: the need to ensure the survival of the organization by means of asymmetry-producing functions is flanked by the impossibility of rendering this asymmetry explicit through its formalization, since, should this happen, the solidarity and the interpersonal relations are subjected to the threat of a breakdown. The strategies employed to resolve this dilemma are not necessarily coherent with one another: they occur at different times, and they take different forms in the various contexts of mobilization. All of them, however, entail the transformation of the decision-making process, compared with the classical model of political decision-making.

A first strategy consists in reducing to the minimum, and at the same time concealing, the decision-making and representation functions. The decisional role of an individual or collective body is simply no longer formally recognized as such. Above all, it is no longer binding. For instance, radios, magazines, cultural agencies, ad hoc committees, campaign promoters, which are often semi-professionalized structures, play an extremely important role in mobilizations. They can orient and support the mobilization process, but they are unable to determine the precise form that it will take, since they lack any sanctions applicable to nonconformist behaviour. The same applies to the bodies responsible for coordinating movements – interorganizational committees, national assemblies. The documents and motions produced by these bodies are, in fact, only proposals presented to the movement. The nonideological nature and the organizational informality of the movements have largely neutralized the weapons previously wielded to ensure compliance with decisions taken by the centre (expulsion, doctrinal excommunication).

A second strategy is to narrow down decision-making occasions, while at the same time postponing *sine die* their implementation. Often this technique is used to reduce internal tensions. A decision which, if taken in an unambiguous manner, might trigger dangerous internal conflicts, is first postponed as far into the future as possible and then taken only under the pressure of organizational and/or conjunctural constraints. This generates a form of leadership which we can call concealed leadership, inasmuch as the decision eventually becomes the exclusive responsibility of whoever, for personal interest or because of the normal division of tasks, has followed up the problem in question. In this case the problem assumes the guise of ineluctability which renders the decision acceptable and to some extent legitimate, even though it had not been subjected to any collective control. The asymmetry is made visible and accepted, while being simultaneously denied in its capacity to threaten the unity of the group.

Thirdly, decision-making power tends to be redistributed as much as possible among the members of a group or among the groups. The multiplication and overlapping of the functions maintains an efficient operation of the group and obstructs the centralization of the resources relevant to it, favoring instead the appearance of a rotating leadership. One member in the group fulfils the ideological role of the leadership, another expresses its creative component, and still another interprets its solidarist-organizational function.

The presence of a diffuse leadership also often leads to the activation of reciprocal control mechanisms among the various leaders which impede the emergence of dominant roles. It is worth stressing that the concept of rotating or diffuse leadership does not refer solely to situations in which various functions are performed simultaneously by different subjects, which is a pattern common among small groups. At the network level, the diffusion of leadership means that positions of predominance are temporarily assumed also by the bodies promoting the specific mobilization in which the movement as a whole is engaged. Very important at this level is the role of information, coordination, and transmission performed by the semi-professionalized structures, as already mentioned.

Fourthly, the function of representation is to a large extent denied. Indeed, the representatives formally delegated by individual groups to the various committees possess only limited powers, and their action stops short at simple organizational coordination. There does exist, however, an informal version of representation, whereby specific individuals or organizational structures constitute what is an essentially symbolic referent, but one that is nevertheless able to express the image of the movement or of the individual group towards the outside. In this manner, some sort of control is exerted over the flux of information by the groups possessing a greater quantity of resources (for example coordination committees, umbrella organizations, radios, bookshops, cultural centres, magazines); those groups are, therefore, taken as a point of reference by people who wish to establish relations with the movement.

There are, finally other means available for handling the tensions caused by the persistence of asymmetric power relationships among members, like the depersonalization of the leadership role. The groups distinguish sharply between the role and the persons occupying it. While the role is in fact the object of systematic contestation, relations with the person are invariably amicable. This enables the personal relation to continue and the organizational structure to be maintained. The depersonalization strategy is used against emerging personalities, when differences can pose a threat to the solidarity of the group. In groups based on technical skills it prevents what could become a permanent asymmetry based on knowledge not shared by all members. At the network level, depersonalization operates primarily through the granting of a predominant role to the semi-professionalized groups. The latter's leadership function attains legitimacy because it is not associable with individuals or specific political organizations, and because it is characterized not by political decision-making but by proposals for issues to stimulate debate, and by a media function towards the movement and toward the outside.

The relationship with power and asymmetry is not easily solved by contemporary movements. The present tendency seems to be a refusal of the formal legitimation of asymmetry, accompanied by acknowledgement of its relative inevitability. In the eyes of many of today's participants, power is a dimension which must be addressed with the fullest possible specification of its mechanisms, thereby increasing the possibility to gain control over it. It is not possible to eliminate power with a simple declaration of intent. From this point of view, the contractualist attitude toward power relationships seems to prefigure a route which collective mobilization is bound to follow. Addressing power as openly as possible is the internal condition for the groups to develop ability to address the societal power in the same way.

18

Collective action and discourse

Ideology and frames

Framing processes, as discussed in the recent literature on social movements (Snow *et al.* 1986; Snow and Benford 1988, 1992; Benford 1993; see also Gamson 1992b) are part of the symbolic production of a social movement. The literature on frames contributes to a better understanding of how actors define their action but it tends to forget the 'ideological' aspect of such a definition. As a relational process, framing activity is related to the particular position of the actor in the social field and carries with itself the partiality, plurality and tensions of that position. Frames are to be defined as the discursive representation of collective action organized according to the position of the actor in the field, and they must be located within a theory of ideology. Even after Mannheim (Mannheim 1960; see also Shils 1968; Manning 1980), sociological thought is still a prisoner to its dualistic inheritance, which considers symbolic production either as a transparent expression of beliefs and values or as a pure reflex of material interests. Recent advances in theory (for a synthesis, see Thompson 1984, 1990; Wuthnow *et al.* 1984, Wuthnow 1987, 1989; Swidler 1986, 1995; Billig 1991, 1992; Billig *et al.* 1988) have contributed to a new awareness of the complexity of cultural and symbolic levels in individual and collective action.

Ideology is a key analytical level for the understanding of social movements and should include the framing activities as part of the representational system of the actor. The way in which the actors represent their own actions is not a simple reflection of more profound mechanisms (economic constraints or unconscious psychological motivations, for example), but it carries the very meaning of action, although this meaning is removed from the system of social relationships of which it is a part. Ideology can neither be written off as false conscience, simply mystifying real social relationships, nor redeemed as the transparent representation of shared social values.

Ideology is a set of symbolic frames which collective actors use to represent their own actions to themselves and to others within a system of social relationships. Such symbolic production is a constituent part of these relationships, but at the same time the actor tends to separate it from the system of which it is a part, turning it to the defence of her/his own particular interests. Hence the interweaving of truth and falsehood that characterizes ideology: it is geared to the reproduction of real social relationships, but at the same time it hides and negates them. The symbolic elaboration of action 'rationalizes' social relationships according to the interests of the actor. It supplies a representation which tends to legitimate and reinforce those interests while at the same time defining the relational field of collective action. The meaning of this action, which is to be found in the system of relations of which the actor is a part, is instead identified with the particular point of view of the actor himself: the field of social relationships, which is always made up of a network of tensions and oppositions, is restructured according to the position occupied by the actor. When sociological analysis takes these representations back to the system of relationships in which they are produced, and there tries to discover the meaning of collective action, it becomes a critique of ideology. Frame analysis should therefore not be separated from a deconstruction of the ideological dimensions of the frames produced by collective actors.

What can, then, be said of the role and the form of ideology within a social movement, during its formative phase and its organizational consolidation? At the most general level, the ideology of a movement always includes, as Touraine has pointed out (Touraine 1977), a (more or less clearly articulated) definition of the actor her/himself, the identification of an adversary, and an indication of ends, goals, objectives for which to struggle. But ideology also stabilizes a set of relationships among these elements which serve on the one hand to legitimize the actor, and on the other to negate any social identity of the opponent. By declaring to be fighting for a goal which belongs to her/him, but which goes beyond her/his own immediate interests, a collective actor always tries to affirm the general legitimacy of her/his action. By at the same time indicating the opponent as the major obstacle to the attainment of such a goal or to the realization of such an objective, the collective actor negates the adversary's right to a social stature or to any form of legitimacy.

The connection between the particularism of the actor and certain general values (truth, freedom, justice, emancipation, and the like) is a key mechanism of the framing activity of a collective actor. A link of necessity is established between the role of the actor and some kind of a totality to be reached through his action. The actor is the true interpreter of this totality, which has always positive attributes in cultural, political, or moral terms. On the other hand, the adversary is seen only as having a negative relationship to the totality: the opponent is, in fact, the very obstacle that prevents general needs from being satisfied or social goals from being attained.

In the ideology of a social movement, it is then always possible to identify, more or less explicitly, a definition of the social actor who is mobilized, of the adversary against whom the movement must struggle, and of the collective objectives of the struggle. These three analytical elements are combined in a complex system of representations that defines the position of the collective actor with respect to the opponent and the collective goals in the following ways: (a) the definition of the social group in whose name actions are undertaken determines the limits of collective identity and the legitimacy of the movement; (b) the undesirable situation which has given rise to the need for collective action is attributed to an illegitimate adversary, usually identified in nonsocial terms; (c) objectives, or desirable goals for which it is necessary to fight, exist for society as a whole; (d) there is a positive relationship between the actor and the general goals of the society, and therefore the actions of the movement go beyond the particular interests of the actor; (e) the adversary is seen as an obstacle to the general goals of the society; and (f) there is thus an irreconcilable opposition between the actor and the adversary.

These constituent elements of the ideology of a social movement take on different cultural contents and vary at different moments in the trajectory of collective action. As far as the birth of a collective actor is concerned, Alberoni (1984) has pointed out the many ways in which the fundamental experience during the *status nascendi* is framed into different ideological contents. In the formative phase, I consider that two elements characterize the ideology of a movement. The first is the *negation of the gap* between expectations and reality. The birth of a movement is marked by 'moments of madness' (Zolberg 1972), when all things seem possible, and collective enthusiasm looks forward to action, confident of a positive outcome. Ideology overcomes the inadequacy of practice: the less capacity for action the still weak and unorganized movement has, the greater will be the production of symbols. This is the moment of the fusion of the various components of a movement into a new form of solidarity, in which the expressive dimensions and emotional identification with collective goals prevail.

The second characteristic is the central role of the theme of *rebirth.*

Collective actors often make reference to a 'mother society' or to a golden age, temporarily rewriting the chronicle of the group's infancy. The ideology of rebirth, of a return to an atemporal past, is closely bound up with the need for a totalizing legitimacy mentioned above. In the moment of its formation, the movement restructures old social allegiances in a new collective framework: the defence of an identity still defined by reference to the past is often the way through which new problems are addressed. When a new conflict arises, the only solid points of reference, the only known language, the only images to be entrusted with the new claims, belong to the past.

A return to a situation of original purity, which can assume a variety of cultural connotations in different cases, allows collective action to combine its ancestral components into a new solidarity, and restructures existing identities projecting them towards the prospect of change. A movement joins past and future, the defence of a social group with a demand for transformation. Symbols and cultural models are sought in the traditions of the group and the social movements that came before the movement now in formation. Symbolic referents and the language in which new collective demands are expressed come from the past. A new movement always views its own action as a rebirth – as a regeneration of the present through a mythic reaffirmation of the past, which in reality is the cocoon in which new needs and new conflicts are formed.

For a long time, the labour movement spoke the language of the French Revolution and dreamed of a return to the community and the solidarity of corporations. Marx's analysis, which tried to scientifically define the specific characteristics of that movement within the capitalist mode of production, was accepted only at a certain phase reached in the movement's development, and it still had to come to terms with the other components – Utopian, humanitarian, religious, solidaristic – coexisting within the movement. The evocation of a Leninist purism or Maoism on the part of many small sects coming out of the youth movement of the 1960s reflects in an analogous manner this taxing, hardening search for a backward-looking identity by a movement in its formative stage. The profound crisis of so many of the political groups stemming from 1968 does not, contrary to how many would rather have it, indicate the end of the movement or its disintegration, but rather the end of a utopian, fragmentary phase of collective action. In the late 1970s, the movements left behind the myths and symbols which had helped to bring it about in the first place; in the 1980s, the new problems and new conflicts which the movement carried with it surfaced and began to manifest their real contents.

I would call this situation of movements in formation a *regressive Utopia*.

The general characteristic of Utopia is the immediate identification between the actor and the goals of a global society. The cultural model of transformation of the society coincides, in the utopian view, with the action of a particular actor, who thus becomes the direct agent of general change. A Utopia is regressive when the transformation is equated with a return to the past and the myth of rebirth. After the nascent phase, these utopian components do not disappear, but progressively give way to an ideological elaboration which is more directly linked to the specific problems of the movement. New languages and new symbols are created to define the field and the actors of the conflict. The mobilized social group, the adversary, and the collective goals are redefined in a more pertinent manner; ideology becomes a more complex and detailed symbolic system. At the same time, the movement finds that it is faced with the necessity to assure internal integration and to improve its position *vis-à-vis* the environment.

Integration and strategy

As the movement grows, two essential aspects of ideology are thus called into play. First of all, ideology fulfils a *function of integration* with respect to the movement as a whole; this function is accomplished by a repeated proposal for values and norms, the control of deviant behaviour, and the stabilization of certain rituals. Secondly, ideology performs a *strategic function* in relation to the environment. Discursive capacity is one of the resources that can be used to reduce the costs and maximize the benefits of action. This process can take place in two ways. On the one hand, there is an effort to widen the margins within which the movement acts within the political system, in order thus to increase the scope of its possibility to exert influence. On the other hand, ideology tries to widen the movement's base and to push the groups which were previously outside the conflict to become involved in it. Both of these processes imply a complex game, in which discursive messages are sent in an effort to turn social interactions to the actor's advantage by symbolically undermining the adversary's position. In particular, one of the fundamental tasks is that of making evident the illegitimacy of the adversary, and the negative nature of its position, in the eyes of both neutral observers and potential supporters. Let us examine the integrative and strategic functions separately.

A movement is subject to strong centrifugal pressures, due to both its own internal fragmentation and the initiatives of the adversary. The need to maintain organizational unity becomes stronger as the movement is consolidated. Ideology emerges as one of the main tools which can be used to guarantee integration. The multiplicity of interests and demands which are always to be found in an organized movement must be mediated and unified. Ideology coordinates, articulates, and makes coherent these demands, associating them with general principles. By reformulating the values and norms of the group, discursive frames solidify the collective identity and prevent internal conflicts from damaging unity (see Fine 1995). At the same time, it fixes the boundaries of belonging (see Gyerin 1983) and the criteria for the identification and punishment of those who deviate from these norms.

Nevertheless, the discursive apparatus of a movement is not a static entity: it is also influenced by tensions, and remains a field of conflict between groups and factions. The control of ideology and, more generally, the flow of information is an important leadership resource, being as it is necessary in the continuous adaptation of symbolic representations to the present state of the movement. The bottom line of the costs and benefits cannot always be directly calculated, particularly when what is in question are non-material resources. Thus ideology, enlisted to minimize costs, to facilitate the perception of rewards, to cover losses or to substitute for resources in short supply, comes to play. The relative rigidity or flexibility of the discursive frames will in turn make the adjustments more or less difficult (see Moaddel 1992).

A last aspect of the integrative function of ideology can be found in ritual practices. Every movement creates rituals which serve to consolidate its components. The adoption of linguistic or gestural codes, of costumes or ways of dressing creates traits common to those who are part of the movement. Actual ceremonies, governed by codified procedures, represent the synthesis of a shared organizational culture. These rituals, through the quasi-sacred crystallization of the norms of the group, tend to guarantee the continuity and the efficacy of ideology, in spite of the tensions at work within it.

The second fundamental need for any movement in the phase of consolidation is that to improve its position in relation to the environment. This is handled by, on the one hand, increasing the movement's influence within the political system while, on the other, simultaneously widening the base of consensus on which it can rely within the overall society. In this sense ideology has a strategic function, for it is through the articulation of the symbolic meaning of the action that the actor can increase her/his advantage over the others. In particular, this means gaining the consensus of components of other organizations, and the support of groups not directly involved in the conflict against the initiatives of the adversary.

With respect to other organizations, ideology must call forth loyalty to the general aims of the movement, while at the same time differentiating the image and the contents of the single organization. Competition between organizations can increase the differentiation of symbolic contents, without any real corresponding conflict in practice. In a situation in which the market of potential supporters is a limited one and there are restrictive margins for action, different organizations will tend to accentuate competition on an ideological level.

As far as the adversary is concerned, ideology will tend to assign the blame for the negative situation to the initiatives of the adversary, attempting to deny the opponent of any legitimacy. Along with this, it is the positive task of ideology to attempt to improve the position of the actor *vis-à-vis* the antagonist in the eyes of a public, from whom support or favor is sought. The contrast must be symbolically articulated in such a way as to turn to the actor's advantage the unbalance of the power relationship. Ideology can be used to obtain a positive identification with the movement on the part of potential supporters and neutral observers, by deflecting all negative feedback onto the adversary. In these 'dramatic encounters' (Klapp 1965), different situations may develop with a variety of symbolic meanings, following, however, no more than a few standard scripts. In the 'victory of the hero' version, the actor makes an attempt to present her/himself as culturally or morally superior to the antagonist; this symbolic tool is often complemented by the 'vanquishing of the villain' variation in which a temporary or occasional disadvantage of the opponent is presented as a due and deserved punishment. When the actor finds her/himself in an uncomfortable or disadvantaged position, then the 'unfair tactics' or 'dirty fighting', or even the 'oppression of the weak', scenarios are used as symbolic means to rebuild a relatively even confrontation with the opponent. And, in case these efforts do not succeed, the 'defeat without dishonor' script is often the last resort to maintain or recapture the attention and support of the potential followers.

All of these symbolic scenarios framing the relationship between a movement and its opponents respond to the strategic function of ideology, which aims at widening the support base of a movement and the space within which it can act inside the political system, subverting at the same time any attempts of the adversary to maintain the legitimacy of its action. This dramaturgical role of ideology (Snow *et al.* 1981; Benford and Hunt 1992) is that of securing the actor's emergence out of every confrontation with the most favorable image possible. In the case of a positive outcome of the conflict, the situation will be symbolically articulated as the victory of the good and the righteous over arbitrary injustice. In the case of a defeat, ideology will retell the story as the battle of the weak against the powerful, with special attention to any unfair tactics. In either case, ideology intervenes on behalf of the actor in an attempt to increase the consensus mobilization and to symbolically redefine the field to its advantage.

It should not be forgotten that these mechanisms also operate, with even greater efficacy, in the area of social control. The attempt to discredit collective forms of protest or to turn public resentment against a movement, thus legitimizing repression, is one of the essential components of the framing activity of the ruling groups. Control over the flow of information and the media guarantees a structural advantage to the powers that be; in social conflict, as in any contention for public consensus, the game is never entirely open and the positions are not those of parity.

The ambivalence of collective frames

The discursive frames of collective action are produced by internal negotiations and conflicts: individuals and groups within a movement construct them, laboriously adjusting the different orientations that express multiple and contrasting requirements of a collective field. But this deep constructive activity of a collective actor is not visible, particularly since some unity and effectiveness must be maintained over time. Ideological patterns and leadership functions are always at work in an attempt to give a durable and predictable order to the continuously negotiated process. One of the main tasks falling on the part of the leaders is precisely that of producing those frames that reinforce the unity and improve the effectiveness of the collective actor.

Ideological dimensions expressed in framing processes are therefore necessarily ambivalent because, on the one hand, they express the actual meaning and goals of collective action, but, on the other, they cover and hide the plurality of orientations and tensions corresponding to the different components of the movement. Leaders claim a unity that they seldom achieve and tend to present the movement as homogeneous and coherent as possible.

The frames produced by a collective actor are ambivalent also in another, even more important respect. The very idea of a social conflict implies the opposition of two actors struggling for the same resources, symbolic or material, which they consider valuable. The adversaries share the same field of action but they interpret it in opposing ways, as part of the effort of trying to submit it to their own control. The actor identifies her/himself with the entire field, while denying any legitimacy and role to the opponent. Conflict is a social relationship, but the actors tend to reify it: each pole of the opposition wants to erase the other, labelling it in non-social terms. A

relational field, constructed by conflicting orientations, is thus reduced to
the particularism of a single actor.

The ideology of a movement carries with it this ambivalence because it
is an interpretation of a social field; but it is also a misinterpretation, guided
by the particularism of the actor. It at once reveals and covers what is at
stake in a conflict. The task of sociological analysis is precisely to discover
the field behind the actors' particularistic frames and to reveal the internal
tensions of the frames themselves.

Both movements and their opponents speak the same language; they
define a common field from opposite poles. In fact, they both address the
same basic dilemmas of social life in a planetary world, problems which
have no solutions and which define the cultural and social boundaries of
complexity. They constitute polarities which represent impossible choices,
inasmuch as the roots of the tension between them are located at the core
of a highly differentiated system. They bring forth the problems which
society cannot but try to solve, but whose solution only transfers the uncertainty elsewhere. Society copes with the situation by making decisions,
attempting thereby to reduce uncertainty within the range of possible
action. But a decision, which thus would permit action, is also an attempt
at escape, a denial and cover-up of the dilemmas implicit in the decision
itself. A decision may be tantamount to avoidance of a tension which has
become unbearable, a means for neither seeing nor speaking of such dilemmas.

Both movement activists and ruling groups deal with these dilemmas,
framing them in opposite ways while denying any truth to the opponent's
frames. They also tend to hide their internal plurality. Sociological analysis can detect the ambivalence of these discourses and recognize a conflictual field common to the adversaries. The enormous expansion of
individual capacities and room for choice contrasts with the parallel tendency for creation of capillary systems of behavioural manipulation; the
fact that social systems have extended their power of action beyond the
boundaries known to any society of the past bears witness to the unprecedented capacity of contemporary societies to consciously produce themselves to the extreme measure of potential self-destruction; the tendency to
continuously expand the capacity of human systems to intervene even in
their very own development runs counter to the need to respond to the
limits given in internal and external nature; the irreversible accumulation
of scientific knowledge is governed by the administrative rationality of
organizational and political apparatuses, whose choices are reversible;
inclusion in the world culture tends toward a levelling of cultural differences, and resistance to the pressures towards homogeneity produces self-

exclusion or marginalization – contemporary movements deal with all these dilemmas. They challenge the technocratic power on a symbolic ground, opposing to its instrumental rationality cultural codes which reverse the logic of the dominant techno-scientific, political, and industrial-economic apparatuses: they assert the need for autonomy and meaning, call for awareness of the limits of human action, urge for the search for a new scientific paradigm, alert for the respect due to the marginalia of human cultures. Revealing the shadowy side of the technological power, movements allow society to take responsibility for its own action.

But when producing these challenging codes, movements also frame the dilemmas just discussed, in accordance with their particular standpoint: they reject the field in which they partake in the shared trust in science, rationalization, and efficiency. The affirmative and negative side of ideology, the revealing and the covering function, are simultaneously present: ambivalence marks the consciousness of collective actors and reminds us that social action is never transparent.

Reversing the symbolic order

An analysis of the ideological dimensions of collective action is made today more difficult by the fact that societal processes are increasingly located at the symbolic level (Klapp 1969, 1991; Moscovici 1993). The struggle of contemporary movements is aimed at the foundations of power in complex societies, at its more extreme claim to impose the codes governing our relation with the world. The importance of this endeavour becomes central if one acknowledges that the act of *nomination* is a crucial factor in the construction of social life. And that act becomes even more crucial in a society in which the distinction between the real and its representation has all but disappeared. Contemporary movements strive to reappropriate the capacity to name through the elaboration of codes and languages designed to define reality, in the twofold sense of constituting it symbolically and of regaining it, thereby escaping from the predominant forms of representation.

The movements have waged a critical struggle against the representation of the world served up by the dominant models, denying their claim to uniqueness and challenging the symbolic constitution of politics and culture; they have refused the predominant communicative codes and they have replaced them with sounds, idioms, recognition signals that break the language of technical rationality (Melucci 1985). Through social practices that are not solely the object of thought but lived experiences, movements have introduced a breakdown in the norms of perception and production of reality, from which different ways of addressing things and of imagining them, new languages and new scriptures struggle to emerge. They have prompted the redefinition of Nature itself in her rhythms, spaces, odours, and colours, beyond those inscribed in the hegemonic codes of scientific and technological discourse.

The transformation of codes is equally substantial when they stress the spiritual dimension of human experience, when they attempt to modify the symbolic relationship with the world – which is not what one is induced to perceive by the most diffuse criteria of codification. Hence derives the impossibility of sharing the dominant social language, and the destructuring of meaning which opens up the way for other modalities of experience beyond instrumental rationality and which affects the forms of knowledge themselves. One finds an endeavour to subvert shared criteria of codification, the obligatory set of signs with which the social order seeks to impose a reality which is solely its own. Though easily incorporated into the market, these languages remain a powerful challenge to the functional neutrality of the dominant discourse. Contrary to the case of relationships based on material strength or physical power, in which those in possession of the greatest share of resources hold sway, here the relationship hinges on the symbolic capacity to reverse meaning to demonstrate the arbitrariness of the power and its domination. And it is enough to structure reality using different words for the power monopoly over reality to crumble.

In the neutralized scenario of signs, with the fragmentation of identities and the breakdown of every unitary symbolic principle, individuals and groups are propelled into an anguished state of uncertainty. Contemporary movements resist the destructuring of the symbolic universe, and *symbolic reintegration* is one of the terrains on which they pit themselves most forcefully against established power. In complex societies the incoherent flux of the signs entail the legitimation of a rationality which feeds upon itself and upon its operational results. We witness the risk of a radical draining and deprivation of the individual's symbolic life, the loss of those symbolic functions which govern the social expression of desire and imagination and their integration into the social texture. In movements, symbolic reintegration patterns itself as an attempt to heal this breach, and the adoption of alternative codes constitutes a first step towards that end. If it is possible to remake the world by adopting new ways to nominate, perceive, and imagine reality, it may once again become possible – at a remove from the imperatives of operational functionality – to recompose the various parts of the self. This objective is pursued by contemporary movements in a variety of ways but always by disputing the very meaning of social production. Movements orient their strategies towards the recovery of the dimensions of symbolic existence eradicated by the operational model of technical rationality: Resistance to instrumental investment and to deferred satisfaction of relational and affective needs, the recovery of fantasy and play, the symbolic relationship between humankind and the environment, the revival of the mind/body relationship.

The movements' challenge is also evident in the *non-negotiability* of their goals. Their marked indifference towards the political does not stem from an inability to formulate demands designed to pass through the filters of the system, but rather from a shift in the arena of confrontation. The struggle no longer centres on the definition of the terms of exchange acceptable to both parties as in every political strategy. They are, instead, simply ignored and the action is carried forward elsewhere: at the level not of real efficacy but of symbolic efficacy. The radical nature of the challenge derives precisely from that which evades negotiation; not because collective actors refuse to compromise with power – indeed, they have shown proneness to a reckless pragmatism in their dealings with the political institutions – but inasmuch as they address forms of symbolic relation non reducible to any instrumental logic.

Finally, movements' action is geared primarily to *offering*. To offer instead of asking represents another breakdown in the rules of the game, another challenge whose impact is incomprehensible on the basis of strategic and instrumental logic but perfectly justifies itself on the basis of symbolic logic. At the symbolic level, domination is accomplished when the possibility of the reversion of the gift into the countergift is successfully precluded (Baudrillard 1993). It is the unilateral power of giving, of generating and providing cultural models which constantly reproduces the predominance of the apparatuses in complex societies. Movements attempt to extricate themselves from this asymmetry, with the offer of alternative models which the system itself cannot replicate, because they are non-negotiable. Hence, movements tend to lose their claimant thrust and develop forms of action aimed at the autonomous and gratuitous production of cultural models not governed by cost-benefit calculations but by symbolic waste.

The significance assumed by *forms* of action in movements gives us a better understanding of the decline in the importance of general ideological messages. Hence derives the transfer of conflict potentiality from contents to the modalities of symbolic relation, or to the medium. The means of communication is not the support for the content communicated; on the contrary, it is the latter which serves to support the means. And it is here, at the level of codes, that movements distance themselves most radically from the prevailing norms. The strategic use of the media is to be found in all contemporary movements: music, bodily signals and clothing, radios and images, theatre and art, communication networks and vitual reality are all media through which the mental, sensory, and emotional perception of the world is altered and tries to evade the codification imposed by mass society. These media, of course, can be easily incorporated into the market, but new forms tend to reappear elsewhere with other actors involved.

19

Forms of action

Revolutions

In this chapter I shall focus on several forms of collective action which are frequently associated with the study of social movements. The discussion of these forms should demonstrate the utility of an analytical approach to collective action which is able to differentiate levels and meanings, particularly when complex historical phenomena are considered.

Let us start with revolutions. After many classic studies (Johnson 1964; Brinton 1965; Hobsbawm 1962), writing and discussion on revolution still continues steadily. No other topic is so resistant to analysis as revolution. Apart from the affective investments and political implications that characterize it, the difficulty stems from the fact that revolution is always a global phenomenon whose analytical meanings are extremely difficult to unravel.

Evidence of this situation is provided by the wide variety of the definitions given to the term, and the equally wide variety of misunderstandings that continue to surround it (for a general introduction, see Aya 1990; De Fronzo 1991). Only twenty years ago, one of the most systematic bibliographies on the topic, published in 1976 (Blackey 1976), comprised about 2,400 titles, and since then the list has considerably increased in length (see the most recent studies by Tilly 1993 and Skockpol 1994). Nevertheless, as before the confusion of languages reigns supreme. The object of identification or rejection, a goal pursued or an event expected, a phenomenon to be observed and analysed, revolution still retains the glamour of a controversial myth and still prompts people to take sides.

It is difficult to find a coherent definition of revolution in the studies on the subject. One need to look no further than the many sociological theories and analyses of the phenomenon (Paige 1975; Foran 1994; Taylor 1988; Wood 1991) to realize that the opinions vary considerably.

Heterogeneous phenomena are lumped together under the same heading 'revolution'; at times the category is extended to include every form of social revolt, and again sometimes restricted to the processes of violent institutional change. The difficulty seems to stem from the fact that the concept of revolution is not an analytic notion, but an historical-descriptive one; this is the sense, at least, in which it is used in most studies concerned with the subject (as in the ongoing debate on French Revolution: see Hunt 1984; Chartier 1991; Ozouf 1988; Sewell 1985, 1990; Skockpol 1985). Accordingly, the term subsumes under its scope the whole breadth of the empirical phenomena encountered and loses all analytical consistency. I shall give only one classic example to show the uselessness of such definitions in the face of the multitude of empirical phenomena that they must take into account. Johnson (1964) defines revolution as change brought about by the use of violence in the government and/or the regime and/or the society. But this is to extend the concept of revolution to embrace virtually all phenomena of violent political and social change.

It seems to me that the only solution is to attribute an analytical content to revolution which fixes the minimal conditions for the phenomenon to exist. The presence of such conditions would entitle us to talk of revolution, in the analytical sense. On the empirical level, the phenomena that the actors or adversaries call revolutions should then be disassembled into their multiple analytical components, thereby highlighting the differences between, and often the incomparability of, specific empirical phenomena. A definition which respects these methodological criteria should be able to establish no more than the minimal analytical conditions for the existence of the phenomenon. The one proposed years ago by Tanter and Midlarsky (1967), for example, seems to fulfil this requirement. The authors contend that revolution occurs when a social group illegally and/or with force attacks the political system in order to occupy the roles in the political power structure.

This is an apparently reductive definition of the phenomenon, which certainly does not reflect the expectations and images of global change which often accompany revolutionary phenomena in the ideology of the actors involved, or in the readily available plethora of *post factum* justifications. None the less, it seems methodologically correct, for two reasons. First of all, by fixing minimal conditions it enables one to graduate the phenomenon, by progressively introducing further levels of analysis and differentiations not on an empirical basis but according to the analytical complexity of the phenomenon. It is thus possible to talk of processes which only affect the political system, and of others which relate rather to other levels of the social structure. Secondly, the definition emphasizes the essentially *political* nature of revolution. The specific feature differentiating revolution from other forms of collective action is that it necessarily, although not exclusively, affects the political system and the structure of political power.

On the basis of an approach of this kind criteria can be used to distinguish among the *various types of revolution*. It is possible to identify several degrees of intensity (change of political personnel, change in the rules of the political system, and so forth); the different ways in which power may be seized (military *coup d'état*, war, revolutionary party, and the like); the different ways in which power may be lost (for example, a split in the elite, abdication, or a collapse).

Another type of analysis concerns the diachronic *process of revolution*. There certainly exist empirical regularities which enable identification of certain phases typical of revolutionary processes. Concepts like the transfer of loyalty by the intellectuals, polarization, precipitating factor, phase of celebration and collective enthusiasm, doctrinaire phase, and the formation of sects, seem to identify significant stages in the revolutionary process. They fix the sequence of the phenomenon but they tell us nothing about its sociological meaning. Once again, it is on the analytical level that these categories can be used and the passage from a description of historical phases to a succession of systems of social relations, defined analytically, accomplished.

A final level of analysis concerns the *structural conditions of revolution*. It seems to me that the concepts best suited to this purpose are those of *revolutionary situation* and *revolutionary potential*. The first indicates a certain state of the structure – that is, a particular combination of the specific conditions characterizing the different levels of the social structure. The revolutionary situation defines a state of *emergency* in the system. This situation develops when the variability margins of the various action systems which constitute the structure all shift towards their negative values: the predominance of aspects of domination over those of innovation in class relationships, the closure and rigidity of the political system, crisis and breakdown in the social organization. The simultaneous occurrence of these conditions – which in historically specific contexts may take different forms – seems to define the concept of revolutionary situation.

Closely connected here is the notion of revolutionary potential. This establishes a relationship between the conditions and the forces which foster the appearance of action seeking to bring down the system and the conditions and forces which oppose it. Given a certain state of the structure, it is possible to specify this relationship, which varies from one concrete situation to another. The category of revolutionary potential is the link between a structural analysis and an analysis of the *conjuncture*.

Among the recent contributions to the topic, Theda Skocpol (1976, 1994) has certainly made the most systematic effort to date to define the revolutionary phenomenon. She accomplishes this on the basis of painstaking comparison between the great revolutions of modern history (primarily the French, the Russian, and the Chinese), which she considers in terms of their common character as 'social revolutions'. Despite their diversity, these phenomena analysed by Skocpol exhibit a number of shared features and lend themselves to reduction to sociological categories without overcontrivance. The theoretical principles on which Skocpol has based her analysis are those of a perspective in which class conflicts, the state, and the imperialist relationships at the international level play an essential role.

What, then, is a 'social revolution'? It is a rapid and radical transformation of a state society and its class structure, which is accompanied and supported by class mobilizations. Social revolutions imply two distinctive characteristics: a structural change in society which affects the class structure and a coincidence of political change and social change. Based on this definition, Skocpol identifies a relatively rare historical type, of which the three cases mentioned above are the most significant examples. Once defined, social revolutions can be linked to a set of shared structural causes, which the author identifies as follows: the crisis of an autocratic state, internally weakened due to its relationships with parasitical agrarian classes and exposed to external pressures (war) which hasten its collapse; the existence of agrarian class structures which create the conditions for peasant insurrections; the possibility of building a new state from revolutionary resources of organization, leadership, and ideology. The outcome of social revolution is apparently the formation of a state characterized by a powerful, dynamic, and centralized bureaucracy which is no longer distinct from society but wholly absorbs it.

Skocpol's definition of her subject is certainly useful on a historical-comparative level, but it appears to do little to advance theoretical reflection on the concept of revolution itself. Indeed, specification of the entity 'social revolution', to which Skocpol restricts her analysis, still contains the term revolution and only serves to postpone the problem. To be sure, the definition of an historically specific type, characterized by change in the class structure and by change in the setup of the state, undoubtedly helps to unclutter the range of phenomena to be classified; but it tells us nothing about the analytical value of the concept of revolution.

Nevertheless, Skocpol's analysis highlights two crucial elements for critical examination, although she herself does not seem to have fully grasped their significance (or they might simply lie outside the range of an historical-comparative approach to which she subscribes). Revolution is an historically burdened concept which is inextricably bound up with its constitutive link with modern transformations in society and thought. Industrialization as an endeavour to transform and dominate Nature was accomplished through the wilful effort of politics, where the weakness of the elites and the disintegration of society made other methods for channelling collective resources impossible. In the modern age the order of politics and the state organize social energies where they are unable to raise their voice autonomously.

We are immediately brought to the second point in Skocpol's work: the unbreakable nexus conjoining revolution and the state structure. Without the clash with a state apparatus unable to ensure the integration of society except through a resort to force, and without the concentration of collective energies in the building of the 'new' state, revolution is a concept bereft of meaning.

I believe that these two propositions, for which Skocpol's rich and detailed analysis provides substantial empirical support, enable us to advance theoretical reflection on the analytical significance of the concept of revolution. From the sociological point of view, in fact, the theoretical leap consists in the passage from an historical typology to an identification of the analytical components of collective action. In this sense, revolution takes the form of the *conjunctural coincidence* of diverse and analytically distinct phenomena. Historically, it is possible to identify the causes of this coincidence (as Skocpol does for the cases she analyses), and it is also possible to describe the types of social structure most likely to bring it about. Yet the nature of the phenomenon must be recognized as analytically multiple. In it converge, conjuncturally, heterogeneous elements (tied to class relationships, to the political structure, to problems of the integration and functioning of society, to the dynamics of collective behaviour).

Hence, in my view, the only possible analytical definition of revolution is one which sets the minimum conditions for the phenomenon to be recognized as being such, and which subsequently makes it possible to break down that phenomenon into diverse analytical meanings. The relationship with the political system and the state structures seems, from this point of view, to be the unifying criterion: I propose to define it analytically, as in the foregoing, as an action prosecuted with the use of force in order to occupy the existing roles in the political power structure of a state. This seems to me to be the essential minimum requisite for any definition of a revolution. By establishing the minimal requirement to be met, such a definition stresses the preeminently political nature of the revolutionary phenomenon and leaves open the possibility for more complex typologies comprising also other analytical levels. Skocpol's 'social revolutions', for example, are broader phenomena that certainly include action aiming at violent changes in the power structure of the state, but also comprise action aimed at deep transformations in class relationships.

Revolution as a sociological concept may thus become a well-circum-scribed instrument, one utilizable for cases involving certain societies and certain historical conjunctures. Analyses such as those conducted by Tilly (1984, 1993) in precisely this manner shed substantial light on the factors that bring about or accelerate the coincidence of elements that can lead to a revolutionary situation. One passes from the description of global phenomena to the singling out of individual processes defined analytically with reference to a theory of collective action (mobilization, availability of resources, opportunity, and so forth). A self-restrained utilization of the concept of revolution, however, is only possible if one moves from the historical-comparative level to an analytical definition of the concept: I am proposing to transform the concept of revolution into an analytical tool to be applied to historical cases. One can speak of a revolution once the minimal conditions I have posed are fulfilled (violent changes in the power structure of the state), and one can hence detect other elements which possibly converge in the same historical event: behaviours that occur 'below' the political level (for example crowd behaviour) and forms of action that reach social relationships beyond politics (such as action aimed at producing changes in the structure of social production).

Having briefly explored this line of inquiry, we may now address the question of what is left of the concept of revolution in highly complex and differentiated societies, as they progressively move further away from the model of industrial society. Accumulating knowledge about the complexity of power and of integration mechanisms, about the ambivalent role of the mass parties, and about the risks of manipulated participation will deprive the concept of revolution of much of its evocative allure. In societies in which power becomes fragmented and diffuse, and in which the apparatuses of control and regulation extend their scope to reach down to the everyday life level, the historicist idea of revolution is fading. Social changes are not the result of necessary laws, which a vehicle of an elite of professional revolutionaries interprets and embodies through its action. On the contrary, they stem from a variable combination of factors internal and external to the system in question: more specifically, they spring from the combined workings of the internal and international political system, which in complex systems increasingly assumes the role of the regulator and accelerator of conflict. The concrete forms assumed by the change depend more and more on the modes of political mediation and regulation.

The need for systems to continuously adjust to changes in the environment and to the exigencies of internal equilibrium means that change today is a phenomenon of crucial importance for the reproduction of the system. Yet, precisely for this reason, the pace and frequency of change highlight its specific, circumscribed, non-transposable nature. The problem, therefore, is to define the goals of possible transformation, delimit analytically the system or systems which the transformation can affect, and project the effects on other systems.

Viewed in these terms, Skocpol's analysis is at once useful and unsatisfactory. Its usefulness, in my view, lies in its demonstration that 'social revolutions' are an historical phenomenon confined to specific conditions of societal evolution of modernity. At the same time, however, the contribution to conceptual clarification of a research of such magnitude remains markedly inadequate: the crucial issue – namely, how the concept of revolution can still be useful for sociological analysis – is left entirely unresolved.

My purpose here has been not to provide an answer to this question, but to merely forward some suggestions as regards the issue of method. Sociology can productively employ the notion of revolution only if it shifts from a historical-descriptive account to an analytical concept which identifies a particular form of collective action. I have suggested that framing the concept of revolution in terms of political change may fashion it into an instrument with which diverse historical phenomena can be usefully interpreted. Such an approach, however, would be at odds with the tradition of study that has treated revolution as a global historical entity, if not an ideological option altogether. The approach I propose considers the processes of collective action as a result from the interaction of diverse analytical components. The theoretical task thus becomes that of identifying these components and explaining how they aggregate in a specific conjuncture in a given historical society.

Violence in collective action

Violence as a social phenomenon is another recurrent theme in the study of collective action. Definitions of collective violence agree on certain features of this type of behaviour. Violence is the aberrant use of force resorted to in order to threaten or damage an adversary, usually so as to force that adversary to act against his/her own will. This, however, is only the phenomenological aspect of violent action. Its analytical significance varies considerably according to the system of relations of which it is part. To say that the United States is the industrialized country with the highest rate of homicides involving firearms does not clarify the quality and meaning of this violence. Violence is always a 'sign' of more complex social phenomena. The functionalist tradition has listed a number of social functions of violence. It is a phenomenon which expresses the collective problems of the most oppressed groups; it is an alarm signal as well as a catalyst which causes the tensions present in a society to explode.

But by talking of functions we have already embarked on an analysis which assumes that violence is action endowed with meaning. For many years, the legacy of 'crowd psychology' (see Moscovici 1981) fostered the growth of an attitude within the social sciences which reduced violence to irrational and distorted behaviour only so as to buttress the dominant ideology and its repressive acts. Historical and sociological studies of collective violence (Tilly, 1970, 1986; Tilly *et al.* 1975; Maffesoli 1979; Rule 1988; Aya 1990; Della Porta 1992b) have made a definitive break with this model, showing that crowd behaviour and collective violence possess their own rationality and obey a logic which can be captured by an analysis of social relationships.

Analysis of rioting in the black North American ghettos has shown that collective violence is not the random and confused behaviour that the official ideology and the apparatuses of repression would have us believe. Rather, it operates within set restrictions, which are and must be internally respected. There is a selectivity of goals which makes manifest the type of problems underlying the action, as well as the motives of its participants. Actors, in truth, shape their action according to the means available to them: violence is only one of these means and is used in specific situations. There are collective rituals and a set of group relations among those participating in episodes of violence. Hence violence, like other forms of collective action, is subject to norms, involves the calculation of advantages and risks, and is geared towards meaningful goals.

Having acknowledged the sensibility of violent action, typologies of violence do not seem to serve any good purpose beyond the mere descriptive function: they tend to annul the complex of analytical meanings conveyed by the action. The only useful classifications possible, it seems, are historical ones which record the changes over time in forms of violence, or those which refer to the predominant type of force used. Tilly (1970) has proposed a classical distinction between primitive violence, reactionary violence, and modern violence. The first is the violence employed by rival communitarian groups in the social structure of precapitalist Europe. The second is the violence with which communitarian groups resisted the loss of traditional rights and the new demands imposed by the emerging national state. The third is the violence which characterizes the social and political conflicts of urban-industrial capitalism. As regards the type of force invoked, the distinction proposed by several authors between instrumental force, symbolic force, and expressive force seems also useful. Three different kinds of violence derive from the prevalence of one or another dimension. Instrumental force is directly oriented towards the achievement of a specific purpose; symbolic force is used to convey a message, to assert the social position of those who resort to it; and expressive force manifests the actor's deep-seated needs and/or situation of crisis.

The most interesting problem, however, is providing an explanation for the genesis of violence, and specifying the conditions under which violent behaviour rather than any other form of collective action appears. The reply that attributes the phenomenon to a subculture of violence – violence as a marginal offshoot from the parent culture, a sort of transmitted cultural pathology – strikes me as decidedly unsatisfactory. Accounts of this sort risk to repeat, in contemporary guise and using the language of the social sciences, the old statements of a pessimistic doctrine of human nature and its innate dispositions. The cultural climate in which individuals are raised can certainly account for a predisposition to violent behaviour at the individual level, but the extension of such a model to collective violence cannot survive the scrutiny of empirical observation.

Historical analysis of collective violence shows, in fact, that to an overwhelmingly large extent it constitutes a response to the violence by the power. Violence in social conflicts is almost always first resorted to by the agents of social control. The obstinate defence of traditional rights, or the voicing of urgent demands, often provokes violent action by the repressive apparatuses. From this point of view, violence can be rightly called a technique of social control and an instrument to preserve the existing forms of power. Not incidentally recourse to violence by elites is often a decisive factor in collective explosions.

Viewed in these terms, popular violence is a self-fulfilling prophecy. Power usually justifies its actions as measures to prevent the situation from degenerating further and thus creates the conditions for a violent response. When examining concrete episodes of collective violence, the analyst must concentrate on the features and behaviour of the agents of social control as well as on violent action by protesters. A great number of situations comprise the self-fulfilling prophecy exhibited by these examples. The aggressive presence, the techniques of intervention, and the preventive or demonstrative violence of the repressive agencies of the state are often the cause of the violent response characteristic of so many episodes of collective action.

However, violence is not a necessary attribute of collective action. It only arises under certain sociologically discernable conditions. The most convincing definition, I believe, is the one that treats violence as the point at which a crisis and a conflict meet. The presence of a conflict is expressed in the appearance of social demands directed principally at the political system. These demands only take violent form *vis-à-vis* a rigid closure of the channels transmitting demand and of a diffuse breakdown in the mechanisms of social organization. It is the crisis, the clash with an order at once blocked and inefficient, that gives collective action its violent character. This means that violence as such cannot be taken to indicate the presence of antagonist action and that, conversely, collective action with deep conflictual orientation is not necessarily violent.

Violence is born of the inability of the political system to absorb the demands created by change, of its rigidity, and of the incoherence of its functioning. The closure of the channels of political communication, the disequilibrium or inefficiency of the principal functional subsystems, and possibly also a grave economic crisis and the use of repressive measures to control demand explain the violent character of social protest. Violence alone is not a sufficient condition to account for the analytical features of a collective action, for its antagonist nature for instance. There are two reasons for this: First, because there are forms of violence which are clearly not based on social antagonism, but on simple reaction to the crisis of social order; second, because antagonist action also assumes non-violent forms, according to the features of the political system or of the social organization.

The 'issueless riots' described by Gary Marx (1972) are forms of 'expressive' violence which appear when social controls slacken (public holidays, absence of the police, and the like). In this case, violence is a limited and temporary response to a breakdown in the social order – a breakdown which in the case of issueless riots is circumscribed and short-lived, but still offers insights into the general process. One may also advance a hypothesis concerning the structural significance of these random explosions of collective violence (to which one might add the violence associated with sports). The presence of structural antagonism and the need to control it at all levels of society require the dominant system to make constant investment in the direction of integration/repression, although this will never suffice to contain the conflict entirely. Marginal outbreaks occur which never reach collective dimensions and which accumulate as latent tensions in some corner or other of the system. The slackening of social control in situations of collective enthusiasm or in the absence of repressive agents causes repressed and marginalized tensions to explode.

On the other hand, antagonist action is not necessarily violent in form, at least during certain of its phases. If the margins of tolerance – of the political system in particular – are sufficiently elastic, antagonist action (that is, the advancing of demands which go beyond the system's compatibility limits) may occur without resorting to violence. Although collective action already lies outside the limits fixed by the system, it is tolerated. It is evident, however, that the closer the conflict advances towards the vital nodes of the system, the more probable repressive reaction and recourse to violence become, if political channels are not able to transform collective pressures into reformist policies and democratization of decision-making.

Crowd behaviour

Crowds, insofar as they are distinct from more formally structured movements, also present ample material for reflection on the way individuals come to constitute a collective reality (see Moscovici 1981; Oliver 1989). Studies on crowds, for their part, represent one of the best examples of the confusion between the empirical unity of the phenomenon itself and the plurality of analytical dimensions that can be discerned within that apparent unity. An initial precaution therefore concerns the necessity of distinguishing the empirical crowd from the analytical concept of aggregation. The latter implies atomized relations between individuals who act in a contiguity of space and time without being bound by mutual ties of solidarity. While in crowds this analytic dimension is certainly predominant, the phenomena, nevertheless, cannot be reduced to it at the expense of the others: here again we have a plurality of meanings and orientations that require elucidation.

According to the current literature, the traits characteristic of crowds are: *imitation*, the dominant role of *number* (in the concept of 'critical mass', for example), and *spatio-temporal* aspects (for instance, in a riot or in a panic, where the simultaneous concentration of people in the same place is critical). The facilitating factors might be described as a *crisis* and *necessity*. In a crisis situation, unexpected systemic countereffects tend to encourage stimulus-response behaviour; chance may foster the spatio-temporal contiguity of many individuals; and finally climatic or natural factors, such as earthquakes or floods, may well provoke collective effects.

However, were we to assume that crowds are nothing but mere aggregates it would be difficult to grasp their profound ambivalence. Bearing in mind the fact that crowds are composite phenomena, the experience of the crowd can be located somewhere on the axis between *attraction* and *threat*. On the one hand, the individuals are attracted to the crowd: it permits *the feeling of being part of something* without *taking part*. Within a crowd individuals can participate without paying the price of participation – they can 'lose

themselves in the crowd'. But what do we feel part of when we lose ourselves in the crowd? Can we properly speak of a crowd's collective identity?

The crowd offers individuals the chance to take part in a 'collective' that
remains undefined, that *leaves the options open*. By definition, the more
structured entities are also more closed – they limit the range of possibilities. The crowd offers an open field in which the individual may project her
or his expectations, desires, dreams. In this respect, the crowd can be seen
as the most elementary example of a potential collective, and therefore one
in which individuals already interact in the production of meanings and
orientation.

On the other hand, though, the crowd is seen as a threat. In a crowd, individuals sense the danger of losing themselves, they see their individual
differences eradicated, they cease to exist as unique and singular individuals. Number and concentration in space are determining factors in feeding
the perception of that danger, as ethological studies on territory have
demonstrated. To the perception of this threat the individuals respond by
introversion, withdrawal, or aggression. Along this axis the crowd moves
towards the maximum destructuring of the 'collective.'

This ambivalence is always present in crowd phenomena and is
suspended in a delicate balance which is easily upset. The characteristic
eruptions of crowds should be understood in terms of a *loss of equilibrium*.
A temporary shift of balance taking away from the side of the threat jerks
the crowd towards jubilant and unrestrained exploration of the possible,
that is, towards the feast. If, however, the balance is tipped taking away
from side of the attraction, panic and violence express its atomized and
reactive dimension.

Individual involvement in the crowd, then, is held in this unstable equilibrium between attraction and threat, and can readily shift from one pole
to the other. The eruption of ambivalence sends collective action off
towards its extremes, towards those limit situations that can only be of an
exceptional and short-lasting nature. In ordinary crowd situations, it is as
though the two poles hold each other mutually under control, keeping the
collective action within the bounds of normal everyday life.

A typical example of crowd behaviour characteristic of complex societies
is given when individual and collective actors face a situation of emergency.
I will address this issue by combining a sociological perspective on the
structure of collective processes in this kind of situation with a brief
examination of individual emotional experience – an approach which I
believe will be of interest because of the light it sheds on the actual experience of individuals when caught up in an emergency.

An emergency is a social situation produced by an event or series of events whose principal features are their *unpredictability* and *rapidity*, and the *concentration* in time and space of the stressful event; these describe three morphological characteristics of an emergency situation. From the point of view of social relations, an emergency is a situation in which habitual modes of conducting relationships, of solving problems, and of handling everyday situations are suspended. Such a *state of suspension*, however, should be more precisely specified. For this purpose, the functionalist tradition on collective behaviour has introduced a set of distinctions which may prove useful. The level at which the suspension of habitual relations comes about creates a diversity – analytical more than empirical – of types of emergency. A first level is the suspension of the habitual means whereby problems are solved. For example, a minor emergency in the urban environment arises when all the traffic lights break down; such an event would be a dysfunction at the level of means which creates a micro-emergency in the city traffic. A blackout is a broader suspension of functionality of means, and it already introduces a different level, namely a suspension of rules (during blackouts there is an increase in criminal activities, but also the emergence of new forms of solidarity). Even finer distinctions can be drawn, but as a first approximation we may distinguish three levels: the level of means, the level of norms or shared rules, and the level of values or general orientations.

Matters differ according to whether the emergency situation – connoted by unpredictability, rapidity, and the concentration of the stressful event – suspends or prevents from functioning the habitual means employed in order to solve problems, the customary rules which govern problem-solving, or the value criteria usually applied in such activity. This distinction is of course an analytical one, since concrete situations may and also do arise which involve one or more of these levels. However, it suggests a hierarchy of emergency situations, which are not all identical because their meaning changes for the subjects involved and the response may vary according to the type of social relations involved.

This distinction also helps to shed light on the difference between *risk* and *uncertainty*. Risk is usually a situation of uncertainty at the level of means, that is to say, a situation in which the solution is usually highly predictable. To return to the example of the traffic lights, the signals are still obeyed even if their particular medium breaks down, and this is all that happens: the traffic lights stop working and the traffic wardens take over to direct the traffic. The highway code is not called into question or suspended. If, however, drivers refuse to stop at red lights even when the traffic light system is in operation, we have at hand another kind of emergency. If, out of madness or rebelliousness, drivers no longer respected traffic lights, the level involved would be evidently different, and the type of action required and the type of effect anticipated would change considerably. A state of uncertainty arises when conventional strategies are unable to solve the problem. This is, in my definition, a true situation of uncertainty.

When traffic lights break down the risk of accidents increases, but there is, properly speaking, no uncertainty. At the level of means, as the economists put it, one can refer to frequencies as an operational criterion with which to render the risk amenable to empirical inquiry and quantification. But the problem is qualitatively different when the conventional strategies or the habitual instruments cannot be used, so that the true state of uncertainty arises when something is called into question at the level of rules and values.

Complexity increases the interdependence of functional levels of social life, particularly in urban contexts, and exposes them to greater vulnerability. Many of the problems of everyday life in complex societies often stem from the absence of an appropriate culture of user-friendly means, from a lack of risk-reducing facilities as a fundamental level of a more humane civil society. However, a true situation of uncertainty arises when there is no longer agreement, or simply when there is a suspension of the rules, and even more so when value orientations, ends, collective goals are suspended. Thus, uncertainty is truly uncertainty because what happens from the point of view of the subjects involved is that in the new situation created by the event, uncertainty affects their very identity. True uncertainty arises when we no longer know who we were before the event because it has triggered something of crucial importance.

All the rest remains in the order of risk; thereafter the problem is whether the community is equipped or not to cope with risk. Many of the differencies among societies in coping with emergency relate to the treatment of risk as a component of predictability, as a deep-rooted cultural component. One needs only to compare the North American or Northern European with the Latin cultures, in order to realize the far greater significance of the culture of risk, as the capacity to predict, prevent, and to organize beforehand, in the 'cold' cultures, and understand how much more substantial it is in situations of great risk.

But it seems to me that the problem of uncertainty goes somewhat further. The 'hard' situation occurs when the event suspends rules, values, and goals and thereby affects the capacity of individuals, groups, and collectivities to respond with certitude to the question of identity; that is, to the question of who we were before, and who we are now. In such a situation the differences among cultures that I have just mentioned are probably reversed. The flexibility and adaptability of Latin cultures become invaluable resources in accommodating to the new situation, whereas more rigid cultures experience greater difficulties in coping with true uncertainty.

The suspension of rules and values becomes even more evident if we examine the emotional side of the situation. What is the experience of individuals involved in an emergency situation which affects norms and values? Their situation is profoundly ambivalent because – apart from the amount of shock produced by the rapidity and unpredictability by the event – it is accompanied by fear, anxiety over what has been lost or left behind and over the new situation created by the emergency. However, it is also connoted, in some way, by positive attitudes which relate to curiosity, to hope, to a will to renewal now that everything that existed previously no longer does so. Therefore the subjects involved display a profound ambivalence, especially when they have recovered from the immediate shock. It is as if they have suffered a blow of bereavement but must now reconstruct their world. There is always an ambivalence and, in certain cases, a feeling of relief that the old order has been destroyed or overthrown by the event. Consequently, emergency emphasizes the negative and destructive elements but also this curiosity, hope, and potential for renewal, which varies according to the circumstances, the type of event and its gravity, and so on.

It should therefore be stressed that there are always different outcomes to the collective processes that follow an emergency. In fact, disintegration occurs so that certain groups in the community assimilate the negative, destructive, and depressive component of the event and are thus confined within a state of shock, impotence, and inertia, as in the most extreme cases of subordination or cultural death. The analogy as regards the collective aspect of this process of inertia and total subjugation is with the Nazi extermination camps, or those extreme cases of colonialism in which there occurs something akin to the cultural death of the subordinate group, a sort of collective psychosis, a collective catatonia, as it were, but at the cultural level and in the group, not in individuals as pathological cases. This, however, is only the extreme outcome.

In addition, there is the marginal deviant outcome, reactive in the sense of breakdown, such as looting, violence, rape – all phenomena that have been closely studied for example after blackouts or earthquakes. But these are also extremely interesting cases of the coexistence of the two aspects because, simultaneously, destructuring is accompanied by restructuring and the revival of collective energies through the formation of the new identities and of new collective solidarities which, very frequently, are created and made manifest after the event.

How do these two outcomes function, and what determines the prevalence of one over the other? There is no general answer, but a number of conditions can be indicated which help or hinder the outcome of restructuring, rather than destructuring, or the capacity to respond positively instead of retreating into passivity. There are three of such conditions:

(i) The first refers to the quality of the preexistent institutional bonds. What preexistent representation channels and preexistent relations and forms of authority survive, and what credibility or legitimacy did they previously enjoy? What is left of the old order that is still reliable and credible? Consequently, the amount of reliability and credibility that had previously been produced is extremely important. The existence of a previous emergency culture is very important in this respect: an authority which has already demonstrated its credibility when it has foreseen, prearranged, and proved itself able to control emergencies in the past, remains credible even when everything else collapses. This is a problem of the quantity, but also and especially of the quality, of the previous institutional bonds.

(ii) The second condition is very important and has been much studied by analysts of mobilization processes in social movements. It concerns the existence of informal networks, of everyday solidarity circles. This finding can be applied more generally to social mobilization processes in any circumstance or situation. An extremely important factor from this point of view is therefore the density and vigor of the hidden networks of belonging, of preexisting solidarity networks, the associative experiences that individuals have accumulated. This applies even more forcefully to the autonomy of communities in an emergency situation. Indeed, the mobilization resources present are those which can be directed towards new goals because they were already in place: if they did not exist, the situation could not have created them. The situation restructures them, it redirects and reshapes them. It produces new ones out of those that already exist, but it does not invent them *ex novo*. Thus informal networks, hidden resources, all the heritage present in the community determines the type of response to an emergenecy.

(iii) The third condition is one that is difficult to label; I will call it the presence of space to listen, the presence of civic listening spaces. The point is this: if the true emergency situation is not one of risk but one in which previous norms and/or values are suspended, then the situation is one of uncertainty and no one knows what is to be done. If those concerned already knew what to do, then the situation would not be a real emergency but a risk which is already being responded to. Hence, the greater the degree of preparation, the less the amount of real emergency. And a true emergency is a situation in which nobody now or ever before knows what to do. Therefore it is extremely important in these circumstances that the community, the group, or the authorities that intervene, should be able to listen at various levels. Listening means really paying attention to what is taking place, truly listening to what people need, truly learning from what people have begun to do. This entails looking, taking account, truly acknowledging the solutions that people have already invented in emergency situations.

These three conditions determine whether and to what extent restructuring processes predominate in an emergency situation, and vice versa. My final point relates to a dilemma often posited when dealing with emergency situations: autonomy or authority. Which one is more important and which one is to be favoured in order to increase a positive outcome of the emergency? I believe this is a false dilemma and that both these headings subsume a certain potential for restructuring created by the emergency situation, which has been proved in studies of collective phenomena. I shall only mention three processes which account for people's autonomous capacity to restructure social life in emergencies: There are forms of self-organization; the creation of new rites and new languages; and, finally – although seemingly paradoxical, given that we usually talk about tragic, dramatic, and indeed catastrophic events – there is always an element of celebration, which is mourning, but also liberation, among those who have survived the danger. All these great events generate expressive forms of celebration. For example, during the famous New York blackout dozens of bands and theatre groups formed in the course of that week's collective street life. The earthquake in Friuli led to the formation of a number of theatre, dance, and visual arts groups. This is an impressive aspect because it is not merely a marginal or residual effect of these kinds of event: from a sociological point of view it is interesting to note this odd coincidence whereby tragic events also generate something new and creative.

As regards the option of authority, here, too, there are three elements that may be significant – again as potentials for innovation created by the catastrophic event. The first is that there is almost always an upwards shift in the level of invested authority. That is to say, when norms and values are called into question, it is rare for the authority which previously enjoyed legitimacy to be directly called upon to solve the problem. Smelser has stressed this point in his classic work, namely, that legitimation shifts to a higher level: if the problem is local it shifts to the national state, if the problem is national it is assigned to the international community in the people's hopes and expectations. This latter aspect is striking, because it is not merely a matter of delegation to a higher authority; through the catastrophic event the possibility and the awareness of wider belonging gain ground, a new social perspective opens up. The other two aspects are more overtly institutional. There is the potential formation of a new leadership which usually grows out of the informal networks already in operation; and there is a redistribution among the old leaderships that have already proved themselves worthy by being ready for a possible catastrophe, reliable, and so on.

In short, the situation of pronounced ambivalence which I have described as regards the individual subject also applies to the collective, to the group. And whether the outcomes take one form or another depends on certain conditions which help or hinder destructuring or restructuring processes to come about.

Direct action and conflictual participation

The term 'direct action' encompasses numerous forms of collective action whose common analytical features are not always easy to identify (see Carter 1973; Sharp 1973; Favre 1990). Direct action includes marches, demonstrations, petitions, sit-ins, picket lines, boycotts, wildcat strikes, refusal to pay taxes, draft evasion, acts of civil disobedience, and other such phenomena of noninstitutional confrontation with authorities.

What is common to all these forms of collective action? Is there any basis for using the notion of direct action? I believe that it is possible to fix a set of essential requisites allowing this analytical usage. I define direct action as a form of resistance or of collective intervention which possesses a minimum of organization; which breaks the rules of the political game and/or the norms of the organization without, however, undermining the foundations of the system of domination; which does not involve the deliberate use of violence; and which seeks to change the rules of the political game and/or to intervene in the political system.

Let us examine this definition analytically. Direct action is a form of resistance or of intervention: it may involve a refusal to apply a norm (law) or a deliberate breach of a norm through active mobilization. For this to be possible, a minimum degree of organization is required, although this does not necessarily entail the creation of a formal organization. Direct action is distinct from normal political action because it involves to some extent a transgression of the rules of the political game and of social norms (the most direct indicator is that it always comprises some margin of illegality). In itself it is not oriented to provoke changes in the system of dominant social relationships and it is therefore analytically distinct from antagonist action. This does not mean, however, that an antagonist movement may not resort to forms of direct action.

The deliberate and continuous use of violence is not a necessary characteristic of direct action. It is thus distinct from guerrilla warfare, which in certain respects may be considered direct action but which structurally involves violence (see White 1989). Direct action may be violent or non-violent. Non-violence is a form of direct action which may come about in the presence of certain structural conditions and of certain responses by the adversary. Direct action seeks to have an effect on the political system. It is not expressive but instrumental action, although it may attain symbolic and expressive dimensions. In this sense, direct action always possesses a strategic dimension; it involves a choice of means and interlocutors, as well as the calculation of the effects on the public and of the costs and benefits of the action.

So defined, the features of certain borderline cases become clearer. One of them is guerrilla warfare, in particular urban guerrilla warfare and all those situations in which the military structure does not resemble that of a conventional army. The deliberate and continuous use of violence and a military-type organization distinguish guerrilla warfare from direct action. A similar case is that of sabotage and terrorism. On the other side lies symbolic action, in which expressive components are prevalent (consider, for example, street theatre, certain youth or feminist events). In these cases, the instrumental and strategic dimension of direct action diminishes or disappears.

Direct action also has a constructive dimension, in the sense that it seeks to create institutions parallel to those being contested or resisted. Hence it also always constitutes an experience of alternative participation and the exercise of some form of direct democracy.

20

Research on collective action

The object of knowledge constructed by the study of collective action attains a significance that expands beyond the strict boundaries of the subject matter at hand. Probably no other field of sociological inquiry today is brought, through multiple linkages, to such a close contact with other areas of sociological research. In systems with a capacity for self-production that far exceeds the achievements of any society in the past, the forms of action most distant from reproduction and the maintenance of social order signal processes that involve the system in its entirety: they affect the fundamental orientations of society, the direction of change, the basic moral and political choices. Precisely for this reason, analysis of movements provides insights that point behind the back of the collective actors as empirical facts. By their action that challenges the dominant discourse and mobilizes the creative energies in society, movements force us to reflect on the question of how social action – and perhaps individual action as well – constitutes itself in systems where the available resources overwhelmingly exceed reproductive needs.

If social action in complex systems has prominently shifted from the inherited to the constructed, society can no longer be conceived as the replication of the social order embedded in institutions and roles; rather, it has become a field of cognitive and emotional investment which creates its own meaning. If movements are the social domain which most readily escapes the confines of the inherited, and most perceptibly reveals the manner and locus of the society's self-constructive processes, collective action can become the terrain for exploration of the possible.

The last thirty years have witnessed a growth of interest in collective action and social movements to the point that the subject has now become a fully accredited branch of study all on its own, with a considerable amount of literature already produced and a variety of schools of thought established. What, we may ask, is behind this upsurge of interest? For an answer, we must start looking at things from the perspective of sociology, if, as is the case in the situation of increasing complexity and social capacity for heightened self-reflexivity, the construction of social phenomena and the construction of cognitive processes stand in a circular relationship.

The unprecedented interest in collective action derives mainly from the obvious fact that the same past decades have also seen the emergence in all advanced societies of forms of collective mobilization which call the conventional categories of analysis into question. The inadequacy of theory has become increasingly evident as new movements have revealed their non-conjunctural nature, and as they have demonstrated their irreducibility to mere variants of the more familiar forms of collective action. Researchers in this situation have found themselves in the unfortunate position of having to pick their way through a *terra incognita* without the help of a map. As it happens, some have returned back to the beginning in order to study the existing, well-worn charts in order to square their familiar outlines with the hazy recollections of the territory they have just glimpsed. Others strike off blindly in all directions, squandering their energies and ending up travelling in circles. Others still, however, have recorded the first landmarks so as to mark out the new domain, with the results as sketchy as they are undiminished in utility.

A second reason for the growing interest in social movements is no doubt the fact that this branch of knowledge and inquiry provides a useful training for those who wish to address the central problem of social theory concerning the relationship between the actor and the system. In no other area of sociology does the dualistic tradition handed down to us from the nineteenth century clash as evidently with the object of study.

Mobile and 'in action', an expression of emerging needs and of nascent conflicts, social movements locate themselves at the opposite extreme from that opaque stuff of the institutions that so easily makes us identify the society with its established setup. Perhaps for this reason forms of collective action have been either seen as a token of, as it were, hidden energy, a collective *élan vital* that generates change in the heart of the order; or they have been banished to the shadowy margins where reside those social phenomena which, more than just expressions of resistance to the order, escape it altogether as its own pathology; or, again, they have been forced into the impossible role of the interpreters and standard-bearers of 'contradictions' intrinsic in the thick matter of the structure.

Density of structures versus mobility of actors, last-instance determination versus revolutionary voluntarism – these are the poles between which the inherited theory of the nineteenth century has oscillated; poles which indelibly mark conceptual models and research practices in the field of collective action. Given the fact, it is obvious that an examination of the study of collective action itself promptly guides us towards theoretical and methodological reflection of a more general nature, as we pursue the possibilities to overcome the legacy of dualism.

How a 'we' is formed

The historical transformation of the phenomena observed and the change in conceptual models – have given rise to a perception of collective action which is no longer satisfied with the inherited framework of analysis, the dualistic legacy of the past which essentially ascribes collective action either to the structural location of actors or to the values, ideologies, and suggestions which guide them. Today, questions are raised which the dualistic framework could have never been able to handle, regardless of the pole – structural determination or representations – assigned the priority.

Such probing questions can none the less be formulated in extremely simple terms: By what processes do actors construct their collective action? How is the unity we observe in a collective phenomenon produced? Answering them, however, entails abandoning the dualistic assumption at the very outset; for an *a posteriori* recovery of unity between 'structure' and 'action', between 'objective social condition' and 'representations' has proven impossible. Should one fail to establish an original circular relation between the actor and the system, the analysis is trapped again in an inescapable impasse. Deciding between determinism and voluntarism becomes merely a matter of taste, or of circumstance; but, in any case, one is still confronted with the necessity to introduce a *tertium*, an intermediate element bridging the gap between the 'objective' and the 'subjective', the 'structural' and the 'cultural'. Such a third term, perhaps, need no longer be the Leninist revolutionary party connecting the exploited classes to the true consciousness of their interests; yet it may still be posed in the image of the intellectual who, carried away in omnipotent frenzy, believes it her/his duty to relate the constraints and opportunities of the system to the consciousness of the actors.

The collective actor is a composite, constructed reality which, however, is empirically observed as a unit. There are two reasons for this. Actors tend to create of themselves a unitary definition which reinforces, at least ideologically, their capacity for action and confrontation with their interlocutors, adversaries, and allies. Observers and witnesses tend to attribute such unity to the empirical phenomenon itself, transforming it into a 'subject' endowed with that substantial unity characterizing the common sense notion. Unity is thus taken as the starting datum for inquiry, owing to the fact that, on one hand, the actors themselves attribute it to their action for ideological and practical reasons, and because, on the other, observers' interaction with the actors takes place in close correspondence with these actors and their ordinary assumptions.

It seems to me essential that analysis accept this unity not as a given but solely as a point of departure for empirical observation. It is of course true that we can and do observe a set of individuals who, through coordinated action, define themselves as a 'we' to which such unity is attributed. In journalism and in everyday conversation, we frequently resort to the artless realism that paradoxically takes for granted a quasi-metaphysical existence of the actor. In sociological research, however, it is precisely this datum that has to be carefully reexamined. As accumulating evidence is gradually subjected to the scrutiny of analysis, it becomes clear that unity is the result of exchanges, negotiations, decisions, and conflicts, constantly activated by actors but not apparent on the surface. These processes are not immediately visible, since the actors tend to conceal themselves and their fragmentation. Action, in fact, entails the unification of the field by means of some common representation and the force of ideology.

We should not forget, then, that when unification comes about it is already a product. The construction process have outcomes of varying degree of success, but when we observe actual collective action taking place, it should be assumed that such a process is active and is perpetuated through time. The observed unity is the datum to be investigated, not the evidence from which to proceed. It is here that the questions formulated above assume their importance. When they are posed, collective action ceases to be a concrete entity, and can, instead, be conceived as end-directed behaviour constructed by means of social relations within the field of possibilities and limits that the actors perceive.

This perspective clearly differs from that of an historical analysis of collective action. When one seeks to reconstruct the genesis and development of an historical actor, questions must be answered which are very different from the ones raised above. Current historical analyses of social movements often yield useful information on specific topics, but they almost always rely on the ingenuous assumption of realism criticized above. They presume that the collective actor, the 'movement', exists; that, like an historical personage, it was born in a certain period, that it developed in another, and that it manifested this or that behaviour. But the question is, Who acted, who spoke for the movement, and what happened to the 'movement' internally in the meantime? We discover that those who spoke were its leaders, that some of its components acted differently from others, and that the sociological reality of the actor is quite distinct from the unity attributed to it by the observer.

The question that has most fired my interest is the problem of how a 'we' can become a we. How and why do social aggregates arrive at a collective definition of their joint action? This is the research problematic I have set for myself within the restricted sphere of social movements and, in particular, of those of them that most recently emerged in complex societies.

Research procedures

I would like now to discuss the consequences that posing the question of collective identity has for research practice. In the field of social movements, research has reflected the actor/system dualism inherited from the nineteenth century legacy. This dualism has been present in three major and recurrent practices.

First and most commonly, in the observation of behaviours variously defined as movements, protest, mobilizations and so on, the researcher seeks to discover a particular social condition. This has meant investigating whether the structural conditions which define the actor, or rather the alleged actor, are capable of explaining the types of behaviour observed.

The second area deals with the perceptions, representations and values of actors regarding their own action. In this case, surveys are conducted, normally about activism, to delve into the motivations of individuals to participate in social movements. A sub-category of this approach, is the analysis of documents produced by collective actors, that is, of the ideologies which have been articulated in written form. This entails working on organized representations (and also organizational ones, given that the documents are usually produced by organizations). In this case, one can take the framing activity of 'movement' leaders (those who have the power to speak on behalf of a movement) as a point of reference. Obviously a constant and recurring possibility is that of relating these two levels: certain representations and opinions are correlated with certain structural conditions.

The third type of research practice concerns the quantitative analysis of collective events, a relatively recent approach which Charles Tilly has systematically developed with very important results (see also, in the same direction, Tarrow 1989a). With it, he has achieved some extremely interesting results, and not the least so from a purely technical point of view. In this approach, the most circumscribed protest events possible and singular collective phenomena are used as units of analysis. Such events, further classified by their specific characteristics (size, type of actors, repertoire of actions used, response on the part of the authorities), are then correlated with structural factors or different states of the political, economic or other systems.

Each of the foregoing research practices provides useful information and helps clarify some aspect of collective action. Each of them indicates a research path that, if explicitly confined to its own epistemological limits, could increase our understanding of collective action. But when an approach becomes the only tool for the interpretation of 'a movement as such', then it easily becomes an undue extension and generalization which is also coloured by a metaphysics of the actor which tends to consider it as an 'essential' subject instead of a system of relationships. The methods considered adopt the attitude of ingenuous realism so as to be able to assign the status of collective actor to a set of empirical behaviours manifesting itself within a certain spatio-temporal context. Subsequently, this set is attributed with a fictitious sociological unity and a 'real' substance which, in fact, reside nowhere outside the presuppositions of the observer.

In the first case it is assumed that the structural 'thickness' of a social condition should explain action, which is not able in itself to carry the 'true' meaning of what is observed. One has to refer to a more substantial reality beyond the appearance of the phenomenon. A self-restrained application of this approach could provide useful information on the social profile of participants in social movements and on some societal macro-processes affecting collective action.

In the second case, when inquiries concern the participants' motivation, the assumption is that by comparing individual opinions and representations and by relating them to some structural variables (e.g. social condition) one can draw a picture of the movement as a collective actor, which is supposed to be the sum or the combination of those individual opinions. When, on the other hand, one refers to documents, the discourse of the leaders and their framing activities are taken, mostly implicitly, as representative of the movement as a whole: the actor is conceived therefore as a unified reality which is interpreted in a transparent way by the leaders and by the organizational discourse. Here too, a self-restrained use of these sources and methods could tell us what participants and leaders think.

The third case is concerned with protest events and it is based on public records. In this case the reification of the collective actor is produced first by the fact that it is reduced to a political actor: given the nature of the data, the only forms of action that can be considered are those who challenge a public authority and are recorded by the police, the press or other public sources. Secondly, in the definition of the movement all the submerged relationships, the everyday life activities which are part of a movement culture cannot be taken into account, but indirectly. A self-restrained use of this method could give us important answers to the question of how an actor confront a public authority and how his action is affected by the opponent.

When these approaches are used to provide general interpretations of 'a movement as such', what disappears from the scene in all the three cases is collective action as a social production, as a purposive, meaningful and relational orientation, which cannot simply be derived from structural constraints (first case), cannot be reduced to the unity of leaders discourse or to the sum of militants' opinions (second case), cannot be reduced to being merely public behaviour (third case).

Either action is deprived of its meaning altogether – it is transposed elsewhere, in some structural preconditions – or that meaning is reduced to the opinions or beliefs expressed by the actors, without placing this discourse within the actual field of social relationships. Another drawback inherent in the method of data gathering is its often heavy reliance on questionnaires or interviews and other written documents produced by the actors (a notable exception to this, however, is the technique used by Tilly). These research practices inevitably focus attention on the opinions of the actors; they are based, that is to say, on the equally crude assumption that the meaning of the action coincides with the actors' verbal representation of it.

The recent developments of discourse analysis have opened up new ways of understanding discourses as dialogic and controversial constructions of meaning (see Bakhtin 1981, 1986; Simons 1990; Van Dijk 1972; Stubbs 1983; Billig et al. 1988; Edwards and Potter 1993; Potter et al. 1993; Potter and Wetherell 1987; Palmer 1990; Parker 1992; Parker and Shotter 1990; Sampson 1993); mental models and contexts play an important role in this construction (Johnson-Laird 1983; Hormann 1986). The students of social movements are becoming aware of this complexity and try to creatively approach the multiplicity of levels implied in a collective discourse (Johnston 1994). These advances are also the background of the analysis of political discourse (see Gamson 1992b; Donati 1992; Wilson 1990b). All these approaches bring a different point of view that is more concerned with meaning and its relational construction.

Also, the recent wave of interest for biographical narratives and subjective accounts (see Bertaux 1981; Della Porta 1992a; Rice 1992; Viney and Bousfield 1991; Richardson 1991) has brought a new attention to the personal and discursive dimensions of collective action. Recourse to this method seems to reflect the evident inadequacy of quantitative methodologies in handling the everyday and subjective dimensions of social action, and all the problems involved in their uninhibited, totalizing self-understanding as to their status as a 'hard'science. However, there are also some risks related to a new version of the naive assumption that the meaning of a collective action will be the sum of the representations of individual actors (see Melucci 1992); in a parallel way action as experience (Dubet 1994) might be reduced to pure subjective perception, instead of being recognized as part of a field, as a constant relation between intentions and constraints, possibilities and limits (Melucci 1996).

Moreover, the assumption that a narrative will somehow adequately reveal the meaning of an action, above and beyond the relationship with the researcher in which the narrative is produced, and the particular relationship of the narrator with his own memory, can easily end up identifying action with the ideology of the actor (and of the researcher), instead of revealing the nature of action as an interactive construct. If attention is not paid to the field of action, to the conditions of production of a text, to the reception and interpretation of it by the researcher, a new kind of 'objectivism' can be the outcome of a very 'subjective' source as biographical data or personal narratives. Without a careful focus on the relational and affective dimensions that the biographical methods always imply when referring to personal accounts, and without a methodological clarification of the selective role of memory, the narrative methods easily become but yet another form of simple-minded clinical interviewing. The particular relational setting in which the narrative is produced, the quality of the affective link with the interviewer, and the narrator's particular relationship with her/his memory are all important dimensions in the construction of a narrative (see Briggs 1986; Steier 1991; Alasuutari 1995; Moustakas 1994; Ellis and Flaherty 1992; Van Maanen 1995).

Over the last thirty years, specific research methods have been developed which seek to grasp action as it actually unfolds. We could classify them under the shared denomination 'action research', or 'intervention research', as the approach has also been called.

Participatory action research (see Whyte 1991; Reason 1994) and research-intervention, particularly as developed by Alain Touraine (1981), directly address the question of how action is constructed and attempts to observe action as it takes place, as a process built by actors. With regard to the premises of the dualistic legacy embedded in the conventional methodologies, these approaches represent, at least in intention, an important attempt to bridge the seemingly insuperable gulf between representations and structural determinants. However, the tools and techniques they operationalize suffer from three limitations which the practicants of the approach have been unable to overcome, and which represent a residual encrustation of such dualism still persisting even in the more unconventional approaches to research. Firstly, these approaches assume a kind of missionary task on the part of the researcher who ends up playing the role of *deus ex machin*a, providing the actors with a consciousness which they are apparently not able to produce for themselves (this is particularly true for Touraine). Secondly, they ignore the relationship between the observer and the observed, a problem which is crucial for any form of research which entails a direct interaction between the researcher and his subject. The problem is seldom addressed directly, and has been habitually ignored by methodological reflection as regards its constitutive role in research. A prominent exception to such inattention, however, is represented by those research procedures which in the French tradition go by the name of *analyse institutionelle*; in them the dimension of the relationality of the research situation explicitly enters the field of observation. But inspite of the successful thematization of the problem, the approach ultimately still remains captive to a bias in its definition of the role of the analyst. The researcher continues proceeding with a missionary intent: her/his role still is to bring to the light the hidden energies lying below the encrusted surface of institutions and push them against the powers that be (*l'instituant contre l'institué*, to borrow the title of Lourau's famous book filtering the spirit of May '68). Finally research-intervention methods underestimate the fact that a researcher intervening into a field of action does not work under 'natural' conditions but he/she modifies the field and may even manipulate it, beyond his/her intentions (this point has been particularly developed by the French *analyse institutionnelle*, see Lapassade 1981; Lourau 1977).

These difficulties cannot be resolved merely by recognizing that action can itself be a significant object of research. What we need is a deliberate and unambiguous transcendence beyond the dualistic premises that underlie current research methods, and that entails a new conception of action as a field of meanings constructed by social relations within a set of resources and constraints. The innovative character of the methods of action research should be pushed much further than what has been achieved so far by the practicants of the approach. The three persistent problems I pointed out behind its apparent novelty mean that their techniques are still of very limited validity and remain persistently threatened by the risks of manipulative intentions or conceptions of a 'sacred' role of the intellectual-cum-enlightener.

What we must recognize is that actors themselves can make sense out of what they are doing, autonomously of any evangelical or manipulative interventions of the researcher. And in the disenchanted world of consummate systemic processes where epistemological privileges have been divested together with everything hereditary and natural, all meaning is judged not by the correctness of its content but by the processes of its creation.

Secondly, we need to recognize that the researcher-actor relation is itself an object of observation, that it is itself part of the field of action, and thus subject to explicit negotiation and to a contract stipulated between the parties. This, however, entails the assumption that the interests and roles in the play are not identical, that the researchers and the actors are not located in the same position in the social field and must therefore acknowledge and articulate their mutual differences, together with their common (and often provisional) goals in collecting and sharing information.

Lastly, we must recognize that every research practice which involves intervention in the field of action creates an artificial situation which must be explicitly acknowledged. The researcher cannot make any claims as to the naturalness of the phenomena investigated, and s/he must be able to shift the level of observation and communication: a capability for meta-communication on the relationship between the observer and the observed must therefore be incorporated into the research framework.

In order to reach the level where causal connections can be assigned within an explanatory framework, we must thus first assume a 'phenomenological' attitude: it is necessary to explicate and bring out into the open our vantage point, our specific location within the field of relations constituting the research practice, and raise it to self-awareness. Only after this methodological step beginning the observation does it become possible to assume the full responsibility for the analytical tools operationalized in the process and for the act of establishing causal relationships among phenomena in its course, without losing sight of the fact that they nevertheless always retain a generative connection to the particular context clarified in the beginning. Thus they inevitably remain provisional and exposed to a dialogic challenge from other subjects, other discourses. For such a dialogue to be possible, though, the partners to the research practice must show capability for self-reflexion, for locating themselves in a field that includes them all, and for self-justifying their respective perspectival viewpoints; only then can the space for establishing such a metalevel emerge in which a dialogue transcending each particular situation becomes possible. Any totalizing assumptions concerning such a point of view that fail to be thematized in self-consciousness, and thereby verified as limited, will however at once forestall the possibility for communication and dialogue; whereas a realization of the necessary rootedness in a particular location in the field of social relationships, languages, and discourses will allow the preconditions to develop for adopting the vantage point of the other.

A method that is mindful of, and responsive to, these requisites should concentrate increasingly more on processes and increasingly less on contents. It is in this direction that my own research into new forms of collective action has moved, and in that process I have become convinced that the three conditions I just outlined provide a testing ground for any method that is to seek escape from the dualism between structure and intentions, observer and observed: Firstly, that is, the need to recognize that the actors have the capacity to define the meaning of their own action; secondly, the need to recognize that the relation that is the basis of knowledge formation must be made an explicit object of observation, negotiation, and contract, under the assumption that analysts and 'actors' are mutually and irreducibly different social actors and that they must reach an agreement on their relationship; thirdly, the need to recognize that research constructs an artificial field, that it does not observe 'natural' action but, instead, always action in relation to the observer; and this field can be analysed only if the researcher is able to engage in metacommunication about it. Metacommunication is, then, the capacity to temporarily locate oneself at a level outside the relational field, enabling the possibility of subjecting that relation itself to discursive treatment.

Social research thus discards the illusion that it in some way mirrors 'true' reality and moves closer to a recognition of its proper nature: namely, that it is a social activity, a self-reflexive process constructed within the possibilities and the constraints of a social field and of an ecosystem. The particular form of action that we call research introduces into the field of social relations new cognitive inputs, which derive from the action itself and from the observation of collective processes and effects. Research is that particular kind of social action where chances or opportunities for self-reflexivity are higher. It thus becomes a form of second-degree learning – as a development of those formal abilities that an age of accelerated change such as ours demands of knowledge.

This provides the foundation for new reflection on the social function of knowledge. The social actor, in fact, is never entirely in control of his or her own action. S/he acted upon by the process of constructing a 'we' as s/he enacts and lives that process. There is a margin of opacity in collective action which corresponds to the actor's inability to simultaneously occupy her/his position as actor, and assume the point of view of the relations in which s/he is involved as a contributor. Although the point of view of the relation is not inaccessible to the actor, the latter cannot be simultaneously both an actor and an analyst of her/himself in that capacity – as each of us knows from our personal experience. Sufficient distance is needed for one to be able to assume the point of view of the relation and engage in metacommunication regarding the constraints and possibilities that characterize it.

Only by taking this distance and at the same time by being close to the action itself, one can observe that intense, plural and sometimes contradictory system of meanings that constitute the collective identity of a social movement. Without an access to the invisible network of negotiations and interactions among different parts and levels of an empirical movement, it is difficult not to reduce action to behaviours and opinions. But this access requires some conditions in the relationship between researchers and collective actors.

Ways out

Knowledge on collective identity assumes a decisive role in rendering accessible a specific potential for action; it can function as a multiplier of processes for change, because it gives the actors responsibility for the choices they make. Action research is sometimes close to this purpose and result, but it is often led by a missionary spirit that too easily transforms the researcher in an activist or in a preacher. In a highly differentiated and variable system, therefore, knowledge becomes a desirable resource for actors. Hereby is also opened up the way for recognition of the fact that the functions and interests of the actor and the researcher are different. The researcher possesses cognitive resources that can help render the point of view of relationality more transparent. It is thus possible for a negotiative relationship to arise between, on the one hand, actors with professional skills and control over specific cognitive resources and, on the other, actors whose needs call for a greater transparency of their own action, but who nonetheless possess skills and information relative to such action as well.

The point at which the two can meet can only be contractual in character. There is nothing of the missionary about this, and the contractual meeting allows no researcher expectations as to the destinies of the actors. The researchers may be involved as individuals, as citizens, as political militants, but not as specialists. As such, they have the task of performing a professional role within knowledge-producing institutions. They therefore are bearers of the ethical and political responsibility for the production and allocation of cognitive resources; but they do not have the right to orient the destinies of society as 'counsellors of the Prince' or as ideologues of protest.

The ground on which the researcher encounters the actor (and here I am thinking not only of social movements) consists in the recognition of a demand for cognitive resources. Two interests – the researcher's interest in gathering information, the actor's interest in increasing her/his capacity for action – may temporarily converge and make an exchange possible.

Through reflection on the actor-researcher relationship, we can thus gain a novel insight into action – not because of any duty or mission incumbent on the researcher, but on account of the contractual situation that allows metacommunication on the relations that tie the actor to her/his interlocutors and adversaries. These relationships both delimit a field of action and create opportunities. However, opportunities and constraints are never 'objective': they are what they are to particular actors. The actors possess the cognitive, motivational, and perceptive resources with which to recognize and define the limits and possibilities of their action. Knowledge, therefore, has a decisive role to play in rendering more accessible the potential for action that is present in a given situation. It may, likewise, operate as a multiplier in the processes of change, as it serves as a tool in making actors responsible for their own choices.

In my own research practice, which is based on group experiential and videorecorded sessions (see Melucci 1989, 1994), I have tried to apply these methodological guidelines to different social movement networks. The goal of my methodology is to break the apparent unity of the discourse of movements and to observe the interactive construction of the unity through differences and conflicts. The particular methodology is intended to address not individual opinions, but the system of interactions in its making. It assumes that it does not address only discourses but, discourses constructed through actual interactions, involving the internal and external action field: actors are confronted with their internal tensions and with the external relationships with researchers, leaders, other actors, observers, opponents. The procedure is intended to allow the multilevelled, multifaceted, often contradictory aspects of identity to emerge. Through a structured and process-oriented intervention it aims at the reconstruction of a field of meanings and relationships which is often dilemmatic (as the rhetorical approach in social psychology has also shown, see Billig 1995).

Through the reconstruction of the collective identity this methodology tries to detect the action system of the collective actor and the ways the different components of its action are kept together and translated in visible mobilization. The analysis reveals the tensions between various orientations that are present within the movement, but also within a single group, or portion of the movement. The integration of these orientations is assured in contemporary movements by the organization that, starting from this identity structure, assumes the characteristic double-level (visibility-latency) form: brief and intense public mobilization compaigns which are fed by the submerged life of the networks and their self-reflective resources.

The example of contemporary movements shows how important can be the notion of collective identity in revealing collective action as a system of tensions. If applied to empirical cases it accounts for different outcomes of the movement, which are related to the different internal field and to different answers from the external environment.

Collective action should be thought of as a construct, putting an end to the structure-intentions duality. Action is an interactive, constructive process within a field of possibilities and limits recognized by the actors. The accent on the limits to the process of construction, which always take place within the boundaries of a given field, avoids the risk of a radical constructivism which would be difficult to sustain. Nevertheless without the capability of perceiving and making sense of its boundaries, action would not be possible. In fact, radical constructivism finishes by destroying the relational dimension of social action and presents itself as the ultimate version, perhaps more sophisticated, of a voluntaristic paradigm.

Moral and political implications

At this point I would like to discuss some more general consequences concerning the position of the researcher and the role of scientific knowledge. We are witnessing today the decline of the great collective certainties, and an emergence of fragmented and multiple social actors. The apparent 'weakness' of social actors may have us mourn the passing of the heroic era when the course of history assigned each to her/his proper place, and when the researcher's only task was to unravel the plot. But if the plurality, the temporariness, and the multilocationality of actors do not exhaust their significance as mere symptoms of decline, it becomes necessary for the observer to adjust her/his analytical perspective and inquire into the meaning of these changes. The demise of actor-personages conceived as essences forces us to shift our attention to the processes whereby social action is constructed.

Recent studies on living systems (Maturana and Varela 1980; Morin 1980, 1986; Roszak 1992) support this requirement and bring to the fore the need to define human action as the construction of the possible within specific boundaries. The reference to boundaries is to be understood in a dual sense: the term 'boundary' denotes finiteness, the recognition of mortality and death as the confines of the human condition; but it also stands for frontier, for separation, and thus for the recognition of the other, the different, the irreducible. The emphasis on possibility signals, firstly, the uncontainable impulse of human action to overcome the limits of pain and death. Secondly, it is a testimony to the species tendency to cerebralize, to 'elevate' the body through the meaning produced by its higher faculties. Thirdly, it makes the dimension of solidarity and communication tangible as the urge to render diversity less opaque and irreducible.

The tension between limits and possibilities affects in particular the concept of rationality, as defined in modern Western culture. As the precariousness of a rationality based exclusively on the calculation of means and ends has become increasingly evident, the way has been opened up for other modes of knowledge. The emotions, intuition, creativity, and the 'feminine' perception of the world are now fully part of the process of construction of our social and individual realities. One must recognize these factors, not seek to conceal them. Ethical capacity also loses the certainty of absolute ends and is relegated to the responsibility and risk of co-living. When relations among people are increasingly more founded on choice, social links become fragile and unstable. The threat of catastrophic disaggregation is imminent. But if it is accepted that not everything in social relationships can be subjected to calculation in the light of pure rationality, then difference and uncertainty can become the foundation for a new solidarity. From this well-known fragility arises the change in the ethical attitudes that underpin communal life.

Today scientific knowledge increasingly enters into the constructive process of collective action, as a particular form of social action with a high self-reflective capacity. Knowledge is not a mirror revealing in a linear way the causal chains that govern reality. Instead, it is a circular process of modelling (of its subjects) and self-modelling (of its instruments). It is a process that is anything but 'pure', in which the contaminating factors of emotions, subjective evaluations, and the limitations of the observer interact in a decisive manner.

But also different fields of knowledge interact to an ever-greater degree, continuously calling into question the conventional disciplinary boundaries and their institutional settings. Thus defined, scientific knowledge takes on the aspect of a bricolage, the gathering and combining of cues, whose meanings depend upon variations in point of view, from the particular perspective of the observer (Bateson 1972, 1979). The arrogance with which science as a public institution expresses its certainties does not correspond to the reality of scientific research, nor does it reflect the new awareness of a growing number of scientists (Gilbert and Mulkay 1984, Latour 1987). The limits of knowledge, the hypothetical character of research, and the disproportionate area of uncertainty in which the choices and decisions of scientists take place are all elements which ought to enter into the public discussion of science. And thus they will contribute to a weakening, if not a dismantling, of the foundations of a faith in technology which turns to science as the new God, hoping for salvation from the catastrophes which threaten us today.

To study collective action means redefining the relationship between the observer and the observed, because we are not dealing with a thing, but with a process continuously activated by social actors. Acknowledging both in ourselves as scientists and in the collective actors the limited rationality that characterizes social action, researchers can no longer apply the criteria of truth or morality defined a priori, outside of the relationship. Researchers must also participate in the uncertainty, testing the limits of their instruments and of their ethical values. They cannot avoid freezing in a definition 'what a social movement is', as very often is the case for actors themselves. But they must be aware that collective identity is just a tool for the analysis, not a reality in itself.

Thus the two models which have always characterized the relationship between researcher and actor in social sciences fall to pieces before our very eyes: that of identification, and that of distance. The 'understanding' or 'empathetic' researcher shares with the ideologue, from whom he nevertheless intends to distance himself, the illusion of the power to destroy the gap between reflection and action. The myth of transparency or of total communication seems to feed in a recurrent manner the need to transform the scientific work into maieutics or into pedagogy, exposing the 'cold' body of science to the fire of action. But the model of distance, of the neutrality of the researcher, high priest of a 'truth' and a 'reality' that are beyond the comprehension of the actors, also seems to be obsolete. After all, just what is this 'reality' of which the researcher speaks, if not that constructed together in a circular interaction with his/her 'subjects'?

From this perspective, the opposition between quantitative and qualitative research, between 'soft' and 'hard' methods, is a false problem – but one which nevertheless contains within itself a real one. Behind the quantity-quality dichotomy lies a change in the objects and modes of knowledge, the ongoing crisis of methods (quantitative and qualitative) centred on opinion and representation rather than on action; of methods based on a model of 'pure' actor rationality which often consigns the intuitive and emotional dimensions of behaviour to the sidelines; of methods not prepared to capture the meaningfulness of behaviour which does not follow the stipulations of instrumental rationality, but which, none the less, is not 'irrational', either; of methods that lay claim to an 'objectivity' that excludes the observer from the field of observation.

In differentiated and highly variable systems, there is a growing need to predict and control uncertainty. Research inevitably becomes part of the game of demands, expectations, and interests which ties together or puts in opposition actors, researchers, and consumers. It is difficult to believe that social research will be able to handle the new tasks that lie in store for it without a high level of self-reflexivity; and this is to speak of both quantitative and qualitative methods.

This is not a question of innovative techniques alone. It entails, as a part of the very process of research, rendering ever more explicit the social relations and the options that provide the procedure with its basis and which make it possible. In other words, what is called for is, as it were, a situational epistemology, which social research increasingly needs if it is to break out of the illusion that it stands outside or above the circular observer-actor game. Such circularity is not vicious when it involves a recognition of the partiality of, and limits to, the partners' respective 'standpoints' and allows metacommunication about them: a limited, situated knowledge can become 'true' when it carries with it the awareness of its own limitations.

The observer/observed relationship becomes an arena of responsibility, a space comprising a cognitive and ethical contract between the researchers and the actors. This encounter is a difficult one as it hinges upon successful recognition between diverse entities, and also because it entails acknowledgment of two interconnected requisitions made on us by the age of complexity: to exist and to exist-with. Responsibility is, in the first place, the ability to assume one's own being, one's own finitude, one's own value. But such an assumption entails responsibility towards the 'other', the definition of a space for living together. 'Time to be' and 'time to care' are inextricably woven together as the patterns and imperatives of a livable human life.

Giving up the role of the demiurge, the great suggestor or the eye of God, the researcher can take responsibility of his work of knowledge and he can offer the actors a possibility to develop their capacity to learn how to learn, to produce their own codes. By renouncing the role of the great mentor, the researcher, however, cannot resume the role of the sorcerer's apprentice, of the ingenuous manipulator of forces beyond his control. To speak of the actors' weakness is not only to call attention to the necessary process of freeing oneself from the mentality that ascribes metaphysical substance to the subject and still thinks of strong historical actors as protagonists of a shining future; that weakness at once refers to new imbalances, submission to new forms of power, and exclusion from, and deprivation of, the word.

Researchers can indeed escape from their role as demiurges or pedagogues. The accomplishment, however, does not relieve them of their responsibility to make the word more accessible by enabling weaker actors to become actors in the contract. Researchers do not have a monopoly over cognitive resources, but they can provide actors with the instruments they need in order to develop their capacity for action. Such responsibility thus governs the process of construction of the objects of knowledge, but is also manifest in the omissions, the silences, the voids in that operation. Recognizing the twin-faceted nature of this responsibility paves the way for an ethics and politics of the work of knowledge. Research is a form of social action which introduces its own outcomes into the social field. In complex societies, research becomes a process of metacommunication, a self-reflective learning process. Providing an account of the plurality and tensions constituting collective life, it can contribute to a practice of freedom.

References

Abel, Emily K. and Nelson, Margaret K. (eds.) 1990, *Circles of Care: Work and Identity in Women's Lives*, Albany: SUNY Press.

Abelson, Robert P. 1981, 'The Psychological Status of the Script Concept', *American Psychologist* 36: 715–29.

Abrams, Dominic and Hogg, Michael A. (eds.) 1990, *Social Identity Theory*, Hemel Hempstead: Harvester.

Abrams, Philip and McCulloch, Andrew 1976, *Communes, Sociology and Society*, Cambridge University Press.

Abu-Lughod, Lila 1990, 'The Romance of Resistance: Tracing Transformations of Power through Bedouin Women', *American Ethnologist* 17: 41–55.

Adam, Barbara E. 1990, *Time and Social Theory*, Cambridge: Polity Press.

Adam, Barry D. 1987, *The Rise of a Gay and Lesbian Movement*, Boston: Twayne.

Adams, Nassau A. 1993, *Worlds Apart: The North–South Divide and the International System*, London: Zed Books.

Aggleton, Peter, Davies, Peter and Hart, Graham (eds.) 1990, *AIDS: Individual, Cultural and Policy Dimensions*, London: Falmer Press.

Agor, Weston H. (ed.) 1989, *Intuition in Organizations*, Newbury Park: Sage.

Aguirre, B. E., Quarantelli, E. L. and Mendoza, Jorge L. 1988, 'Collective Behaviour of Fads: The Characteristics, Effects, and Career of Streaking', *American Sociological Review* 53: 569–84.

Ahlemeyer, Heinrich W. 1995, *Soziale Bewegungen als Kommunikationssystem*, Opladen: Leske und Budrich.

Alasuutari, Pertti 1995, *Researching Culture: Qualitative Methods and Cultural Studies*, London: Sage.

Alberoni, Francesco 1984, *Movement and Institution*, New York: Columbia University Press.

Alexander, Jeffrey C. 1987, 'The Social Requisites for Altruism and Voluntarism: Some Notes on What Makes a Sector Independent', *Sociological Theory* 5: 165–71.

Alexander, Jeffrey C. 1988a, *Action and Its Environment: Towards a New Synthesis*, New York: Columbia University Press.

Alexander, Jeffrey C. (ed.) 1988b, *Durkheimian Sociology: Cultural Studies*, Cambridge University Press.

Alexander, Jeffrey C. 1989, *Structure and Meaning: Relinking Classical Sociology*, New York: Columbia University Press.

Alexander, Jeffrey C. 1990, 'Analytic Debates: Understanding the Relative Autonomy of Culture', in Alexander, Jeffrey C. and Seidman, Steven (eds.) 1990, 1–27.

Alexander, Jeffrey C. and Seidman, Steven (eds.) 1990, *Culture and Society: Contemporary Debates*, Cambridge University Press.

Almond, Gabriel A. and Verba, Sidney (eds.) 1980, *The Civic Culture Revisited*, Boston: Little, Brown and Co.

Anderson, Benedict 1991, *Imagined Communities: Reflections on the Origins and Spread of Nationalism*, London: Verso.

Arato, Andrew and Cohen, Jean 1992, *Civil Society and Social Theory*, Cambridge. MA: MIT Press.

Arendt, Hannah 1973, *The Origins of Totalitarianism*, New York: Harcourt, Brace.

Arrighi, Giovanni, Hopkins, Terence H. and Wallerstein, Immanuel 1989, *Antisystemic Movements*, London: Verso.

Arutyunyan, Yuri V. 1990, 'On the Development of Nations in their Own and International Context', *Innovation* 3: 381–92.

Avritzer, Leonardo (ed.) 1994, *Sociedade Civil e Democratizaçao*, Belo Horizonte: Livraria del Rey.

Aya, Rod 1990, *Rethinking Revolutions and Collective Violence: Studies on Concept, Theory and Method*, Amsterdam: Het Spinhuis.

Badie, Bertrand 1976, *Stratégie de la gréve*, Paris: Presses de la Fondation Nationale des Sciences Politiques.

Bakhtin, Michail M. 1981, *The Dialogic Imagination*, Austin: University of Texas Press.

Bakhtin, Michail M. 1986, *Speech Genres and Other Late Essays*, Austin: University of Texas Press.

Barglow, Raymond 1994, *The Crisis of the Self in the Age of Information: Computers, Dolphins and Dreams*, London: Routledge.

Barkan, Steven E. 1984, 'Legal Control of the Southern Civil Rights Movement', *American Sociological Review* 49: 552–65.

Barnes, Samuel, Kaase, Max *et al.* 1979, *Political Action: Mass Participation in Five Western Democracies*, London: Sage.

Barthes, Roland 1970, *Writing Degree Zero*, Boston: Beacon.

Barthes, Roland 1975, *The Pleasure of the Text*, New York: Hill and Wang.

Bartholomew, Anne and Mayer, Margit 1992, 'Nomads of the Present: Melucci's Contribution to "New Social Movement" Theory', *Theory, Culture and Society* 9, 3: 141–59.

Bateson, Gregory 1972, *Steps to an Ecology of Mind*, New York: Ballantine.

Bateson, Gregory 1979, *Mind and Nature*, New York: E. P. Dutton.

Baudrillard, Jean 1975, *The Mirror of Production*, St. Louis: Telos.

Baudrillard, Jean 1993, *Symbolic Exchange and Death*, London: Sage.

Bauman, Zygmunt 1991, *Modernity and Ambivalence*, Cambridge: Polity Press.

Bauman, Zygmunt 1992, *Intimations of Postmodernity*, London: Routledge.

Bauman, Zygmunt 1993a, *Mortality, Immortality and Other Life Strategies*, Cambridge: Polity Press.

Bauman, Zygmunt 1993b, *Postmodern Ethics*, Oxford: Blackwell.

Beck, Ulrich 1992, *Risk Society. Towards a New Modernity*, London: Sage.

Beckford, James A. 1989, *Religion and Advanced Industrial Society*, London: Unwin Hyman.

Bellah, Robert N., Marsden, Richard, Sullivan, William M., Swidler, Ann and Tipton, Steven M. 1985, *Habits of the Heart. Individualism and Commitment in American Life*, Berkeley: University of California Press.

Benedikt, Michael (ed.) 1991, *Cyberspace: First Steps*, Cambridge. MA: MIT Press.

Benford, Robert D. 1993, 'Frame Disputes Within the Disarmament Movement', *Social Forces* 71: 677–701.

Benford, Robert D. and Hunt, Scott A. 1992, 'Dramaturgy and Social Movements: The Social Construction and Communication of Power', *Sociological Inquiry* 62: 3–55.

Bennett, W. Lance 1988, *News: The Politics of Illusion*, New York: Longman.

Berejikian, Jeffrey 1992, 'Revolutionary Collective Action and the Agent–Structure Problem', *American Political Science Review* 86: 649–57.

Berger, Peter L., Berger, Brigitte and Kellner, Hansfried 1973, *The Homeless Mind*, Harmondsworth: Penguin.

Berger, Suzanne (ed.) 1981, *Organizing Interests in Western Europe*, Cambridge University Press.

Berkowitz, Leonard (ed.) 1969, *Roots of Aggression: A Re-examination of the Frustration-Aggression Hypothesis*, New York: Atherton Press.

Berkowitz, Leonard 1972, 'Frustrations, Comparisons, and Other Sources of Emotional Arousal as Contributors to Social Unrest', *Journal of Social Issues* 28: 78–91.

Berkowitz, Leonard (ed.) 1988, *Social Psychological Studies of the Self: Perspectives and Programs*, San Diego: Academic Press.

Berman Paul (ed.) 1992, *Debating P. C.: The Controversy Over Political Corectedness on College Campuses*, New York: Dell.

Bertaux, Daniel 1981, *Biography and Society*, London: Sage.

Billig, Michael 1978, *Fascists: A Social Psychological View of the National Front*, London: Academic Press.

Billig, Michael 1991, *Ideology and Opinions: Studies in Rhetorical Psychology*, London: Sage.

Billig, Michael 1992, *Talking of the Royal Family*, London: Routledge.

Billig, Michael 1995, 'Rhetorical Psychology, Ideological Thinking and Imagining Nationhood', in Johnston and Klandermans (eds.) 1995, 64–81.

Billig, Michael, Condor, Susan, Edwards, Derek *et al.* 1988, *Ideological Dilemmas: A Social Psychology of Everyday Thinking*, London: Sage.

Blackey, Robert 1976, *Modern Revolutions and Revolutionists: A Bibliography*, Oxford: Clio Press.

Blackmer, Donald L. M. and Tarrow, Sidney (eds.) 1975, *Communism in Italy and France*, Princeton University Press.

Blee, Kathleen 1991, *Women of the Klan*, Berkeley: University of California Press.

Bobbio, Norberto 1987, *Which Socialism: Marxism, Socialism and Democracy*, Cambridge: Polity Press.

Bobbio, Norberto 1989, *Democracy and Dictatorship: The Nature and Limits of State Power*, Cambridge: Polity Press.

Bobbio, Norberto 1994, *Destra e Sinistra*, Roma: Donzelli.

Boggs, Carl 1986, *Social Movements and Political Power*, Philadelphia: Temple University Press.

Bonnicksen, Andrea L. 1989, *In Vitro Fertilization: Building Policies from Laboratories to Legislatures*, New York: Columbia University Press.

Bourdieu, Pierre 1977, *Outline of a Theory of Practice*, Cambridge University Press.

Bourdieu, Pierre 1984, *Distinction: A Social Critique of the Judgement of Taste*, London: Routledge.

Bourdieu, Pierre 1990a, *In Other Words: Essays Towards a Reflexive Sociology*, Cambridge: Polity Press.

Bourdieu, Pierre 1990b, *The Logic of Practice*, Stanford University Press.

Braden Johnson, Ann 1990, *Out of Bedlam: The Truth about Deinstitutionalization*, New York: Free Press.

Brand, Karl-Werner 1990, 'Cyclical Aspects of New Social Movements: Waves of Cultural Criticism and Mobilization Cycles of New Middle-class Radicalism', in Dalton and Kuechler (eds.) 1990, 23–42.

Breakwell, Glynis M. (ed.) 1992, *Social Psychology of Identity and the Self Concept*, London: University of Surrey Press.

Breines, Wini 1982, *Community and Organization in the New Left, 1962–68*, New York: Praeger.

Briggs, Charles L. 1986, *Learning How to Ask*, Cambridge University Press.

Bright, Charles and Harding, Susan (eds.) 1984, *Statemaking and Social Movements: Essays in History and Theory*, Ann Arbor: The University of Michigan Press.

Bryman, Alan 1992, *Charisma and Leadership in Organizations*, London: Sage.

Brinton, Crane 1965, *Anatomy of Revolution*, New York: Knopf.

Bromley, David G. and Hammond, Phillip E. (eds.) 1987, *The Future of the New Religious Movements*, Macon, Ga.: Mercer University Press.

Brown, Helen 1992, *Women Organising*, London: Routledge.

Bruner, Jerome 1986, *Actual Minds, Possible Worlds*, Cambridge, MA: Harvard University Press.

Bruner, Jerome 1990, *Acts of Meaning*, Cambridge. MA: Harvard University Press.

Buechler, Steven M 1990, *Women's Movements in the United States*, New Brunswick: Rutgers University Press.

Burke, Kenneth 1969, *A Rhetoric of Motives*, Berkeley: University of California Press.

Burke, Peter 1992 'We, the People: Popular Culture and Identity in Modern Europe', in Lash and Friedman 1992, 293–308.

Burkitt, Ian 1991, *Social Selves: Theories of the Social Formation of Personality*, London: Sage.

Busfield, Joan 1989, *Managing Madness: Changing Ideas and Practice*, London: Unwin Hyman.

Calderon, Fernando 1986, *Los Movimientos Sociales ante la Crisis*, Buenos Aires: United Nations University.

Calhoun, Craig 1982, *The Question of Class Struggle: Social Foundations of Popular Radicalism during the Industrial Revolution*, University of Chicago Press.

Calhoun, Craig 1983, 'The Radicalism of Tradition: Community Strength or Venerable Disguise and Borrowed Language?', *American Journal of Sociology* 88: 886–914.

Calhoun, Craig 1993, 'New Social Movements of the Early Nineteenth Century', *Social Science History* 17: 385–427.

Calhoun, Craig (ed.) 1994, *Social Theory and the Politics of Identity*, Oxford: Blackwell.

Capek, Stella 1993, 'The 'Environmental Justice' Frame: A Conceptual Discussion and an Application', *Social Problems* 40, 1: 5–24.

Carter, April 1973, *Direct Action and Liberal Democracy*, London: Routledge.

Cassell, Joan 1977, *A Group Called Women: Sisterhood and Symbolism in the Feminist Movement*, New York: David McKay.

Castells, Manuel 1983, *The City and the Grassroots: A Cross-cultural Theeory of Urban Social Movements*, Berkeley: University of California Press.

Castleman, Craig 1982, *Getting Up: Subway Graffiti in New York*, Cambridge. MA: MIT Press.

Caute, David 1988, *The Year of the Barricades: A Journey through 1968*, New York: Harper and Row.

Chambers, Iain 1985, *Urban Rythms: Pop Music and Popular Culture*, London: Macmillan.

Chambers, Iain 1986, *Popular Culture: The Metropolitan Experience*, London: Methuen.

Chambers, Iain 1994, *Migrancy, Culture and Identity*, London: Routledge.

Chartier, Roger 1991, *The Cultural Origins of the French Revolution*, Durham, NC: Duke University Press.

Chodorow, Nancy 1978, *The Reproduction of Mothering: Psychoanalysis and the Sociology of Gender*, Berkeley: University of California Press.

Chong, Dennis 1991, *Collective Action and the Civil Rights Movement*, University of Chicago Press.

Cicourel, Aaron V. 1974, *Cognitive Sociology*, New York: Free Press.

Cicourel, Aaron V. 1982, 'Interviews, Surveys, and the Problem of Ecological Validity', *American Sociologist* 17: 11–20.

Clark, David (ed.) 1993, *The Sociology of Death*, Oxford: Blackwell.

Clastres, Pierre 1977, *Society against the State*, Oxford: Blackwell.

Clifford, James 1988, *The Predicament of Culture*, Cambridge. MA: Harvard University Press.

Coakley, John 1992, *The Social Origins of Nationalist Movements*, London: Sage.

Cohen, Jean L. 1985, 'Strategy or Identity: New Theoretical Paradigms and Contemporary Social Movements', *Social Research,* 52, 4: 663–716.

Colburn, Forrest D. (ed.) 1989, *Everyday Forms of Peasant Resistance*, Armonk, NY: M. E. Sharpe.

Coleman, James S. 1982, *The Asymmetric Society*, Syracuse University Press.

Coleman, James S. 1990, *Foundations of Social Theory*, Cambridge, Mass.: Harvard University Press.

Collins, Randall 1975, *Conflict Sociology*, New York: Academic Press.

Collins, Randall 1981, 'On the Microfoundations of Macrosociology', *American Journal of Sociology* 86: 984–1014.

Collins, Randall 1988, 'The Micro Contribution to Macro Sociology', *Sociological Theory* 6: 242–53.

Collins, Randall 1989, 'Toward a Neo-Meadian Sociology of Mind', *Symbolic Interaction* 12: 1–32.

Comor, Edward A. (ed.) 1994, *The Global Political Economy of Communication: Hegemony, Telecommunication and the Information Economy*, London: Macmillan.

Cornell, Stephen 1988, *The Return of the Native: American Indian Political Resurgence*, Oxford University Press.

Costain, Anne N. 1992, *Inviting Women's Rebellion: A Political Process Interpretation of the Women's Movement*, Baltimore: Johns Hopkins University Press.

Costain, Anne N. and Costain W. Douglas 1987, 'Strategy and Tactics of the Women's Movement in the United States: The Role of Political Parties', in Katzenstein and Mueller (eds.)1987, 196–214.

Coupland, Douglas 1991, *Generation X*, London: Abacus.

Crook, Stephen, Pakulski, Jan and Waters, Malcolm 1992, *Postmodernization: Change in Advanced Society*, London: Sage.

Crompton, Rosemary, *Class and Stratification: an Introduction to Current Debates*, Cambridge: Polity Press.

Crouch, Colin and Pizzorno, Alessandro (eds.) 1978, *The Resurgence of Class Conflict in Western Europe since 1968*, London: Macmillan.

Crozier, Michel and Friedberg, Erhard 1978, *L'acteur et le systéme*, Paris: Seuil.

Dahrendorf, Ralph 1972, *Class and Class Conflict in Industrial Society*, rev. edn, Stanford University Press.

Dahrendorf, Ralph 1988, *The Modern Social Conflict*, London: Weidenfeld and Nicolson.

Dalton, Russell 1994, *The Green Rainbow: Environmental Groups in Western Europe*, New Haven: Yale University Press.

Dalton, Russell and Kuechler, Manfred (eds.) 1990, *Challenging the Political Order: New Social and Political Movements in Western Democracies*, Oxford University Press.

D'Anieri, Paul, Erst, Claire and Kier, Elizabeth 1990, 'New Social Movements in Historical Perspective', *Comparative Politics* 22: 445–58.

Daragan, Natalia 1991, 'Social Portrait of Nationalist Activists in the Soviet Union', *Innovation* 4: 133–42.

Darnowsky, Marcy, Epstein, Barbara and Flacks, Richard (eds.) 1995, *Cultural Politics and Social Movements*, Philadelphia: Temple University Press.

Davies, James C. 1969, 'The J-Curve of Rising and Declining Satisfaction as a Cause of Some Great Revolutions and a Contained Rebellion', in Graham, Hugh D. and Gurr, Ted R. (eds.), *Violence in America: Historical and Comparative Perspectives*, New York: Praeger, 690-730.

Davies, Karen 1989, *Women and Time*, University of Lund.

Davis, Kingsley and Moore, Wilbert E. 1945, 'Some Principles of Stratification', *American Sociological Review* 10: 242–9.

De Certeau, Michel 1984, *The Practice of Everyday Life*, Berkeley: University of California Press.

De Certeau, Michel 1986, *Heterologies: Discourse on the Other*, Manchester University Press.

De Fronzo, James 1991, *Revolutions and Revolutionary Movements*, Boulder: Westview Press.

Deleuze, Gilles and Guattari, Felix 1977, *Anti-Oedipus: Capitalism and Schizophrenia*, New York: Viking Press.

Della Porta, Donatella 1988, 'Recruitment Processes in Clandestine Political Organizations: Italian Left-wing Terrorism', in Klandermans, Kriesi and Tarrow (eds.) 1986, 155–69.

Della Porta, Donatella 1992a, 'Life Histories in the Analysis of Social Movements Activists', in Diani and Eyerman (eds.) 1992, 168–93.

Della Porta, Donatella (ed.) 1992b, *Social Movements and Violence: Participation in Underground Organizations*, International Social Movement Research, vol. 4, Greenwich, Conn.: JAI Press.

D'Emilio, John 1983, *Sexual Politics, Sexual Communities*, University of Chicago Press.

D'Emilio, John 1992, *Making Trouble. Essays on Gay History, Politics and the University*, London: Routledge.

D'Emilio, John and Freedman, Estelle B. 1988, *Intimate Matters: A History of Sexuality in America*, New York: Harper and Row.

Di Nardo, James 1985, *Power in Numbers. The Political Strategy of Protest and Rebellion*, Princeton University Press.

Diamond, Edwin 1975, *The Tin Kazoo: Television, Politics, and the News*, Cambridge, MA: MIT Press.

Diani, Mario 1992, 'The Concept of Social Movement', *Sociological Review* 40: 1–25.

Diani, Mario 1995, *Green Networks. A Structural Analysis of the Italian Environmental Movement*, Edinburgh University Press.

Diani, Mario 1996, 'Linking Mobilization Frames and Political Opportunity

Structure: Reflections on Italian Regional Populism', *American Sociological Review* 61: forthcoming.

Diani, Mario, and Eyerman, Ron (eds.) 1992, *Studying Collective Action*, London: Sage.

Donald, James and Rattansi, Ali (eds.) 1992, *Race, Culture and Difference*, London: Sage.

Donati, Paolo 1992, 'Political Discourse Analysis', in Diani and Eyerman (eds.) 1992, 136–65.

Donzelot, Jacques 1979, *The Policing of Families*, London: Hutchinson.

Donzelot, Jacques 1984, *L'invention du social*, Paris: Fayard.

Douglas, Mary 1970, *Purity and Danger*, Harmondsworth: Penguin.

Douglas, Mary 1986, *How Institutions Think*, Syracuse University Press.

Douglas, Mary 1992, *Risk and Blame*, London: Routledge.

Downton, James V. 1973, *Rebel Leadership: Commitment and Charisma in the Revolutionary Process*, New York: Free Press.

Dubet, François 1987, *La Gal-re. Jeunes en survie*, Paris: Fayard.

Dubet, François 1994, *Sociologie de l'expérience*, Paris: Seuil.

Dubois, Pierre 1976, *Le sabotage dans l'industrie*, Paris: Calmann-Levy.

Dumont, Louis 1983, *Essai sur l'individualisme*, Paris: Seuil.

Eckstein, Harry 1965, 'On the Etiology of Internal Wars', *History and Theory* 4, 2: 133–63.

Edelman, Murray J. 1988, *Constructing the Political Spectacle*, University of Chicago Press.

Eder, Klaus 1993, *The New Politics of Class: Social Movements and Cultural Dynamics in Advanced Societies*, London: Sage.

Eder, Klaus 1995, 'Does Social Class Matter in the Study of Social Movements? A Theory of Middle-class Radicalism', in Maheu (ed.)1995, 21–54.

Edwards, Derek and Potter, Jonathan 1993, *Discursive Psychology*. London: Sage.

Eiser, John R. 1980, *Cognitive Social Psychology*, London: McGraw-Hill.

Eisinger, Peter K. 1973, 'The Conditions of Protest Behaviour in American Cities,' *American Political Science Review* 67: 11–28.

Ekins, Paul 1992, *A New World Order: Grass Root Movements for Global Change*, London: Routledge.

Elias, Norbert 1991, *The Society of Individuals*, Oxford: Blackwell.

Elias, Norbert 1993, *Time: An Essay*, Oxford: Blackwell.

Elias, Norbert 1994, *The Civilizing Process*, Oxford: Blackwell.

Ellis, Carolyn and Flaherty, Michael G. 1992, *Investigating Subjectivity: Research on Lived Experience*, London: Sage.

Elster, Jon (ed.) 1985, *The Multiple Self*, Cambridge University Press.

Elster, Jon 1992, *Local Justice: How Institutions Allocate Scarce Goods and Necessary Burdens*, New York: Russel Sage.

Epstein, Barbara 1990a, *Political Protest and Cultural Revolution: Nonviolent Direct Action in the 1970s and 1980s*, Berkeley: University of California Press.

Epstein, Barbara 1990b, 'Rethinking Social Movement Theory', *Socialist Review* 20: 35–66.

Epstein, Edward J. 1973, *News from Nowhere*, New York: Random House.

Epstein, Steven 1987, 'Gay Politics, Ethnic Identity: The Limits of Social Constructionism', *Socialist Review* 17: 9–54.

Escobar, Arturo and Alvarez, Sonia E. (eds.) 1992, *The Making of Social Movements in Latin America: Identity, Strategy and Democracy*, Boulder CO: Westview Press.

Esman, Milton J. (ed.) 1977, *Ethnic Conflict in the Western World*, Ithaca: Cornell University Press.

Esping-Andersen, Gosta (ed.) 1993, *Changing Classes: Stratification and Mobility in Post-Industrial Societies*, London: Sage.

Etzioni, Amitai 1968, 'Mobilization as a Macro-Sociological Conception', *British Journal of Sociology* 19: 243–53.

Etzioni, Amitai 1993, *The Spirit of Community*, New York: Crown.

Evans, Peter B., Rueschemeyer Dietrich and Skocpol, Theda (eds.) 1985, *Bringing the State Back In*, Cambridge University Press.

Evans, Sara 1980, *Personal Politics: The Roots of Women's Liberation in the Civil Rights Movement and the New Left*, New York: Vintage.

Evans, Sara, and Boyte, Harry 1986, *Free Spaces*, New York: Harper and Row.

Eyerman, Ron 1994, *Between Culture and Politics: Intellectuals in Modern Society*, Cambridge: Polity Press.

Eyerman, Ron and Jamison Andrew 1991, *Social Movements: A Cognitive Approach*, University Park: Pennsylvania University Press.

Fabian, Johannes 1983, *Time and the Other: How Anthopology Makes Its Other*, New York: Columbia University Press.

Falk, Pasi 1994, *The Consuming Body*, London: Sage.

Falk, Richard A. 1992, *Exploration at the Edge of Time: The Prospects for World Order*, Philadelphia: Temple University Press.

Fancher, Robert 1994, *Cultures of Healing: Correcting the Image of American Mental Health Care*, New York: W. H. Freeman.

Fantasia, Rick 1988, *Cultures of Solidarity*, Berkeley: University of California Press.

Farr, Robert M. and Moscovici, Serge (eds.) 1984, *Social Representations*, Cambridge University Press.

Favre, Pierre (ed.) 1990, *La manifestation*, Paris: Presses de la Fondation Nationale des Sciences Politiques.

Featherstone, Mike 1992, *Consumer Culture and Postmodernism*, London: Sage.

Featherstone, Mike (ed.) 1988, *Postmodernism*, London: Sage.

Featherstone, Mike (ed.) 1990, *Global Culture: Nationalism, Globalization and Modernity*, London: Sage.

Featherstone, Mike and Burrows, Roger (eds.) 1995, *Cyberspace/Cyberbodies/Cyberpunk*, London: Sage.

Featherstone, Mike, Hepworth, Mike and Turner, Bryan S. (eds.) 1991, *The Body: Social Process and Cultural Theory*, London: Sage.

Feldman, Steven P. 1990, 'Stories as Cultural Creativity: On the Relation between

Symbolism and Politics in Organizational Change', *Human Relations* 43: 809–28.

Ferguson, Marjorie (ed.) 1990, *Public Communication: The New Imperatives*, London: Sage.

Fernandez, Roberto M. and McAdam, Doug 1989, 'Multiorganizational Fields and Recruitment to Social Movements', in Klandermans (ed.) 1989, 315–43.

Ferree, Myra Marx 1992, 'The Political Context of Rationality: Rational Choice Theory and Resource Mobilization', in Morris and Mueller (eds.) 1992, 29–52.

Ferree, Myra Marx and Martin, Patricia Yancey (eds.) 1994, *Feminist Organizations: Harvest of the New Women's Movement*, Philadelphia: Temple University Press.

Field, David 1989, *Nursing the Dying*, London: Routledge.

Field, Martha A. 1988, *Surrogate Motherhood: The Legal and Human Issues*, Cambridge, MA: Harvard University Press.

Fine, Gary A. 1995, 'Public Narration and Group Culture: Discerning Discourse in Social Movements', in Johnson and Klandermans (eds.) 1995, 127–43.

Fineman, Stephen (ed.) 1993, *Emotions in Organizations*, London: Sage.

Fireman, Bruce and Gamson, William H. 1979, 'Utilitarian Logic in the Resource Mobilization Perspective', in Zald and McCarthy (eds.) 1979, 8–44.

Fiske, John 1987, *Television Culture*, London: Methuen.

Fiske, John 1989, *Understanding Popular Culture*, Boston: Unwin Hyman.

Flacks, Richard 1967, 'The Liberated Generation: An Exploration of the Roots of Student Protest', *Journal of Social Issues* 23: 52–75.

Flacks, Richard 1988, *Making History: The American Left and the American Mind*, New York: Columbia University Press.

Flacks, Richard 1994, 'The Party's Over. So What Is to be Done?' in Larana, Johnston and Gusfield (eds.) 1994, 330-51.

Flam, Helena (ed.) 1994, *States and Anti-nuclear Movements*, Edinburgh University Press.

Foran, John (ed.) 1994, *A Century of Revolution: Social Movements in Iran*, Minneapolis: University of Minnesota Press.

Forman, Frieda Johles and Sowton, Caoran 1989 (eds.), *Taking Our Time: Feminist Perspectives on Temporality*, Oxford: Pergamon Press.

Fornas, Johan and Bolin, Goran 1995, *Youth Culture in Late Modernity*, London: Sage.

Foucault, Michel 1970, *The Order of Things*, London: Tavistock Publications.

Foucault, Michel 1979, *Discipline and Punish: The Birth of Prison*, New York: Vintage/Random.

Foucault, Michel 1980a, *A History of Sexuality*, New York: Vintage.

Foucault, Michel 1980b, *Power/Knowledge: Selected Interviews and Other Writings, 1972–1977*, New York: Pantheon.

Foweraker, Joe and Craig, Ann L. (eds.) 1990, *Popular Movements and Political Change in Mexico*, Boulder: Linner Rienner.

Fraser, Nancy 1989, *Unruly Practices: Power, Discourse, and Gender in Contemporary Social Theory*, Minneapolis: University of Minnesota Press.

Fraser, Ronald, Bertaux, Daniel *et al.* 1988, *1968: A Student Generation in Revolt: An International Oral History*, New York: Pantheon Books.

Freeman, Jo 1975, *The Politics of Women's Liberation*, New York: David McKay.

Freeman, Jo 1983 (ed.), *Social Movements in the Sixties and Seventies*, New York: Longman.

Freeman, Jo 1987, 'Whom You Know versus Whom You Represent: Feminist Politics in the United States', in Katzenstein and Mueller (eds.) 1987, 215–44.

Friedman, Debra and McAdam, Doug 1992, 'Collective Identity and Activism: Networks, Choices, and the Life of a Social Movement', in Morris and Mueller (eds.) 1992, 156–73.

Friedman, Jonathan 1994, *Cultural Identity and Global Process*, London: Sage.

Frith, Simon and Goodwin, Andrew (eds.) 1990, *On Record: Rock, Pop and the Written Word*, New York: Pantheon Books.

Frykman, Jonas 1995, 'The Informalization of National Identity', *Ethnologia Europaea* 25: 5–15.

Gadamer, Hans Georg 1976, *Philosophical Hermeneutics*, Berkeley: University of California Press.

Galtung, Johan 1994, *Human Rights in Another Key*, Cambridge: Polity Press.

Gamson, Josh 1989, 'Silence, Death, and the Invisible Enemy: AIDS Activism and Social Movement "Newness"', *Social Problems*, 36: 351–67.

Gamson, William A. 1988, 'Political Discourse and Collective Action', in Klandermans, Kriesi and Tarrow (eds.) 1988, 219–44.

Gamson, William A. 1990, *The Strategy of Social Protest*, Belmont, CA: Wadsworth.

Gamson, William A. 1992a, 'The Social Psychology of Collective Action', in Morris and Mueller (eds.) 1992, 53–76.

Gamson, William A. 1992b, *Talking Politics*, Cambridge University Press.

Gamson, William A. 1995, 'Constructing Social Protest', in Johnston and Klandermans (eds.) 1995, 85–106.

Gamson, William A., Fireman, Bruce and Rytina, Steven 1982, *Encounters with Unjust Authority*, Homewood, Ill.: Dorsey.

Gamson, William, and Modigliani, Andre 1989, 'Media Discourse and Public Opinion on Nuclear Power', *American Journal of Sociology* 95: 1–37.

Gans, Herbert J. 1979, 'Symbolic Ethnicity: The Future of Ethnic Groups and Cultures in America', *Ethnic and Racial Studies*, 2: 1–20.

Gans, Herbert J. 1988, *Middle American Individualism*, New York: Free Press.

Garfinkel, Harold 1967, *Studies in Ethnomethodology*, Englewood Cliffs NJ: Prentice-Hall.

Garner, Roberta Ash and Zald, Mayer N. 1985, 'The Political Economy of Social Movement Sectors', in Suttles and Zald (eds.) 1985, 119–45.

Geertz, Clifford 1973, *The Interpretation of Cultures*, New York: Basic Books.

Geertz, Clifford 1983, *Local Knowledge*, New York: Basic Books.

Gelb, Joyce 1987, 'Social Movement Success: A Comparative Analysis of Feminism in the United States and the United Kingdom', in Katzenstein and Mueller (eds.) 1987, 267–89.

Gellner, Ernst 1983, *Nations and Nationalism*, Oxford: Blackwell.

Gellner, Ernst 1987, *Culture, Identity and Politics*, Cambridge University Press.

Gergen, Kenneth J. 1982, *Towards Transformation in Social Knowledge*, New York: Springer.

Gergen, Kenneth J. 1985, 'The Social Constructionist Movement in Modern Psychology', *American Psychologist* 40: 266–75.

Gergen, Kenneth J. 1989, 'Social Psychology and the Wrong Revolution', *European Journal of Social Psychology* 19: 463–84.

Gergen, Kenneth J. 1991, *The Saturated Self: Dilemmas of Identity in Contemporary Life*, New York: Basic Books.

Gerhards, Jurgen, and Rucht, Dieter 1992, 'Mesomobilization: Organizing and Framing in Two Protest Campaigns in West Germany', *American Journal of Sociology*, 98: 555–95.

Gerlach, Luther P. and Hine, Virginia H. 1970, *People, Power, Change: Movements of Social Transformation*, Indianapolis: Bobbs-Merrill.

Gerlach, Luther P. and Hine, Virginia H. 1973, *Lifeway Leap: The Dynamics of Change in America*, Minneapolis: University of Minnesota Press.

Gershuny, Jonathan I. and Miles, Ian D. 1983, *The New Service Economy: The Transformation of Employment in Industrial Societies*, London: Pinter.

Gherardi, Sivia 1995, *Gender, Symbolism and Organizational Cultures*, London: Sage.

Geschwender, James A. 1968 'Explorations in the Theory of Social Movements and Revolutions', *Social Forces* 47: 127–35.

Giddens, Anthony 1984, *The Constitution of Society*, Cambridge: Polity Press.

Giddens, Anthony 1985, *The Nation State and Violence*, Berkeley: University of California Press.

Giddens, Anthony 1987, *Social Theory and Modern Sociology*, Cambridge: Polity Press.

Giddens, Anthony 1990, *The Consequences of Modernity*, Cambridge: Polity Press.

Giddens, Anthony 1991, *Modernity and Self-Identity: Self and Society in the Late Modern Age*, Cambridge: Polity Press.

Giddens, Anthony 1992, *The Transformation of Intimacy*, Cambridge: Polity Press.

Giddens, Anthony 1994, *Beyond Left and Right: The Future of Radical Politics*, Cambridge: Polity Press.

Gieryn, Thomas F. 1983, 'Boundary-Work and the Demarcation of Science from Non-Science: Strains and Interests in Professional Ideologies of Scientists', *American Sociological Review* 48: 781–95.

Gilbert, G. Nigel and Mulkay, Michael J. 1984, *Opening Pandora's Box: A Sociological Analysis of Scientists*, Cambridge University Press.

Gilligan, Carol 1982, *In a Different Voice*, Cambridge, MA: Harvard University Press.

Gilroy, Paul 1987, *There Ain't No Black in the Union Jack*, London: Hutchinson.

Gilroy, Paul 1993a, *Small Acts*, London: Serpent's Tail.

Gilroy, Paul 1993b, *The Black Atlantic*, Cambridge MA: Harvard University Press.

Gitlin, Todd 1980, *The Whole World Is Watching: Mass Media Unmaking of the New Left*, Berkeley: University of California Press.

Gitlin, Todd 1987, *The Sixties: Years of Hope, Days of Rage*, New York: Bantam Books.

Giugni, Marco 1995, *Entre strategie et opportunité: les nouveaux mouvements sociaux en Suisse*, Zurich: Seismo.

Glendon, Mary Ann 1991, *Rights Talk: The Impoverishment of Political Discourse*, New York: Free Press.

Goldfarb, Jeffrey C. 1991, *The Cynical Society*, University of Chicago Press.

Granovetter, Mark 1973,'The Strength of Weak Ties: A Network Theory Revisited', *American Journal of Sociology* 78: 1360-80.

Graumann, Carl F. and Moscovici, Serge (eds.) 1987, *Changing Conceptions of Conspiracy*, New York: Springer.

Greenfield, Liah 1992, *Nationalism: Five Roads to Modernity*, Cambridge MA: Harvard University Press.

Gregory, Derek and Urry, John (eds.) 1985, *Social Relations and Spatial Structures*, London: Macmillan.

Gurr, Ted R. 1970, *Why Men Rebel*, Princeton NJ: Princeton University Press.

Gurr, Ted R. 1988, 'Empirical Research on Political Terrorism: The State of the Art and How it Might Be Improved', in Slater and Stohl (eds.) 1988, 115–54.

Gusfield, Joseph R. 1963, *Symbolic Crusade*, Urbana: University of Illinois Press.

Gusfield, Joseph R. 1981, *The Culture of Public Problems: Drinking and Driving and the Symbolic Order*, University of Chicago Press.

Gusfield, Joseph R. 1995, 'The Reflexivity of Social Movements: Collective Behaviour and Mass Society Theory Revisited', in Johnston and Klandermans (eds.) 1995, 58–78.

Habermas, Jurgen 1976, *Zur Rekonstruktion des Historichen Materialismus*, Frankfurt: Suhrkamp.

Habermas, Jurgen 1984, *The Theory of Communicative Action: Vol. I: Reason and Rationalization of Society*, Cambridge: Polity Press.

Habermas, Jurgen 1987, *The Theory of Communicative Action: Vol. II: The Critique of Functionalist Reason*, Cambridge: Polity Press.

Habermas, Jurgen 1989, *The Structural Transformation of the Public Sphere*, Cambridge: Polity Press.

Habermas, Jurgen 1990, *The Philosophical Discourse of Modernity*, Cambridge: Polity Press.

Halbwachs, Maurice 1975, *Les cadres sociaux de la mémoire*, Paris: Mouton (original edition 1925).

Halebsky, Sandor 1976, *Mass Society and Political Conflict*, Cambridge University Press.

Hall, Stuart and Jefferson, Tony (eds.) 1979, *Resistance Through Rituals: Youth Subcultures in Post-war Britain*, London: Macmillan.

Hall, Stuart and Jacques, Martin (eds.) 1989, *New Times: The Changing Face of Politics in the 1990s*, London: Lawrence and Wishart.

Hardin, Russell 1982, *Collective Action*, Baltimore: Johns Hopkins University Press.

Harding, Sandra 1991, *Whose Science? Whose Knowledge?*, Ithaca: Cornell University Press.

Harré, Rom and Gillett, Grant 1994, *The Discursive Mind*, London: Sage.

Harvey, D. 1989, *The Condition of Post-Modernity*, Oxford: Blackwell.

Hassard, J. (ed.) 1990, *The Sociology of Time*, London: Macmillan.

Heath, Anthony 1976, *Rational Choice and Social Exchange: A Critique of Exchange Theory*, Cambridge University Press.

Hebdige, Dick 1979, *Subcultures: The Meaning of Style*, London: Methuen.

Hechter, Michael 1975, *Internal Colonialism*, London: Routledge.

Hegedus, Szusza 1989, 'Social Movements and Social Change in Self-Creative Society: New Civil Initiatives in International Arena', *International Sociology* 4, 1: 19–36.

Hellman, Judith Adler 1987a, *Journeys Among Women: Feminism in Five Italian Cities*, Oxford University Press.

Hellman, Stephen 1987b, 'Feminism and the Model of Militancy in an Italian Communist Federation', in Katzenstein and Mueller (eds.) 1987, 132–52.

Hellman, Stephen 1988, *Italian Communism in Transition: The Rise and Fall of the Historic Compromise in Turin, 1975–1980*, Oxford University Press.

Hilgartner, Steven, and Bosk, Charles 1988, 'The Rise and Fall of Social Problems: A Public Arenas Model', *American Journal of Sociology*, 94: 53–78.

Hill Collins, Patricia 1990, *Black Feminist Thought*, New York: Routledge.

Hirsch, Eli 1982, *The Concept of Identity*, Oxford University Press.

Hirsch, Eric L. 1986. 'The Creation of Political Solidarity in Social Movement Organizations', *Sociological Quarterly* 27: 373–87.

Hirsch, Eric L. 1990a, *Urban Revolt: Ethnic Politics in the Nineteenth Century Chicago Labour Movement*, Berkeley: University of California Press.

Hirsch, Eric L. 1990b, 'Sacrifice for the Cause: Group Processes, Recruitment and Commitment in a Student Movement', *American Sociological Review* 55: 243–54.

Hirschman, Albert O. 1975, *Exit, Voice and Loyalty: Responses to Decline in Firms, Organizations and States*, Cambridge MA: Harvard University Press.

Hirschman, Albert O. 1982, *Shifting Involvements: Private Interest and Public Action*, Princeton University Press.

Hobsbawm, E. J. 1959, *Primitive Rebels*, New York: Norton.

Hobsbawm, Eric J. 1962, *The Age of Revolution: 1789–1848*, London: Weidenfeld and Nicolson.

Hobsbawm, Eric J. and Ranger, Terrence (eds.) 1983, *The Invention of Tradition*, Cambridge University Press.

Hochschild, Arlie 1979, 'Emotion Work, Feeling Rules, and Social Structure', *American Journal of Sociology* 35: 551–73.

Hochschild, Arlie 1983, *The Managed Heart*, Berkeley: University of California Press.

Hoffer, Eric 1951, *The True Believer. Thoughts on the Nature of Mass Movements*, New York: Harper and Row.

Hollander, Edwin P. 1964, *Leaders, Groups, and Influence*, Oxford University Press.

Hollander, Edwin P. 1978, *Leadership Dynamics*, New York: Free Press.

hooks, bell 1993, *Sisters of the Yam: Black Women and Self-Recovery*, Boston: South End Press.

Hormann, Hans 1986, *Meaning and Context*, New York: Plenum.

Hornborg, Alf 1994, 'Environmentalism, Ethnicity and Sacred Places: Reflections on Modernity, Discourse and Power', *Canadian Review of Sociology and Anthropology* 31: 245–267.

Horowitz, Donald L. 1977, 'Cultural Movements and Ethnic Change', *Annals of the American Academy of Political and Social Sciences* 433: 6–18.

Hugues, Robert 1993, *Culture of Complaint: The Fraying of America*, Oxford University Press.

Hunt, James G. 1991, *Leadership: A New Synthesis*, London: Sage.

Hunt, Lynn 1984, *Politics, Culture and Class in the French Revolution*, Berkeley: University of California Press.

Hunt, Scott A., Benford, Robert D. and Snow, David A. 1994, 'Identity Fields: Framing Processes and the Social Construction of Movements Identities', in Larana, Johnston, Gusfield (eds.) 1994, 185–208.

Hviding, Edvard 1995, *Guardians of Marovo Lagoon: Practice, Place and Politics in Maritime Melanesia*, Honolulu: University of Hawaii Press.

Inglehart, Ronald 1977, *The Silent Revolution: Changing Values and Political Styles among Western Publics*, Princeton University Press.

Inglehart, Ronald 1990, *Culture Shift in Advanced Industrial Society*, Princeton University Press.

Iyengar, Shanto 1991, *Is Anyone Responsible?: How Television News Frames Political Issues*, University of Chicago Press.

Iyengar, Shanto, and Kinder, Donald R. 1987, *News That Matters*, University of Chicago Press.

Jacobus, Mary, Keller, Evelyn Fox and Shuttleworth, Sally (eds.) 1990, *Body/Politics: Women and the Discourses of Science*, London: Routledge.

Jahn, Detlef 1993, 'The Rise and Decline of New Politics and the Greens in Sweden and Germany', *European Journal of Political Research* 24: 177–94.

Jameson, Fredric 1991, *Postmodernism, or the Cultural Logic of Late Capitalism*, London: Verso.

Jelin, Elizabeth (ed.) 1987a, *Movimientos sociales y democracia emergente*, Buenos Aires: Centro Editor de America Latina.

Jelin, Elizabeth (ed.) 1987b, *Ciudadania y identidad. Las Mujeres en los movimientos sociales latino-americanos*, Geneva: UNRISD.

Jelin, Elizabeth (ed.) 1990, *Women and Social Change in Latin America*, London: Zed Press.

Jenkins, J. Craig 1983, 'Resource Mobilization Theory and the Study of Social Movements', *Annual Review of Sociology* 9: 527–53.

Jenkins Craig J. and Klandermans, Bert (eds.) 1995, *The Politics of Social Protest:*

Comparative Perspectives on States and Social Movements, Minneapolis: University of Minnesota Press.

Jenson, Jane 1987, 'Changing Discourse, Changing Agendas: Political Rights an Reproductive Policies in France', in Katzenstein and Mueller (eds.) 1987, 64–88.

Jenson, Jane 1995, 'What's in a Name? Nationalist Movements and Public Discourse', in Johnston and Klandermans (eds.) 1995, 107–26.

Johnson, Chalmers 1964, *Revolution and Social System*, Stanford University Press.

Johnson-Laird, Phillip N. 1983, *Mental Models*, Cambridge MA: Harvard University Press.

Johnston, Hank 1991, *Tales of Nationalism: Catalonia, 1939–1979*, New Brunswick NJ: Rutgers University Press.

Johnston, Hank 1993, 'Religio-Nationalist Subcultures under the Communists: Comparisons from the Baltics, Transcaucasia and the Ukraine', *Sociology of Religion* 54, 3: 237–55.

Johnston, Hank 1995, 'A Methodology for Frame Analysis: From Discourse to Cognitive Schemata', in Johnston and Klandermans (eds.) 1995, 217–46.

Johnston, Hank and Klandermans, Bert (eds.) 1995, *Social Movements and Culture*, Minneapolis: University of Minnesota Press.

Johnston, Hank, Larana Enrique and Gusfield Joseph R. 1994, 'New Social Movements: Identities, Grievances and Ideologies of Everyday Life', in Larana, Johnston and Gusfield (eds.) 1994, 3–35.

Kanter, Rosabeth 1972, *Commitment and Community*, Cambridge MA: Harvard University Press.

Kanter, Rosabeth 1973, *Communes: Creating and Managing the Collective Life*, New York: Harper and Row.

Katsiaficas, George 1987, *The Imagination of the New Left*, Boston: South End Press.

Katzenstein, Mary Fainsod and Mueller, Carol McClurg (eds.) 1987, *The Women's Movements of the United States and Western Europe: Consciousness, Political Opportunity and Public Policy*, Philadelphia: Temple University Press.

Katznelson, Ira and Zolberg, Aristide R. (eds.) 1986, *Working Class Formation: Nineteenth Century Patterns in Western Europe and the United States*, Princeton University Press

Kauffman, L. A. 1990, 'The Anti-Politics of Identity', *Socialist Review* 20: 67–80.

Keane, John 1988a, *Democracy and Civil Society*, London: Verso.

Keane, John (ed.) 1988b, *Civil Society and the State*, London: Verso.

Keating, Michael 1988, *State and Regional Nationalism*, London: Harvester-Wheatsheaf.

Kepel, Gilles 1987, *Les banlieues de l'Islam*, Paris: Seuil.

Kepel, Gilles 1994, *A l'Ouest d'Allah*, Paris: Seuil.

Kemper, Theodore D. 1978, *A Social Interactional Theory of Emotions*, New York: Wiley.

Kemper, Theodore D. 1981, 'Social Constructionist and Positivist Approaches to the Sociology of Emotions', *American Journal of Sociology* 87: 33–62.

Kemper, Theodore D. (ed.) 1990, *Research Agendas in the Sociology of Emotions*, Albany: SUNY Press.

Kerbo, Harold R. 1982 'Movements of Crisis and Movements of Affluence: A Critique of Deprivation and Resource Mobilization Theories', *Journal of Conflict Resolution* 26: 645–63.

Kitschelt, Herbert P. 1986, 'Political Opportunity Structures and Political Protest: AntiNuclear Movements in Four Democracies', *British Journal of Political Science* 16: 57–85.

Kitschelt, Herbert P. 1989, *The Logic of Party Formation: Ecological Politics in Belgium and West Germany*, Ithaca, N.Y.: Cornell University Press.

Kitschelt, Herbert 1991, 'Resource Mobilization: A Critique', in Rucht (ed.) 1991, 323–47.

Kitsuse, John I. 1975, 'The New Conception of Deviance and Its Critics', in Gove, Walter R. (ed.), *The Labeling of Deviance: Evaluating a Perspective*, New York: Wiley/Halstead Press, 273–84.

Kivisto, Peter 1986, 'What's New about the 'New Social Movements'?: Continuities and Discontinuities with The Socialist Project', *Mid-American Review of Sociology* 11, 2: 29–44.

Klandermans, Bert 1984, 'Mobilization and Participation: Social-Psychological Expansions of Resource Mobilization Theory', *American Sociological Review* 49: 583–600.

Klandermans, Bert 1988, 'The Formation and Mobilization of Consensus', in Klandermans, Kriesi and Tarrow (eds.) 1988, 173–96.

Klandermans, Bert 1989a, 'Grievance Interpretation and Success Expectations: The Social Construction of Protest', *Social Behaviour* 4: 113–25.

Klandermans, Bert 1992, 'The Social Construction of Protest and Multiorganizational Fields', in Morris and Mueller (eds.) 1992, 77–103.

Klandermans, Bert 1993, 'A Theoretical Framework for Comparison of Social Movement Participation', *Sociological Forum* 8, 3: 383–402.

Klandermans, Bert 1994, 'Transient Identities?: Membership Patterns in the Dutch Peace Movement', in Larana, Johnston and Gusfield (eds.) 1994, 168–84.

Klandermans, Bert (ed.) 1989b, *Organizing for Change: Social Movement Organizations in Europe and the United States*, International Social Movement Research, vol. 2, Greenwich, Conn.: JAI Press.

Klandermans, Bert, Kriesi, Hanspeter and Tarrow, Sidney (eds.) 1988, *From Structure to Action: Comparing Movement Participation Across Cultures*, International Social Movement Research, vol. 1, Greenwich, Conn.: JAI Press.

Klandermans, Bert and Oegema, Dirk 1987, 'Potentials, Networks, Motivations and Barriers', *American Sociological Review 52*: 519–31.

Klandermans, Bert and Tarrow, Sidney 1988, 'Mobilization into Social Movements: Synthesizing European and American Approaches', in Klandermans, Kriesi and Tarrow (eds.) 1988, 1–38.

Klapp, Orrin 1965, *Symbolic Leaders*, Chicago: Aldine.

Klapp, Orrin 1969, *Collective Search for Identity*, New York: Holt, Rinehart and Winston.

Klapp, Orrin 1991, *Inflation of Symbols*, New Brunswick, NJ: Transaction.

Kleidman, Robert 1993, *Organizing for Peace: Neutrality, The Test Ban and the Freeze*, Syracuse University Press.

Klein, Ethel 1984, *Gender Politics*, Cambridge MA: Harvard University Press.

Klein, Ethel 1987, 'The Diffusion of Consciousness in the United States and Westem Europe', in Kazenstein and Mueller (eds.) 1987, 23–43.

Koopmans, Ruud 1993, 'The Dynamics of Protest Waves: Germany, 1965 to 1989', *American Sociological Review* 58: 637–58.

Koopmans, Ruud, Duyvendak, Jan Willem and Giugni Marco G. 1992, 'New Social Movements and Political Opportunities in Western Europe', *European Journal of Political Research* 22: 219–44.

Kornhauser, William 1959, *The Politics of Mass Society*, Glencoe IL: Free Press.

Kramer, Ralph M. 1981, *Voluntary Agencies in the Welfare State*, Berkeley: University of California Press.

Kriesi, Hanspeter 1988, 'Local Mobilization for the People's Petition of the Dutch Peace Movement', in Klandermans, Kriesi and Tarrow (eds.) 1988, 41–81.

Kriesi, Hanspeter 1993, *Political Mobilization and Social Change: The Dutch Case in Comparative Perspective*, Avebury: Aldershot.

Kriesi, Hanspeter, Koopmans, Ruud, Duyvendak, Jan Willem and Giugni, Marco G. 1995, *New Social Movements in Western Europe: A Comparative Analysis*, Minneapolis: University of Minnesota Press.

Laclau, Ernesto 1990, *New Reflections on the Revolution of Our Time*, London: Verso.

Laclau, Ernesto and Mouffe, Chantal 1985, *Hegemony and Socialist Strategy*, London: Verso.

Laidi, Zaki 1994, *Un monde privé de sens*, Paris: Fayard.

Lalive d'Epinay, Christian 1983, 'La vie quotidienne. Essai de construction d'un concept sociologique et anthropologique', *Cahiers Internationaux de Sociologie*, 74: 13–38.

Lamont, Michelle and Fournier, Marcel 1992, *Cultivating Differences: Symbolic Boundaries and the Making of Inequalities*, University of Chicago Press.

Lange, Peter, Irvin, Cynthia and Tarrow, Sidney 1989, 'Phases of Mobilization: Social Movements and the Italian Communist Party since the 1960s', *British Journal of Political Science*, 22: 15–42.

Lapassade, Georges 1981, *L'analyse et l'analyste*. Paris: Gauthier Villars.

Larana, Enrique 1995, 'Continuity and Unity in New forms of Collective Action: A Comparative Analysis of Student Movements', in Johnston and Klandermans (eds.) 1995, 209–33.

Larana, Enrique, Johnston, Hank and Gusfield, Joseph R. (eds.) 1994, *New Social Movements: From Ideology to Identity*, Philadelphia: Temple University Press.

Lasch, Christopher 1978, *The Culture of Narcissism*, New York: Norton.

Lasch, Christopher 1984, *The Minimal Self*, London: Pan Books.

Lasch, Christopher 1991, *The True and Only Heaven: Progress and Its Critics*, New York: Norton.

Lash, Scott and Friedman, Jonathan (eds.) 1992, *Modernity and Identity*, Oxford, Blackwell.

Lash, Scott and Urry, John 1987, *The End of Organized Capitalism*, Cambridge: Polity Press.

Lash, Scott and Urry, John 1994, *Economies of Signs and Space*, London: Sage.

Latour, Bruno 1987, *Science in Action*, Milton Keynes: Open University Press.

LeBon, Gustave 1960, *The Crowd: A Study of the Popular Mind*, New York: Viking.

Lefebvre, Henri 1991, *The Production of Space*, Oxford: Blackwell.

Levinson, Daniel *et al.* 1978, *The Seasons of a Man's Life*, New York: Knopf.

Lindblom, Charles E. 1977, *Politics and Markets*, New York: Basic Books.

Lipietz, Alain 1992, *Towards a New Economic Order: Postfordism, Ecology and Democracy*, Oxford University Press.

Lipsky, Michael 1968, 'Protest as a Political Resource', *American Political Science Review* 62: 1144–58.

Lo, Clarence 1982, 'Counter-Movements and Conservative Movements in the Contemporary US', *Annual Review of Sociology* 8: 107–34.

Locke, Don C. 1992, *Increasing Multicultural Understanding: A Comprehensive Model*, London: Sage.

Lofland, John 1993, *Polite Protesters: The American Peace Movement of the 1980s*, Syracuse University Press.

Lofland, John 1985, *Protest: Studies of Collective Behaviour and Social Movements*, New Brunswick, NJ: Transaction.

Lorber, Judith 1994, *Paradoxes of Gender*, Yale Universtiy Press.

Loureau, René 1977, *Le gai savoir des sociologues*, Paris: Editions 10/18.

Loye, David 1977, *The Leadership Passion: A Psychology of Ideology*, San Francisco: Jossey-Bass.

Luard, Evan 1990, *The Globalization of Politics: The Changed Focus of Political Action in the Modern World*, London: Macmillan.

Luhmann, Niklas 1987, 'The Future Cannot Begin: Temporal Structures in Modern Society', *Social Research*, 53: 130–52.

Lumley, Robert 1990, *States of Emergency: Cultures of Revolt in Italy from 1968 to 1978*, London: Verso.

Luske, Bruce 1990, *Mirrors of Madness: Patrolling the Psychic Border*, New York: Aldine.

Lyotard, Jean-François 1984, *The Postmodern Condition: A Report on Knowledge*, Minneapolis: University of Minnesota Press.

MacLeod, Arlene Elowe 1991, *Accommodating Protest: Working Women, the New Veiling, and Change in Cairo*, New York: Columbia University Press.

Maffesoli, Michel 1979, *La violence totalitaire*, Paris: Presses Universitaires de France.

Maffesoli, Michel 1995, *The Time of the Tribes*, London: Sage.

Maheu, Louis (ed.) 1995, *Social Movements and Social Classes: The Future of Collective Action*, London: Sage.

Mannheim, Karl 1960, *Ideology and Utopia*, London: Routledge.

Manning, David J. (ed.) 1980, *The Form of Ideology*, London: Allen and Unwin.

Martin, Joanne 1992, *Cultures in Organizations*, Oxford University Press.

Martin, Patricia Yancey, 1990, 'Rethinking Feminist Organizations', *Gender and Society* 4, 2: 182–206.

Marullo, Sam and Lofland, John (eds.) 1990, *Peace Action in the Eighties*, New Brunswick, NJ: Rutgers University Press.

Marwell, Gerald and Oliver, Pam 1993, *The Critical Mass in Collective Action: A Micro-Social Theory*, Cambridge University Press.

Marx, Gary T. 1972, 'Issueless Riots' in Short, James F. and Wolfgang, Marvin E. (eds.), *Collective Violence*, Chicago: Aldine, 47–59.

Marx, Gary T. and Useem, Michael 1971, 'Majority Participation in Minority Movements: Civil Rights, Abolition, Untouchability', *Journal of Social Issues* 27: 81–104.

Marx, Gary T. and Wood, James L. 1975, 'Strands of Theory and Research in Collective Behaviour', *Annual Review of Sociology* 1: 363–428.

Marx, John H. and Holzner, Burkart 1975, 'Ideological Primary Groups in Contemporary Cultural Movements', *Sociological Focus* 8: 311–29.

Massolo, Alejandra 1992, *Por amor y coraje: mujeres en movimientos urbanos de la Ciudad de Mexico*, Mexico City: El Colegio de Mexico.

Maturana, Humberto and Varela, Francisco 1980, *Autopoiesis and Cognition*, Boston: Reidel.

Mayer, Margit and Roth, Roland 1995, 'New Social Movements and the Transformation to Post-Fordist Society', in Danrnovsky, Epstein and Flacks (eds.) 1995, 299–319.

McAdam, Doug 1982, *Political Process and the Development of Black Insurgency 1930-1970*, University of Chicago Press.

McAdam, Doug 1988, *Freedom Summer*, Oxford University Press.

McAdam, Doug, McCarthy, John D. and Zald, Mayer N. 1988, 'Social Movements' in Smelser, Neil J. (ed.), *Handbook of Sociology*, Beverly Hills: Sage, 695–739.

McAdam, Doug and Rucht, Dieter 1993, 'The Cross-National Diffusion of Movement Ideas', *Annals of the American Academy of Political and Social Sciences* 528: 56–74.

McCarthy, John D. 1987, 'Pro-Life and Pro-Choice Mobilization: Infrastructure Deficits and New Technologies' in Zald and McCarthy (eds.) 1987, 49–66.

McCarthy, John D. 1994 'Activists, Authorities and the Media Framing of Drunk Driving', in Larana, Johnston and Gusfield (eds.) 1994, 133–67.

McCarthy, John D., Britt, David and Wolfson, Mark 1991, 'The Institutional Channelling of Social Movements by the State in the United States', in Kriesberg, Louis (ed.), *Research in Social Movements, Conflict and Change* 13: 45–76.

McCarthy, John D. and Wolfson, Mark 1992, 'Consensus Movements, Conflict Movements, and the Cooptation of Civic and State Infrastructures', in Morris and Mueller (eds.) 1992, 273–97.

McCarthy, John D. and Zald, Mayer N. 1973, *The Trends of Social Movements in*

America: Professionalization and Resource Mobilization, Morristown NJ: General Learning Press.

McCarthy, John D. and Zald, Mayer N. 1977, 'Resource Mobilization and Social Movements: A Partial Theory', *American Journal of Sociology* 82: 1212–41.

McCrone, David 1992, *Understanding Scotland: The Sociology of a Stateless Nation*, London: Routledge.

McGrew, Anthony G. and Lewis, Paul G. (eds.) 1992, *Global Politics: Globalization and the Nation State*, Cambridge: Polity Press.

McPhail, Clark 1991, *The Myth of the Madding Crowd*, New York: Aldine De Gruyter.

McQuail, Denis 1992, *Media Performance*, London: Sage.

Melucci, Alberto 1980, 'The New Social Movements: A Theoretical Approach', *Social Science Information* 19: 199–226.

Melucci, Alberto 1984, 'An End to Social Movements?', *Social Science Information* 23, 4–5: 819–35.

Melucci, Alberto 1985, 'The Symbolic Challenge of Contemporary Movements', *Social Research* 52: 781–816.

Melucci, Alberto 1988, 'Getting Involved: Identity and Mobilization in Social Movements', in Klandermans, Kriesi and Tarrow (eds.) 1988, 329–48.

Melucci Alberto 1989, *Nomads of the Present: Social Movements and Individual Needs in Contemporary Society*, Philadelphia: Temple University Press.

Melucci, Alberto 1992, 'Frontier Land: Collective Action between Actors and Systems', in Diani and Eyerman (eds.) 1992, 238–58.

Melucci, Alberto 1994, 'The Process of Collective Identity', in Johnston and Klandermans (eds.) 1994, 41–63.

Melucci, Alberto 1996, *The Playing Self. Person and Meaning in a Planetary Society*, Cambridge University Press.

Melucci, Alberto and Diani, Mario 1992 (1983), *Nazioni senza stato. I movimenti etnico-nazionali in Occidente*, Milan: Feltrinelli.

Meyer, David S. 1990, *A Winter of Discontent: The Nuclear Freeze and American Politics*, New York: Praeger.

Meyer, David S. 1993, 'Institutionalizing Dissent: The United States Structure of Opportunity and the End of the Nuclear Freeze Movement', *Sociological Forum* 8: 157–79.

Meyer, David S. and Whittier, Nancy 1994, 'Social Movement Spillover', *Social Problems* 41: 277–98.

Meyer, John W. and Scott, W. Richard 1992, *Organizational Environments: Ritual and Rationality*, London: Sage.

Middleton, David and Edwards, Derek (eds.) 1990, *Collective Remembering*, London: Sage.

Miliband, Ralph 1973, *The State in Capitalist Society*, London: Quartet Books.

Miliband, Ralph 1989, *Divided Societies: Class Struggle in Contemporary Capitalism*, Oxford: Clarendon Press.

Miller, Mark Crispin 1988, *Boxed-In: The Culture of TV*, Evanston IL: Northwestern University Press.

Mirowsky, John, and Ross, Catherine E. 1989, *Social Causes of Distress*, New York: Aldine de Gruyter.

Misztal, Bronislaw 1995, 'The Uses of Freedom: PostCommunist Transformation in Eastern Europe', in Darnowsky, Epstein and Flacks (eds.) 1995, 264–86.

Mitterauer, Michael 1992, *A History of Youth*, Oxford: Blackwell.

Moaddel, Mansoor 1992, 'Ideology as Episodic Discourse: The Case of the Iranian Revolution', *American Sociological Review* 57: 353–79.

Modleski, Tania (ed.) 1986, *Studies in Entertainement: Critical Approaches to Mass Culture*, Bloomington: Indiana University Press.

Molotch, Harvey 1979, 'Media and Movements', in Zald and McCarthy (eds.) 1979, 71–93.

Moore, Barrington Jr. 1978, *Injustice: The Social Bases of Obedience and Revolt*, Armonk, N.Y.: M. E. Sharpe.

Morgan, Jane 1987, *Conflict and Order: The Police and Labour Disputes in England and Wales, 1900-1939*, Oxford University Press.

Morgen, Sandra 1983, 'Towards a Politics of Feelings: Beyond the Dialectic of Thought and Action', *Women's Studies* 10, 2: 203–23.

Morin Edgar 1980, *La méthode: 2. La vie de la vie*, Paris: Seuil.

Morin Edgar 1986, *La méthode: 3. La connaissance de la connaissance*, Paris: Seuil.

Morley, David 1992, *Television: Audiences and Cultural Studies*, London: Routledge.

Morris, Aldon 1984, *The Origins of the Civil Rights Movement: Black Communities Organizing for Change*, New York: Free Press.

Morris, Aldon D., and Mueller, Carol McClurg (eds.) 1992, *Frontiers in Social Movement Theory*, New Haven: Yale University Press.

Moscovici, Serge 1979, *Psychologie des minorités actives*, Paris: Presses Universitaires de France.

Moscovici, Serge 1981, *L'âge des foules*, Paris: Fayard.

Moscovici, Serge 1988, 'Notes Towards a Description of Social Representations', *European Journal of Social Psychology* 18: 211–50.

Moscovici, Serge 1993, *The Invention of Society*, London: Polity.

Moscovici, Serge and Doise, Willem 1994, *Conflict and Consensus: A General Theory of Collective Decisions*, London: Sage.

Moscovici, Serge, Mugny, Gabriel and Van Avermaet, Eddy 1985, *Perspectives on Minority Influence*, Cambridge University Press.

Mosse, George 1975, *The Nationalization of the Masses: Political Symbolism and Mass Movements in Germany from the Napoleonic Wars Through the Third Reich*, New York: H. Fertig.

Moustakas, Clark 1994, *Phenomenological Research Methods*, London: Sage.

Mueller, Carol McClurg 1987, 'Collective Consciousness, Identity Transformation, and the Rise of Women in Public Office in the United States', in Katzenstein and Mueller (eds.) 1987, 89–108.

Mueller, Carol McClurg 1992, 'Building Social Movement Theory', in Morris and Mueller (eds.) 1992, 3–25.

420   References

Mueller, Carol McClurg 1994, 'Conflict Networks and the Origins of Women's Liberation', in Larana, Johnston and Gusfield (eds.) 1994, 234–63.
Mugny, Gabriel and Perez, Juan A. 1991, *The Social Psychology of Minority Influence*, Cambridge University Press.
Namer, Gérard 1987, *Mémoire et société*, Paris: Méridiens Klincksieck.
Nava, Mica 1992, *Changing Cultures: Feminism, Youth and Consumerism*, London: Sage.
Nederveen Pieterse, Jan (ed.) 1992, *Emancipations, Modern and Postmodern*, London: Sage.
Neisser, Ulrich 1976, *Cognition and Reality*, San Francisco: Freeman.
Nicholson, Linda (ed.) 1990, *Feminism/Postmodernism*, London: Routledge.
Novotny, Helga 1992, 'Time and Social Theory. Towards a Social Theory of Time', *Time and Society* 1: 421–54.
Oberschall, Anthony 1973, *Social Conflict and Social Movements*, Englewood Cliffs, N.J.: Prentice-Hall.
Oberschall, Anthony 1978, 'The Decline of the 1960s Social Movements', in Kriesberg, Louis (ed.), *Resarch in Social Movements, Conflict and Change* 1: 257–89.
Oberschall, Anthony 1993, *Social Movements: Ideologies, Interests and Identities*, New Brunswick: Transaction Books.
O'Donnell, Guillermo and Philippe Schmitter 1986, *Transition from Authoritarian Rule: Tentative Conclusions About Uncertain Democracies*, Baltimore: Johns Hopkins University Press.
Offe, Claus 1984, *Contradictions of the Welfare State*, London: Hutchinson.
Offe, Claus 1985a, 'New Social Movements: Challenging the Boundaries of Institutional Politics', *Social Research* 52: 817–68.
Offe, Claus 1985b, *Disorganized Capitalism: Contemporary Transformations of Work and Politics*, Cambridge: Polity Press.
Offe, Claus 1990, 'Reflections on the Institutional Self-Transformation of Movement Politics: A Tentative Stage Model', in Dalton and Kuechler (eds.) 1990, 232–50.
Oliver, Pam 1984, 'If You Don't Do It, Nobody Else Will: Active and Token Contributors to Local Collective Action', *American Sociological Review* 49: 601–10.
Oliver, Pam 1989, 'Bringing the Crowd Back: The Non-Organizational Elements of Social Movements', in Kriesberg, Louis (ed.), *Research in Social Movements, Conflict and Change* 11: 1–30.
Oliver, Pamela E. and Marwell, Gerald 1993, 'Mobilizing Technologies for Collective Action', in Morris and Mueller (eds.) 1993, 251–72.
Olson, Mancur 1965, *The Logic of Collective Action*, Cambridge MA: Harvard University Press.
Orum, Anthony M. 1974, 'On Participation in Political Protest Movements', *Journal of Applied Behavioural Science* 10: 181–207.
Ost, David 1990, *Solidarity and the Politics of Anti-Politics: Opposition and Reform in Poland Since 1968*, Philadelphia: Temple University Press.

Ostrom, Elinor 1990, *Governing the Commons: The Evolution of Institutions for Collective Action*, Cambridge University Press.

Ozouf, Mona 1988, *Festivals and the French Revolution*, Cambridge MA: Harvard University Press.

Paige, Glenn D. 1977, *The Scientific Study of Political Leadership*, New York: Free Press.

Paige, Jeffrey M. 1975, *Agrarian Revolutions: Social Movements and Export Agriculture in the Underdeveloped World*, New York: Free Press.

Pakulski, Jan 1991, *Social Movements: The Politics of Moral Protest*, Melbourne: Longman Cheshire.

Pakulski, Jan 1995, 'Social Movements and Class: The Decline of the Marxist Paradigm', in Maheu (ed.) 1995, 55–86.

Palmer, Bryan D. 1990, *Descent into Discourse*, Philadelphia: Temple University Press.

Parfit, Derek 1984, *Reasons and Persons*, Cambridge University Press.

Parker, Ian 1992, *Discourse Dynamics*, London: Routledge.

Parker, Ian and Shotter, John (eds.) 1990, *Deconstructing Social Psychology*, London: Routledge.

Peterson, Abby 1994, 'Racist and Anti-Racist Movements in Post-Modern Societies: Between Universalism and Particularism', paper presented at the XIII World Congress of Sociology, Bielefeld.

Pickvance, Chris 1995, 'Social Movements in the Transition from State Socialism: Convergence or Divergence?', in Maheu (ed.) 1995, 121–50.

Piven, Frances Fox and Cloward, Richard A. 1971, *Regulating the Poor*, New York: Vintage.

Piven, Frances Fox and Cloward, Richard A. 1977, *Poor People's Movements*, New York: Vintage.

Piven, Frances Fox and Cloward, Richard A. 1992, 'Normalizing Collective Protest, in Morris and Mueller (eds.) 1992, 301–25.

Pizzorno, Alessandro 1978, 'Political Exchange and Collective Identity in Industrial Conflict', in Crouch and Pizzorno (eds.) 1978, 277–98.

Pizzorno, Alessandro 1986, 'Some Other Kind of Otherness: A Critique of Rational Choice Theories', in Foxley, Alejandro, McPherson, Michael S.. and O'Donnell, Guillermo (eds.), *Development, Democracy and the Art of Trespassing: Essays in Honor of Albert O. Hirschman*, University of Notre Dame Press, 355–73.

Pizzorno, Alessandro 1993a, 'All You Can Do with Reasons', *International Studies in the Philosophy of Science*, 7, 1: 75–80.

Pizzorno, Alessandro 1993b, *Le radici della politica assoluta*, Milan: Feltrinelli.

Potter, Jonathan and Wetherell, Margaret 1987, *Discourse and Social Psychology*, London: Sage.

Potter, Jonathan, Edwards, Derek and Wetherell, Margaret 1993, 'A Model of Discourse in Action', *American Behavioural Scientist* 36: 383–401.

Powell, Walter W. and Di Maggio, Paul (eds.) 1991, *The New Institutionalism in Organizational Analysis*, University of Chicago Press.

Prior, Lindsay 1989, *The Social Organisation of Death: Medical Discourse and Social Practices in Belfast*, London: Macmillan.

Proietto, Rosa 1995, 'New Social Movements: Issues of Sociology', *Social Science Information* 34: 355–88.

Putnam, Robert D. 1993, *Making Democracy Work: Civic Traditions in Italy*, Princeton University Press.

Ramirez Saiz, Juan Manuel 1995, *Los movimientos sociales y la politica*, Guadalajara: Universidad de Guadalajara.

Reason, Peter (ed.) 1994, *Participation in Human Inquiry*, London: Sage.

Rice, John S 1992, 'Discursive Formation, Life Stories, and the Emergence of Codependency: 'Power/Knowledge' and the Search for Identity', *Sociological Quarterly* 33: 337–64.

Richardson, Laurel 1991, 'Speakers Whose Voices Matter: Toward a Feminist Postmodernist Sociological Praxis', *Studies in Symbolic Interactionism* 12: 29–38.

Richardson, Laurel and Taylor, Verta (eds.) 1993, *Feminist Frontiers III*, New York: McGraw-Hill.

Ricoeur, Paul 1974, *The Conflict of Interpretations: Essays in Hermeneutics*, Evanston IL: Northwestern University Press.

Ricoeur, Paul 1976, *Interpretation Theory: Discourse and the Surplus of Meaning*, Fort Worth: Texas Christian University Press.

Ricoeur, Paul 1981, *Hermeneutics and Human Sciences: Essays on Language, Action, and Interpretation*, Cambridge University Press.

Ricoeur, Paul 1984, *Time and Narrative*, University of Chicago Press.

Robbins, Tim 1988, *Cults, Converts and Charisma: The Sociology of New Religious Movements*, London: Sage.

Robertson, Roland 1992, *Globalization: Social Theory and Global Culture*, London: Sage.

Rochon, Thomas R. 1988, *Mobilizing for Peace: The Antinuclear Movements in Western Europe*, Princeton University Press.

Rokkan, Stein and Urwin Derek W. (eds.) 1982, *The Politics of Territorial Identity: Studies in European Regionalism*, London: Sage.

Rootes, Chris 1995, 'A New Class? The Higher Educated and the New Politics', in Maheu (ed.) 1995, 220-35.

Rorty, Richard 1989, *Contingency, Irony and Solidarity*, Cambridge University Press.

Rose, Margaret A. 1991, *The Post-Modern and the Post-Industrial*, Cambridge University Press.

Rosenau, Pauline M. 1992, *Post-Modernism and the Social Sciences*, Princeton University Press.

Roszak, Theodore 1992, *The Voice of the Earth*, New York: Simon and Schuster.

Rucht, Dieter 1988, 'Themes, Logics, and Arenas of Social Movements: A Structural Approach', in Klandermans, Kriesi and Tarrow (eds.) 1988, 305–28.

Rucht, Dieter 1990, 'The Strategies and Action Repertoires of New Movements', in Dalton and Kuechler (eds.) 1990, 156–75.

Rucht, Dieter (ed.) 1991, *Research on Social Movements: The State of the Art in Western Europe and the USA*, Boulder, CO.: Westview.

Rule, James B. 1988, *Theories of Civil Violence*, Berkeley: University of California Press.

Rule, James B. 1989, 'Rationality and Non-rationality in Militant Collective Action', *Sociological Theory* 7: 145–60.

Rupp, Leila J. and Taylor, Verta 1987, *Survival in the Doldrums: The American Woman's Rights Movement, 1945 to the 1960s*, Oxford University Press.

Ryan, Barbara 1992, *Feminism and the Women's Movement*, New York: Routledge.

Ryan, Charlotte 1991, *Prime Time Activism*, Boston: South End Press.

Salmon, Charles T. (ed.) 1989, *Information Campaigns*, London: Sage.

Salmon, J. Warren (ed.) 1984, *Alternative Medicine: Popular and Policy Perspectives*, London: Tavistock.

Salvati, Michele 1981, 'May 1968 and the Hot Autumn of 1969: The Responses of Two Ruling Classes', in Berger (ed.) 1981, 329–63.

Sampson, Edward E. 1993, *Celebrating the Other*, Hemel Hempstead: Harvester/Wheatsheaf.

Schank, Roger C., and Robert P. Abelson. 1977, *Scripts, Plans, Goals and Understanding*, Hillsdale, N.J.: Erlbaum.

Scheff, Thomas J. 1990, *Microsociology: Discourse, Emotion, and Social Structure*, University of Chicago Press.

Schelling, Thomas C. 1978, *Micromotives and Macrobehaviour*, New York: Norton.

Schennink, Ben 1988, 'From Peace Week to Peace Work: Dynamics of the Peace Movement in the Netherlands', in Klandermans, Kriesi and Tarrow (eds.) 1988, 247–79.

Scherer-Warren, Ilse 1993, *Redes de movimientos sociais*, Sao Paulo: Loyola.

Scherer-Warren, Ilse and Krischke, Paulo (eds.) 1987, *Uma revoluçao no cotidiano? Os novos movimientos sociais na America Latina*, Sao Paulo: Brasiliense.

Schlesinger, Philip 1991, *Media, State and Nation*, London: Sage.

Schmitter, Philippe C. and Lembruch, Gerhard (eds.) 1979, *Trends Towards Corporatist Intermediation*, Beverly Hills: Sage.

Schwartz, Michael and Paul, Shuva 1992, 'Resource Mobilization versus the Mobilization of People', in Morris and Mueller (eds.) 1992, 205–23.

Scott, Alan 1990a, *Ideology and the New Social Movements*, London: Unwin Hyman.

Scott, James C. 1986, *Weapons of the Weak: Everyday Forms of Peasant Resistance*, New Haven: Yale University Press.

Scott, James C. 1990b, *Domination and the Arts of Resistance*, New Haven: Yale University Press.

Seidman, Steven and Wagner, David G. 1992, *Postmodernism and Social Theory*, Oxford: Blackwell.

Sen, Amartya K. 1992, *Inequality Reexamined*, New York: Russell Sage.

Sennett, Richard 1993, *The Conscience of the Eye: The Design and Social Life of Cities*, London: Faber.

Sewell, William H. 1980, *Work and Revolution in France: The Language of Labour from the Old Regime to 1848*, Cambridge University Press.

Sewell, William H. 1985, 'Ideologies and Social Revolutions: Reflections on the French Case', *Journal of Modern History* 57: 57–85.

Sewell, William H. 1990, 'Collective Violence and Collective Loyalties in France: Why the French Revolution Made a Difference', *Politics and Society* 18, 4: 527–52.

Sewell, William H. 1992, 'A Theory of Structure: Duality, Agency, and Transformation', *American Journal of Sociology* 98: 1–29.

Sharma, Ursula 1993, 'Contextualizing Alternative Medicine: The Exotic, the Marginal and the Perfectly Mundane', *Anthropology Today* 9, 4: 15–18.

Sharp, Gene 1973, *The Politics of Nonviolent Action*, Boston: Porter Sargent.

Shelton, Beth Anne 1992, *Women, Men and Time*, Westport, Conn.: Greenwood Press.

Shields, Rod (ed.) 1992, *Lifestyle Shopping: The Subjects of Consumption*, London: Routledge.

Shilling, Chris 1993, *The Body and Social Theory*, London: Sage.

Shils, Edward 1968, 'The Concept and Function of Ideology', *International Encyclopedia of the Social Sciences* 7, New York: Macmillan, 66–76.

Shils, Edward 1981, *Tradition*, University of Chicago Press.

Shorter Edward 1992, *From Paralysis to Fatigue: A History of Psychosomatic Illness in the Modern Era*, New York: Free Press.

Shotter, John 1993a, *Cultural Politics of Everyday Life*, Buckingham: Open University Press.

Shotter, John 1993b, *Conversational Realities: Studies in Social Constructionism*, London: Sage.

Shotter, John and Gergen, Kenneth J. (eds.) 1989, *Texts of Identity*, London: Sage.

Shusterman, Richard 1992, *L'art à l'etat vif*, Paris: Les Editions de Minuit.

Simonds, Wendy 1992, *Women and Self-Help Culture*, New Brunswick, NJ: Rutgers University Press.

Simons, Herbert W. (ed.) 1990, *The Rhetorical Turn*, University of Chicago Press.

Sims, Henry P. and Lorenzi, Peter 1992, *The New Leadership Paradigm: Social Learning and Cognition in Organizations*, London: Sage.

Sirianni, Carmen 1988, *Work, Time and Inequality*, Oxford University Press.

Skevington, Suzanne and Baker, Deborah (eds.) 1989, *The Social Identity of Women*, London: Sage.

Skockpol, Theda 1976, *States and Social Revolution: A Comparative Analysis of France, Russia and China*, Cambridge University Press.

Skocpol, Theda 1985, 'Cultural Idioms and Political Ideologies in the Revolutionary Reconstruction of State Power: A Rejoinder to Sewell', *Journal of Modern History* 57: 86–96.

Skockpol, Theda 1994, *Social Revolutions in the Modern World*, Cambridge University Press.

Slater, David 1994a, 'Power and Social Movements in the Other Occident: Latin

America in an International Context', *Latin American Perspectives* 21, 2: 11–37.

Slater, David (ed.) 1985, *The New Movements and the State in Latin America*, Dordrecht: CEDLA.

Slater, David (ed.) 1994b, *Social Movements and Political Change in Latin America*, *Latin American Perspectives* 21, 2.

Slater, Robert O. and Stohl, Michael (eds.), *Current Perspectives on International Terrorism*, London: Macmillan.

Smart, Barry 1992, *Modern Conditions, Postmodern Controversies*, London: Routledge.

Smelser, Neil J. 1962, *Theory of Collective Behaviour*, New York: Free Press.

Smelser, Neil J. 1968, *Essays in Sociological Explanation*, Englewood Cliffs, NJ: Prentice-Hall.

Smith, Anthony D. 1981, *The Ethnic Revival*, Cambridge University Press.

Smith, Anthony D. 1991a, *National Identity*, Reno: University of Nevada Press.

Smith, Christian 1991b, *The Emergence of Liberation Theology: Radical Religion and Social Movement Theory*, University of Chicago Press.

Smith, Dorothy 1988, *The Everyday World as Problematic: A Feminist Sociology*, Milton Keynes: Open University Press.

Smith, Dorothy 1990, *The Conceptual Practices of Power*, Boston: Northeastern University Press.

Smith, Hedrick 1992, *The Media and the Gulf War*, Washington: Seven Locks Press.

Snow, David A. and Benford Robert D. 1992, 'Master Frames and Cycles of Protest', in Morris and Mueller (eds.) 1992, 133–55.

Snow, David A. and Benford Robert D. 1988, 'Ideology, Frame Resonance, and Participant Mobilization', in Klandermans, Kriesi and Tarrow (eds.) 1988, 197–218.

Snow, David A., Rochford, E. Burke, Worden, Steven K. and Benford, Robert D. 1986, 'Frame Alignment Processes, Micromobilization and Movement Participation', *American Sociological Review* 51: 456–81.

Snow, David A., Zurcher, Louis A. and Eckland-Olson, Sheldon 1980, 'Social Networks and Social Movements,' *American Sociological Review* 45: 787–801.

Snow, David A., Zurcher, Louis A. and Peters, Robert 1981, 'Victory Celebrations as Theater: A Dramaturgical Approach to Crowd Behaviour', *Symbolic Interaction* 4: 21–41.

Spector, Malcolm and Kitsuse, John I. 1973, 'Social Problems: A Reformulation', *Social Problems* 21: 145–59.

Spivak, Gayatri C. 1987, *In Other Worlds*, London: Methuen.

Staggenborg, Suzanne 1991, *The Pro-Choice Movement: Organization and Activism in the Abortion Conflict*, Oxford University Press.

Steier, Frederick (ed.) 1991, *Research and Reflexivity*, London: Sage.

Stein, Arthur 1985, *Seeds of the Seventies*, Hanover NH: University Press of New England.

Steinem, Gloria 1992, *Revolution from Within*, Boston: Little, Brown.

Strathern, Marilyn 1991, *Partial Connections*, Savage MD: Rowan and Littlefield.

Strathern, Marilyn 1992, *Reproducing the Future: Essays on Anthropology, Kinship and the New Reproductive Technologies*, Manchester University Press.

Streek, Wolfgang and Schmitter, Philippe C. (eds.) 1985, *Private Interest Government: Beyond Market and State*, Beverly Hills: Sage.

Stryker, Sean D. 1994, 'Knowledge and Power in the Students for a Democratic Society 1960-1970', *Berkeley Journal of Sociology* 38: 89–138.

Stubbs, Michael 1983, *Discourse Analysis*, University of Chicago Press.

Suttles, Gerald and Zald, Mayer N. (eds.) 1985, *The Challenge of Social Control: Citizenship and Institution Building in Modern Society*, Norwood NJ: Ablex.

Swidler, Ann 1986, 'Culture in Action: Symbols and Strategies', *American Sociological Review* 51: 273–86.

Swidler, Anne 1995, 'Cultural Power and Social Movements', in Johnston and Klandermans (eds.) 1995, 25–40.

Szasz, Andrew 1994, *Ecopopulism: Toxic Waste and the Movement for Environmental Justice*, Minneapolis: University of Minnesota Press.

Sztompka, Piotr 1994, *The Sociology of Social Change*, Oxford: Blackwell.

Tanter, Raymond and Midlarsky, Manus 1967, 'A Theory of Revolution', *Journal of Conflict Resolution* 11, 3: 264–80.

Tarde, Gabriel 1969, *L'opinion et la foule*, Paris: Presses Universitaires de France.

Tarrés, Maria Luisa (ed.) 1994, *Transformaciones sociales y acciones colectivas: America Latina en el contesto de los Noventa*, Mexico City: El Colegio de Mexico.

Tarrow, Sidney 1988a, 'Old Movements in New Cycles of Protest: The Career of an Italian Religious Community', in Klandermans, Kries and Tarrow (eds.) 1988, 281–304.

Tarrow, Sidney 1988b, 'National Politics and Collective Action: Recent Theory and Research in Western Europe and the United States', *Annual Review of Sociology* 17: 421–40.

Tarrow, Sidney 1989a, *Democracy and Disorder. Protest and Politics in Italy, 1965–1975*, Oxford University Press.

Tarrow, Sidney 1989b. *Struggle, Politics and Reform: Collective Action, Social Movements and Cycles of Protest*, Cornell University, Western Societies Paper no. 21.

Tarrow, Sidney 1992, 'Mentalities, Political Cultures, and Collective Action Frames: Constructing Meanings through Action', in Morris and Mueller (eds.) 1992, 174–202.

Tarrow, Sidney 1993a, 'Modular Collective Action and the Rise of the Social Movement: Why the French Revolution Was Not Enough', *Politics and Society* 21: 69–90.

Tarrow, Sidney 1993b, 'Cycles of Collective Action: Between Moments of Madness and the Repertoire of Contention', *Social Science History* 17: 281–307.

Tarrow, Sidney 1994, *Power in Movement: Social Movements Collective Action and Politics*, Cambridge University Press.

Taylor, Charles 1989, *Sources of the Self: The Making of the Modern Identity,* Cambridge, Mass.: Harvard University Press.

Taylor, Charles 1992, *Ethics of Authenticity*, Cambridge MA: Harvard University Press.

Taylor, Charles 1992, *Multiculturalism and 'The Politics of Recognition'*, Princeton University Press.

Taylor, Michael (ed.) 1988, *Rationality and Revolution*, Cambridge University Press.

Taylor, Verta, and Rupp, Leila J. 1993, 'Women's Culture and Lesbian Feminist Activism: A Reconsideration of Cultural Feminism', *Signs* 19: 32–61.

Taylor, Verta and Whittier, Nancy E. 1992, 'Collective Identity in Social Movement Communities: Lesbian Feminist Mobilization', in Morris and Mueller (eds.) 1992, 104–29.

Thompson, John B. 1984, *Studies in the Theory of Ideology*, Berkeley: University of California Press.

Thompson, John B. 1990, *Ideology and Modern Culture*, Oxford: Polity Press.

Thorson, James A. 1995, *Aging in a Changing Society*, Belmont: Wadsworth.

Tillock, Harriett and Morrison, Denton E. 1979, 'Group Size and Contributions to Collective Action: An Examination of Olson's Theory Using Data from Zero Population Growth, Inc.', in Kriesberg, Louis (ed.), *Research in Social Movements, Conflict and Change* 2: 131–58.

Tilly, Charles 1970, 'The Changing Place of Collective Violence', in Richter, Melvin (ed.), *Essays in Theory and History*, Cambridge. MA.: Harvard University Press, 139–64.

Tilly, Charles (ed.) 1975, *The Formation of National States in Western Europe*, Princeton University Press.

Tilly, Charles 1978, *From Mobilization to Revolution*, Reading. MA.: Addison-Wesley.

Tilly, Charles 1984, *Big Structures, Large Processes, Huge Comparisons*, New York: Russell Sage.

Tilly, Charles 1986, *The Contentious French*, Cambridge MA: Harvard University Press.

Tilly, Charles 1990, *Coercion, Capital, and European States, A.D. 990-1990*, Oxford: Blackwell.

Tilly, Charles 1993, *European Revolutions 1492–1992*, Oxford: Blackwell.

Tilly, Charles, Tilly, Louise and Tilly, Richard 1975, *The Rebellious Century 1830-1930*, Cambridge MA: Harvard University Press.

Tomlison, Alan (ed.) 1990, *Consumption, Identity and Style: Marketing, Meanings and the Packaging of Leisure*, London: Routledge.

Toulmin, Stephen E. 1990, *Cosmopolis: The Hidden Agenda of Modernity*, New York: Free Press.

Touraine, Alain 1977, *The Self-Production of Society*, University of Chicago Press.

Touraine, Alain 1981, *The Voice and the Eye*, Cambridge University Press.

Touraine, Alain 1985, 'An Introduction to the Study of Social Movements', *Social Research* 52: 749–87.

Touraine, Alain 1988a, *Return of the Actor: Social Theory in Postindustrial Society*, Minneapolis: University of Minnesota Press.

Touraine, Alain 1988b, *La parole et le sang. Politique et société en Amerique Latine*, Paris: Odile Jacob.

Touraine, Alain 1994a, *Critique of Modernity*, Oxford: Blackwell.

Touraine, Alain 1994b, *Qu'est-ce que la démocratie?*, Paris: Fayard.

Touraine, Alain, Dubet, François, Hegedus, Szusza and Wieviorka, Michel 1981, *Le pays contre l'-tat. Luttes occitanes*, Paris: Seuil.

Touraine, Alain, Dubet, François, Wiewiorka, Michel and Strzelecki, Jan 1982, *Solidarité. Analyse d'un mouvement social*, Paris: Fayard.

Tronto, Joan C 1987, 'Beyond Gender Difference to a Theory of Care', *Signs* 12: 644–63.

Tumin, Melvin M. 1967, *Social Stratification: The Forms and Function of Inequality*, Englewood Cliffs NJ: Prentice-Hall.

Turner, Bryan S. (ed.) 1990, *Theories of Modernity and Postmodernity*, London: Sage.

Turner, Bryan S. 1992, *Regulating Bodies: Essays in Medical Sociology*, London: Sage.

Turner, Ralph H 1969, 'The Theme of Contemporary Social Movements', *British Journal of Sociology*, 20: 390-405.

Turner, Ralph H 1983, 'Figure and Ground in the Analysis of Social Movements', *Symbolic Interaction*, 6, 2: 175–81.

Turner, Ralph H. and Killian Louis M., 1987, *Collective Behaviour*, 3rd edn., Englewood Cliffs NJ: Prentice-Hall.

Turner, Victor 1969, *The Ritual Process*, Chicago: Aldine.

Turner, Victor 1982, *From Ritual to Theatre*, New York: Performing Arts Journal Publications.

Urry, John 1995, *Restructuring Place*, London: Routledge.

Useem, Bert 1980, 'Solidarity Model, Breakdown Model, and the Boston AntiBusing Movement', *American Sociological Review* 45: 357–69.

Valdés, Teresa and Winstein, Marisa 1993, *Mujeres que suenan. Las organizaciones de pobladores en Chile: 1973–1989*, Santiago: Flacso.

Van Dijk, Teun A. 1972, *Some Aspects of Text Grammars*, The Hague: Mouton.

Van Dijk, Teun A. 1987, *Communicating Racism: Ethnic Prejudice in Thought and Talk*, London: Sage.

Van Dijk, Teun A. 1992, 'Discourse and the Denial of Racism', *Discourse and Society* 3: 87–118.

Van Maanen, John (ed.) 1995, *Representation in Ethnography*, London: Sage.

Verba, Sidney, Schozman, Kay Lehman and Brady, Henry E., *Voice and Equality: Civic Voluntarism in American Politics*, Harvard Universtiy Press.

Villasante, Tomas R. (ed.) 1994, *Las ciudades hablan. Identitades y movimientos sociales en seis metropolis latinoamericanas*, Caracas: Nueva Sociedad.

Viney, Linda L., and Bousfield, Lynne 1991, 'Narrative Analysis: A Method of Psychosocial Research for AIDS-Affected People', *Social Science Medicine* 32: 757–65.

Wagner-Pacifici, Robin E. 1986, *The Moro Morality Play: Terrorism and Social Drama*, University of Chicago Press.

Walsh. Edward J. 1988, *Democracy in the Shadows: Citizen Mobilization in the Wake of the Accident at Three Mile Island*, Westport, Conn.: Greenwood.

Walzer, Michael 1992 (1977), *Just and Unjust Wars*, New York: Basic Books.

Wardwell, Walter I. 1994, 'Alternative Medicine in the United States', *Social Science and Medicine*, 38, 8: 1061–8.

Watney, Simon 1987, *Policing Desire: Pornography, Aids and the Media*, London: Comedia.

Weigert, Andrew J., Teitge J. Smith and Teitge, Dennis W. 1986, *Society and Identity*, Cambridge University Press.

Weller, Jack M. and Quarantelli, E. L. 1974, 'Neglected Characteristics of Collective Behaviour', *American Journal of Sociology* 79: 665–85.

Werbner, Pnina and Anwar, Muhammad (eds.) 1991, *Black and Ethnic Leadership: The Cultural Dimension of Political Action*, London: Routledge.

Wetherell, Margaret and Potter, Jonathan 1992, *Mapping the Language of Racism*, Hemel Hempstead: Harvester/Wheatsheaf.

Whalen, Jack, and Flacks, Richard 1989, *Beyond the Barricades: The Sixties Generation Grows Up*, Philadelphia: Temple University Press.

White, Harrison C. 1992, *Identity and Control: A Structural Theory of Social Action*, Princeton University Press.

White, Robert W. 1989, 'From Peaceful Protest to Guerrilla War: Micromobilization of the Provisional Irish Republican Army', *American Journal of Sociology* 94: 1277–1303.

Whittier, Nancy E. 1995, *Feminist Generations: The Persistence of the Radical Women's Movement*, Philadelphia: Temple University Press.

Whyte, William Foote (ed.) 1991, *Participatory Action Research*, London: Sage.

Wiewiorka, Michel 1988, *Sociétés et terrorisme*, Paris: Fayard.

Wiewiorka, Michel 1995, *The Arena of Racism*, London: Sage.

Willis, Paul 1990, *Common Culture: Symbolic Work at Play in the Everyday Cultures of the Young*, Milton Keynes: Open University Press.

Wilson, Brian R. 1990a, *The Social Dimensions of Sectarianism*, Oxford University Press.

Wilson, John 1990b, *Politically Speaking: The Pragmatic Analysis of Political Language*, New York: Basil Blackwell.

Wilson, Kenneth L. and Orum, Anthony M. 1976, 'Mobilizing People for Collective Political Action', *Journal of Political and Military Sociology* 4: 187–202.

Wolpe, Paul Root 1994, 'The Dynamics of Heresy in Profession', *Social Science and Medicine* 39, 9: 1133–48.

Wolton, Dominique 1991, *Wargames: L'information et la guerre*, Paris: Flammarion.

Wood, Gordon S. 1991, *The Radicalism of the American Revolution*, New York: Vintage.

Woolley, Benjamin 1992, *Virtual Worlds*, London: Penguin.

Wuthnow, Robert 1987, *Meaning and Moral Order: Explanations in Cultural Analysis*, Berkeley: University of California Press.

Wuthnow, Robert 1989, *Communities of Discourse: Ideology and Social Structure in the Reformation, the Enlightenment, and European Socialism*, Cambridge MA: Harvard University Press.

Wuthnow, Robert 1991a, *Acts of Compassion: Caring for Others and Helping Ourselves*, Princeton University Press.

Wuthnow, Robert (ed.) 1991b, *Between States and Markets: The Voluntary Sector in Comparative Perspective*, Princeton University Press.

Wuthnow, Robert, Hunter, James D., Bergesen, Albert and Kurzweil, Edith 1984, *Cultural Analysis*, London: Routledge.

Wuthnow, Robert and Witten, Marsha 1988, 'New Directions in the Study of Culture', *Annual Review of Sociology* 14: 49–67.

Yanitsky, Oleg 1991, 'Environmental Movements: Some Conceptual Issues in East-West Comparison', *International Journal of Urban and Regional Research* 15: 524–41.

Yiannis, Gabriel and Lang, Tim 1995, *The Unmanageable Consumer: Contemporary Consumption and Its Fragmentations*, London: Sage.

Young, Michael D. 1988, *The Metronomic Society*, Cambridge MA: Harvard University Press.

Zald, Mayer N. 1991, 'The Continuing Vitality of Resource Mobilization Theory: Response to Herbert Kitschelt's Critique', in Rucht (ed.) 1991, 348–54.

Zald, Mayer N. 1992, 'Looking Backward to Look Forward: Reflections on the Resource Mobilization Research Program', in Morris and Mueller (eds.) 1992, 326–48.

Zald, Mayer N. and Ash, Roberta 1966, 'Social Movement Organizations: Growth, Decay and Change', *Social Forces* 44: 327–41.

Zald, Mayer N. and McCarthy, John D. (eds.) 1979, *The Dynamics of Social Movements*, Cambridge, Mass.: Winthrop.

Zald, Mayer N. and McCarthy, John D. (eds.) 1987, *Social Movements in Organizational Society*, New Brunswick, NJ: Transaction.

Zald, Mayer N. and Useem, Bert 1987, 'Movement and Countermovement Interaction: Mobilization, Tactics and State Involvement', in Zald and McCarthy (eds.) 1987, 247–72.

Zelizer, Viviana A. 1994, *The Social Meaning of Money*, New York: Basic Books.

Zerubavel, Eviatar 1981, *Hidden Rythms*, University of Chicago Press.

Ziehe, Thomas 1991, *Zeitvergleiche: Jugend in Kulturelle Modernisierung*, Munich: Juventa.

Zolberg, Aristide R. 1972, 'Moments of Madness', *Politics and Society* 2: 183–207.

Index